an introduction to
exceptional children

an introduction to

Third Edition

exceptional children

William R. Van Osdol
Central State University,
Edmond, Oklahoma

Don G. Shane
Central State University
Edmond, Oklahoma

wcb

Wm. C. Brown Company Publishers
Dubuque, Iowa

wcb group

Wm. C. Brown, Chairman of the Board
Mark C. Falb, Executive Vice President

Book Team

Susan J. Soley, Editor
Julia A. Scannell, Designer
Barbara J. Rowe, Production Editor
Faye Schilling, Visual Research

wcb

Wm. C. Brown Company Publishers, College Division

Lawrence E. Cremer, President
Raymond C. Deveaux, Vice President/Product Development
David Wm. Smith, Vice President/Marketing
David A. Corona, Assistant Vice President/Production Development and Design
Janis M. Machala, Director of Marketing Research
Marilyn A. Phelps, Manager of Design
William A. Moss, Production Editorial Manager
Mary M. Heller, Visual Research Manager

Contents

Preface

The implications for a thorough understanding of all children by all school personnel are evident in a comment by Dr. Haim Ginott: "I've come to the frightening conclusion that I am the decisive element in the classroom. It is my personal approach that creates the climate, it's my daily mood that makes the weather. As a teacher, I possess tremendous power to make a child's life miserable or joyous. I can be a tool of torture or an instrument of inspiration. I can humiliate or humor, hurt or heal. In all situations, it is my response that decides whether a crisis will be escalated or defused and a child humanized or dehumanized." (California Association for Neurologically Handicapped Children, CANHC Gram 1976).

This revised edition presents adequate information which offers graduate and undergraduate special education majors, regular class teachers, psychologists, administrators, guidance counselors, and parents a realistic and functional approach to exceptional children's needs in school, at home, and in the community. Any area of specific interest should be pursued further by the individual reader.

The introductory course in special education on a college or university level attracts students who are preparing for professional services in many areas different from the field of special education, but who may wish to become aware of exceptional children. Students may also take the introductory course to determine whether they wish to enter the field of special education. Of course, the introductory course is required of majors in special education.

The authors of this revision were concerned about the relative importance of different topics. A cutoff point for a textbook is necessary; therefore, we provide a comprehensive introduction to exceptional children with a limited number of statistics, graphs, charts, case studies, and anecdotal records.

In this revision, adequate statistics are generally offered in narrative form rather than graphically. Only a number of specific statistics are included, primarily because of rapid change in the services for exceptional children. There also appears to be a certain aversion to statistical approaches. How many times, for example, have you heard a speaker or professor reflect negative attitudes by approaching an audience with a statement such as, "Now I shall bore you with some statistics"? The authors do imply, though, that statistics are useful. The point is that in this introductory text, general statements regarding statistics about exceptional children are presented as a basic component of concepts rather than as static, detailed information.

Some authors use case studies and anecdotal records, which may or may not contribute to a student's understanding of special children. We believe that the reader can acquire realistic concepts of exceptional children from professors who teach from their own experiential frameworks with exceptional children. The professor certainly needs to be resourceful. We emphasize that all exceptional children must be viewed as unique individuals, and in this textbook sufficient information is provided for problem-oriented discussions and lecture teachings.

We have chosen to discuss the different exceptionalities by categories. Special education professionals have varying opinions about labels and categories, but the fact remains that children who are, for example, deaf, blind, or mentally retarded, have to have special provisions for education and social growth. Schools throughout the United States plan and provide for categorically identified children, and the federal government uses a categorical funding formula. Therefore, this book is written within the framework of categories, which offers the reader the information necessary for an awareness and understanding of the different exceptionalities.

This 1982 edition has been changed considerably to include revolutionary trends in special education. The book contains twelve chapters. Chapter 1, on history and program development, has been completely revised to include the many implications of the Handicapped Children's Act, Public Law 94–142; integration (least restrictive environment—mainstreaming) of the exceptional child into regular classes; the history and program development of special education (attitudinal and program changes). Special education testing guidelines, test descriptions, and definitions of frequently used test abbreviations are in Appendix A.

Seven different chapters introduce different exceptionalities: mental retardation; the gifted and talented; physical, chronic, multiple, and severe handicaps; visual and hearing impairments; speech and language impairments; learning disabilities; and emotional and behavioral maladjustments.

Chapter 2, on mental retardation, distinctly integrates the areas of the trainable and educable programs into the four basic school levels: primary, intermediate, junior high, and senior high. Additional emphasis is given to severely and profoundly mentally retarded children. Adaptive behavior as a part of the definition of mental retardation is discussed in depth, because it is an essential area in the diagnosis of mental retardation.

The authors realize that chapter 3, on disadvantaged children, is not a special education category for special class placement. We felt the need, though, to reflect specifically the relationship of disadvantaged conditions of birth and adaptive life to the incidence of exceptional children.

Chapter 4, "Gifted and Talented Children," includes an emphasis on current trends in the education and identification of gifted children. Several projects for gifted children are described, and trends in the identification and education of disadvantaged gifted children are discussed.

We have expanded chapter 5 to include physically, chronically, multiply, and severely handicapped children in order to offer current, comprehensive information. Special equipment and materials that are necessary for the education and treatment of students who are physically and chronically handicapped are included in this revised edition.

Current information was added to chapter 6, on visual and hearing impairments, which includes special materials and equipment and recent medical treatment.

Chapter 7, on speech and language impairments, is now offered as a separate chapter. The new emphasis is primarily in the area of language disorders.

Chapter 8, on learning disabilities, offers current references and some of the newer developments in this area.

Chapter 9, on emotional and behavioral maladjustments, now includes a section on autism, and more emphasis is given to the area of behavior modification.

The final three chapters—chapter 10, "Practicum"; chapter 11, "Teachers, Administrators, and Parents"; and chapter 12, "Trends and Services in Special Education"—were revised to contain recent information regarding parent conferences, parent training, parent's rights, and emerging trends in the field of Special Education.

The chapters present an awareness of special education methods and materials, but the reader should remember that this is primarily an introductory textbook, not a procedures book for special education. The purpose of each chapter is to present basic concepts and introductory material, to create an awareness of the various exceptionalities, and to present the services that are or should be offered to exceptional children. Study questions are included at the end of each chapter. These questions are intended to serve as materials for individual study, oral reports, outside readings, and test exercises.

an introduction to
exceptional children

1

history and program development in special education

Who Are Exceptional Children?

Exceptional children, within the context of this book, are those who are mentally, emotionally, or physically unable to cope with the regular school program on a full- or part-time basis. These areas of exceptionalities include children who are identified as mentally retarded; disadvantaged; gifted; physically, chronically, multiply, and severely handicapped; visually and hearing impaired; speech and language impaired; learning disabled; and children who are emotionally or behaviorally disturbed.

Because of their limitations, whether permanent or temporary, exceptional children require special modification in their school programs if they are to succeed as individuals and become worthwhile, contributing members of society. Of course, many exceptional children also require modifications in their living arrangements and in community services. Special modifications appropriate for these children will be discussed in this chapter and throughout the text.

Brief History of Special Education

We have chosen to focus on attitudinal and program changes because they seem to be more important than a year-by-year analysis of developments in the field of special education.

Early History (1800-1950)

In years past, when exceptional children were first recognized as different or strange, the majority of them were ignored, rejected, or punished. There were few, if any, medical, social, or educational solutions to the problems encountered by exceptional children and their families. Consequently, they had to find their own solutions. The public's lack of knowledge, rather than deliberate negligence of the exceptional child, led to superstitions, fear, and a lack of meaningful programs. Generally, the early approaches either did nothing, placed the person in a residential center, or administered punishment.

During this early period, there were no specific curricula for exceptional children. They had to cope with what was offered to everyone, and if they could not cope, they were excluded. Any training provided in the early residential centers and other programs tended to focus on the development of personal skills. Very little emphasis was placed upon adaptive behavior that would enable such children to return functionally to the community.

Very few professional personnel were involved initially in working with exceptional children. Probably the largest professional group showing a concern for exceptional children were medical doctors. In addition, a few psychologists and educators were pioneers in the area of study and the provision of services. There were no professional training programs during this period. The people who were working intensively with exceptional children were doing so primarily on a one-to-one basis. A good example of this focus was evident in Itard's research in the eighteenth century with the wild boy of Aveyron (1962). This early emphasis provided the beginning in such areas as Montessori methods, perceptual and language training, and the provision of structured learning environments.

Little, if any, public school emphasis was evident from parents during this time. Because of the social stigma attached to having an exceptional child, many parents may have hidden such children and not told anyone outside the immediate family. Services for parents were not available primarily because no one knew which services might be appropriate. If services for the exceptional child were not indicated, then certainly services for parents were considered unnecessary.

Communities were not open to exceptional children prior to the stage (1950s) of concentrated program development. They really had no place in the community, and community services were certainly not available. With the primary emphasis being on the development of institutional programs, there was no need for communities to develop or offer services. Exceptional children resided within institutions and the community did not need to demonstrate a concern for them.

Virtually no long-range planning for the development of community programs or professional training was in existence at this time (1900s–1950s). The further growth of institutional programs led to what were later called, "human warehouses." The growth of these centers was accepted as the answer for the problems of exceptional children and their family. This solution accomplished the specific objectives of "caring for" the exceptional child and created the rationale that no additional planning was necessary.

The Period of Rapid Growth (1950–1970)

When interventions other than the institution began for the exceptional child, then progress was made in attitudinal changes. Changes in a positive direction did not happen overnight, and many professionals still believed that the provision of services was a waste of monies and effort. After all, there was no evidence nor trend to indicate that services would offer any return to the community. Perhaps the most obvious aspects of this transition from almost total isolation, ignoring, and rejection were that exceptional children were more tolerated and were included in community programs, although they were still separated.

The move of exceptional children from institutional settings into community settings was a slow process. In the early days of this move, the majority of recognized exceptional children were still in institutional settings. Movement of exceptional children into the community was not the result of drastic changes in public attitudes. The change resulted mainly from the demand for services from parents and parent groups. The parents insisted that exceptional children had as much right to community services as anyone. A gradual awareness of exceptionalities helped open the doors of the community to parents and children. In some instances, even though exceptional children were provided with a facility, they actually were just tolerated, subtly rejected, or isolated.

The early curriculum and instructional material development was based on the collective thinking of a few professionals who were working with exceptional children. This early program development was almost entirely teacher oriented with a few curriculum "specialists" included. Perhaps the most obvious trend was the attempt to adapt the regular curriculum and instructional materials to the needs of the exceptional child. There was also evidence of instructional programs which were focusing on the development of physical skills. Such areas as basketweaving, occupational handwork, arts and crafts, etc., were emphasized almost to the exclusion of any focus on reading, writing, arithmetic, or the development of cognitive skills. Many of the materials required for these programs were inexpensive and could be "scrounged" from the local merchants. In fact, if a special class teacher were not willing to scrounge, the instructional program probably suffered tremendously.

The total curriculum emphasis was to make exceptional children happy by giving them something to do with their hands. Many of the early programs stressed that the educational goals for the exceptional child were the same as the goals for the normal or regular class youngsters; however, a different curriculum had to be provided. Most of the curriculum guides prepared by state departments and local districts at this time were "watered down" versions of the regular class curriculum. The efforts were not, by any means, a total waste because at least the students who were included in such programs were given a curriculum. Many of the curriculum guides were very good and are still appropriate as general outlines for instructional programs.

After community programs began for the exceptional child, generally the professional training was similar to the present concept of in-service training. There were few books published pertaining to the exceptional child and very few institutions of higher education were preparing future teachers and other professionals to work with exceptional children. The early training had to be provided by those who had worked with the exceptional child and the training was usually provided on site.

Recruitment into the field of special education was a very difficult task because of the lack of training available, the small number of programs, and the limited future viewed for this field. Those who were recruited no doubt received training which focused on the needs of the individual child.

As programs became more established within community settings, training programs grew somewhat rapidly within the public schools and institutions of higher education. At least one college or university in the majority of states offered training programs initiated at the graduate level. In fact, many states required prior experience in the regular classroom before a person could be certified to teach exceptional children. Of course, training programs also began for other professionals. One could obtain training in the areas of psychology and social work pertaining to the exceptional child; however, these programs were not widespread.

The development of programs such as early public school classes tended to neglect parents or, at best, tolerate them. Professional services almost entirely excluded the parents. A thorough examination of this period would probably reveal the general attitude that parental intervention was not appropriate. What could the parents offer to the education and training of the exceptional child? Certainly parents were not viewed as having any expertise in providing training. Education and training were the responsibility of the professionals who had formal training.

Contrarily, though, parents usually were not asking for specific kinds of services. They were demanding that their children be included in a community program, but there was little awareness of quality programs. The parents wanted something done, but they did not see it as their role to demand particular types of services. Any service available was definitely better than nothing. Experience indicated little or no hope for the future for exceptional children; therefore, parents were complacent. They accepted programs as they were conceived and developed by professionals.

The above statements should not be construed to mean that no counseling services were available for parents of exceptional children. Counseling services have been provided for many years for parents; however, the majority of counselors did not consider the vital role that parents could play in improving the development of an exceptional child. Many of the early counseling programs were very directive and emphasized helping the parents to be more accepting of their child. If the parents did not like or accept the services, they could always search for another agency counselor.

With the opening of community services to the exceptional child, many community agencies and people became involved in attempting to meet their needs. The exceptional child's needs were beginning to be recognized as more than custodial; therefore, more agencies had to offer services. Professionals agreed that intensive and comprehensive services were required if exceptional children were to reach their potential.

During the phase of rapid growth, public schools were not the only agencies providing services. Sheltered workshops, halfway houses, vocational training programs, early childhood programs, hospital settings, etc., were developed for the exceptional child. As a result of these expanding community services, many agencies and professionals became involved in providing direct and indirect services for exceptional children.

In addition to professional services, many organizations, such as the Shriners, Jaycees, Business and Professional Women's Groups, Lions Clubs, Rotary Clubs, became involved in promoting services for exceptional children. These services provided funds for research, summer camps, scholarships for professional training, physical facilities, hospitals, and many other areas. Without the involvement of these organizations, the exceptional child would not have been provided the comprehensive services needed.

The exceptional child's visibility in the community was also evident in many vocational areas. With the implementation of work-oriented school programs, vocational training, and improved attitudes of many employers, exceptional individuals began to take their places in the work force of the community. Because the services provided for them had led to productive full-time employment, the average citizen began to see the exceptional individual in meaningful work stations, which had a tremendous effect on attitudes and further acceptance. The general public gradually became more involved with and accepting of the exceptional individual's access to the resources of the community.

The primary emphasis in program planning during this period of growth was consistently to encourage more programs. We had neglected or isolated the exceptional individual for so long that many different programs were required; therefore, the focus on providing more services was very appropriate.

Although many programs developed during this time, some of them developed without much planning. A few years ago, professionals were stating that if only we had comprehensive assessment services, resource centers, instructional materials, public school classrooms, and vocational training programs, we could really meet the needs of exceptional children. These programs and services developed into existence rapidly, yet we are still not meeting the children's needs.

Many programs were good. However, when the building of programs is the primary focus, quality is sometimes overlooked. Instead of planning ahead for the type and number of programs which might be required, programs were planned and implemented after the need for them was demonstrated. Planning as an afterthought does not always accomplish the same objective as planning for the services before they are required.

Recent Program Emphasis

Recent programs are providing services which tend to enhance the position of the exceptional individual in society. Evidence is accumulating that the exceptional individual with appropriate services can succeed and definitely can learn and become a contributing member of society.

There are still skeptics in our society and those who do not wish to discuss the problems or the life chances of the exceptional child. However, if one will take the time to listen to the news broadcasts, read the newspapers, and visit schools and other programs, the evidence is that more positive attitudes are developing. The exceptional individual is probably more a part of society today than ever before.

By no means do all people have positive or even wholesome attitudes toward the exceptional child. There are people who still put down exceptional children and believe that if they can't make it in society, then it's certainly not the fault of society. Even some school administrators try to hide the fact that they have an exceptional individual within their school population because special services or modifications in services are too much of a hassle. Special educators will still have battles to improve attitudes and services for exceptional children, but objectively demonstrating that such children can learn and be successful in the work-a-day world will continue to enhance their positions in society.

Certainly the curricula provided for exceptional children today are much more sophisticated than they were a few years ago. In recent years very few commercially published materials were available, but today there is an overwhelming variety. In fact, special educators must select appropriate instructional materials with a great deal of discretion and study, because some commercially published materials are not adequate for exceptional children. Consequently, the person choosing materials should examine carefully the claims of the publisher. Another consideration is cost. Commercially published materials will not meet all of the needs for education and training. Therefore, professional personnel must be trained to develop their own materials to supplement commercial publications. This training should exist within colleges and universities on a pre-service basis, and within agency programs as in-service training.

The curriculum of today is beginning to place a strong emphasis on the development of competencies. Also, there is more emphasis on vocational education and career education for the exceptional child. These additions to the instructional programs create more comprehensive curricula for the total life space of these children.

There are probably very few colleges or universities which do not provide at least one course pertaining to exceptional children. Many university training programs developed extensively after the exceptional child was integrated into community programs. The university programs offer professional training for teachers, psychologists, physical and speech therapists, social workers, vocational educators, counselors, and even paraprofessionals.

Large sums of federal monies were available for the original development of many of these programs. Monies are still provided for the development of programs relative to the current emphasis which is determined by a needs analysis indicated by state plans for exceptional children.

In addition to university and college training, many in-service training programs are offered by regional resource centers, public schools, residential centers, parent groups, and interested associations. These numbers will continue to expand as more exceptional children are identified and placed in appropriate educational facilities.

The training of professionals focuses more than ever on their abilities to meet adequately the individual needs of exceptional children. Such areas as prescriptive teaching, individualization of instruction objectives and techniques, and computerized instruction are receiving considerable professional attention. Emphasis is directed toward regular and special classroom teachers and their abilities to understand and to teach the individual exceptional child. A part of this current trend is indicated by competency-based training programs. The preprofessional can no longer demonstrate competency by earning passing grades on course examinations. Professional trainees must also demonstrate that they can effectively apply the skills they learned in their training programs. The field application of learned skills will probably continue to be a part of training programs and should result in an overall improvement in services for exceptional children.

The variety in professional training today is unlimited. If one has a feasible approach, the consumer of professional training is usually willing to engage in it if it appears to be an improvement. The future, unquestionably, will reveal many interesting and challenging trends yet to be developed in the area of professional training.

Recent programs for exceptional children have progressively changed because parents have worked diligently toward the desired goals. As parents realized the need for additional planning and delivery of services, they organized themselves into powerful lobbying and pressure groups. Such organizations as the National Association for Retarded Citizens and the National Association for Children with Learning Disabilities receive most of their support from parents, who have demanded more services and better quality in existing programs.

The passage and implementation of Public Law 94–142 requires that programs develop more cooperation and contact with parents regarding their exceptional child. This law, as well as a greater acceptance of the importance of the role of the parents, has made parents a viable part of programs for exceptional children. Consulting with parents, training them as a part of the intervention team, and seeking their approval for placement of their child in special programs or for changes in their child's programs are essential.

Several current programs have demonstrated that parents can be very effective as trainers of their exceptional child. This emphasis will continue and increasingly become a part of the programs provided. Developing the skills of professionals to work more effectively with parents will also increase in momentum.

Parents have become more sophisticated and knowledgeable regarding their exceptional children. They continue to provide meaningful lobbying and resources for other parents as well as professionals. Their knowledge, concerns, and vital roles will continue to influence the direction of programs and the services offered by professionals. Certainly there will be some parents who don't cooperate, but those who care and are involved will tend to control the direction of professional growth.

During recent years, community involvement for exceptional children has been more of an expansion of existing services rather than continual new growth. The period of rapid growth produced most of the increase of community services for and visibility of exceptional children.

The expansion of services by schools requires a comprehensive transitional program from the elementary to the secondary level. These services should provide a continuum of programs for exceptional children that reflects cautious and realistic needs assessments.

In addition to public schools' expanded services, many vocational education or vocational technical programs are implementing services. Such programs will further enhance the vocational futures of exceptional children, and also give more realistic assessments of their vocational potentials.

Physical barriers are being eliminated when buildings are constructed, and in some instances architectural barriers are being removed in existing buildings. These developments should continue which will offer more programs for exceptional children and also allow more visibility in everyday society.

There is probably more positive awareness of exceptional children today than ever before in our history. The handicapped person's performance as a contributing member of society becomes more evident each year. There are many examples of success stories: a blind person has completed medical school, a person with artificial legs has learned to fly his own airplane and give flying lessons, deaf people master requirements for teaching degrees and jobs, physically disabled people hold high level political offices, etc.

As community rehabilitation centers, respite care, sheltered workshops, and public schools programs continue to grow, there will be more involvement from people within communities. The involvement of professionals or paraprofessionals will continue to enhance the image of exceptional children and promote further development of meaningful programs.

Planning programs for exceptional children is increasingly important in our technological, complex society. Programs must be planned to provide early interventions and also a continuum of services throughout the life of the exceptional individual. A broadening emphasis is being placed on the development of career education programs and the development of personal competencies. If professionals plan these programs for appropriate implementation, the exceptional child will be better prepared to become a well-adjusted adult.

As the emphasis in planning becomes a part of interagency services for exceptional children, we will begin to close the gap between services offered and services needed. This type of planning should also help agencies to better use their personnel and facilities. If we do not incorporate intensive planning as a part of program services, many programs will be hurriedly conceived and staffed.

Program planning has become more evident because every state has to submit a state plan for meeting the needs of exceptional children. These plans have to consider the number of children presently served, the services offered, and how the new delivery of services will be implemented for the unserved and the underserved. Through the development of these plans and consistent revision, services will be implemented on the basis of priority groups rather than on a "first come, first served" basis. Of course, these state plans will also determine the types of new or re-trained professionals who will be in demand. Program planning has to consider the services which will have an appropriate impact on the lives of exceptional children and their families.

Goals of Special Education

The ultimate goal of the education of children, both handicapped and non-handicapped, ". . . is a productive, satisfying life as a member of society," (Martin 1972). Special educators have often failed to achieve this goal in existing programs for handicapped children.

From two-thirds to three-fourths of all special education programs are at the elementary school level, and in many, preparation for the world of work is only indirectly involved. Only twenty-one percent of handicapped children leaving school in the next four years will be fully employed or go on to college. Another forty percent will be underemployed, and twenty-six percent will be unemployed. An additional ten percent will require at least a partially "sheltered" setting and family, and three percent will probably be almost totally dependent. (Martin 1972)

In order to reach the goals suggested by Martin, educators must have practical, short-term objectives for exceptional children at various periods during their development. Perhaps one of the first goals should be to improve continuously the ways in which exceptional children are identified. As identification techniques are improved, all personnel should focus on developing quality educational programs and related services within the continuum of services to be provided to all exceptional children and youth.

Quality educational programs and related services include remediation, physical restoration services, developing academic and personal skills, and learning to cope with the environment and ever-changing modern technology.

Quality education programs through which the teacher can focus on improving the child's abilities and skills are goals for all educators. Educating parents to become significant contributors to their child's total development is an additional goal which is attained through parent and home intervention programs.

Goals for exceptional children must evolve consistently based on the best current information. Educators must never allow their goals to become static. Exceptional children will continue to need early identification and intervention programs if they are to become functioning and contributing members of society.

Early Identification of Exceptional Children

The improvement of educational services for exceptional children includes the early identification of their problems in learning, adjustment, and health. Professional personnel have hesitated too long in identifying exceptional children at an early age. Hesitation in identifying children as exceptional in order to "wait and see" can only cause frustration on the part of children, parents, and teachers. Waiting until a child has continuously failed in the regular school program in order to contribute information to the existing diagnostic assessment certainly cannot help the development of the child's self-concept; nor can it enhance the attitude the child will develop toward learning and adjustment.

Exceptional children must be provided adequate and functional educational services at an early age in order to prevent a significant loss of human potential. In this sense, special education services must be viewed as habilitative. Some exceptional children may be directly helped to overcome problems before the severity reaches a point of total debilitation. With appropriate supportive personnel and a prevailing attitude that special education is a positive approach, all professional personnel should strive to identify the child's problems and place him or her in an adequate learning environment as soon as possible.

Of course, the early identification of exceptional children means that professional persons must stop viewing special education placement as a social stigma. The training of the teacher in the field of Special Education and the small number of children in the special class should enable the Special Education program to provide meaningful instruction when the child is in a time of greatest need. Placement in a special education class should never mean that the child is destined to spend the remainder of the educational program within the special class setting. All exceptional children cannot and should not be moved in and out of special education classes, but a few children who exhibit severe problems during the early elementary school years, or even the preschool years, may be assisted to the extent that they will be able to move into the mainstream of education. These statements imply that the school principal, school superintendent, and any other person who may be responsible for teacher selection and assignment must strive to find and hire the best special education teachers to implement appropriate programs for exceptional children.

Provision of Services for Exceptional Children

Even though great strides have been made in establishing programs and preparing professional personnel to serve exceptional children, we estimate that adequate provisions are available for 60 to 80 percent of all exceptional children. This percentage may appear to be quite sufficient; however, when one conservatively estimates that approximately 15 to 18 percent of the school age population may be categorically identified within at least one exceptional group; then progress in meeting the needs of these children is very inadequate.

Estimates of Exceptional Children Receiving Services

In 1971, Weintraub, Aberson, and Braddock reported on estimates of the numbers of exceptional children and compared the total estimated to the number who were receiving some type of special education program. This report indicated that a large majority of exceptional children are still not receiving special services. For example, the estimated number of trainable and educable mentally retarded children was reported to be in excess of 1,330,000 but only 703,000 (approximately) were receiving special services. This means that nearly 53 percent of all moderately and mildly retarded children were receiving special services as of 1971. Approximately the same percentage of speech impaired children and only about 2 percent of the children with learning disabilities were being served. The reader should note that these figures are from 1971 data, and there has been improvement during the 1970s. The 1980s, we hope, will indicate nearly 100 percent served.

Because state and federal legislation has not closed the gap between the demand and supply of special services for exceptional children, educators are questioning the foundation in legislation, programs, teacher training, and certification on which special education policies and practices are based. The shift to self-analysis is a painful process which will help educators to reexamine the basic principles and structures that presently strengthen special education programs (Gallagher 1972).

A considerable amount of current discussion is centered around the issue of labeling and the effectiveness of etiological categories in developing programs for exceptional children. Although categorization according to disabilities was once an effective method for public recognition and funding, it is presently being criticized. Lilly (1971) states:

Substantial public support has been developed for special education programs, and as a result the frequency of outright exclusion of children from public education has been decreased. The accomplishments of special educators in the areas of public opinion and positive recognition of individual differences is commendable. These past activities have been both necessary and effective; however, in combination with a number of parallel forces, they may have changed the educational system to such an extent that as solutions, they are no longer appropriate. In solving the original problems facing special education, new problems have been created which demand new solutions. Thus come the present forces for change in the field of special education.

The Problem of Labels and Categories

Reynolds and Balow (1972) suggested that numerous problems may be created when labels and categories are assigned to groups of people. These problems are: (1) each label carries with it certain characteristics which do not necessarily fit each individual within the group; (2) stigmas attached to a group may result in "scapegoating" and serve as an excuse for inadequate educational procedures; (3) lower expectations by those working with handicapped children may be seen in their rapport with students and in curriculum development; and (4) categorical labels may be equated with special educational techniques which disregard individual differences.

We recognize the need for changes in the field of special education. However, if noncategorization goes too far and there is a tendency to eliminate all information directly related to the use of labels, then problems which existed in special education programs of the past may be rediscovered. If we hesitate to disseminate information with respect to the functioning level of some exceptional children, then a special educator may apply too much pressure for performance from a child who cannot meet these expectancies. Certainly, we do not want to promote the use of labels and categories which create or continue to create stigma. However, labels and categories, if used properly, can aid communication and need not create stigma and lowered expectations.

Regardless of views to the contrary, current trends in definitions assigned to exceptional children are becoming more flexible. They tend to define the functioning level of a child rather than the disabling condition. The trend is away from the precise clinical diagnosis to one that emphasizes behavioral and learning characteristics (Weintraub, Aberson, and Braddock 1971).

Lilly (1971) described a mildly handicapped child as one

. . . whose problems can be seen as relatively mild, those children traditionally labeled as educable mentally retarded, emotionally disturbed, behaviorally disordered, educationally handicapped, learning disabled, or brain injured . . . referred from regular education programs because of some sort of teacher perceived behavioral or learning problems.

With an awareness of a few of the current arguments and issues in the field of special education, the reader should recognize that constructive changes are being made. However, until the majority of changes being implemented and proposed are effective, many programs that have been in existence for several years will remain ineffective.

Alternatives for Placement of Exceptional Children

Exceptional children should be placed in educational programs designed to meet their particular needs and abilities. Programs for exceptional children have been presented as a cascade of services described by Deno (1971) to involve a hierarchy of services. Public Law 94–142, which is described in detail later in this chapter, mandates that an appropriate educational program be provided for all handicapped children. The question remains as to whether this mandate can be served through a hierarchy of services or a continuum of services. For example, instead of implementing a resource room for *all* learning disabled children and adolescents, a continuum of services should be available in order to meet their needs and abilities. The components of Deno's cascade of services should be in operation at all times in order to comply with Public Law 94–142.

One of the requirements of Public Law 94–142 is to educate the handicapped with the nonhandicapped to the greatest extent possible. The main focus should be to provide an appropriate and quality education for the handicapped and the gifted. A continuum of services is an approach which includes both the letter of the law, and the intent of the law.

We propose a continuum of services which would place the handicapped child or adolescent in an existing program which is designed to serve individual needs. The proposed continuum of services (see figure 1.1) demonstrates the overlap of all educational programs which should be offered. In this type of structure, the handicapped individual may be moved into any program which provides the least restrictive environment. All programs within the continuum of services are equal in that each offers an appropriate and quality instructional and training program designed to meet an individual's needs and abilities. The placement team recommends placement based upon the diagnosis of handicapped individuals and their immediate needs. These guidelines interpret the least restrictive environment as the one in which the child or adolescent can best perform. As a student progresses in a particular placement, he or she may be moved to any appropriate part of the continuum. In the continuum of services, the residential center or the self-contained special class is not perceived as less desirable placement. They are viewed and accepted as integral parts of the entire continuum of programs available.

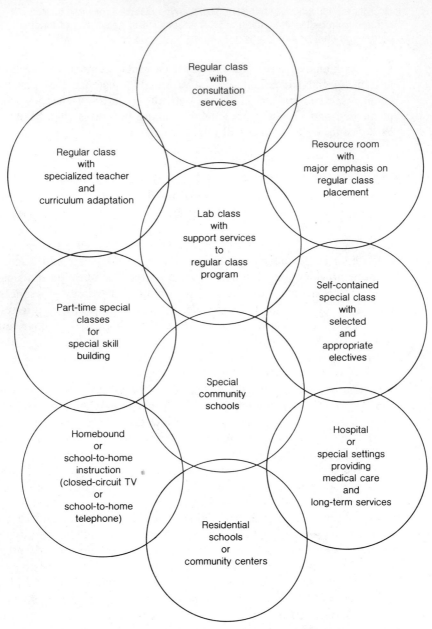

Figure 1.1 Continuum of services for handicapped children.

In figure 1.1, a continuum of services for the handicapped child is presented. After a brief study of this table, the various areas which should be offered on a consistent and continuing basis for the handicapped child are discussed.

Residential Schools or Community Centers

Residential schools continue to play an important role in the care and education of the handicapped child. Most states provide residential services by providing state facilities or paying for private schools located either in the home state or in neighboring states (Cruickshank and Johnson 1975).

In the early history of special education, the majority of handicapped children were placed in residential schools or kept at home. As local school districts assumed increasing responsibility for the education of handicapped children, the complexion of state schools changed. Children presently enrolled in residential schools are those who are so severely handicapped that they cannot participate in or profit from public school programs, or who reside in sparsely populated areas without access to special classes (Calovini 1968).

The Wisconsin program has created an alternate solution for children residing in rural areas. This plan is designed for students who live too far to commute to special education programs. Instead of residential placement, these children live with boarding home parents during the week and attend special programs within the local schools (Melcher 1969).

Residential schools have received serious criticism in recent years. Essentially the criticism has revolved around three specific issues: (1) the handicapped child is isolated from both home and society; (2) there is a stigma attached to residential schools; and (3) generally the quality of the teaching staff and curriculum development is not equal to that of other types of education programs (Cruickshank and Johnson 1975).

Even though there has been criticism of residential centers, many of them have improved their services and their staffs. Residential schools and community centers provide services when no other appropriate service is available. Improved criteria for staff employment and reduction of enrollment in residential schools or community centers have improved services vastly. Some of the improvements in residential schools and community centers are offered through supportive services such as physical therapists, recreation specialists, speech therapists, and psychological care. Programs provide special trips away from the grounds of the residential or community center; therefore, students receive education outside the restrictions of their usual environment.

Hospital or Special Settings

Many educational programs with hospital or special settings are administered by local school systems, and the teachers are employed by that school system rather than the hospital program. This procedure provides the teachers with a salary commensurate with the salaries of the local school system. It also provides them with the same benefits.

The children in the special setting are counted in the local school system's average daily attendance, and funding is on the local level. A close liaison must be maintained with the child's local school system since he or she may be away from home. This liaison will provide the local school system with the child's academic progress and also recommend special provisions which may be necessary when the child returns home.

There are times when a handicapped child must be placed in a hospital setting or a very specialized setting in order to receive appropriate medical care as well as continued educational services. Children requiring these services include those who have been burned severely, children with advanced cystic fibrosis, children or adolescents who have become handicapped as a result of a serious injury, and some children who are multiply and severely handicapped from birth. In some situations, the child who is in the specialized setting may have a terminal illness. This requires counseling for the child, the parents, and the educators who are involved.

As the educational program continues in a hospital setting or a very specialized setting, school activities often must be planned around the medical services required. Children may be scheduled for surgery, special medical treatment, or physical therapy, and the educators must adapt to scheduled treatments which are vital to the child's life and welfare.

There may be a need for specially equipped wheelchairs which are breath controlled for the paralyzed individual, special standing and tilt tables, tape recorders, taped programs, and a variety of other audiovisual aids. The special equipment adds considerable cost to the educational program, but it is essential if the needs and abilities of the individuals are to be met.

Homebound or School-to-Home Instruction

As a result of Operation Child Find, which is in effect in every state, many preschool handicapped children are receiving educational services through homebound instruction. Other children, such as those who are seriously ill or recuperating at home as a result of surgery or serious injury, receive homebound instruction or school-to-home instruction. Homebound instruction is somewhat limited in most states in that educational services must be provided a minimum of three to four hours per week. Although this limitation exists, remember that the instruction is on a one-to-one basis, and the child is required to complete assignments throughout the week.

School-to-home instruction is provided by a special telephone circuit from the school to the home. Through this circuit, the student at home may listen to all class discussions and also ask questions or contribute to class discussions. A much more specialized version of school-to-home instruction is through a closed circuit television system. This permits the student to see the classroom, and the class can see the student at home. School-to-home instructional programs are expensive, but they enable the student to maintain close contact with the regular education program.

A school system may provide special homebound instructors who serve children in the entire school district through central office coordination. In many cases these teachers must have a state teaching certificate or license but are not required to have a special education teaching certificate or license. Full-time homebound instructors are found more frequently in large, metropolitan school systems. Smaller school systems offer homebound instruction through teachers who travel to children's homes after school hours for additional compensation.

Special Community Schools

Special schools were developed as an alternative to residential placement and can generally be defined as one of two types. The first type serves children of a single etiological classification; for example, the physically handicapped, the mentally retarded, or any other specific group of handicapped children. The second type of special school is one in which children with many different types of handicaps are educated (Cruickshank and Johnson 1975). The purpose of special residential school facilities is to meet the needs of seriously handicapped children who (1) are unable to cope with the normal school situation; (2) require a sheltered environment; or (3) need specialized equipment for treatment (Cruickshank and Johnson 1975).

The authors' experiences indicate that a special school may also be organized and established for the purposes of having a central location for providing the services of supplementary professional personnel, such as a physical therapist, occupational therapist, speech therapist, and school psychologist. Rather than requiring such personnel to spend time traveling throughout a school district, they may be assigned to one special school. They can then spend more of their time in serving the individual needs of handicapped children.

The special school has been subjected to the same criticism as that directed toward the residential schools. The primary objection is the lack of integration with the nonhandicapped members of society. Calovini suggests that a few children from special schools have difficulty in adjusting after

Special school settings are an important part of services for handicapped children. (Courtesy of June Maddox, Children's Convalescent Center, Bethany, Oklahoma Public Schools.)

they return to a regular school environment. Although the disadvantages of the special schools are numerous, these schools are preferred to residential schools, or to no placement at all in a special setting.

Self-Contained Special Classes

The special class provides for a group of handicapped children of a given classification and should be located in a regular elementary or secondary school. The number of special classes in a particular school building may vary. Often the number is increased to a point where programs may resemble a modified special school. This type of program is being used with all categories of handicapped children, both severely and mildly handicapped (Cruickshank and Johnson 1975).

These classes may be varied in their operation. A few of them are completely set apart from the rest of the school. We have seen special classes so segregated from the rest of the school that even the teachers could not share the same lounge with regular classroom teachers. This was an extreme case; however, such cases do exist in many school systems. Contrary to this isolated program, special room programs allow for integration of the handicapped into the mainstream of school activities. The degree of integration is determined by the physical and academic abilities of the child (Calovini 1968). If exceptional children can function with success in the mainstream of education, they certainly should be permitted to do so.

Lilly suggests that the real focus of the controversy in special education is on children who have been labeled mildly handicapped and have been placed in self-contained special classes. Studies concerning special class programs have produced conflicting evidence. The majority of researchers have reported that special class programs show very little superiority over programs provided in regular classes (Lilly 1970).

In reviewing the literature, Lilly quotes several professional educators who question the effectiveness of special class programs. It is from this reference point that he suggests traditional special education services as represented by self-contained special classes be discontinued immediately for all mildly handicapped children.

This is, in all fairness, a commendable recommendation from Lilly. However, we question whether or not the majority of regular classroom teachers are ready to accept mildly handicapped individuals back into their classrooms on a full-time basis. If the recommendation were to be implemented in the near future, many of these children would be further alienated from school and learning. Administrators and regular classroom teachers are not prepared for quick and total mainstreaming. If mainstreaming is done slowly, and appropriate training is given to regular classroom teachers, such a plan might be effective.

Martin (1972) comments on special classes, stating:

> The predominant strategy today, in its most oversimplified sense, is to reduce the complexity of educating handicapped children by reducing the task to dealing with small, relatively homogeneous groups called special classes. We have discovered, however, that using etiological labels to establish homogeneity is less efficient than we expected. And so we are exploring other categorization systems, the relevant behaviors of the child, the type of process to be learned, etc. The ultimate reduction of this process is to move beyond small groupings to individualized instruction.

Resource Rooms, Itinerant Teaching, and Lab Classes

The resource room and itinerant programs are used in an effort to respond to some of the criticisms of the special class approach to the education of the mildly handicapped and to achieve more fully an integrated experience for them. The function of the two programs is very similar. The basic difference is that the itinerant teacher goes to the child in the regular schools; consequently the teacher may serve more than one school building. The resource room teacher rarely serves more than one school building.

Although there is no stereotyped resource or itinerant program, the programs involve the presence of a special education teacher in a regular school building, serving the needs of handicapped children who have been placed in regular class programs. Scheduling for these children depends on (1) the number of students involved in the programs, and (2) the type of instruction needed to allow the child to function adequately and remain in the regular program.

One variation of the resource room approach is operating in the school district of Buffalo, New York. The Board of Cooperative Education Services (BOCES) operations grew from eleven resource rooms in the 1969–70 school year to twenty-three such rooms in 1970–71. Two unique features of this program are its operation of a Child Evaluation Center, and teacher roles. The purpose of the Child Evaluation Center is to help teachers to understand problem children in their rooms. There are several features of the evaluation center that are unique: (1) a "confidential" or "restricted" label is not applied to anything that happens within the center; (2) the entire evaluation process is done by the teacher; (3) parents are allowed to observe the entire evaluation process; and (4) children who are already enrolled in a BOCES special education class may not be referred to the center.

The necessity of close communications between the regular classroom teacher and the resource room teacher is common to all resource room programs. Usually the regular teacher is the assistant in the learning program established for the child. In the BOCES program, the feeling is generated that the regular teacher is the learning coordinator. The resource room teacher is an assistant who helps further the goal established primarily by the learning coordinator (Reger and Kappman 1971).

A very interesting adaptation and expansion of the resource room concept was implemented in the State of Washington. According to Affleck, Lehning, and Brow (1973), this adaptation involved a resource school which provided special services to a variety of exceptional children and eliminated the need for self-contained classrooms.

There were forty-eight children who were identified as mildly handicapped and in need of special services and an additional fifty-one who needed special academic services. The program provided many supportive services to regular classroom teachers and, of course, to children with special needs. Training was also provided for special education practicum students and master's degree interns. The model improved existing services for practical training of the future special educator. Hopefully, this concept will expand and be implemented by more states.

In addition, there are part-time special classes provided for the primary purpose of assisting the mildly handicapped in special skill building. For example, the primary task of the special education teacher in this setting is to provide a special emphasis in reading, math, or spelling. Students receiving the service do not require intensive tutorial or remedial programs; therefore, the part-time special class can meet their needs without extensive removal from a regular class.

The resource room, lab class, and part-time special class must allow the teacher time to serve as a support and liaison person to regular teachers. Some authorities suggest that the special class teachers, in one of the above mentioned settings, should have one to two hours per day set aside as a part of their regularly assigned duties to consult with and support regular teachers. The services offered through the resource room, lab class, and part-time special class would improve considerably if support and liaison were to become a reality.

Regular Class with Specialized Teacher Training and Curriculum Adaptation

Time and time again, one can find resources which advocate regular class placement (mainstreaming) for the mildly handicapped. In-service training has been conducted throughout the states in order to assist regular class teachers with the education of the handicapped. In fact, such training appears to be ongoing for all regular teachers whether they want to provide educational services for the handicapped or not. If regular class placement is as successful as it should be for the mildly handicapped, specialized teacher training should be accomplished through specific programs of curriculum adaptation, and with in-service training of regular teachers in small groups of eight to ten over a period of an entire school year.

The rapid pace at which in-service training programs are generally conducted, and the concurrent large numbers of teachers in a single training session, merely satisfies the requirement that such training has been conducted. Those rapid-fire programs offer little value or change in instructional programs. They are a farce. In-service training must be intensive and result in significant teacher and instructional changes, or it is not training.

Regular Class With Consultation Services

As a part of the continuum of services required for handicapped children and adolescents, the regular class with consultation services is the final connecting link. Consultation is not necessarily the last resource to use, but it should be used only when the regular class with specialized teacher training and curriculum adaptation has proven successful. After regular class teachers have received specialized training and assistance in adapting the curriculum, they should be able to provide an appropriate educational program with periodic consultation.

If the entire continuum of services is accepted as a step-by-step approach in providing services for the handicapped as well as in training special educators, regular educators, vocational educators, school counselors, school administrators, and making adaptations in the curriculum; then the handicapped will receive quality educational programs designed to meet their special needs and abilities.

Issues and Trends in Placement of Exceptional Children

A Training Based Model

Lilly (1971) proposes in "A Training Based Model for Special Education," an alternative to the special services model presently used by special education. In this model plan, the focus is on children who are referred from the regular educational programs because of teacher-perceived behavioral or learning problems. The goal of this model is very similar to the BOCES program. The objective is to equip regular classroom teachers with the skills necessary to cope with problem situations. The roles of the special educators would be to provide support and training for the classroom teachers, rather than to provide repositories for children from whom teachers need relief.

The implementation of this model will require more thorough training of special education teachers, and an acceptance of the special educator as a resource person. In addition, training programs for special education personnel will have to prepare teachers to become more proficient in conducting informal evaluations and in demonstrating competency in the use of procedures that may eliminate or alleviate learning or behavioral problems. These adjustments are possible in a majority of special education training programs and should, if implemented properly, enhance the educational placements and environments provided for mildly handicapped children.

The Special Education Contract

Gallagher (1972) describes a contract that must be signed between both parents and educators before mildly handicapped children can be placed in a special education unit. This contract is designed for a specific time limit, a maximum of two years. It is not renewable and contains specific educational goals. With the termination of the contract period, the responsibility for education of the handicapped child is shifted back to the regular educational program.

Proficiency in stating and accomplishing specific instructional and behavioral objectives is relatively new to all fields of education. If contracts, as suggested by Gallagher, were to be required, the special educator would designate specific tasks to be accomplished by the handicapped child within specified periods of time. This procedure would require the special educator to develop and use skills in preparing tasks by specific steps and sequencing educational and behavioral activities. Several programs have started an emphasis in this area and would certainly enhance the feasibility of special education contracts.

A Comprehensive Plan for Programming

Programs and services for the handicapped are so diversified that some services appear to overlap in some areas and are seriously deficient in other areas. A portion of these difficulties could be corrected or alleviated through the establishment of a voluntary organization in each state which would collect information relative to all services available. This organization could be developed through existing governmental agencies; it would not necessitate the implementation of a new state organization (Cogan and Ohrtman 1971).

The entire system is based on a continuous and computerized record-keeping system, containing information on each handicapped person within a state from birth throughout the educational process. This system of record keeping makes possible longitudinal studies, evaluation of diagnostic procedures, and a method by which professional terminology may be standardized. The authors of this plan propose that the consolidation of activities currently existing and the proper use of agencies would not only be more effective, but also result in less expenditures.

Teacher Training Programs

The traditional practice of organizing services for handicapped children on the basis of disability categories and the preparation of teachers in terms of specializations is presently used in most colleges and universities. These programs appear to reflect the legislation and program development of the 1960s. The United States Department of Education gives its support to the categorical system in both legislation and in programming. Somewhat recent federal legislation that reflects this support is Public Law 91–230, which specifically defines an additional group of handicapped children—children with specific learning disabilities.

More flexibility in training programs has been suggested by the Office of Education, and this trend will probably remain in existence for a number of years. This flexibility will aid universities and colleges in developing programs that will train teachers to provide instructional programs for children with learning or adjustment problems regardless of their disabilities. Different emphasis in teacher training programs will also involve changes in the special education services described above.

Contemporary Approaches in Teacher Training
The National Education Association's National Commission on Teacher Education and Professional Standards identified three trends which may be significant in changing the standards for the preparation of teachers of handicapped children. "These trends are (1) alternate routes into certification through the use of performance criteria, (2) student-teacher reforms, and (3) differentiated staffing" (Position Paper on Standards 1970).

Andrews (1970) proposed an innovative program of teacher certification. The plan was program-centered and performance-centered. Certification as a teacher would be based on competencies, that is, one's ability to teach.

Schwartz (1971) in "A Clinical Teacher Model for Interrelated Areas of Special Education" states:

Clinical teaching, i.e., diagnostic, prescriptive, and individualized instruction, is not new or innovative, but rather is the renewed and continuing aspiration toward a fundamental goal of special education. The coupling of the heritage of the field with the emerging sophistication in instructional systems and technology provides a conceptual framework for testing and building a data base for proposed changes in teacher education for the decade of the Seventies

With this as his rationale, he describes a teacher preparation model for interrelated areas in special education. This model provides instructional objectives for training teachers as well as for educating handicapped children in the schools. The main emphasis is upon (1) using behavioral descriptions of desired competencies; (2) assessment procedures for measuring entry and proficiency levels of performance; and (3) a variety of instructional plans designed to accomplish the objectives of the program (Schwartz 1971).

Curriculum Development in Special Education
When implementing and planning materials for the special classes, the teacher must be very considerate of the child's particular level of growth and age range. As exceptional children move through the school program, they may have a mental or performance age that is significantly different from that of other children. They are faced with many new needs and social expectations which may be extremely frustrating. Students who mature physically compatible with their chronological age range, but not emotionally or mentally, are unable to understand or possibly cope with additional demands placed upon them. If one is to be able to help constructively and

meaningfully in what is perhaps the greatest hour of need, then one must meet the challenge of the individual exceptional child.

For example, a youngster may be faced with a newly developed sex interest and may not be able to sustain the boy-girl interaction. The concept of self at this time is important if students are to maintain a reasonable degree of logic and understanding of the social skills required in boyfriend-girlfriend communication. Consequently, there must be the right kind of curriculum planning in the special education or regular class to help these students understand themselves and society's demands.

Exceptional children need help in learning how to function harmoniously in society. They need to learn how to work, play, and communicate with others, and to be accepted by others. If they are to become efficient socially, economically, and personally, they must learn to develop adequate social relations in a special class. To develop a more complete self-awareness of the here and now, they must also be aided in transferring these learned skills into the realm of the total school program and their own total functioning as individuals. The teacher's instruction must be coordinated to meet the three objectives of social, economic, and personal efficiency. Learning how to function properly in society should be a part of a curriculum that affords students the opportunity to learn how to find a place in life that is worthwhile to themselves and to society.

In planning the curriculum for exceptional children, the school is faced with a number of developmental needs and very little time to meet them. These students enter school on an academic and social level significantly different from the regular school student. The special class teachers have the responsibility of helping these students to become integrated, functional members of society in the same period of time that is granted to the regular student population. This is a very difficult assignment for the special teacher, particularly if the exceptional child has been exposed to failure for long periods of time in the regular classroom program. However, in the majority of cases, the special class teacher should have more individual resources than most other teachers. Consequently, special class teachers should be able to integrate their own resources with those of the community, vocational rehabilitation, the state department of education, and current literature, with a continuity that enables the exceptional student to achieve social, economic, and personal efficiency. In some cases, these objectives may be realized in spite of the system to which the child is exposed.

Resourceful teachers will not permit a rigid enforcement of academic requirements for their students. Special class teachers must remember that they are working with students who usually have difficulty learning incidentally and, therefore, must have concrete application in all or most areas of instruction. (Of course, this does not generally include the gifted child.) A teacher who enforced rigid academic standards upon these students would meet instant failure. The academic program must be integrated with the objectives of social, economic, and personal efficiency. Special class teachers should constantly remind themselves that they must afford opportunities to their students to do work that can be associated with life and society. These special students may have little ability to form true concepts. The teacher has to provide instruction that is meaningful to the student as a person and as a member of society, and this meaning cannot be transmitted through abstractions and theories. Instruction has to be practical.

It is understood that exceptional students will not be operating at a grade level consistent with that of other students; therefore, the teacher should not expect an academic commitment from the special class students to compete with the rest of the student body. The special class students will not remain in class for the entire school day. They will interact with other students at lunch, on the playground, at social functions, at athletic functions, and many other school activities. In some instances special class students have actively participated in athletic, musical, art, and driver's education programs, and in other classes which are chosen according to their appropriateness for the individual child. Many of the activities in which exceptional children become involved are not as functionally easy for the special student as they are for the regular class student. Some special class students may be physically larger than the other students, and they may be chronologically older. Even if the students are the same age, the exceptional students will not have, in many cases, mental and physical coordination that is consistent with the chronological age range of their peers.

These problems of exceptional students do not remain at school when they go home in the evening. They meet similar situations which remind them of their failures and deficiencies at home with their siblings, in the community with their peers, and many times with adults who do not have realistic insights into the exceptional student's characteristics. Therefore, it is very important that special class teachers concern themselves with the total environment—exceptional and normal—in which these students must live and learn, if they are to be successful in helping these students become functional citizens. A teacher must constantly remain aware that the main difference between the special class and the regular class is not so much in the instructional, academic subject areas as it is in the emphasis which needs to be placed upon the application to daily life situations.

Legislation for Exceptional Children

Direct involvement of the federal government in the education of exceptional children developed as a result of a serious shortage of qualified personnel in the field of special education. In 1959, Public Law 85–926 provided annual appropriations of one million dollars to college, universities, and state educational agencies, whereby graduate fellowships could be awarded to qualified individuals wishing to prepare for a career in the field of mental retardation (Tompkins 1969). Since special education programs at the graduate level were few, the appropriated funds were spent largely developing leadership personnel (McCarthy and McCarthy 1969).

Appropriations of 1.5 million dollars were authorized in 1961 through Public Law 87–276 for the preparation of teachers of the deaf. These funds were made available over a three-year period to colleges and universities, and were not restricted to graduate students (McCarthy and McCarthy 1969).

In 1962, Public Law 85–926 (Title III, as amended), provided stipends and dependency allowances for persons preparing for careers as teachers, supervisors, speech correctionists, specialists, and administrators in the areas of mental retardation, emotional disturbance, speech and hearing impairment, deafness, visual impairments, crippling conditions, and other health impairments (McCarthy and McCarthy 1969). This Public Law provided incentive to both institutions and students, and accounted for a rise in the number of personnel trained for careers in special education. Classes for the exceptional child were also either developed or expanded as a result of this legislation.

Legislative funding during the sixties expanded to include projects and programs for the exceptional child at various age levels. A new decade of legislation was initiated on April 13, 1970, when President Nixon signed Public Law 91–230, the Elementary and Secondary Education Act Amendments of 1969; Title VI, The Education of the Handicapped Act. The purpose of this law was to combine newly created and existing legislation into a single statute. This act had seven parts which included provisions for general areas such as a Bureau for Education and Training of the Handicapped in the Office of Education; financial and consultant assistance to states; centers and services for the handicapped; training of personnel to serve handicapped children; research in education for the handicapped; instructional media; and

Continuing legislative efforts are vital to programs for exceptional children.

special programs for children with learning disabilities. For a detailed description of the seven parts of this law, the reader is referred to Martin, Bryan, LaVor, and Scheflin (1970).

By combining newly created and existing legislation into a single statute, Congress (1) established guidelines for identifying handicapped children as a major target population; (2) increased expenditure authorizations to prepare for a total response to the needs of the handicapped; (3) stimulated special education programs to continue an emphasis on humanity toward the handicapped individuals, and resisted rigid categorical classification; and (4) encouraged state agencies, local agencies, and university programs to implement cooperative endeavors in the field of special education (Martin, Bryan, LaVor, and Scheflin 1970).

Categorical versus General Aid

A controversy in legislation is rooted in the ultimate determination as to whether the form of federal aid granted to schools or agencies should be categorical or general. In categorical aid, unlike general aid, the use of funds is specified. General aid involves the distribution of federal funds on a formula basis and reserves the rights of the respective states to decide the educational purpose for which the funds would be used (McCarthy and McCarthy 1969).

Special educators tend to favor categorical aid in which funds are earmarked. If funds are categorically specified for special education, then one is relatively assured that the funds will directly serve the needs of exceptional children. If federal assistance is in the form of generalized aid, many special educators believe that the existing needs of regular education could siphon off these special funds. Earmarking of federal funds insures that they will be spent on education of a particular category of exceptional children (McCarthy and McCarthy 1969).

Reynolds and Balow (1972) comment on categorical aid and reflect the current views of a number of professional educators:

Special education should shift major attention to ways of inserting itself back into mainstream educational structures. The legislation, the "earmarks," and the special bureaucracies produced over the past decade have made their point in strong fashion; but, in the process, special educators have failed to win the leadership and concern of most progressive leaders in general education. Categorical aid should be used to build special education into broad programs rather than to build separate systems and to excuse general educators from concern with the handicapped.

Based upon these viewpoints, special educators are not advocating the elimination of categorical aid to the field of special education. They are emphasizing that the funds should be expended for purposes other than maintaining the present programs of rigid categorical classifications.

In the latter part of 1972 and the early part of 1973, federal revenue sharing began. This procedure of providing federal funds to state, county, and city governments was initially viewed as "soft" monies for which there may not be any direct accounting. When federal cutbacks were announced for such programs as the Elementary and Secondary Education Act Amendments of 1969, the Office of Economic Opportunity, and other programs, it was quickly realized that there should be a method of accounting with respect to federal revenue sharing. The full impact of federal revenue sharing and federal cutbacks in funding various programs is not evident; however, these procedures certainly seem to emphasize general federal aid as compared to categorical federal aid.

A Bill of Rights for the Handicapped: Public Law 94-142

Public Law 94-142 will bring schools closer to the principles of democracy on which the Nation was founded by opening classrooms to a new student clientele. (Goodman 1976)

By any standards, Public Law 94-142—enacted in November, 1975 as the Education for All Handicapped Children Act and scheduled for full implementation in Fiscal Year 1978—is blockbuster legislation. Schools in every part of the nation are destined to feel its impact, and to be sturdier and more broadly "American" as a consequence.

The most recent in a series of refinements of the Education of the Handicapped Act, PL 94–142 has been hailed as a "Bill of Rights for the Handicapped," promising an end to the custom of treating persons with disabilities as second-class citizens.

It gives national imprimatur to the proposition that the claim of a handicapped individual to first-rate schooling (and by extension to all other privileges offered by our society) is no less compelling than that of any other American.

It opens the way for the nation's schools to broaden their horizons, no longer focusing their operations solely on "regular" students but giving equal consideration to those with handicaps—including placing such youngsters in regular classroons to the fullest extent that doing so would be in their best interests.

PL 94–142 is remarkable among federal education laws for being permanent, voted by margins of 404 to 7 in the House and 87 to 7 in the Senate to serve the nation's schools in perpetuity.

Moreover, many of the advances it calls for have specific implications for the education of nonhandicapped youngsters as well. Two are especially noteworthy. The first, a practice that enlightened educators have been advocating for many years, requires that children served by the Act be educated in accordance with individual plans tailored to their particular needs and capacities. The second calls for making what is now termed "preschool" education a standard part of the elementary-level operation. It provides free public education to all handicapped children starting at age three. Over the next few years these important innovations can be expected to receive careful study not just by the special education community but by educators in general, and doubtless by parents as well.

PL 94–142 is in any case a big, ambitious law. In the view of one of its sponsors, Sen. Harrison Williams (D.–N.J.), it represents "the most significant development" in federal school legislation since the enactment of Title I of the Elementary and Secondary Education Act of 1965. Its magnitude is suggested by the scope of some of the challenges it sets out to deal with, as cataloged in its opening passages:

"There are more than eight million handicapped children in the United States today," and those children have special educational needs that are not being fully met.

"More than half" of them "do not receive appropriate educational services."

"One million" are in fact "excluded entirely from the public school system."

Many other handicapped children are not "having a successful educational experience because their handicaps are undetected."

The state and local agencies have the responsibility for solving such problems in the training of teachers and in developing improved diagnostic and instructional procedures and methods to assure that the states and localities can do the job. The hitch, PL 94–142 says, is that they can't tackle it properly because they do not have the resources.

Against that background—and picking up on guarantees introduced in PL 93–380 enacted two years ago—PL 94–142 sets out to make certain that without exception, every one of the nation's handicapped children (defined as "mentally retarded, hard of hearing, deaf, speech impaired, visually handicapped, seriously emotionally disturbed, orthopedically impaired, or other health impaired children, or children with specific learning disabilities") receives "special education and related services."

The scope of this goal might seem to suggest that the most noteworthy aspect of the bill is the size of the outlays it implies, and in fact the numbers do get big. What most observers see as being of greater significance, however, is that the policies expressed in the law are binding regardless of the size of appropriations. Those policies clearly are worth noting, and they include the following:

A free public education will be made available to all handicapped children between the ages of three and eighteen by no later than September of 1978 and all those between three and twenty-one by September of 1980. Coverage of children in the three-to-five and eighteen-to-twenty-one ranges will not be required in states whose school attendance laws do not include those age brackets. Nevertheless, it is now national policy to begin the education of handicapped children by at least age three and to encourage this practice. PL 94–142 authorizes incentive grants of $300 over the regular allocation for each handicapped child between the ages of three and five who is afforded special education and related services.

For each handicapped child there will be an "individualized educational program," (IEP). This is a written statement jointly developed by a qualified school official, the child's teacher and parents or guardian, and if possible the child himself. This statement will include an analysis of the child's present achievement level, a listing of both short-range and annual goals, an identification of specific services that will be provided toward meeting those goals, and an indication of the extent to which the child will be able to participate in regular school programs. It will also include a notation of when these services will be provided and how long they will last, and a schedule for checking on the progress being achieved under the plan and for revising it.

Handicapped and nonhandicapped children will be educated together to the maximum extent appropriate. The former will be placed in special classes or separate schools "only when the nature or severity of the handicap is such that education in regular classes," even if they are provided supplementary aids and services, "cannot be achieved satisfactorily."

Tests and other evaluation material used in placing handicapped children will be prepared and administered in such a way as not to be racially or culturally discriminatory, and they will be presented in the child's native tongue.

There will be an intensive and continuing effort to locate and identify youngsters who have handicaps, to evaluate their educational needs, and to determine whether those needs are being met.

In the overall effort to make sure education is available to all handicapped children, priority will be given first to those who are not receiving an education at all and second to the most severely handicapped within each disability who are receiving an inadequate education.

In school placement procedures and in any decisions concerning a handicapped child's schooling, there will be prior consultation with the child's parents or guardian. In general, no policies, programs, or procedures affecting the education of handicapped children covered by the law will be adopted without a public notice.

The rights and guarantees called for in the law will apply to handicapped children in private as well as public schools. Youngsters in private schools will be provided special education at no cost to their parents if the children were placed in these schools or referred to them by state or local education agencies.

The states and localities will undertake comprehensive personnel development programs, including in-service training for regular as well as special education teachers and support personnel. Procedures will be launched for acquiring and disseminating information about promising educational practices and materials coming out of research and development.

In implementing the law, special effort will be made to employ qualified handicapped persons.

The principles set forth a few years ago in federal legislation aimed at the elimination of architectural barriers to the physically handicapped will be applied to school construction and modification, with the commissioner authorized to make grants for these purposes.

The state education agency will have jurisdiction over all education programs for handicapped children offered within a given state, including those administered by a noneducation agency (a state hospital, for example, or the welfare department).

An advisory panel will be appointed by each governor to advise the state's education agency of unmet needs, comment publicly on such matters as proposed rules and regulations, and help the state develop and report relevant data. Membership on these panels will include handicapped individuals and parents and guardians of handicapped children.

Many of these policies have been advocated by individual educators or by professional associations. Several have been established within particular states, either by legislative action or as a consequence of court suits brought on behalf of handicapped children. And for more than five years, OE's Bureau of Education for the Handicapped (and particularly its Deputy Commissioner, Edwin W. Martin) have been urging a national goal of providing education for all handicapped children and of doing so by 1980—a principle and a target date now spelled out in the law. In short, the concepts involved are not new. The difference is that through PL 94–142 they have become requirements, and accommodation to them is a condition of being eligible to receive support under the Act's funding provisions.

Like so many other aspects of the Act, those provisions are both lofty and innovative, entailing some noteworthy changes in the ways by which federal education dollars have traditionally been distributed. Allocation of the current $100 million annual appropriation for the state grant program, for example, is based on a funding formula by which the number of children in a state between the ages of three and twenty-one is multiplied by $8.75. Starting with FY 1978, however, state allocations are to be determined by a radically different formula that both rewards extra effort to educate handicapped children and calls upon the federal government to take on an increasing share of the cost.

The first element of the new formula's equation again involves the three-to-twenty-one age range but includes only those youngsters who are handicapped and receiving special education. Thus, the more handicapped children the state sets out to educate, the more money it will be entitled to. The second element is a specified percentage of the national average public school expenditure per child. For FY 1978 the proportion of the overall allocation for which a given state will be eligible is to be determined by multiplying the number of handicapped children being served by 5 percent of the national average expenditure. At the current expenditure rate that would translate into an estimated overall authorization of $378 million.

For FY 1979 the multiplication factor doubles, with the number of children being served multiplied by 10 percent of the national per pupil expenditure. Thereafter it continues to rise by an additional 10 percent annually for another three years, to a permanent level of 40 percent—that is, the number of handicapped children being served in the state times 40 percent of the national average per pupil expenditure.

Based on the current per pupil expenditure, that could mean a FY 1981 authorization of more than $3.16 billion. Even that figure might be low, depending on whatever changes inflation or other factors might work on national average expenditures. It is important to note, however, that the actual amounts of money to become available will depend in large measure on the President's budget and the subsequent actions of the Congressional Appropriations committees. Authorization amounts frequently far exceed actual appropriations.

Accompanying the new formula is a new system by which funds are to be distributed. Under this formula, the states passed along 50 percent of the FY 1978 funds they received to their local education agencies. In FY 1979 and thereafter the states are to retain only 25 percent of their total, with the local districts receiving 75 percent.

State and local education agencies alike must take into account certain limitations in how the new formula may be applied in determining allotments. As regards the first part of the equation—the number of handicapped children receiving special education—Congress sought to deflect any temptation to stack the deck by limiting the total to no more than 12 percent of the state's overall five-to-seventeen population (a provision also aimed at discouraging questionable identification of youngsters as being handicapped). Similarly, not more than one-sixth of the 12 percent may include children identified as having "specific learning disabilities" (a term the law incidentally instructs the Commissioner of Education to more clearly define).

Such limitations aside, PL 94–142 portends a major expansion of the nation's commitment to handicapped children. To participate in that expansion, the states must have taken two steps. First, they must have adopted a "full service" policy of assuring all handicapped children the right to a free appropriate public education. Second, they must have prepared for submission to the Commissioner of Education a plan for implementing that policy. In essence the state plan—it must be revised annually—is a document reporting on the current situation in the states as regards education of the handicapped. It also spells out the methods, procedures, and resources it pledges to employ toward putting into practice the various policies set forth in the law—serving all handicapped children, opening up regular classrooms to such children, the September 1978 and September 1980 benchmarks, priorities for unserved and severely handicapped children, and the like.

For its part the local education agency (LEA) must submit a formal application to the state education agency (SEA) similarly endorsing these policies and giving assurance that it will carry them out. This application must then be supplemented by regular reports to the SEA. If along the way the state finds evidence that an LEA is failing to comply with all the provisions of the law, it may, after having given proper notice, hold up further payments to the district until the problem is corrected, meanwhile using these funds to make other arrangements for serving the affected children.

The Office of Education is similarly made responsible for riding herd on the states through mechanisms which begin with notifying a noncomplying state of OE's intention to take action. This could go as far as the federal circuit court in the instance of a state that appealed an adverse OE ruling.

If the Commissioner finds there to be a "substantial" failure to meet the various provisions of PL 94–142—either by a state or by an intermediate or local agency within the state—the law says he or she "shall" withhold further payments under the Act and "may" withhold funds earmarked for education of the handicapped under the Elementary-Secondary and Vocational Education Acts.

Action also might be taken by the parents of individual children, for the Congress went to considerable pains to spell out various procedural safeguards. It is now required, for example, that parents or guardians have an opportunity to examine all relevant records bearing on the identification of children as handicapped, on evaluating the nature and severity of their disability, on the kind of educational setting in which they are placed. The latter issue is expected to be of particular concern to parents who feel their handicapped children have unfairly been denied access to regular classes. Schools are called upon to give written notice prior to changing a child's placement (and a written explanation if they refuse a parent's request for such a change). Statements of this kind are to be in the parents' native tongue.

In the event of objections to a school's decision, there must be a process by which parents can register their complaints. That process must also include an opportunity for an impartial hearing that offers parents rights similar to those involved in a court case—the right to be advised by counsel (and by special education experts if they wish), to present evidence, to cross-examine witnesses, to compel the presence of any witnesses who do not appear voluntarily, to be provided a verbatim report of the proceedings, and to receive the decision and findings in written form.

The advances called for in PL 94–142 entail such a break from the traditional suppression of the handicapped that some people in education might imagine that the Act's language represents only the ideal. Not so. Congress plainly expects specific, substantial, sustained progress, and it calls upon the Commissioner to report at least annually and in detail as to precisely what gains are being made.

For each state and within each disability, for example, there are to be data for the overall number of handicapped children "who require special education and related services;" the number receiving a "free appropriate public education" contrasted with the number who should be but aren't; and the number participating in regular classrooms together with the number who have been placed in separate classrooms or "otherwise removed from the regular education environment." And there must be figures for the number of handicapped children enrolled in public and private institutions, with a breakdown in each for those receiving an appropriate education and those receiving something less than that.

In addition to providing this statistical information, OE is called upon to evaluate the Act's overall annual performance. Among other things, that evaluation must include an assessment of the effectiveness of procedures established by the states and education agencies within the states to assure the handicapped children are placed in the least restrictive environment commensurate with their needs; and a report on arrangements made to prevent erroneous classification of children as eligible to be counted (and thus funded) under the Act.

In short, Congress is four-square for accountability, and it has instructed OE to keep score on how the states and local education agencies are doing. That's quite an assignment, given the fact that there are more than 16,000 school districts in the United States, and the Bureau of Education for the Handicapped is busy now trying to gear up for carrying it out.

Members of the BEH staff prepared the various regulations required by Congress as a preliminary step to the law's full implementation. In all, these regulations address a dozen or so different topics, some minor and some of general impact. The drafting process involved numerous steps, including a series of ten "input" conferences to get comments and suggestions from state and local education officials, teachers, handicapped individuals, parents of handicapped children, advocacy groups, state legislators, and others with a direct stake in the law.

These and other suggestions received by BEH were then used as the basis for deliberations by an "input" team of some 100 persons from around the nation chosen to represent the broadest range of "consumers" and "users" of PL 94–142. The documents they produced were reviewed and where necessary refined by officials of BEH and the HEW Office of General Counsel, and final versions were published in the Federal Register.

State departments of education and local school districts across the country prepared for the day on which all of the PL 94–142 revisions of the Education of the Handicapped Act would be in effect, October 1, 1977—the start of the 1978 Fiscal Year and the date on which American education entered a new era.

PL 94–142 will most obviously affect the 10 to 12 percent of the school population who are handicapped. But its benefits will be felt by all other students as well, and by all teachers and administrators. The fundamental promise of PL 94–142 is that it will strengthen public education in general by strengthening what has been one of its weakest links. And in opening classroom doors to a new student clientele, it will bring the nation's schools far closer to the principles of democracy and justice on which it was founded (Goodman 1976).

Implementation of Public Law 94-142

At this time, the full impact of Public Law 94–142 has been felt by all of the nation's schools. All handicapped individuals between the ages of three and twenty-one should be receiving a free, appropriate public education. As of February, 1980 (Office of Special Education) almost 75 percent of all school-age handicapped individuals were receiving special education and related services. This represents an increase of approximately 230,000 handicapped individuals receiving services since Public Law 94–142 became law. These figures have continued to increase since February, 1980, and the mandate of Public Law 94–142 moves closer to reality.

To what extent has Public Law 94–142 been funded by Congress? This may appear to be a moot point since the requirements of the law are to be met whether there is funding or not. However, the implementation of the law has required increased expenditures of LEAs (Local Educational Agencies). Such local funds are crucial without appropriate congressional funding. According to the plan of the law, by Fiscal Year (FY) 1981 there was to be 40 percent federal funding provided, and the proposed (FY) 1981 budget reflected a continuation of 12 percent funding. The FY 1981 budget authorized $25 million for preschool incentive grants, which was no increase from the previous year. The original authorization for preschool incentive grants was $300 per child, and FY 1981 authorized approximately $105 per child. There are slight increases in the FY 1981 budget for special education personnel development, special studies, and regional vocational, adult, and postsecondary programs. Centers for the deaf-blind, severely handicapped projects, early childhood education, innovation and development, media services and captioned films, regional resource centers, and recruitment and information will be maintained through the FY 1981 budget at FY 1980 levels. Because of inflation and the increase in the numbers served, the end result of FY 1981 budget will be a decrease in services (Council for Exceptional Children 1980). The information given above may seem irrelevant, but if federal funding continues in a pattern similar to FY 81, local school systems will be burdened beyond their capacities to provide full educational services for the handicapped.

An important part of Public Law 94–142 is concerned with due process. Due process is provided for parents or the school if they have objections to their child's educational evaluation, educational placement, or educational program. Parents have the right to examine their child's school records and must agree in writing to having their child tested and placed in a special program. If parents do have an objection regarding their child's program, a conference must be held with the goal of solving any differences between the school and the parents. If this conference is not successful, the parents or school have the right to request a due process impartial hearing in order to resolve the problems.

Parents must specifically request a due process hearing by writing to the school principal, school superintendent, and the state department of education. Once requested, a conference should be held within a designated time. If it is not successful, an impartial hearing will be scheduled. A LEA must complete several steps in the process of arranging for the impartial hearing:

1. Inform the parents of their rights regarding due process.
2. Give parents an opportunity to obtain an independent evaluation of their child.
3. Notify the parents that they have a right to legal counsel.

4. Parents should have access to their child's school records and obtain copies.
5. Parents have the opportunity to compel any school person knowledgeable about their child's needs, abilities, or status to attend the hearing.
6. Parents are given the assurance that their child will remain in the present educational placement (unless the child's health or safety is endangered) until a hearing officer makes a decision.
7. Parents have the right to be notified five days prior to the time and actual location of the hearing.
8. Parents have the right to present evidence and witnesses during the hearing.
9. Parents must be given a verbatim report of the hearing in their native language.

Due process is a procedural safeguard in that the parents or school are given the right to agree or disagree regarding any aspect of a child's program. The job of the impartial hearing officer is not a simple one. The hearing officer must accept evidence presented by both the LEA and the parents and then make a decision regarding the child's testing and placement based on Public Law 94–142, the Rehabilitation Act of 1973, Section 504, the state school law, the state's plan for providing services and programs for handicapped children, and any state regulations regarding the education and training of the handicapped. When making the decision, the hearing officer must quote the sources from which the decision was made. If the parents or the LEA disagree with the officer's decisions, they may appeal to the state department of education. If the result of this appeal is unsatisfactory, the parents or the LEA may take the matter to legal court. It should be noted that the LEA also has the right to due process if the parents disagree with their recommendations. An LEA may pursue an impartial hearing and legal court action if the representatives believe a particular child needs special services and the parents refuse to accept the diagnosis or placement of their child.

According to Public Law 94–142, there will be no racial or cultural discrimination in the preparation or administration of tests or evaluations of handicapped individuals. Concern about test bias is evident in all states and, in some cases, has resulted in lawsuits. The elimination of test bias and placement decisions is difficult and perhaps not totally possible. A noncategorical and nondiscriminatory assessment procedure has been suggested which would eliminate the use of norm-referenced tests. This plan places all children in regular classes. Then if a child is not progressing the teacher must document the use of at least three intervention strategies before the child may be moved to another part of the continuum of services. Although this plan requires regular class teachers to make meaningful curriculum adaptations and requires close coordination of services, it may be an appropriate procedure to eliminate test and evaluation bias (Ysseldyke and Regan 1980).

Another essential part of Public Law 94–142 is the development of an Individual Education Plan, commonly referred to as an IEP. Every handicapped child must have a written IEP. It must be written prior to the child's placement in a special education program. IEPs may vary in form but must include certain information regarding the child. One version of the IEP is presented in figure 1.2.

The version of an IEP shown in the figure is not universal. The information included on the IEP will vary from state to state and even from school district to school district. The basic premise of the IEP is that it depicts the plan of the team members for a child's education program and support services. This plan should be based upon the diagnostic information pertaining to the child, so that it will serve that child's needs and abilities.

To develop IEPs for all handicapped children is a time-consuming and expensive process. There is no doubt that IEPs have increased the responsibility and time involvement of special education teachers. A recent report by Price and Goodman (1980) indicates the complications inherent in IEP development. Their report is the result of a study conducted during the 1977–78 school year which included 75 teachers and 807 special education students who were in regular school settings and special schools. The teachers kept a special time log to report their IEP activities from the first of October to the last of March. The time spent included telephone calls, conferences regarding the IEP, gathering information for IEP development, writing the IEP, and other related activities. The areas of exceptionality represented in the sample included the learning disabled; emotionally disturbed; educable, trainable, severely and profoundly mentally retarded; physically handicapped; and the visually, hearing, and speech impaired. Time spent in IEP preparation was highest for the hearing impaired and lowest for the trainable mentally retarded. Of the total sample of 807 students, teachers spent an average of 390 minutes in IEP development. Of these 6.5 hours, 68 percent (265 minutes) was during school time and 32 percent (125 minutes) was the teacher's personal time while away from school. In the school setting, teachers reported most of the time used for IEP preparation was during their release time or instructional time. Price and Goodman project that with their data one could assume that a teacher with twelve children would spend twenty hours of their release time and twenty-four hours of their instructional time in the development of IEPs.

Price and Goodman further report that more experienced teachers and teachers with at least four days of in-service training on IEP preparation require less time to complete an IEP. Time for the IEP was not affected by whether the student was in elementary or secondary programs. Resource teachers, however, spent more school time, and self-contained teachers spent

INDIVIDUAL EDUCATION PLAN

Child's name _____   Strengths and weaknesses

Date _____

_____

Prioritized goals _____

_____

_____

_____

_____

_____

Short-term objectives	Methods and materials	Persons responsible for IEP development	Beginning date	Ending date

Transportation provided _____   Physical education _____

Amount of time in regular class _____

Justification for Placement _____

_____

Evaluation procedures (at least annual) _____

_____

Parent and/or student present _____   IEP team members:
LEA rep: _____

Comments: _____

Teacher: _____

_____

Special teacher: _____

_____

Psychologist: _____

_____

Others: _____

Plan recorded by: _____

_____

_____

Figure 1.2 Individual education plan.

more personal time on the IEP. Price and Goodman conducted their study in Pennsylvania; therefore, their report of the costs for IEP development should not be projected as an average for other states. It is noteworthy that the average cost per student for IEP preparation was $66.81 and this figure represents only the cost as related to the teacher involved. The lowest cost per student was for the speech impaired ($25.35) and the highest was for the hearing impaired ($193.62). The range for the other exceptionalities was $48.59 to $85.98.

Considering the time factors and costs for IEP development as presented above, do IEPs make a difference in a child's program? Are special education teachers doing better jobs and presenting more appropriate education programs because of the IEP? These questions and many more will have to be answered in the near future in order to demonstrate that a good IEP makes a significant difference in programs offered the handicapped.

There are many resources available for developing the IEP. One may find variations in the comprehensiveness of the resources. A few of these are presented here for those readers who need more information on the IEP.

Resources

Arena, John. *How To Write An IEP*. Novato, Ca.: Academic Therapy Publications, 1978.
————. *Developing and Implementing Individual Education Programs*. Oklahoma City, Okla.: Oklahoma State Department of Education, 1980. (Contact any state department for a similar publication.)
————. *Exploring Issues in Implementation of PL–94–142*. Philadelphia, Penn.: Research for Better Schools.
Lerner, Janet W., and Dawson, David K. *Cases in Learning and Behavior Problems: A Guide To Individualized Education Programs*. Boston, Mass.: Houghton Mifflin, 1980.
Myers, Donald G., and Sinco, Michael E. *Individual Education Programming For All Teachers Of The Special Needs Learner*. Springfield, Ill.: Charles C Thomas, Publishers, 1979.
Nazzaro, Jean. *Preparing For The IEP Meeting: A Workshop For Parents*. Reston, Va.: The Council for Exceptional Children, (Stock No. 188), 1979.

Overview

Special education was conceived and nurtured as a separate field within the broad spectrum of education. Amid much controversy, this separatism of services is still the most common approach to special education. States, individuals, citizen groups, and their agencies are beginning to recognize the fallacies of methods currently used to educate the handicapped child. They are proposing many approaches to change existing programs (the reader is referred to the chapter on trends for an overview of proposed and existing approaches for improved delivery systems in special education). The extent to which model programs become a reality will depend upon the degree to which legislators, professional educators, and lay citizens are willing to implement such procedures. Because of existing legislation in the various states, the establishment of new programs and new approaches for dealing with the problems of the handicapped child will not become a reality immediately. Changes proposed on each state level will have to consider many factors relevant to existing or future programs for the handicapped child.

We agree with Blatt (1972) who indicates that existing programs are still not reaching the majority of handicapped children and that many in need of specialized services are either not placed or are misplaced within our schools and institutional settings.

Most states provide education as a fundamental right which is guaranteed to both handicapped and nonhandicapped children. Yet statistics indicate that 30 to 40 percent of the approximately seven million handicapped children are denied the help offered by special education programs. Only 10 percent of those receiving special education services, in many metropolitan school systems, are returned to regular classroom situations.

Today educators in local, state, and college systems cannot afford the luxury of separateness. We must show how college teachers of teachers, classroom teachers of normal and exceptional children, school administrators, and the other parties involved in the education of children can forget our own comforts and biases and cooperate for the benefit of the children we purport to serve. (Melcher 1972)

Categorization or separatism of the handicapped are only two of the many variables to be examined in maintaining or developing improved education programs for exceptional children. In order to prevent the creation of new problems, educators must test a variety of ways to improve existing services. At the same time, they must continue to develop different approaches and programs to increase the level and appropriateness of the services necessary for handicapped children.

Surely the development of new models and approaches in attempting to meet the needs of handicapped children will result in the improvement of many services for the nonhandicapped. Caution must be exercised in the development of these programs so that the handicapped child is not "forgotten" in the process of developing new delivery systems. If we develop or return to an integrated educational system which does not understand the needs of handicapped children, we will be no better off than with our present form of segregation (Valletutti 1969).

In conclusion, the foremost consideration in the development of new or different models is whether or not they will increase and improve services which are available for handicapped children. If new emphasis on reintegrating the handicapped child into the mainstream of education serves only to lessen the use of labels or categories and does not successfully reach more handicapped children and improve the quality of services, then we have not served their needs.

Study Questions

1. In what ways do you believe current attitudes toward the exceptional individual have changed in the past five years?
2. What are the advantages and disadvantages of early identification?
3. Why should state and local educational agencies know estimates of the number of exceptional children?
4. From library resources find two or three definitions of exceptional children.
5. How do labels and categories serve a constructive purpose for planning special education programs?
6. How may a resource room provide appropriate educational services for the mildly handicapped child?
7. What are the objectives and the needs for special education programs?
8. List the advantages and disadvantages of a community special school.
9. Select one group of exceptional children and discuss advantages and disadvantages of residential placement for that group.
10. What effect does the implementation of Public Law 94–142 have upon parents of exceptional children.
11. What effect does the implementation of Public Law 94–142 have upon regular classroom teachers?
12. What are the general ramifications of Public Law 94–142 relative to teachers, parents, schools, communities, public and private agencies, psychologists, and children?
13. Discuss how a local system can develop a continuum of services for handicapped children.
14. Briefly present your ideas regarding the advantages and disadvantages of placing a mildly handicapped child in a lab class or resource room.
15. List the various items that should be included in an IEP.

Bibliography

Affleck, James Q.; Lehning, Thomas W.; and Brow, Kateri D. 1973. "Expanding the Resource Concept: The Resource School." *Exceptional Children* 39, no. 6 (March).

Andrews, Theodore E. 1970. "New Directions in Certification." *Improving State Leadership in Education.* Olympia, Washington: Department of Health, Education and Welfare, Office of Education, Institution of Washington State Board of Education.

Blatt, Burton. 1972. "Public Policy and the Education of Children with Special Needs." *Exceptional Children* 38, no. 7 (March).

Calovini, Gloria. 1968. *The Principal Looks at Classes for the Physically Handicapped.* Springfield, Illinois: State Office of Superintendent of Public Instruction.

Cogan, Victor, and Ohrtman, William. 1971. "A Comprehensive Plan for Services for the Handicapped." *Journal of Special Education* 6, no. 1 (Winter–Spring).

Council for Exceptional Children. 1980. "The 1981 Budget Report: A Dismal Outlook for Exceptional Education." *UPDATE* 11, no. 3 (Spring).

Cruickshank, William M., and Johnson, G. Orville, eds. 1975. *Education of Exceptional Children and Youth.* 3rd ed. Englewood Cliffs, N.J.: Prentice-Hall.

Deno, Evelyn. 1971. "Strategies for Improvement of Educational Opportunities for Handicapped Children: Suggestions For Exploitation of EPDA Potential." *Exceptional Children In Regular Classrooms,* ed. M.C. Reynolds and M.D. Davis. Minneapolis: University of Minnesota Press.

Gallagher, James J. 1972. "The Special Education Contract for Mildly Handicapped Children." *Exceptional Children* 38, no. 7 (March).

Goodman, Leroy V. 1976. "A Bill of Rights for the Handicapped." *American Education Journal,* (July).

Itard, Jean-Morc-Gaspard. 1962. *Wild Boy of Aveyron.* Reprint. Translated by George and Muriel Humphrey. Englewood Cliffs, N.J.: Prentice-Hall. (Originally published, 1799).

Lilly, Stephen. 1971. "A Training Based Model for Special Education." *Exceptional Children* 37 (Summer).

————. 1970. "Special Education: A Teapot in a Tempest." *Exceptional Children* 37, no. 1 (September).

Martin, Edwin W. 1972. "Individualism and Behaviorism as Future Trends in Educating Handicapped Children." *Exceptional Children* 38, no. 7 (March).

Martin, Edwin W.; Bryan, Trudy; LaVor, Martin; and Scheflin, Rhonda. 1970. "Law Review." *Exceptional Children* 37, no. 1 (September).

McCarthy, James J., and McCarthy, Joan F. 1969. *Learning Disabilities.* Boston: Allyn and Bacon.

Melcher, John. 1969. "A Boarding Home Program for Handicapped Children." *Eric* (October). Wisconsin State Department of Public Instruction, Division for Handicapped Children.

————. 1972 "Some Questions from a School Administrator." *Exceptional Children* 38, no. 7 (March).

"Position Paper on Standards for Professional Preparation of Special Education Personnel." 1970. Discussion Draft, Division of Special Education, Texas Education Agency (September 24).

Price, Marianne, and Goodman, Libby. 1980. "Individual Education Programs: A Cost Study." *Exceptional Children* 46, no. 6 (March).

"Public Law 94–142: Excerpts from Update on the Implementation of P. L. 94–142 Prepared by the Bureau of Education for the Handicapped." 1980. *The Exceptional Parent* 10, no. 1 (February).

Reger, Roger, and Kappman, Marion. 1971. "The Child Oriented Research Room." *Exceptional Children* 37, no. 6 (February).

Reynolds, Maynard C., and Balow, Bruce. 1972. "Categories and Variables in Special Education." *Exceptional Children* 38, no. 5 (January).

Schwartz, Louis. 1971. "A Clinical Teacher Model for Interrelated Areas of Special Education." *Exceptional Children* 37, no. 8 (April).

Tompkins, James R. 1969. "An Analysis: Needs, Progress and Issues in the Education of Emotionally Disturbed Children." *Journal of Special Education* 3, no. 1 (Winter-Spring).

U.S. Department of Health, Education, and Welfare; Office of Education. 1970. "Breakthrough in Early Education of Handicapped Children." Reprint from *American Education* (January–February).

U.S. Department of Health, Education, and Welfare; Office of Education; Bureau of Education for the Handicapped. 1971. *Four Programs for Educational Services to Handicapped Children*. Washington D.C.: Government Printing Office.

Valletutti, P. 1969. "Integration vs. Segregation: A Useless Dialectic." *Journal of Special Education* 3.

Weintraub, Fredrick J.; Aberson, Albert R.; and Braddock, David L. 1971. *State Law and Education of Handicapped Children: Issues and Recommendations*. Arlington, Va.: The Council for Exceptional Children.

Ysseldyke, James E., and Regan, Richard R. 1980. "Nondiscriminatory Assessment: A Formative Model." *Exceptional Children* 46, no. 6 (March).

2

mentally retarded children

Definition

A discussion of mental retardation must begin with a definition which will functionally describe children who are mentally retarded. Many definitions are available which attempt to provide a meaningful understanding of mental retardation. We will present several older definitions of mental retardation, and then focus on the most current and acceptable definitions.

Some of the early definitions of mental retardation emphasized such factors as a lack of ability, incurability, and problems in adjustment. For example, Tredgold (1963) defined mental retardation as a state of incomplete mental development of such a kind and degree that the individual is incapable of adapting to the normal environment in such a way as to maintain existence independently of supervision, control, or external support. In 1941, Doll indicated that mental deficiency is a state of social incompetence obtained at maturity, resulting from developmental arrest of intelligence because of constitutional (hereditary or acquired) origin: the condition is essentially incurable through treatment and unremediable through training except as treatment and training instill habits which superficially compensate for the limitations of the person so afflicted while under favorable circumstances and for more or less limited periods of time. A definition which approximates more closely a modern acceptance of mental retardation is that of Benoit (1959). Benoit indicates that mental retardation is a deficit of intellectual function resulting from varied intrapersonal and/or extrapersonal determinants, but having as a common proximate cause a diminished efficiency of the nervous system thus entailing a lessened general capacity for growth in perceptual and conceptual interpretation and consequently in environmental adjustment.

These definitions are no longer acceptable in the professional field, because they focus on the lack of potential of the mentally retarded individual and do not present educationally relevant information. Most professionals prefer a definition that not only describes the mentally retarded individual, but also provides some guidelines for instructional purposes.

A comprehensive definition that gives more than just a description of the mentally retarded was presented by Heber (1959), who was commissioned by the American Association on Mental Deficiency. This definition is as follows:

Mental retardation refers to subaverage general intellectual functioning which originates during the developmental period and is associated with impairment in adaptive behavior. (Heber 1959)

Instead of presenting all of the descriptive material covered by Heber's definition, we will summarize the main points. By subaverage intellectual functioning, Heber is referring to a child who scores one or more standard deviations from the mean on an individual intelligence test, such as The Revised Stanford-Binet Intelligence Scale or the Wechsler Intelligence Scale for Children. In more specific terms, the IQ portion of the definition refers to individuals who score below 84 or 85 on an IQ instrument.

For many professionals, Heber's definition is somewhat incompatible because it includes too many children. Many states do not go above an IQ range of 70 to 75 for identifying the educable mentally retarded. However, the reader should be aware that Heber included in his definition children who were considered to be borderline mentally retarded, more commonly referred to as slow learners.

By including the time in one's life during which subaverage general intellectual functioning occurs, Heber attempted to eliminate other learning problems which might be interpreted as mental retardation. He specified that the developmental period is the time during which mental retardation occurs, and set the age limits for the developmental period at approximately birth to sixteen. Perhaps a more realistic definitive period would be prior to and during the school age years.

Adaptation to one's environment may be assessed during several phases of life, and specific impairments in adaptive behavior would be a possible indication of mental retardation. Heber divided the abilities of a person to adapt to his environment into three distinct and yet overlapping areas. The first is that of maturation and applies most appropriately to the preschool age child. If a child in this age group is slow in developmental skills, such as crawling, walking, talking, or developing self-help skills, then one might suspect that the child may be mentally retarded. However, upon further assessment, if the child did not obtain a low score on an individual intelligence test, then other problems should be considered.

During the school years, academic and social learning is the primary task of the child. If a child is not learning at a level compatible with his or her age, achievement tests should be administered to determine whether the learning lag is indicative of mental retardation. If a child has fallen one, two, or more years behind peers in academic subjects, mental retardation certainly becomes a possibility.

Adapting to one's environment also includes adequate social adjustment, which is particularly important during the adult years. If a person has reached adulthood and is unable to maintain a job or a home, or to establish meaningful adult relationships, then mental retardation may be indicated. Of course, the lack of adaptive behavior and social adjustment should be observed and corrected during the school age years.

An important aspect of Heber's definition is comprehensiveness. For example, if an individual has problems in social adjustment, but does not score one or more standard deviations below the norm on an individual intelligence test, then other problems are suspected instead of mental retardation. In addition, if an individual's score on an intelligence test is within the range of mental retardation, but the person continues to mature, learn, and socially adjust in accordance with levels expected, then possibly mental retardation should be excluded and other problems considered (Heber).

Consequently, educators, parents, and professionals should understand that failure in one test area does not necessarily mean that an individual is relegated to a category of mental retardation. Many factors of human development and functioning must be examined. Professionals must not be hasty in deciding to place labels on children for singularly assumed reasons.

If professional educators were to examine closely Heber's definition of mental retardation, they would also learn that he never intended for mental retardation to be a rigid, lifelong classification. Heber specifically indicates that his definition should focus on the current functioning and behavior of the individual. Under a variety of circumstances, the child's functioning and behavior may change. We believe that Heber's emphasis on *current* functioning and behavior is most important, because this trend implies that mental retardation, particularly mild mental retardation, can change. If temporary placement in special programs causes a change in a young educable mentally retarded child's life, then his or her level of functioning can and often will change to a level above that of mental retardation. Changes in functioning will not be brought about as a result of miracles. Changes can be experienced, though, if teachers and other professionals believe that the child is a worthwhile individual, who can learn and can make progress in academics and daily living.

Through his definition, Heber has issued a challenge for comprehensive evaluations, thorough and well-formulated education and training programs. These should focus on the child's current needs, and periodic comprehensive reevaluations to keep in tune with the child's functioning. They should also consider removal from special class programs either on a full-time or part-time basis. Heber's definition reflects an emphasis for appropriate evaluations, which tend to lessen the use of rigid labels and allow flexible programming.

In 1970, the Board of Directors of the National Association for Retarded Citizens adopted a position statement on classification and placement of mentally retarded persons in special education (NARC 1971). This statement was prompted by growing controversy over the mislabeling of culturally disadvantaged and bilingual children and their inappropriate placement in special education classes intended for mentally retarded students.

The 1970 position statement contained the following guidelines concerning classification procedures:

No child should be classified as mentally retarded until he or she has been evaluated by an evaluation team composed of qualified diagnosticians who bring to bear skills needed to assess medical, psychological, social educational and vocational factors, as applicable. The team should assume responsibility for proposing and interpreting an individual educational plan for the child in the school setting, with provisions for ongoing evaluation of the child's progress and/or needs. The team should also develop suggestions for assisting the child and his family to maximize his growth potentials within his out-of-school hours.

The classification of retardation should not be applied until the child's adaptive behavior has been assessed in relation to the community and family situation, taking into account the cultural norms of this natural milieu. Where adaptive behavior in any life situation is found to be significantly discrepant from intellectual expectations, the label retardation should not be used, at least until further observation has justified it.

The classification of retardation should be applied only to those children who continue to function at a significantly subnormal level even after various remediation attempts. Special attention should also be given to the identification and treatment of debilitating physical conditions such as auditory or visual impairments, malnutrition, epileptic seizures, or other sensory-motor impairments.

Psychological evaluation for the purpose of classification should always include the use of individual test procedures which measure a range of skills and which are appropriate to a child's cultural and linguistic background. Testing should assess specific learning disorders, if any, and the extent to which inferior performance is due to the reversible environmental factors such as repeated failure, cultural dissonance, inappropriate expectations by teachers, situational anxieties, personality disorders, or inadequate motivation.

A child who is suspected of being mentally handicapped should be observed in his regular class setting. However, classroom behavior alone should never be used as the criteria for labeling a child mentally retarded. Regular classroom teachers should be assisted to ascertain the wide variety of reasons other than retardation which may contribute to inappropriate responses to the school academic environment and to underachievement. They should be assisted to implement behavior modification procedures, when appropriate, both to enhance learning and to help the child develop behavior which is more acceptable to his peers.

No assessment of a child should be considered complete unless the parents have been actively involved in the evaluation process as significant observers of the child and his performance. In addition, assistance to parents in the home management problems related to optimal child development should be offered through a trained home visitor, where appropriate.

Since 1970, considerable controversy has continued regarding the evaluation procedures and instruments used to collect data for making classification and placement decisions. Critics still contend that current tests do not accurately measure or predict learning, and that large numbers of children continue to be classified incorrectly as mentally retarded because of problems that are essentially behavioral, cultural, or linguistic. Even if adequate test instruments exist, the opinion has been strongly expressed that many examiners are not adequately trained to administer the tests or interpret the results.

Another definition of mental retardation provided by the American Association on Mental Deficiency was formulated by Grossman (1973).

Mental retardation refers to significantly subaverage general intellectual functioning existing concurrently with deficits in adaptive behavior, and manifested during the developmental period.

This definition is very similar to Heber's, with the following exceptions. Grossman has stated that the general intellectual functioning must be significantly subaverage. Through this qualification in intellectual functioning, Grossman has eliminated the earlier concerns regarding the inclusion of the borderline mentally retarded. In essence, this feature of his definition places the upper range of intellectual functioning at two or more standard deviations below the norm in order for an individual to be considered mentally retarded. Numerically this means that the upper limits on IQ scores would be either 68 or 70. This feature alone has made Grossman's definition more acceptable.

Grossman also raised the developmental period from Heber's original designation of birth to sixteen to a designation of birth to eighteen. This increment provides a definition that is more inclusive of the school age population.

Intellectual functioning and adaptive behavior, according to Grossman, must coexist if an individual is considered mentally retarded. In brief, mental retardation must be considered as a current condition with no statement of prognosis, and the individual must demonstrate a deficiency in both intellectual functioning and adaptive behavior. We should emphasize that the individual's adaptive behavior must be compared to that of his or her own age and cultural group.

As Grossman's definition gains more recognition and acceptance, the concept of mental retardation will change even more than it did through Heber's definition. One should be aware, though, that any definition or label of mental retardation should be applied with a great deal of caution and only by a thorough study of the individual being evaluated.

The definitions of mental retardation as offered by Heber and Grossman through the American Association on Mental Deficiency (AAMD) have caused concern among educators. This concern resulted in the proposal of a new definition of mental retardation to be considered for inclusion in the

1980 edition of the AAMD's *Manual On Terminology and Classification.* The proposal, submitted by the Committee on Definition and Terminology of the Division on Mental Retardation of the Council for Exceptional Children, calls for the upper level of IQ for classification of mental retardation be increased from the present 68 to 75 ± SE (Standard Error) (Kidd et al. 1979). The members of this committee stress that the determination of mental retardation should not be on the basis of a single IQ score, and that current testing with a standardized individual intelligence test by a competent examiner is absolutely essential. In addition, the test should be as free as possible of bias toward language, culture, ethnic group, race, sex, and other disabilities.

The primary emphasis of this committee is that the current upper level of 68 IQ has been adopted by eleven states. Twenty-five other states have eliminated reference to IQ altogether, and the remaining states have retained the upper level IQ of 75. According to this report, the adoption of an upper level IQ of 68 has caused many mildly (educable) mentally retarded individuals to fail totally in the mainstream. These committee members are not requesting a complete return of all individuals with IQs under 75 to special classes. They do stress, however, that they are opposed to an incorrect exclusion of individuals from the classification of mental retardation based on the IQ limit of 68. The proposed definition is as follows:

Mental retardation refers to subaverage general human cognitive functioning, irrespective of etiology(ies), typically manifested during the developmental period, which is of such severity as to markedly limit one's ability to (a) learn, and consequently to (b) make logical decisions, choices, and judgments, and (c) cope with one's self and one's environment. (Kidd et al. 1979)

This committee also proposes a change in the classification of mental retardation on the Binet IQ, equivalent to 51 to 75 for the educable mentally retarded, 26 to 50 for the trainable mentally retarded, and 1 to 25 for the severe and profound area.

If this definition and classification is accepted by the AAMD, there should be determination of the student's ability to learn, to make logical decisions, and to cope with one's self and environment. These areas will need clarification if the proposed definition is to be understood and used appropriately. The acceptance of this definition may halt or curtail the unrealistic practice of placing students who have IQs between 68 and 75 in programs for the learning disabled. This AAMD definition would enable the schools to provide more appropriate educational programs and related services to individuals who are mildly mentally retarded.

Another concern regarding the definition of mental retardation is expressed by Huberty, Koller, and Ten Brink (1980). These authors indicate that adaptive behavior is an important part of the AAMD definition of mental retardation and that several states do not refer to it in their state guidelines. They report that only eight states have adopted the AAMD definition of mental retardation, and six states have similar definitions. This information was compiled from a survey to which forty-one states responded. Huberty, Koller, and Ten Brink also stress the importance of using adaptive behavior as a part of the criteria for determining if a child is diagnosed as mentally retarded. To train future teachers adequately and provide them with meaningful guidelines for estimating the incidence of mental retardation, these authors propose that all states use adaptive behavior as part of the criteria for determining mental retardation.

The issues concerned with the definition of mental retardation emphasize that approaches in identifying mental retardation are not static. Meaningful changes pertaining to methods used for diagnosing mental retardation should be given serious consideration. Therefore, continued efforts are necessary to refine appropriate methods of identification.

Estimates of Prevalence

Estimates of the number of persons who may be classified as mentally retarded vary considerably. Some authors formulate estimates from the normal curve by using only school-age children; others use the entire population as a base. This may cause some misunderstanding, because the reader may not understand which population base was used to formulate the estimate. However, an estimate of 2–3 percent of the general population prevails throughout the literature. With a general population in the United States exceeding 220 million in the 1980s this means that approximately 4.5 to 6.5 million or more are mentally retarded. Most resources use the 6.5 million figure.

Of this number the authors estimate that approximately 85 percent, or 2 to 2.5 percent of the general population, are within the range of mild (educable) mental retardation. The mildly or educable mentally retarded population (IQ range 50 to 70 or 75) would be nearly 5.5 million. The moderately or trainable mentally retarded population (IQ range 30–35 to 50–55), using a percentage of .3 percent, would number approximately 650,000. About .1 percent of the population falls within the range of the severely and profoundly mentally retarded (IQ range 1 to 30–35), which represents approximately 225,000 persons.

Estimates are valuable in that they help professionals predict how many children are in need of services as compared with the number of children who are receiving services. Planning for comprehensive community services, such as special classrooms, sheltered workshops; and planning for training of professional personnel, such as teachers, psychologists, and speech therapists, is based on these estimates. Estimates also provide guidance in requesting and preparing legislative programs to help provide for the needs of these citizens. Figure 2.1 offers the incidence estimates of the mentally retarded population. The graph shows clearly that the mildly mentally retarded population is much greater than other groups of retarded individuals.

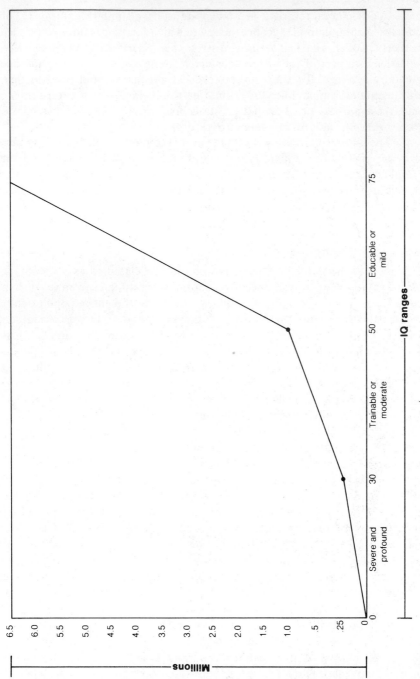

Figure 2.1 Estimates of the prevalence of mental retardation.

Caution should be exercised in applying estimates of the prevalence of mental retardation to all samples of the population, because many mentally retarded children are only mildly handicapped. Tremendous variations in population subgroups may be found when searching for the prevalence of mild mental retardation. For example, in a suburban population of high-middle to lower-upper socioeconomic groups, a very low percentage of the population may be educably mentally retarded. However, in a ghetto area or in an inner city area of lower socioeconomic groups, as high as 6 to 7 percent of the population may be within the range of educable mental retardation.

Methods of Identification

Methods of identifying retarded individuals must be related to the symptoms exhibited. When attention is drawn to children because of learning or behavioral difficulties, tests are usually administered to determine the cause or extent of the problems. The type of testing is usually related to the behavior and adaptive symptoms observed, and the learning areas in which the child has difficulties. By symptoms, we mean behaviors such as low intellectual functioning, slow maturation, or a behavior problem which causes difficulties in social adjustment.

Mental retardation may be the result of a child's culture, emotional problems, organic conditions, hereditary factors, or a combination of these factors (Robinson and Robinson 1976). Determining the possible cause of mental retardation is usually a very difficult, if not impossible, task. Mental retardation is generally considered to be multidetermined. However, if a child is discovered to be functioning as a mentally retarded person because of an emotional disturbance rather than an organic or unknown condition, then the instruction procedures for this child might take an entirely different direction. Perhaps the most important point in discussing methods of identification is that the retarded individual should be reevaluated continuously. This reevaluation should help provide the most meaningful available program for the child.

Standardized testing instruments have been widely accepted as methods for the evaluation of the mentally retarded child. Although tests are only a part of the total evaluation system, they are important and should never be regarded lightly. Professionals who plan to work with mentally retarded individuals should familiarize themselves with some of the more commonly used test instruments in order to provide beneficial formal evaluations of the child. Test information has been used too long for the purpose of making administrative decisions; teachers especially should focus on the educational importance of formal evaluations. Otherwise, the evaluation and placement of mentally retarded children will not serve their needs. It will only serve to provide labels and classification systems.

The following chart of educational tests (table 2.1) provides the reader with the name of the test, individual or group administration, the purpose

Table 2.1 Summary of educational tests

Name	Type	Purpose	Age or Level	Score or Information
Stanford-Binet Intelligence Scale, 1972	Individual	Intellectual Assessment	2 years–Adult	I.Q., Basal Age, Mental Age
Wechsler Intelligence Scale for Children (WISC) R	Individual	Intellectual Assessment	5–15 years	Verbal I.Q., Performance I.Q., Full-Scale I.Q.
Slosson Intelligence Test (SIT)	Individual	Screening test for Intellectual Assessment	Preschool–Adult	I.Q., Basal Age, Mental Age
California Test of Mental Maturity	Group	Mental Ability	Different test for K–Adults	I.Q.
Henmon-Nelson Tests of Mental Ability	Group	Mental Ability	3 sets—Grades: 3–6, 6–9, 0–12	I.Q.
Marianne Frostig Developmental Test of Visual Perception	Individual or Group	Visual Perception	3–9 years	Perceptual Age, Perceptual Quotient
Columbia Mental Maturity Scale	Individual	Intelligence	Mental ages: 3–12	I.Q., Mental Age
Gesell Developmental Schedules	Individual	Maturation, Motor development, adaptive behavior, etc.	4 weeks–6 years	Maturation age, Developmental age
Goodenough-Harris Draw-a-Man Test	Individual or Group	Intellectual Assessment	4–12 years	I.Q., Mental Age
Illinois Test of Psycholinguistic Abilities	Individual	Linguistic Ability	3–9 years	Language Age, Profile of Language strengths and weaknesses
Vineland Social Maturity Scale	Individual	Interview with parents to obtain social maturity	Birth–maturity	Social quotient
Durrell Analysis of Reading Difficulty	Individual	Diagnostic reading test	Grades 1.5–6.5	Reading skills
Gates McKillop Reading Diagnostic Test	Individual	Analysis of Reading Difficulties	Grades 1.6–8.5	Reading problems, Percentile Rank
Wide Range Achievement Test	Individual and Group	Reading, Spelling, Arithmetic Achievement	Preschool–College	Achievement scores, Standard scores

Wepman Test of Auditory Discrimination	Individual	Auditory discrimination deficits	5–8 years	Standard score
Hiskey-Nebraska Test of Learning Aptitude	Individual	Nonverbal test of intelligence	4–10 years	Learning age
Purdue Perceptual Motor Survey	Individual	Perceptual-motor development	6–10 years	Laterality, Directionality, Perceptual-Motor matching

Adapted from data in *Mental Retardation: Diagnosis and Treatment*, Charles M. Polser et al., Harper & Row, 1967.

of the measure, the age or grade level for which the test is appropriate, and the scoring information. Knowledge of these tests should provide a foundation on which a teacher can develop skills to plan educationally for the child.

The reader should note that the tests in table 2.1 are not inclusive. There are many tests appropriate for the mentally retarded child; we selected only a representative sample of them. Perhaps the information presented in the table will clarify what is meant by a comprehensive evaluation and a battery of tests. None of the tests listed should be used exclusively to evaluate a mentally retarded child. Single tests will provide labels, but generally will not provide information which is essential for improving the learning environment.

The combined school achievement, mental, and language test scores are the most valid for the identification of school age children who are having learning difficulties. A child referred for testing because of possible mental retardation, should be the subject of a comprehensive assessment. The primary objective should be to provide the teacher with the child's mental age, achievement test scores, and current strengths and weaknesses in learning. The evaluation should also describe the child in terms of behavioral objectives and provide the teacher with information which is directly related to the teaching-learning process. Information as to how the teacher may provide an ongoing assessment of the child in the classroom should also be given. If the results of a test battery provide the teacher with nothing more than scores, then the time of the examiner, the child, and the teacher has been wasted.

After assessment, the evaluator should recommend the best educational placement for the child, based on the current level of functioning. Recommendations for educational placement must consider the various programs available in the community. All recommendations should be based upon a reasonable plan which is feasible for the child, the parents, and the professional personnel who will be working with the child.

Characteristics of the Mentally Retarded

In attempting to describe the characteristics of mentally retarded children there must be clarification of intent for presenting this information. The authors recognize that individual mentally retarded children vary considerably when compared with a group of similar children. However, certain characteristics are usually predominant in a large group of mentally retarded children. Therefore, characteristics can be descriptive enough to clarify the differences in the levels of mental retardation, and also to clarify the differences between mentally retarded children and the so-called normal child.

Perhaps the admonition to use caution when attempting to identify the type of problems a child may have has been overstressed, but this point will be reiterated with respect to a description of mentally retarded children. Educators should not assume that a list of characteristics will identify an individual child as having the problem of mental retardation. For example, the reader should not assume that a particular child is mentally retarded because he or she exhibits the characteristics of a group of mentally retarded children. As we have stressed previously, the determinism of mental retardation is multidimensional, and demands a comprehensive evaluation.

Educable or Mildly Mentally Retarded

Children may have the problem of mental retardation for various reasons, and their functioning may be affected to a degree ranging from mild to very severe. Children who are mildly mentally retarded generally have their most difficult problems in the area of learning abstract concepts. These children are referred to as educable mentally retarded. Such children are limited in learning academic skills; however, they can and do learn.

The reader should be reminded that the IQ range for the educable mentally retarded is from 50–55 to 70 or 75 which is two to three standard deviations below the mean. The standard deviation is 16 on the Stanford Binet IQ Test, and 15 on the Wechsler IQ Tests. This places the upper level IQ for the educable mentally retarded at 68 or 70 depending upon the test instrument used. However, many states have extended the upper level IQ to 75. It should be noted that the common abbreviations for the educable mentally retarded/handicapped are EMR and EMH.

The educable mentally retarded child will have a physical appearance that is generally normal. This child does not differ in appearance from other children but may have a smaller stature and even be somewhat underweight. Such children may be well developed physically and very capable of performing physical tasks or functioning in an athletic endeavor. There is no typical physical appearance associated with these children. Their physical appearance and development probably will be as variable as that of the normal population.

The area of greatest difference in the educable mentally retarded population is in learning. They tend to be slower in developing concepts and may require that tasks be presented in a variety of ways. Progress in learning will usually be slower than that of the normal population, and they usually will not attain the same academic achievement level of their peers. Problems may exist in the areas of starting to learn, generalizing, and associating learning, rather than in learning itself. The educable mentally retarded individual can and does learn, and after learning a concept, proficiency in learning is somewhat similar to that of a normal population group.

If the educable mentally retarded students are subjected to periods of failures within the school environment they tend to avoid future learning experiences. Therefore, many teachers assume that the educable retarded individual is not motivated. These teachers have not considered the many reasons why these children appear uninterested in new learning experiences. How many individuals, particularly those with limited intellectual abilities, will continue to strive for success when the past has not provided them with any success? Success in learning is essential as a motivator for future learning experiences.

The educational experiences provided for the educable mentally retarded must reflect the need for variety in learning, for making learning practical, and for providing meaningful learning. If we teach the children to generalize and associate the factors which they have already learned, they can begin to comprehend that learning makes a difference in functioning. If we continue to present the same information over and over; then, like other children's reactions educable mentally retarded children will tend to develop a very poor attitude toward school and learning.

The primary objective of an educational program for the educable mentally retarded is to assist them in becoming well-adjusted and employable adults. In many instances, this objective is teaching basic survival skills in a complex, technological world, and teaching skills which will enhance personal and social development. An interesting point which many people do not realize is that after educable mentally retarded individuals leave the school environment, they tend to lose the classification of mental retardation.

To further elaborate, research indicates that many educable mentally retarded children may have some type of sensory deficit which could affect achievement in school. Chiappone and Libby (1972) conducted a study involving sixty normal children and sixty educable mentally retarded children in which they indicated that the retarded children were significantly more farsighted than the normal children. The primary emphasis of these authors pertains to specific differences among retarded children with regard to such areas as visual acuity rather than farsightedness as a single factor. In short, there may be many factors contributing to the educable mentally retarded child's lack of achievement, and educators may be routinely overlooking numerous problems.

Moderately or Trainable Mentally Retarded

Moderately mentally retarded children are referred to as trainable mentally retarded in school systems. This term is used to denote that the children will have severe difficulties in learning academic skills, but they can be trained to care for themselves. In many cases they can be trained to perform some vocational skills. The IQ range for the trainable mentally retarded/handicapped is generally from 30–35 to 50–55 and the abbreviations used for this area are TMR and TMH.

The trainable mentally retarded child may differ in physical appearance from the normal. Many trainable mentally retarded children will have some clinical syndrome which is characterized as a form of mental retardation with physical manifestations. For example, the child with Down's syndrome (mongolism) is usually a trainable mentally retarded child. Anyone who has seen or worked with a child with Down's syndrome knows that there is something different about the child based solely on his physical appearance and performance. All children who have Down's syndrome are

Many children with Down's syndrome are trainable mentally retarded. (Jim Shaffer)

not trainable mentally retarded. Some mongoloid children are severely retarded, but a few of them may function within the educable range. Possibly some children may indicate a slow learner range of intellectual functioning.

The moderately or trainable mentally retarded child may appear physically different, perform differently, and may manifest differences in physical development. Characteristics such as smaller physical stature, shorter hands, a noticeably larger head in proportion to the rest of the body, clumsy walking or deficiencies in motor activity, a speech impediment, and a visual or hearing difficulty may be obvious. In many cases, trainable mentally retarded children certainly may be considered multiply-handicapped, because their difficulties are not limited to just lower intellectual functioning.

The trainable mentally retarded child will need assistance in learning self-help skills, language skills, motor skills, and social development, because of various and obvious difficulties in adaptive functioning. The program for the trainable mentally retarded will combine training and education. This child is capable of learning, although proficiency in academic skills will usually be very limited.

Severe and Profound Mental Retardation

Within the population of the mentally retarded, the severely and profoundly mentally retarded children are the most handicapped. Fortunately, the profoundly retarded is also the smallest group of this population. The severely and profoundly retarded may be so limited intellectually that they do not develop intelligible speech, form no abstract concepts, and do not develop any academic skills. These children may also have severe multiple handicaps, because they may be nonambulatory, and may not be able to care for their personal needs. They probably will need assistance in caring for all of their personal and physical needs. These children can profit from training; however, the training has to be highly specific, and a one-to-one basis is usually essential. The severely and profoundly mentally retarded generally have IQs between the range of 1 to 30 or 35 and the terms sub-trainable or custodial are synonomous in this area.

The individual who is severely or profoundly mentally retarded may have one or more of the approximately 200 different clinical syndromes. Many of these syndromes may have a cause related to recessive or dominant genes, chromosomal deficiencies or aberrations, toxins, diseases, or unknown etiologies. Consequently, in past years, the severely and profoundly retarded individual has been placed primarily in institutional or residential centers for the mentally retarded. However, with recent emphasis on de-institutionalization, additional children will receive care within community residential centers, respite homes, community sheltered workshops or activity centers, and, in some cases, within the public schools. The reader is referred to in chapter 1 the information pertaining to Public Law 94–142 in order to recognize the development of community programs for this subgroup.

One who works with severely or profoundly mentally retarded individuals must have a great deal of patience. At the same time, this person must acknowledge that the development of personal self-help skills is very important. The sequential development of these skills must be broken into very small steps. Many manuals and guides are now being prepared to assist in teaching these skills.

Perhaps a presentation of the characteristics of the mentally retarded in chart form will convey this information simply and briefly. Table 2.2 presents the characteristics of mentally retarded children by area of functioning and the level of mental retardation.

Anyone who is working with a mentally retarded child should not accept these characteristics as a rigid blueprint for determining the present or future functioning level of a mentally retarded child. One must take the attitude that the child should be enabled to progress as far as possible without any preset ideas as to the level of performance. Such flexibility must be incorporated in any endeavor which attempts to meet the needs of individual children. One must recognize that programs are not presently in existence which can enable the more severely and profoundly retarded children to reach levels of functioning that are higher than those generally assumed for them.

The reader should also be aware that many severely and profoundly mentally retarded are commonly referred to as individuals with clinical

Table 2.2 Characteristics of mentally retarded children

Area of Functioning	Mild or Educable	Moderate or Trainable	Severe and Profound
Self-help skills	Feeds and dresses self and cares for own toilet needs.	Has difficulties and requires training but can learn adequate self-help skills.	No skills to partial, but some can care for personal needs on a limited basis.
Speech and Communication	Receptive and expressive are adequate. Understand communication.	Receptive and expressive language is adequate. Has speech problems.	Receptive language is limited to good. Expressive language is limited to poor.
Academics	Optimal learning environment—3rd to 6th grade.	Very few academic skills, 1st or 2nd grade.	No academic skills.
Social Skills	Has friends, can learn to adjust adequately.	Capable of friends but has difficulties in many social situations.	Not capable of having "real" friends. No social interaction.
Vocational Adjustment	Can hold a job. Competitive to semi-competitive. Primarily unskilled work.	Sheltered work environment. Usually needs constant supervision.	No employment for the most part. May be in an activity center. Usually needs constant care.
Adult Living	Usually marries, has children. Needs help during stress.	Usually doesn't marry or have children. Dependent.	Always dependent on others. No marriage or children.

The authors developed Table 2 from the narrative information by Max L. Hutt and Robert G. Gibby, *The Mentally Retarded Child: Development, Education, and Treatment,* Third Edition, © 1976 by Allyn and Bacon, Inc.

syndromes. The terms applied to them are medical terms, since their problems of mental retardation are often the result of some type of organicity or hereditary disorder. Some examples are microcephaly, hydrocephaly, phenylketonuria, cretinism, galactosemia, Rubella, Rh blood factor, and kernicterus. These conditions involve the use of technical terms and in the majority of cases the educator in public schools does not meet children with these types of problems. However, any person working with the mentally retarded child should be aware of these conditions, and have some exposure to the more serious problems associated with them. From our viewpoint, this exposure is essential, because with proper medical treatment some of the more serious types of mental retardation can be prevented or controlled. The professional working with such children should have an awareness of the controls which are relative to the various conditions.

An example of one of the clinical syndromes is phenylketonuria (PKU). This metabolic disorder is inherited through a recessive gene. Phenylalanine is not metabolized into tyrosine; thus, the individual accumulates excessive phenylalanine which causes severe damage to the central nervous system. PKU may be detected by identification of the recessive trait in both parents or by testing newborns for excessive phenylpyruvic acid in the urine or the blood. PKU may be prevented by dietary controls which provide a minimum of phenylalanine. If detected at the time of or shortly after birth, the individual still has PKU, but does not become severely or profoundly mentally retarded. Many studies have been conducted during recent years in order to assess the results of newborn screening procedures and dietary controls. Generally, these studies report that controlled PKU results in near normal development both physically and intellectually. (Robinson and Robinson 1976). A detailed description of the terms mentioned with respect to clinical syndromes may be found in the Merck Manual (1964) and Robinson and Robinson (1976). The reader is referred to these excellent sources.

Knowledge of these conditions, and the ways in which they can be prevented, will help one to be more aware of the resources parents need when they have questions about possible causes of severe or profound retardation. Also, one should be knowledgeable with respect to programs which encourage the prevention of conditions such as German measles, PKU, and cretinism. Educators often serve as resource persons for parents. Special education teachers in particular should be informed about these more serious types of mental retardation, because of the services they can perform.

Public School Programs for Mentally Retarded Children

One of the primary needs of mentally retarded children is appropriate public school programs. Schools in the United States have made considerable progress in providing educational programs for the mentally retarded since the turn of the century. However, new classes and additional teachers are needed to provide even more comprehensive and sequential programs. This may mean that two school systems will have to develop a cooperative agreement in order to provide programs from the preschool level through the high school level. Cooperative agreements are being formed in various localities for this purpose. One should question a policy of any school system which provides an early elementary school program for the mentally retarded, but does not provide junior and senior high programs.

General Objectives

In order for educational programs for the mentally retarded to be sequential, planning among the teachers of the various levels within the schools must be continuous. As pointed out by Shane (1967), teachers of mentally retarded children must focus upon organizing a system whereby they can and will communicate regarding a child. This communication should involve teachers at all levels, so that effective programs continue to be developed. For example, if the primary special education teacher learns that a child is progressing in any area of development through the use of a particular approach, then, if still appropriate, the intermediate teacher could use the same or a similar approach. This does not mean that teachers should teach exactly the same way or use the same materials. The program should be varied. However, if a teacher in the primary class learns that a child is very capable of following directions and working semi-independently, the intermediate teacher should have the benefit of this information.

We have known several special education teachers of mentally retarded children who have had to spend a few weeks at the beginning of the school year to discover how a child approaches a learning situation. Granted the child may be with a new teacher, a new group of children, and in a new classroom; but his or her learning style will probably not change so drastically as to call for a completely different and perhaps inappropriate approach. The sequencing of a special education instructional program goes far beyond the single factor of a teacher presenting an appropriate curriculum. A sequential program must provide a means of insuring that teachers at all levels of training are building a program in unison, not in isolation.

Perhaps another example will serve to emphasize this point. How many primary special education teachers of educable mentally retarded children know about the work-study programs which are so common in the high schools? How can a program be sequential if teachers don't know what happens within the instructional program at a level above or below that which they are teaching? The sequencing and continuity of a program must be an ongoing developmental process, and cannot be accomplished within one school year through conducting an in-service training program. Because of changes in teaching staff, the bringing of new children into the program, and the changing vocational picture within a community, the development of sequence and continuity in an instructional program for retarded children never ends.

School Programs for Educable Mentally Retarded Children

The school program for mildly (educable) mentally retarded children is structured somewhat differently from that for trainable mentally retarded children. The levels are usually described as follows: primary class (age range six to ten); intermediate class (age range ten to thirteen); junior high class (age range thirteen or fourteen to fifteen); and senior high class (age range fifteen or sixteen to twenty or twenty-one). (See *A Guide for Teachers of Educable Mentally Handicapped Children* 1971.) The levels and age ranges will differ for grouping educable mentally retarded children when one is in a rural area or a small community. There may be smaller groups of children within one school building, and they may have to be grouped into an elementary class with age ranges from approximately eight to fourteen.

We believe that the philosophy and training of teachers of educable mentally retarded children should differ from that provided teachers of trainable mentally retarded children. As pointed out earlier in this chapter, the majority of mentally retarded children fall within the educable or mild range. Classes for them will be more common in the public schools than classes for trainable mentally retarded children. Educable mentally retarded children are capable of reaching higher levels of performance in all levels of functioning, and the teacher should be prepared to help them achieve whatever functioning capacity they may have. Children who are educable will also be more capable of finding and holding jobs in competitive employment fields. They should, therefore, be prepared for the higher levels of responsibility which will be demanded of them.

If training is provided early and is appropriate to their needs, several of these children may be candidates for the regular classroom program on a part-time or full-time basis. In brief, working with these children in the classroom presents a challenge to teachers, because they must provide programs that will benefit the children to such an extent that they will be prepared for possible regular classroom functioning. In essence, this means the instructional program provided by a special education teacher must focus on specific objectives and involve the children in learning. The role of a special education teacher or educable mentally retarded children should never be considered an easy one, or a position in which all the teacher has to do is "take care of" the children.

The training of educable mentally retarded children must focus on the same skills as for the trainable mentally retarded. In other words, it is important to develop alike skills in these children. However, the potential development is greater, will be more progressive, and will reach much higher levels with the educable mentally retarded. According to Telford and Sawrey (1977), this group will need a teacher with objectives that focus on the following areas of development: perceptual-motor, language, social skills, academics, work habits, prevocational skills, practical living skills, and vocational skills. The primary objectives of educational programs for educable mentally retarded children are to help them become functional adult citizens in the areas of family living, employment, homemaking, good citizenship, and self-understanding.

The Primary Special Education Class

The primary special education class is provided for mildly mentally retarded children from ages six through nine or ten. This program is the equivalent of grades one through three and in some cases, depending on the structure of the local school system, might continue through grade four.

Placement in the primary class should be based on a comprehensive diagnostic battery of tests, the child's present level of performance, the regular class teacher's recommendation, and staffing by teachers, parents, and evaluators. Placement should be through careful consideration, and for only one school year at a time. Consistent reevaluation of the child's adjustment and performance is recommended to insure an appropriate educational program. Placement in the primary class should not necessarily be on a full-day basis. The placement of a child should consider educational needs relative to the ability to function in both the special and/or regular class.

We insist that early placement in a special program is necessary for the mildly mentally retarded if they are to be provided maximum individual assistance in learning. The mildly mentally retarded child probably will enter school without the prerequisite skills for learning school-related tasks. Therefore, the teacher will have the responsibility of providing a program that enhances prereadiness and readiness skills for reading, writing, social interaction, and arithmetic. Such a program will require careful sequencing of the instructional material in order to work toward early appropriate learning. The mildly mentally retarded child at age six is certainly capable of learning; however, the teacher must provide successful learning experiences and appropriate methods. Early intervention is necessary and should be mandatory. A good special education teacher at the primary level will help children to overcome some of their learning deficits, which may then enable them to be mainstreamed at various times throughout the school program.

The mildly mentally retarded at the primary school level may have language deficiencies. In many cases, their language may be considered to be a second language in that they do not use grammar appropriately or have not developed descriptive language. Improving language, which enables them to cope with the learning environment, may be one of the teacher's primary objectives. This teaching process is time-consuming and will also require individual assistance. Therefore, a resource person, who is often a speech and language therapist, may need to aid the regular or special class teacher.

The primary class special education teacher must be prepared to emphasize prereadiness and readiness skills. As an example, the child may have to be taught how to distinguish between shapes, sizes, forms, visual objects, sounds, etc. Discrimination skills may be very limited, and the teacher must plan a program to improve these difficulties. The instructional program will have to focus specifically on direct teaching of prerequisite skills for reading, writing, and arithmetic. The more actively the teacher can involve the children, the greater progress the children will make. The teacher cannot expect the child with limited ability to learn by being passive. Activity in learning, novelty in the instructional program, and feedback are essential if the child is to be functional in school.

By the time children are ready to leave the primary special class, they probably should be ready academically to learn fairly proficiently. We do not recommend that mildly mentally retarded children in the primary special class should remain isolated in a special class. Regular class integration should be considered relative to their needs. Their class placement should be planned carefully and should be an *educational decision*. The initial concern regarding mainstreaming is whether the regular class program will be able to provide sufficiently for learning needs. If the program should appear to be detrimental to progress or if it is unable to provide the necessary individual attention, then the regular class program will be more harmful than beneficial.

The Intermediate Special Class

The intermediate special education class is provided for children from ages nine to ten through twelve or thirteen and is representative of grades four through six. If the primary class has provided an optimal program for learning, the child is now ready to pursue academics with more intensity. With a few exceptions, children at the intermediate level demonstrate the skills learned in the primary special class. A variety of instructional materials are required for these children to meet their diffuse levels of academic performance. They should also have the opportunity for integration in selected regular classes.

The special teacher of the intermediate special class should provide opportunities to improve social and emotional adjustment. Through a variety of experiences, such as role playing and group discussions, the mildly mentally retarded child at this age range is very capable of learning new ways to interact with others. Understanding of self and the development of a positive self-concept should be further enhanced at this age level, and many different teaching methods should be used. Meaningful success experiences, learning how to cope with self and others, and developing responsibility for one's own actions are important areas of concentration for this age group.

Teachers at the intermediate special class level have many tasks to perform. They must continue to focus on the learning of academics, the development of appropriate social and emotional behaviors, the awareness of self in more depth, and the application of learned skills. They must also assist in preparing for the transition to junior high or middle school. This transition may appear significant. However, moving from a comparatively small school to a larger school and having to relate to more students and more teachers may be very confusing to the mildly mentally retarded. The preparation for this transition must be planned so that they can continue to develop and not be overwhelmed. Frequent field visits to the junior high or middle school which the children will be attending are necessary. Learning the physical arrangement of the building and different class and room schedules are common experiences which can be very helpful.

The Junior High Special Class

The special education program should continue into the junior high school level because of the needs of children who manifest lower academic performances. The junior high school curriculum should not emphasize unrealistic academics which may cause the mildly mentally retarded child additional unnecessary failure. Provisions must be made which will enable them to continue their educational development and offer them the opportunity for a vocational future.

Learning to accept the consequences of one's behavior is important at the earlier levels of special education programming. Behavioral limitations become even more necessary with junior high students. The age range of this group will be from twelve or thirteen to fifteen or sixteen and the program is the equivalent of grades seven through nine. Generally, children at this age group are permitted more independence and more freedom to move throughout communities. The early adolescent years also bring on many physiological changes which are just as evident in the mildly mentally retarded as in the general population.

Greater independence and the beginning of the adolescent period place the mildly mentally retarded in more situations where behavior will be expected to be appropriate. In many cases, the special class teacher may attempt to protect the child from authority or from critical individuals in the community because of previous embarrassing behavior that the child has exhibited. Attempts to protect the child may be evidenced by the teacher's restriction of the child to the classroom for offending some rule of behavior. The teacher must assume the responsibility of correcting inappropriate behaviors. We do not advocate cruel or ruthless punishment. However, the mentally retarded child must learn through structured teaching, limit setting, and through the consequences of behavior. If serious infractions of rules or behaviors are exhibited, counseling sessions may be necessary, and parents should be involved if we really expect the youngster's behavior to improve. The misbehaviors which may occur at this age level should not be dismissed because the child is mentally retarded. They must be managed as must any other youngster's behavior. Only then will the mildly mentally retarded child begin to realize that behavior has certain consequences. Of course, it is also desirable to begin to teach alternative behaviors. Logically being able to explore the various alternatives of behavior and the consequences of one's behavior is usually not learned incidentally. Therefore, behavior training must receive considerable emphasis within the structure of the school program.

The junior high mildly mentally retarded students will continue to apply the academic skills they have learned. However, during this transitional period, it is necessary to begin vocational exploration. The focus of the instructional program is directed toward functional daily living, academics, and work skills. The junior high special class teacher should not be responsible for providing the entire instructional program at this level. For example, in the development of vocational exploration, the child's learning may be enhanced by placement in a selected, appropriate regular class such as home economics, or industrial arts.

The development of interests and skills which are appropriate for one's future life is essential during the junior high school years. In addition to regular elective courses within the junior high school program, the special class teacher should also use a variety of community resource persons and facilities. The community resource persons can be invited to the class for special demonstrations, information relating sessions, or even individual counseling. The community facilities should be visited periodically by the entire class to provide awareness of the community and stimulate vocational interests.

After junior high academic progress, vocational information and learning more about one's self and the effects of one's behavior, the educable mentally retarded child is ready to progress to the senior high school program. In many localities, the senior high program is commonly referred to as a work-study program.

The Senior High Special Class—Work-Study Programs

To provide continuity in the school program for the educable mentally retarded, senior high special classes that emphasize work-study are mandatory. Adequate preparation for the world of work and living in a complex, technological society is not available to the mildly mentally retarded student unless the high school program focuses on the development of work potential and competencies for living in the adult world. If the programs end at the upper elementary school or in the junior high school, the preparation of these youngsters for future life, school, and work is seriously limited.

The age range for the senior high work-study program is generally from fifteen or sixteen to eighteen or nineteen; the grade equivalent is from ten through twelve. In the senior high program, the teacher must develop an instructional program which is primarily horizontal. That is, it emphasizes the application of learned skills, such as academic performance, rather than the vertical development of academics. The educable mentally retarded youngster at the senior high level should be ready to develop skills in such areas as preparing a budget, seeking and finding a job, preparing a menu, preparing and storing food products, shopping and spending money wisely, learning simple home maintenance skills, learning to care for a child, learning his role as a family member, traveling within the community, developing the wise use of leisure time, learning good grooming habits, applying appropriate safety habits, developing good mental hygiene, learning about sex education and family life planning, learning how to drive a car and how to obtain a driver's license, and many other areas.

To accomplish the many tasks set forth above, the teacher must use appropriate community resources and facilities. Similar to the junior high school program, the work-study program at the senior high level must also use the regular classroom as a resource for the educable mentally retarded. In no way should the special class teacher be given the total responsibility for the development and implementation of the program.

Work-study high school special education offers chances for a job, money, and school. (Courtesy of Dr. Patricia McFarland, Dale Rogers Workshop, Oklahoma City, Oklahoma.)

Because employment is one of the main objectives in the education of mildly retarded children, a large number of school systems have established work-study programs. These classes have grown tremendously since the early 1960s. There are many variations in work-study programs throughout the United States. Some operate essentially with the services of one teacher who may be referred to as a teacher-coordinator or a vocational teacher. Other programs include such positions as a vocational rehabilitation counselor, a job evaluator, a job placement specialist, a psychologist, a speech therapist, and a teacher. A large majority of these programs are established with the cooperation of the state vocational rehabilitation agency either through a formal contract agreement or by using vocational rehabilitation as an appropriate referral agency.

Work-study programs are primarily concerned with employability. Students generally receive an academic program for half a school day and a work program for the other half. The morning session may consist of the academic subjects and the afternoon session may be work-oriented. It is the teacher's responsibility to coordinate the vocational rehabilitation services, to help find job placements for students, and to teach the academic subjects. For a brief historical review of work-study programs for the educable mentally retarded, the reader is referred to Kokaska (1968).

School programs for educable mentally retarded children are viewed as terminal programs, because the children will generally not pursue further formal education. Therefore, it is imperative that they be educated and trained to the greatest extent possible during their school years. There has even been an emphasis on including aspects of the work-study program in an elementary school program for the mildly retarded. This emphasis has focused on the development of positive attitudes toward work and learning the concept of being a worker, as well as other types of skill and attitude development (Allen and Cross 1967). Any elementary teacher of educable mentally retarded children should seriously consider adapting these concepts.

In addition, all teachers of retarded children should be prepared to develop programs to enhance their vocational potential and assist them to prepare for adult life. Cohen (1972) suggested that teacher education programs should involve the placement of future teachers of the retarded in the communities where the children live. They could then gain first-hand experience and information relative to the children's current life styles, available community resources, what children's parents do for a livelihood, and ways in which the team concept can be used to combat the problems of mental retardation. Through a field station the teacher could be prepared to learn how to function within the child's existing community and how to aid in the total rehabilitation program for the mentally retarded.

Work-study programs have taught mentally retarded students how to use simple behavior modification approaches to improve their acceptance in school and on the job. Retarded children were taught techniques such as how to make positive statements to regular classroom teachers and how to avoid students who responded to them in a negative manner (Rosenberg 1973). This training was provided in one-to-one and group settings and gave the junior high age youngsters ample opportunities to "test" their new skills before applying them. The results of the project indicate that retarded youngsters can learn to change attitudes and react to their environments in a positive manner.

Emphasizing the vocational potential as well as the academic potential of the mildly mentally retarded is a goal that is well worth pursuing. Instruction in vocational areas may enhance the achievement of EMR students. Porter (1980) indicates that gains were made in language usage, reading, and math for an experimental group of eighteen EMR students who were from twelve to fourteen years of age. The instructional period was 8 months long. A comparison control group of thirteen to seventeen EMR students showed gains only in language usage. Both groups had IQs ranging from 55 to 80 and also had adaptive behavior and achievement deficiencies. The experimental group studied clusters of vocational areas and had to apply their previous learnings and develop new skills and concepts. This was accomplished through participation in the Darmstadt Enterprise for Career and Individual Development (DECIDE) which was developed by Porter in 1978. Porter concluded that career and vocational education for the mildly mentally retarded does have positive results. Students were observed to have more internal motivation during their training in addition to their gains in academic achievement. Further research is needed in this area to support the growth and development of career and vocational education programs for EMR students. If EMR students in the age range of twelve to fourteen demonstrated significant achievement gains through vocational instruction, surely this has relative importance for the age range of fifteen to eighteen.

School Programs for Trainable Mentally Retarded Children

Public school programs for moderately (trainable) mentally retarded children have been in existence for some time. Although at times there have been controversies regarding the role of the public schools in providing educational services for this group of children, the majority of schools which operate programs for them provide for several age levels. The names applied to the various levels of training usually denote the functional level of the children. For example, these levels are often referred to as preprimary (ages six to ten); primary (ages nine to twelve); intermediate level (ages eleven to fourteen); and teenage (ages thirteen to twenty or twenty-one). (*A Guide for Teachers of Trainable Mentally Retarded Children* 1971.) The names and ages for the various levels are not standardized across the country. In a rural area, for example, one may find only one unit for all trainable mentally retarded children. In smaller communities, one may find two units consisting of an elementary school age group and a secondary school age group. Children who are trainable mentally retarded are not a large group. Therefore, modifications in the way in which they are grouped for education and training must be implemented.

The instructional program for trainable mentally retarded children should be planned to focus on the development of practical skills. These children need training in self-help skills such as learning to dress and feed themselves and learning to care for their bodily needs. Language development should also be included in the program so these children can learn to communicate with one another and with others. Many of these children have speech impediments, and services should be provided to correct or minimize these problems. Trainable mentally retarded children should also be trained to develop social skills. They need to learn how to play with others and how to cooperate in a social situation. The development of appropriate and functional social skills is a very important part of the total curriculum.

In order to help these children become as independent as possible, the teacher should also emphasize the development of work skills. One objective in training trainable retarded children is to help them become as independent as possible during their adult years. As they progress and mature, some of them may be able to develop minimal basic reading and number skills. These skills can be presented in a practical manner (one should not expect a traditional academic level of functioning) for the purpose of improving the children's safety habits, their abilities to travel in the community, their abilities to read high interest and low reading level books, and their abilities to handle money. The children should also be provided a motor development and physical education program that will enable them to improve their functioning. As a group, the majority of trainable mentally retarded children require sheltered employment during their adult years. Much of the prospective teacher's school preparation should consist of exploring the possibilities of preparing children for such employment (*A Guide for Teachers of Trainable Mentally Retarded Children* 1971).

Recognizing the vocational potential of the majority of trainable mentally retarded children should direct the teacher toward helping them develop an ability to follow directions, to travel in the community, to communicate regarding their needs, to use fine and gross motor skills, and to endure physical work from four to eight hours per day. This emphasis should be provided throughout the children's school age years with tasks which are in accord with their ages and levels of development.

Some trainable mentally retarded children will not be able to work in a sheltered workshop, and a few will develop the ability to work in a semi-competitive work environment. Therefore, when working with these children in a school setting, one must be flexible and understand that all of the children will not enter a single type of adult employment. Keeping these possibilities in mind should enable a teacher to realize that a few trainable mentally retarded children will require more intensive training to reach their potentials. For those children who are unable to hold employment in a sheltered environment, the instructional training program should focus on helping them to accomplish meaningful tasks around the home. An important point for the parent, teacher, and other professional persons to keep in mind, is that the child should not be considered employable or unemployable based solely upon an IQ score. It is essential to provide a comprehensive training program for trainable mentally retarded children in such areas as self-help skills, language skills, social skills, and work habits.

School Programs for the Severely and Profoundly Mentally Retarded

Individuals are severely and profoundly mentally retarded (IQ range 1 to 30 or 35) have been considered subtrainable and custodial for many years. It was assumed that the best type of placement for students with this degree of mental retardation would be always within a residential center. Since 1975, public schools have been developing programs for students who are severely and profoundly mentally retarded (SMR, PMR). The large number of such students who are multiply handicapped, and the development of public school programs for them, has necessitated the renovation of facilities.

The teacher-pupil ratio for this group is one teacher to four or five students, because considerable individual attention is required. Teachers are using a task analysis approach combined with behavior modification in working toward the goals of development and growth of self-help skills, physical movement skills, and language development. In addition to trained special education teachers, SMR and PMR students require the services of a physical therapist, a speech and language therapist, and sometimes an adaptive physical education teacher. The program must be multi-disciplinary if the goals are to be met. Also considerable parental involvement is required.

Personnel and teachers who provide education and training programs for the SMR and PMR must present learning tasks in a step-by-step approach. They also must be careful observers of behavior in order to determine when a child is making progress. The progress of a child is generally very slow, and a small step of progress may go unnoticed. The trained teacher must use resourcefulness, skills, and observation with each child in order to reinforce improvements. The teacher also must provide feedback to the school's administration and parents regarding the child's progress.

An effective teacher for the SMR and PMR must have a thorough background in child development, task analysis, behavior modification, and parent conferencing. Without training in these areas, the teacher will experience many difficulties and perhaps will not provide the program required by each child. Certain situations require that the teacher help parents establish a home intervention program or, at least, a home environment that is an extension of the school program. This work requires an individual who desires to keep abreast of changing information; therefore, flexibility and additional time are necessary prerequisites for the successful teacher.

Special equipment is necessary for children who are multiply handicapped. The teacher, therefore, must develop skills in the proper use of the special equipment. This equipment will include items such as communication boards, standing tables, tilt tables, special writing devices, special wheelchairs, and a wide variety of audio-visual materials. Learning how to use these items to the best advantage for each SMR and PMR individual will take time and consultation with the physical therapist, and the speech and language therapist.

Education and training programs for SMR and PMR students will continue to grow in numbers and sophistication. As additional learning devices and skills are acquired, progress in learning will increase and the lives of these citizens will be enhanced to a greater extent than previously thought possible. This does not mean that they will be rehabilitated or habilitated to the extent that they will function normally, but they will no doubt be able to do more than was expected or accepted just a few years ago.

Community Services
In association with residential facilities two services are becoming more common in several communities for retarded children. These services are the halfway house or boarding home and the sheltered workshop.

The Halfway House
The halfway house is an extension of the quarterway house which is becoming popular within the residential facility. The halfway house is a facility in the community which offers closely supervised community living for the retarded. A majority of these services are offered in cooperation with the state division of vocational rehabilitation. The halfway house is a home which has been renovated to serve the function of a boarding home. Several young adults who have been returned to the community from a residential

Sheltered workshops provide jobs for many people of different age levels. (Courtesy of Dr. Patricia McFarland, Dale Rogers Workshop, Oklahoma City, Oklahoma.)

facility live in the halfway house, and usually a married couple live in the home to serve as parents for the young people. The individuals who have returned to the community have been placed on jobs and gradually assume responsibility for themselves. They generally pay partial room and board upon first entering the halfway house. After a period of approximately six to eight months they pay full room and board. As they gain self-confidence and maintain their jobs, they are released from the halfway house to find private living quarters and manage for themselves within the community. The halfway house program has been successful and has been appropriate for many young people who are mentally retarded and who, for diffuse reasons, could not return to their own communities.

The Boarding Home
The boarding home is much the same as the halfway house with one exception: it may, in some communities, be one step beyond the halfway house. In other words, when young adults maintain a job and are responsible for themselves in the community, they may move from the halfway house to a boarding home. The boarding home requires that they pay their own way. However, the boarding home may be subsidized by vocational rehabilitation and require less cost than a private facility.

Sheltered Workshops
Sheltered workshops have also been established as extensions of the services of a residential facility. One may also find sheltered workshops on the campus of a residential facility for those who are capable of performing work, but

need a sheltered living environment. According to *Sheltered Workshops—a Handbook* (1966), prepared by the National Association of Sheltered Workshops and Homebound Programs, a sheltered workshop may be defined as follows:

A work-oriented rehabilitation facility with a controlled working environment and individual vocational goals which utilize work experience and related services for assisting the handicapped person to progress toward normal living and a productive vocational status.

This handbook is an excellent resource for any individual or group who may be contemplating the establishment of a sheltered workshop. It is most comprehensive with respect to planning, programs, operations, staffing, labor laws, and workshop standards.

As the reader will note from the definition given, sheltered workshops are usually for handicapped persons in general rather than for any one type. Upon visiting a sheltered workshop, a person may find many different types of handicapped individuals receiving an opportunity to work and be contributing members of society. There are several hundred sheltered workshops in the United States today. These facilities provide a work and training station for many young people who are unable to compete in the larger labor market. The establishment of sheltered workshops has provided a means for many young retarded individuals to return to community living.

Respite Care
Respite care for the mentally retarded is a concept and a service which had its primary start after the emphasis on de-institutionalization. In some situations, respite care facilities are provided by using former private houses which have been modified to meet the resident and house parent needs of the mentally retarded. Respite care may also obtain services from private individuals who care for mentally retarded children in their homes and give the parents the opportunity to enjoy an evening function or a weekend vacation. Considerable emphasis in respite care has been created by associations for mentally retarded citizens, because babysitters are difficult to obtain.

Leisure Time
Programs for leisure activities within the individual and the economical capabilities of retarded persons are a necessity. All children, including the mentally retarded, need opportunities to participate in programs of leisure. With the advent of shorter working hours, participation in leisure time activities will become more of a necessity in the future. Of course, this particular area is partially the responsibility of the special education teacher who should provide an instructional program which will enhance the development of appropriate leisure activities. As the mentally retarded approach

secondary school age, they should receive specific information regarding leisure activities in which they can participate during their young adulthood and later adult years. Younger children should also receive training which will help them to develop interests in leisure activities and skills which they can use in participating in these activities. During school years, retarded youngsters should be directed to community agencies that will include them in leisure activities. Several communities have formed boy and girl scout troops specifically for mentally retarded children. Other recreational activities sponsored during the summer months by the city, by a school recreational department, or by a voluntary agency should be encouraged to include or provide specific programs for mentally retarded children.

The inability to develop substantial leisure activities is probably one of the greatest deficiencies in many school programs. Mentally retarded children usually need assistance to develop appropriate use of leisure time because in many cases their economic status will not permit them to use the resources available to others. One of the authors has surveyed the leisure activities of senior high school mentally retarded individuals and found that these youngsters tend to spend a considerable amount of time in activities that are easily accessible and cost very little. Surveys of the present use of leisure time will vary considerably depending upon the size of the community and the resources available for the teenager. However, any teacher may profit by discovering how the senior high or any other age group of the mentally retarded spend their leisure hours. Perhaps if teachers perform these surveys consistently, their findings may tend to strengthen the instructional program for leisure activities.

Residential Facilities for the Mentally Retarded

Residential facilities for the mentally retarded are probably the oldest programs offered within the United States for this group of children. At the turn of the century these facilities placed primary emphasis on providing care for the mentally retarded. Admission criteria were extremely lax and there was not much chance for children to be returned to the community with appropriate training for community living. Of course, in recent years the criteria for admission and the training programs have become more appropriate to the needs of the children (Jordan 1966).

For a brief but excellent review of basic facts regarding residential facilities for the mentally retarded, the reader is referred to Butterfield (1969). This source discusses the need for residential facilities, the cost involved in operating the programs, the population served in facilities, and the training of the staff of the residential facility.

Programs offered in residential facilities have changed drastically since the mid 1960s. In a majority of residential facilities, vocational training and evaluation centers have been incorporated as an essential feature of the total training program. The provision of a vocational training and evaluation center within a residential facility should have several objectives. One is to evaluate and train children who can return to the community and to return them, as soon as feasible, with saleable skills. Another is to improve the resident's ability to perform higher levels of work within the residential setting.

One of the authors has visited many residential facilities throughout the Southeastern United States, which have vocational training and evaluation centers that have successfully trained retarded individuals to function in a community work program. Several of these institutions have established quarterway houses on the campus of the residential facility. The quarterway house is a cottage set aside for residents who are preparing to return to the community. When residents are selected for vocational training and evaluation, they are moved into the quarterway house and must gradually assume more and more responsibility for themselves. With supervision, they learn the skills necessary for keeping themselves clean, keeping their quarters clean, washing and ironing their own clothes. Some even prepare their own meals. If they can perform successfully in a quarterway house, then the indication is that they can also do the same in the community. The use of a quarterway house is an efficient method of determining the extent to which a person will be able to develop and maintain a degree of independence.

Residential facilities are also developing short-term training for the more capable trainable mentally retarded individuals, so that they may remain at home during the major portion of a year. The short-term training involves admitting the individual to the residential facility for a period of approximately three months, and providing training in areas such as self-help skills, grooming, controlling behavior, learning appropriate social skills, and learning to be more effective in communication. At the same time the child is being trained, parents are also being trained to help with certain management problems in the home. This trend in residential facilities will provide services to many children who are currently on a waiting list to be admitted, but do not need full-time placement. These services will also enable parents to improve their skills in working with their own child and develop a better understanding of their child. As a result, the children should also increase their level of functioning.

As more professionals see that the residential facility can offer training for retarded children instead of providing merely custodial care, residential facilities will continue to improve in the comprehensiveness and appropriateness of training and evaluation. The institutional setting will then be recognized as an important community service for children who need a program of short-term intensive training and boarding.

Parents of Mentally Retarded Children

Parents have difficulties in coming to grips with the fact that they have a retarded child. Generally, the more severe the child's retardation, the greater the problems the parents will have in facing the impact of mental retardation. Some parents may easily recognize their child's severe retardation, because it may be manifested by hydrocephalus, mongolism, etc. They realize quickly that the situation is severe and that they cannot cling to hopes for drastic changes. It is somewhat like the obvious difference between a broken leg and a muscle strain. Parents do not want to have a defective child and if the ability of the child is severely affected, the parents may need continuous support and guidance to help them change their parental role.

Parent Awareness

Of course, awareness of the retarded child by parents and family will depend, to some extent, on the socioeconomic status of the parents. If the parents are within the lower socioeconomic group of the population, and they have a child who is educably mentally retarded, they may not recognize functioning at a level which is lower than the rest of the siblings in the family. Being told that the child is mentally retarded may have very little, if any, effect. In the higher socioeconomic group of the population, the fact that a child is mentally retarded will have a greater impact, because the parents will readily understand that their child will not be able to achieve their aspirations. The reactions of parents at different levels of socioeconomic structures have nothing to do with their love for their children. The difference in reactions is due primarily to the variance in their expectations. Parents in the higher socioeconomic groups have higher expectations for their children, because of the level they have been able to reach for themselves. Probably the main point which must be remembered when attempting to help parents function with their retarded child is that constructive efforts will not begin until the parents realize that the child is mentally retarded.

Farber (1968) refers to this process as a redefinition of the child. Once the parents have been told that their child is mentally retarded, they must redefine all of their child's characteristics and functioning before the process of acceptance begins. Prior to this time, parents may go from one resource to another attempting to find someone who will tell them that their child is not mentally retarded, and that certain procedures may be undertaken which will cause the child to function in a normal way. Going from one agency to another, and avoiding the fact that their child is mentally retarded, may be a result of the manner in which the parents were first told of the retardation. The acceptance of their retarded child is referred to as a process for the parents, for as the child continues to grow and mature, new problems will develop and new redefinitions will have to be formulated. For example, it may become very difficult for parents to accept their teenage child as retarded when the child continues to grow and mature physically in a way that strongly resembles the growth and development of a normal child. Acceptance of their retarded child will not be a one-time event for the parents. As parents continue to redefine their child, they will also have to redefine continuously their own roles as parents.

Parents may have many reactions when they are first told that their child is mentally retarded. They may immediately reject the definition and attempt to ignore the fact that their child is having difficulties in maturational or adjustment processes. This stage will usually not last long if their child is severely handicapped, because the problems of the child will not go away through parents' ignoring the obvious. As soon as the parents *begin* to realize the retardation of their child, parent growth may continue if they receive periodic support as the child continues to grow and mature.

Of course, the majority of problems occurs when the child is severely, profoundly, or moderately mentally retarded. As Farber explains, the fact of having a mentally retarded child in a family in the upper middle class is viewed as a tragic crisis. In a family in the lower socioeconomic class this fact would be viewed as a role or organization crisis. Thus, the impact of a mentally retarded child on parents and the family will depend upon the socioeconomic status of the family, the severity of the child's retardation, the child's sex, the child's age at the time the condition is identified, the family's orientation with respect to organization, and the time in the parents' lives when the retarded child is born (Farber 1968).

Parental acceptance of a retarded child is a factor which school personnel must consider, because school programs must provide for the moderately retarded. In several communities, school programs for trainable retarded children are established as special schools, because a school building may be designated as the building in which the majority or all of the moderately mentally retarded children will receive their education. This procedure means that many parents will go directly for help to the school program, the school principal, or the classroom teacher. Through parental contacts of this nature, school personnel will begin to realize the impact of mental retardation on parents and should recognize their roles in helping these parents to develop acceptance and understanding.

Parent Counseling

Contact with parents of mentally retarded children in the school setting will require teachers, principals, and school counselors to develop skills which will enable them to conduct parent counseling. In fact, each time a teacher meets with a mother, a father, or both parents to discuss their child's school progress, the teacher will be conducting parent counseling. Educators must learn to work with parents effectively to help them to understand their child's school work. Parents also will often seek assistance from school personnel in order to be better able to cope with their child at home. If asked for this type of assistance, school personnel must remember that the child is the responsibility of the parents, and that the child will be in the home for much longer periods of time than in school. Teachers should be careful to provide realistic assistance that will help parents work through their adjustment problems, and not to give them rigid child-care guidelines to follow. In brief, don't talk to the parents as if the child were not their child, and don't indicate to the parents that the school intends to assume major responsibility for their child. The parents may want you to be frank with them about their child's learning problems, but in other domestic areas they may be seeking guidelines and assistance rather than the advice of an "expert" from the school.

A few programs have been established which have as their main objective the training of parents of mentally retarded children. These programs have concentrated on developing better communication with the child and helping the child to develop language, social, and physical skills. These programs may be beyond the role of the public school. However, if such a program does exist in the community, school personnel should be aware of it and, if necessary, refer the parents to this source.

If at all possible, parent counseling should include both parents. This procedure helps to avoid any misinterpretation in the relaying of information from one parent to the other. It also helps parents to work together to develop an improved home environment. Both parents may not be able to come to the school during school hours, but this should not prevent the teacher, principal, or counselor from making one or two home visits during the school year. Home visits should be accepted as an integral part of the special education program in the area of mental retardation. By making home visits, the teacher will have an opportunity to meet both parents, visit in the child's home to learn about family relationships, and learn about the emphasis which is placed on educational activities in the home. A new teacher should probably contact the school principal about home visits prior to making any. Teachers and parents should understand that a teacher making home visits is doing so for the purposes of improving the child's instructional program by developing a more thorough understanding of the child. A home visit should never be made to satisfy a teacher's curiosity about the child's living conditions.

An inexperienced counselor should not undertake an intensive counseling program with parents of retarded children, because of the background of skill and training necessary to be successful in this endeavor. Again, one of the main roles of the classroom teacher, school principal, or school counselor is to know of possible community resources and to be able to refer parents who may be in need of these services. For further information in the area of providing counseling for parents of mentally retarded children, the reader is referred to Farber or Jordan.

(Courtesy of Michael Hanulak.)

Parent Groups

Parent groups for parents of the mentally retarded have been formed in the majority of the larger communities within the United States. These groups usually become a part of the National Association for Retarded Citizens (NARC) and become known as the local association for retarded citizens (ARC).

In many cases, the local ARC will form a school program for preschool trainable mentally retarded children and will promote appropriate activities within the community. The parents and professionals who become members of the local ARC will also serve as a group to promote needed legislation within a state for all retarded individuals. These groups have been most effective in helping to establish programs, better community awareness of retarded children, and comprehensive legislative programs.

Becoming a member of a local ARC is an additional way for parents to receive support and understanding about their retarded child. Parent counseling may take place during some of the meetings, and this is an additional community resource for parents of mentally retarded children.

Published Materials for Use with the Mentally Retarded

Many publishing companies have printed materials suitable for use with mentally retarded children. A teacher may find resources through publishing companies which were not in existence as recently as the early 1960s. Our experiences in teaching mentally retarded children took place during the years when teaching materials were scarce. Teachers today have many materials available to them, but they need to be very concerned with the suitability of these materials.

An excellent guideline source for teaching materials for mentally retarded children is *Instructional Resources for Teachers of the Culturally Disadvantaged and Exceptional* (1969). Teachers may also use their Regional Instructional Materials Centers as a resource. A list of the location of these centers may be obtained from the national office of the Council for Exceptional Children in Reston, Virginia. The use of these centers is restricted to special education teachers who are employed in school programs.

A sample of published materials follows.

Resources

American Association for Health, Physical Education and Recreation. *A Resource Guide in Sex Education for the Mentally Retarded*. Washington, D.C.: AAHPER (or New York: Sex Information and Education Council of the United States, 1855 Broadway and 61st Street), 1969. (Single copy free upon request to publisher.)

Arena, John L., ed. *Teaching Educationally Handicapped Children*. Novato, Calif.: Academic Therapy Publications, 1967.

Brickman, William W., and Lehrer, Stanley, eds. *Education and the Many Faces of the Disadvantaged*. New York: John Wiley and Sons, 1972.

Cratty, Bryant J. *Development Sequences of Perceptual-Motor Tasks*. Freeport, Long Island, N.Y.: Educational Activities, 1967. (020135)

Egg, Maria. *Educating the Child Who is Different*. New York: John Day, 1968.

Johnson, Vicki M., and Werner, Roberta A. *A Step by Step Learning Guide for Older Retarded Children*, Syracuse, N.Y.: Syracuse University Press, 1977. (13210, Prepared for the Moderate to Severe Mentally Retarded.)

Karnes, Merle B. *Helping Young Children Develop Language Skills: A Book of Activities*. Washington, D.C.: Council for Exceptional Children, 1968.

Kirk, Samuel A. *Diagnosis and Remediation of Psycholinguistic Disabilities*. Urbana, Ill.: University of Illinois Press, 1966. (020036)

Kirk, Samuel A., and Kirk, Winifred D. *Psycholinguistic Learning Disabilities: Diagnosis and Remediation*. Urbana, Ill.: University of Illinois Press, 1971.

Programming for the Mentally Retarded. Washington, D.C.: American Association for Health, Physical Education, and Recreation, 1968.

Smith, Robert M., ed. *Teacher Diagnosis of Educational Difficulties*. Columbus, Ohio: Charles E. Merrill, 1969.

Stephens, Thomas M.; Hartman, A. Carol; and Lucas, Virginia H. *Teaching Children Basic Skills*. Columbus, Ohio: Charles E. Merrill, 1978.

Thomas, Janet K. *Teaching Arithmetic to Mentally Retarded Children*. Minneapolis, Minn.: T. S. Denison and Co., 1968.

———. *Teaching Language Arts to Mentally Retarded Children*. Minneapolis, Minn.: T. S. Denison and Co., 1968.

———. *Teaching Reading to Mentally Retarded Children*. Minneapolis, Minn.: T. S. Denison and Co., 1968.

Wagner, Guy, and Dorlan, Mork. *Free Learning Materials for Classroom Use*. Cedar Falls, Iowa: Extension Service, State College of Iowa, 1967.

Witty, Paul A., ed. *Educationally Retarded and Disadvantaged*. Chicago: National Society for the Study of Education, distributed by University of Chicago Press, 1967.

Study Questions

The following study questions may be used for directed studies for individual students or for the development of special projects for graduate students.

1. Use one of the references listed in the chapter or another source and write a description of a trainable mentally retarded child with Down's syndrome.
   a. Physical characteristics.
   b. Types of Down's syndrome.
   c. Learning characteristics.
2. Locate three or four current references on mainstreaming of the mentally retarded child and discuss the pros and cons of mainstreaming. Also, consider the following questions with regard to the mainstreaming of the mentally retarded.
   a. What criteria should be established in order to determine the feasibility of mainstreaming an individual mentally retarded child?
   b. What criteria should be developed to determine the educational evaluation of the child who has been mainstreamed?
   c. Considering the emphasis in work-study programs at the senior high school level for the educable mentally retarded, discuss how mainstreaming at the secondary school level can contribute to the vocational potential of this population group.
3. Provide the following information about phenylketonuria (PKU):
   a. The cause of PKU.
   b. Prevention and diagnosis of PKU.
   c. Symptoms or characteristics of PKU.
   d. Legislation, if any, relative to PKU in your state.
4. Write a brief summary of the factors relative to the diagnosis, classification, and prognosis of children who are educable mentally retarded.
   a. Diagnosis.
   b. Classification.
   c. Prognosis.
5. Write a brief summary of the factors relative to the child who is trainable mentally retarded, and emphasize the following points:
   a. Diagnosis.
   b. Classification.
   c. Prognosis.
6. Visit a sheltered workshop in your community or a nearby community and discuss the following points:
   a. The type of individuals served by the sheltered workshop.
   b. The number of professional staff in the workshop.
   c. The number of paraprofessionals on the workshop staff and their duties.
   d. The criteria used by the workshop for determining the population group it serves.

e. The various ways used by the workshop to evaluate the progress of an individual being served by the program.

f. The number of contracts held by the workshop, how they obtained the contracts, and a specific discussion of what two or three of the contracts involve.

7. Visit a special education class in your community which is provided for the trainable or the educable mentally retarded and discuss the following points:

a. During your visit what was the emphasis of the instructional program?

b. How much of a variety of instructional materials did you see in the classroom? List at least five of them.

c. At what academic level did the students appear to be performing?

d. Did you observe any behavioral characteristics which might provide you with some insight regarding the mentally retarded?

e. If any discipline problems arose during your visit, how did the special education teacher react to them?

f. If you had an opportunity for some interaction with the children, describe your feelings and reactions during this time.

g. Describe the physical facilities provided in the classroom, such as the location of the class in the building, the classroom setting, and the appropriateness of the room for the needs of the children.

8. Locate several current resources in the library and discuss the conclusions reached by the authors regarding the learning characteristics of the educable mentally retarded and how learning environments can enhance the learning progress of this particular group.

Bibliography

A Guide for Teachers of Educable Mentally Handicapped Children, vols. 1 and 2. 1971. Oklahoma State Department of Education and Oklahoma Curriculum Improvement Commission.

A Guide for Teachers of Trainable Mentally Retarded Children. 1971. Oklahoma State Department of Education and Oklahoma Curriculum Improvement Commission.

Allen, Amy A., and Cross, Jacque L. 1967. "Work-Study for the Retarded—The Elementary School Years." *Education and Training of the Mentally Retarded* 2, no. 1 (February).

Anderson, Robert M., Hemenway, Robert E.; and Anderson, Janet W. 1969. *Instructional Resources for Teachers of the Culturally Disadvantaged and Exceptional*. Springfield, Ill.: Charles C Thomas.

Benoit, E. 1959. "Toward a New Definition of Mental Retardation." *American Journal of Mental Deficiency* 63.

Butterfield, Earl C. 1969. "Basic Facts About Public Residential Facilities for the Mentally Retarded," in *Changing Patterns in Residential Services for the Mentally Retarded*, R. B. Kugel and W. Wolfensberger, eds. President's Committee on Mental Retardation Monograph, Washington, D.C. Also published in *Mental Retardation: Readings and Resources*, 2d ed., Jerome H. Rothstein, ed. New York: Holt, Rinehart & Winston, 1971.

Chiappone, Anthony D., and Libby, Bruce P. 1972. "Visual Problems of the Educable Mentally Retarded." *Education and Training of the Mentally Retarded* 7, no. 4 (December).

Cohen, Julius S. 1972. "Vocational Rehabilitation Concepts in the Education of Teachers of the Retarded." *Education and Training of the Mentally Retarded* 7, no. 4 (December).

Doll, E. A. 1941. "Definition of Mental Retardation." *Training School Bulletin* 37.

Farber, Bernard, 1968. *Mental Retardation: Its Social Context and Social Consequences.* Boston: Houghton Mifflin Co.

Grossman, H. J., ed. 1973. *Manual on Terminology and Classification in Mental Retardation.* Revised ed. American Association of Mental Deficiency. Baltimore: Garamond/Pridemark Press.

Heber, Rick. 1959. "A Manual on Terminology and Classification in Mental Retardation." Monograph Supplement to the *American Journal of Mental Deficiency* 64.

Huberty, Thomas J.; Koller, James R.; and Ten Brink, Terry D. 1980. "Adaptive Behavior in the Definition of Mental Retardation." *Exceptional Children* 46, no. 4 (January).

Hutt, Max, and Gibby, Robert. 1976. *The Mentally Retarded Child: Development, Education, and Treatment.* 3rd ed. Boston: Allyn and Bacon.

Jordan, Thomas E. 1966. *The Mentally Retarded.* 2d ed. Columbus, Ohio: Charles E. Merrill.

Kidd, John W.; Bartlett, Richard H.; Forgnone, Charles; Goldstein, Herbert; Gorton, Chester; Moreno-Milne, Nidia; Roseboro, Dorothy; and White, Ralph. 1979. "An Open Letter to the Committee on Terminology and Classification of AAMD from the Committee on Definition and Terminology of CEC-MR." *Education and Training of the Mentally Retarded* 14, no. 2 (April).

Kokaska, Charles J. 1968. "Secondary Education for the Retarded: A Brief Historical Review," *Education and Training of the Mentally Retarded* 3, no. 1 (February).

National Association for Retarded Children. 1971. "Policy Statements on the Education of Mentally Retarded Children." Arlington, Texas: NARC.

Polser, Charles M., et al. 1967. *Mental Retardation: Diagnosis and Treatment.* New York: Harper & Row.

Porter, Mahlon E. 1980. "Effect of Vocational Instruction on Academic Achievement." *Exceptional Children* 46, no. 6 (March).

Robinson, Halbert B., and Robinson, Nancy M. 1976. *The Mentally Retarded Child*, New York:McGraw-Hill.

Rosenberg, Harry E. 1973. "On Teaching the Modification of Employer and Employee Behavior." *Teaching Exceptional Children* 5, no. 3 (Spring).

Shane, Don G. 1967. "The Role of Special Education in the Habilitation of the Mentally Retarded." *Education and Training of the Mentally Retarded* 2, no. 1 (February).

Sheltered Workshops—A Handbook. 1966. 2d ed. Washington, D.C.: National Association of Sheltered Workshops and Homebound Programs.

Telford, Charles W., and Sawrey, James M. 1977. *The Exceptional Individual.* 3rd ed. Englewood Cliffs, N.J.: Prentice-Hall.

Tredgold, A. F. 1963. *A Textbook of Mental Deficiency.* 10th ed. Baltimore: The Williams & Wilkins Co.

3

disadvantaged children as related to special education

Introduction

To find or formulate a single definition which would adequately describe all disadvantaged children is impossible. Many children would be exceptions to the definition. Therefore, this discussion focuses on children who have experienced serious deprivations of one or more types during fetal development or early childhood—deprivations which caused severe limitations in their ability to learn or gain meaningful information from the environment. These children are born to mothers who have had little, poor, or no medical care during pregnancy, or mothers who have experienced severe dietary deficiencies during their pregnancies. Also included are children who, born into families of lower socioeconomic status, have not had appropriate maternal or paternal care, appropriate diets during early childhood, or adequate stimulation to prepare them for school experiences.

Children who may be described as disadvantaged cannot participate fully or meaningfully in the normal school environment, nor can they be expected to learn in the manner which is typical of most children. This does not mean that these children cannot learn. They most definitely can learn—and profit from educational services. It is the task of educators, psychologists, sociologists, and other professionals to learn more about these children and to implement programs and techniques which will enhance this learning. The positive characteristics of the environments and culture of these children must be learned and accentuated.

Educators should never pity or "look down on" disadvantaged children. If one assumes that they are inferior, one's approach is negative and in many instances the child's reactions will unwittingly become negative. To view them as the "cannots" of society perpetuates cultural disparity and discrimination, and the disadvantaged children will continue to exhibit severe learning deficiencies and social difficulties.

Children who are disadvantaged come primarily from families who live in poverty. There are approximately 11 million children in the United States who live in poverty. What criterion should be used to determine poverty? With wages and prices, as they are in the 80s, the criterion may be difficult to pinpoint, but certainly the situation is becoming worse rather than improving. Can a family of four live adequately on $7,000.00 a year? Obviously not. The barest needs of a family of four would undoubtedly exceed the provisions of a $7,000.00 a year minimum. Budget management will help with these families but will by no means totally alleviate their financial difficulties.

Tremendous improvement in the multiple problems of the disadvantaged is the objective. It cannot be met without a concentrated effort in energy, time, and money as well as innovations which have not yet been tried to any great extent. If educators and other professional personnel are truly concerned about the plight of the disadvantaged, educational programs will be devised which will improve children's opportunities to learn and function in society.

In 1981 approximately 3 percent (7.0 million) of the population was classified as mentally retarded. Of the nation's mentally retarded, approximately three-fourths are found in low socioeconomic areas. Estimated incidence of mental retardation in the inner-city neighborhood is 7 percent or higher (the national average is 2 to 3 percent). Inadequate opportunities to learn and other environmental factors may adversely influence the intellectual development of the children in these lower socioeconomic areas.

The following information is concerned with the areas of prematurity, nutrition, and education in low socioeconomic areas as they relate to mental retardation and learning problems. It is difficult to separate the etiological effects relative to genetic and environmental factors because of the constant interaction between heredity and environment. Therefore, our investigation is limited to descriptive research of environmental causes and means of prevention of mental retardation and learning problems in low socioeconomic areas. The following definitions offer a brief description of the areas of concern.

1. Mental Retardation: specific intellectual deficits which originate during the developmental and postnatal periods, and are associated with impairment in the child's adaptive behavior.
2. Learning Problems: manifestations of academic, social, and behavioral inabilities to perform functionally in a "normal" environment, because of one's disadvantaged environment and lack of proper diet and material care.
3. Intelligence: cognitive behaviors which reflect an individual's capacity to solve problems with insight, to adapt to new situations, to think abstractly, and to profit from experience.
4. Socioeconomic: a combination of social and economic factors (income and social position considered as a single factor).

5. Environment: all the conditions, circumstances, and influences surrounding and affecting the development of an organism or group of organisms (often contrasted with heredity).
6. Heredity: the transmission from parents to offspring of certain characteristics.

Assumptions
1. There is a high incidence of mental retardation and learning problems in lower socioeconomic areas.
2. IQ, as measured by a given test, is subject to change if the life or environment of the individual is changed.
3. There is a constant interaction between heredity and environment.

Prematurity and Mental Retardation

Premature birth appears to be one of the major causes of mental retardation. Koch (1966) indicated that approximately 15 to 20 percent of all cases of mental retardation are associated with prematurity. Cooke (1964) reported that in the United States, prematurity occurs in 7 percent of all births, but runs as high as 12 percent in some communities. Robinson and Robinson (1965) cite Pasamanick (1959) who found, when he compared black and Caucasian groups in Baltimore, that the incidence of prematurity was twice as great in the black group as in the upper portion of the Caucasian group (11 percent as compared to 5 percent), while Caucasian infants born to mothers in lower socioeconomic groups suffered an intermediate risk of prematurity of 8 percent. Hardy (1965) indicated that social factors, such as socioeconomic status play a role in the incidence of premature births and there appears to be an inverse relationship between socioeconomic level and the incidence of premature delivery.

The term prematurity is a misnomer. Many children are born fully developed before the normal nine-month period of gestation. On the other hand, some babies are poorly developed even when delivered after a full-term pregnancy. For this reason, pediatricians now base the diagnosis of prematurity on weight, regardless of when the baby is born. The baby under 5½ pounds is considered to be premature or a "low-birth-weight infant" (Thompson 1968).

Maternal Factors Related to Prematurity

Many maternal factors are related to prematurity, such as alcoholism, heavy smoking, tuberculosis, diabetes, and kidney disease. The age of the mother is one factor in determining the likelihood of premature delivery. Hardy (1965) reported that Battaglia, Frazier, and Hellegevers (1963) published results of a study on approximately seven hundred fifty juvenile patients followed in the Women's Clinic of the Johns Hopkins Hospital. Approximately 25 percent of the girls who were fourteen years of age or less at the time they became pregnant had a premature delivery compared to approximately 16 percent premature births for girls fifteen to nineteen. It has also been found that the more children a mother has had, the greater the chances of her next child being premature. "If there is too rapid a succession of pregnancies, the mother does not have adequate time to replenish her depleted nutritional and emotional needs" (Thompson 1968). In addition, the economic circumstances of the mother are important: poverty and prematurity apparently go together.

Developmental Picture of Premature Infants

A developmental picture can be drawn for most premature infants. Jordan (1966) related that in the first two years, the picture will be one of delayed development, a condition proportional to the degree of prematurity and lower social-class standing. Walking and talking are less likely to be present at the usual point in the first twenty-four months of life. At three years, evidence of cognitive impairment as well as perceptual motor limitations may be present. Hardy (1965) cited research showing that between ages three and five, depressed intellectual and neurological signs can often be found, and by the age of six, perceptual-motor dysfunction, immaturity of speech, as well as comprehension and reasoning difficulties are often present.

Correlation Between Prematurity and IQ

The possibility of a correlation between low birth-weight and low IQ has been investigated. Hardy (1965) reported on intelligence tests administered at the ages of three and five years by Harper, Fischer, and Rider (1959) to approximately one thousand premature infants and a like number of normal controls. They revealed that in the group weighing 1,500 gms. (3.3 lbs.) or less at birth, there was a higher incidence of defective and dull children and fewer above-average children than in the group of larger premature infants or in the group of controls who weighed 2,501 gms. (5.6 lbs.) or above at birth. Also, the larger premature infants were intermediate in performance. The black children in all weight groups performed significantly lower than the Caucasian children in comparable weight groups. Waisman (1966) reported that in premature infants weighing 1,500 gms. or less, Lubchenco et al. (1963) showed that IQ was related to birth weight and they felt that poor performance in school was related to prematurity. Dr. Heinz Berendes of the National Institute of Neurological Diseases and Blindness (Thompson 1968) reported that the IQ's of four-year-old Caucasian youngsters who weighed less than three pounds at birth averaged 94 as compared with IQ's of 105 for the four-year-olds born at normal weight, Waisman (1966) reported, however, that McDonald (1964) showed that children weighing not more than four pounds were mentally inferior to the general population. Whereas it was true that some premature females weighing less than three pounds had lower IQ scores than those weighing between three and four pounds, this same finding could not be confirmed for the males.

Long-Term Effects of Prematurity

The long-term effects of prematurity can be illustrated in the presence of school problems. Jordan (1966) cited several studies which revealed a significant relationship between prematurity and enrollment in special education classes. Other symptoms found in classroom investigations were pervasive disorders such as reading problems, poor concentration, motor disabilities, shyness and immaturity. Hardy (1965) reported that Douglas' study (1960) on some six hundred Caucasian children in England revealed that, based on behavior ratings by teachers, children in the premature group presented more difficulties in school and generated more complaints than those in the mature group. Less than half of the premature children, as

Poverty, malnutrition, retardation, premature birth, birth defects, and high mortality rate are all school-related problems.

compared with the controls, passed the qualifying examination for admission to secondary school.

Koch (1966) expressed concern that the women most likely to bear damaged children—the economically and culturally disadvantaged in our population—must be reached if prematurity is to be reduced. Many of these women depend entirely on public medical and health services for prenatal and postnatal care. Thompson (1968) reported that in 1964 a $30 million dollar program to start pilot clinics to find and treat economically disadvantaged mothers was initiated in the United States. Operating in some eighty hospitals throughout the country, these clinics concentrated on expectant mothers suffering from anemia, chronic illnesses, and other factors linked to prematurity. So far the program has reached only a fraction of the mothers who need it. Of the estimated 1 million babies delivered to "poverty" mothers in 1970, only 83,000 were cared for in these clinics.

Social class should be recognized as one of the great concomitants of prematurity. If positive preventive measures are not taken, we can expect to see lower social classes continue to produce a disproportionate number of premature infants and, consequently, contribute a greater number of mentally retarded and learning disabled children to our society.

Malnutrition and Poverty

Malnutrition and undernutrition are also major causes of mental retardation. One of the most important causes of malnutrition is poverty. Upwards of 25 million Americans live on incomes of less than $3,300 a year for a family of four, and half of these Americans—including some five million children—live in households having annual income of $2,200 or less. To maintain an adequate diet such families would have to spend nearly all of their income for food. A preliminary report of the National Nutrition Survey, in which the United States Public Health Service collected nutrition data on 70,000 persons, found evidence of malnutrition in an unexpectedly large percentage of low income families. Up to a third of the children studied showed malnutrition-associated characteristics similar to those of undernourished populations in some of the world's poorest nations (Department of Health, Education, and Welfare 1970).

Perkins (1977) cited many examples of the relationship of poverty and malnutrition, poverty and maternal health, disease hazards to children, malnutrition and brain development, and malnutrition and mental development. Perkins reports a succinctly stated reference by Margaret Mead (1970) in which she indicated the vital importance of nutrition in the life of the child, particularly at critical stages. Mead stated that food affects not only dignity but the capacity of children to reach their full potential, and the capacity of adults to act from day to day. Additionally, she stated that it is true that starving adults, their efficiency enormously impaired by lack of food, may usually be brought back again to their previous state of efficiency, which is not true of children. What children lose is lost for good—deprivation during prenatal and postnatal growth can never be made up.

Newspaper stories through the years, also, have indicated long-term effects of nutrition deprivation of P.O.W.'s from World War II, Korea, and Viet Nam. Evidently, one's food intake is not only significant to children, but also to adults who will someday be mothers and fathers.

Nutrition and Neurointegrative Development

The time at which malnutrition occurs is crucial to the further development of the child. The earlier the malnutrition the more severe the effects and the more likely that they cannot be reversed. It is now known that the prenatal period and first six months of life are the most important in terms of proper nutrition (Department of Health, Education, and Welfare 1970). According to Bakan (1970) undernutrition from birth to twenty-one days produces a persistent and permanent reduction in brain weight. Undernutrition also results in specific degeneration within brain cells; again, the earlier the restriction, the more severe the damage. Bakan (1970) indicated that Winick (1969) felt that malnutrition curtails the normal rate of increase in head circumference. He believed that this reduced head circumference of the malnourished children, especially during the first six months of life, accurately reflected the reduced number of cells present in their brains.

Bakan also reported that during the preweaning period in the rat an enormous amount of chemical change takes place within the brain and that preweaning is the time when the brain is most sensitive to the detrimental effects of undernutrition. She discovered that the brain of the mature rat which was malnourished during this period was not only physically smaller but showed degenerative cell changes. When the deprivation occurred early in infancy, these changes were irreversible, while the effects of later deprivation were reversible through proper feeding. Other animal studies (Department of Health, Education, and Welfare 1970) have proven that malnutrition or undernutrition of the mother and offspring at certain critical prebirth and postbirth periods of rapid growth can impair both physical and mental development. They can cause permanent and irreversible retardation, regardless of the quality of later nutrition, and are most harmful when they involve a lack of specific nutrients such as certain essential vitamins, amino acids, or proteins. An examination of the brains of infants who had died of marasmus (a starvation-related condition marked by progressive emaciation) revealed that their brains' structure and characteristics were significantly altered and abnormal in the same ways as the brains of young animals that suffer from starvation.

A series of studies by Cravioto and his associates (1966) in Mexico and Guatemala showed that the performance of children on psychological tests was related to nutritional factors, not to differences in personal hygiene, housing, income, or other social and economic variables. Children who were exposed to severe early malnutrition exhibited perceptual defects as well as smaller body size. The earlier the malnutrition, the more profound the psychological retardation. The most severe retardation seemed to occur in children under six months of age who were admitted to the hospital. These children failed to improve even after 220 days of treatment. Children who were admitted later with the same socioeconomic background and the same severe malnutrition, but a different time of onset, did recover after prolonged rehabilitation. Cravioto et al. concluded that nutritional inadequacy may interfere with both the staging and the timing of development of the brain and of behavior.

Studies of animals have indicated that growth in all organs occurs in three phases: (1) hyperplasia, during which the number of cells increases; (2) hyperplasis and hypertrophy, during which the number of cells continues to increase and the size of the individual cells also increases; and (3) hypertrophy, where growth occurs only by increase in cell size (Cravioto et al).

These studies suggest that during the phase of hyperplasia, malnutrition can interfere with cell division, resulting in fewer cells in the brain, which seems to have a permanent effect. Malnutrition during hypertrophy, however, results in smaller than normal cell size, which can be corrected by providing adequate nutrition. In humans, the brain grows most during the fetal period, and by the end of the first year has assumed 70 percent of its adult weight. By the end of two years it is nearly complete in growth.

Relatively free from unfactored environmental contamination are some studies made by Dr. Fernando Monckeberg of the University of Chile who reported the progress of fourteen children with severe marasmus. Those subjects were diagnosed at ages one month to five months, were treated for long periods, discharged, and observed during visits to the out-patient department. As each child was discharged from the hospital, the mother was given twenty liters of free milk per month for each preschool child in her family. Three to six years later the children were clinically normal. Their weight, head circumference, and intelligence quotients, however, were significantly lower than in Chilian children of the same age having no history of clinical malnutrition (Cravioto et al. 1966).

Retardation in physical growth and development is generally found to depend upon family dietary practices and on the occurrence of infectious disease. As previously mentioned, it is not related to differences in housing facilities, personal hygiene, proportion of total income spent on food, or other indicators of social and economic status.

It is clear that under circumstances common to developing countries, malnutrition can interact with infection, heredity, and social factors to bring about physical and mental impairment. The social factors responsible are multiple and difficult to correct, but the elimination of malnutrition and infection among underprivileged populations is a feasible goal.

In industrialized countries a child's inadequate intellectual or social performance is the result of a complex interaction over a period of time of genetic variables and primarily nonnutritional factors in the social or cultural environment. But in developing countries, variations in educational and economic status and in beliefs and customs from family to family may be relatively small. Together with genetic differences, they may actually be insignificant as determinants of intellectual performance, because the children are so greatly affected by problems of nutrition, and by infection (*Profiles of Children* 1970).

According to White (1971) the problem of malnutrition or undernourishment is responsible for poor health, high fatigue level, and insufficient learning. An additional factor related by White pertains to the high absenteeism of these children, which also leads to insufficient or faulty learning. If corrective measures are not employed, many children who are disadvantaged will function as mentally retarded all of their lives. There is no justification for allowing this gross waste of human potential.

Malnutrition and Pregnancy

"The relationship between diet in pregnancy and a healthy offspring has been widely studied. It was formerly believed that the baby was a parasite and could derive any nutrients it needed from the mother's body, but evidence now shows that if the mother has a deficient diet the fetus will suffer" (Inzer 1970). Furst (1970) feels that many children suffer malnutrition before birth because their mothers are poorly fed and poorly developed physically, receive inadequate medical care, or have had children too often.

One of the most intriguing findings reported by Bakan (1970) in this area was that poor nutrition of the infant female may affect the development of her offspring many years later. Robinson and Robinson (1965) cited that Masland (1958) reported that Wolf and Drillien (1958) found a higher correlation between prematurity and the class of the mother's father than between prematurity and the economic class of the child's own father. Masland interpreted these results as indicating the possible influence of nutrition during the mother's childhood. He also pointed out that the mother's early nutritional habits would probably carry over into her marriage.

Naeye, Diener, Dellinger, and Blane's (1969) study reported by Bakan identified undernutrition of poor urban mothers as the cause of the low birthweight of their offspring (prematurity). They felt that since evidence has shown that both low birth-weight and a high infant mortality rate are more common in poor families, the finding that undernutrition appears to be the cause of prenatal growth retardation is an important one. In addition to being 15 percent smaller in body weight, the infants from poor families had irrelevant weights of such organs as the thymus, spleen, and liver. Inzer (1970) reported a study in rural Iowa which evaluated the dietary practices of 404 indigent pregnant women and the incidence of prematurity. Forty-four percent of the mothers were poorly nourished. The study concluded that the increase in prematurity was in direct proportion to the decrease in nutritional status. The lowest birth weight and the highest death rate in the neonatal period occurred among the infants of the most poorly nourished mothers.

Malnutrition, Growth of the Brain, and IQ

The nutrition of a mother is an important variable related to the intellectual performance of her children. Erickson (1967) as reported by Bakan found that when a vitamin supplement was given to pregnant and lactating women with poor nutritional environments, the offspring at four years of age appeared to have an average IQ score eight points greater than the average score of the children whose mothers were given placeboes over the same period. Bakan reported that Kugelmass et al., as far back as 1944, demonstrated an increase in the IQ of both retarded and mentally normal children as a result of prolonged nutritional rehabilitation. The children, ranging in age from two to ten, were divided into two groups: malnourished, and well-nourished. The malnourished retarded children gained ten IQ points and the normal children gained eighteen IQ points after a period of dietary improvement. In contrast, there was relatively little change in the score of the already well-nourished retarded and normal children.

The effects of postnatal malnutrition on animals which have already suffered prenatal malnutrition are more marked than effects of either prenatal or postnatal deprivation separately. It seems the prenatal malnutrition made these animals more susceptible to postnatal undernutrition. If the deprivation occurs early in infancy, these changes are irreversible, while the effects of later deprivation may be reversed through proper feeding (Bakan).

Available evidence from human studies reinforces the findings of experiments with animals and suggests that early infancy is a critical period for the development of the brain. This is also the time when the brain is extremely vulnerable to the effects of malnutrition. Indirect measurements of the brain growth in humans show that malnutrition will curtail the normal rate of increase in head circumference, which accurately reflects the reduced number of cells present in the brain. When a fluid, similar to spinal fluid is used to fill the cavity between the brain and the skull, and a diffused light is used to make the fluid glow, a very small area is shown with normal children. But the malnutritioned child's entire brain case glows, from the forehead to the back of the head.

Follow-up tests of children restored to health showed that they achieved lower scores than children who had not suffered from malnutrition. Similarly, the malnourished children who exhibited reduced head circumference had lower IQ's even after long-term follow-up (Bakan).

In addition to the negative impact of malnutrition on the growth rates and intersensory development of children Cravioto found a relationship between these aspects of development and infection. It has also been shown that certain infections in malnourished children may produce severe and prolonged hypoglycemia, a condition which can by itself cause brain damage. In addition, various biochemical defects of children with malnutrition are accentuated by infection. Infection and malnutrition thus act synergistically to produce a chronically and recurrently sick child less likely to react to sensory stimuli from an already inadequate social environment.

Malnutrition and Education

How can malnutrition and its counterpart, mental retardation, be arrested or prevented in poverty areas? What can be done to insure that every child in America has the same chance of being "created equal" or the opportunity to live a life outside of poverty and hunger? Inzer (1970) indicated that a high priority must be set for greater accessibility to prenatal clinics and positive teaching of all mothers and mothers-to-be in the areas of nutrition and child care. She tells us that efforts must be made to help every prospective mother learn the principles of good nutrition and how to budget her food dollar by using less expensive foods to provide the necessary nutrients. Emphasis must be laid constantly on the importance of a proper diet, and that emphasis reinforced to each school child beginning at the elementary grade level. Perhaps in this way the health of future generations can be improved.

Malnourished children will quite likely have problems in school. They are often apathetic, irritable, and inattentive. They lack a sense of curiosity or a desire for exploration. Dr. Birch, research professor of pediatrics at the Albert Einstein College of Medicine says:

A society genuinely concerned with educating socially disadvantaged children cannot restrict itself merely to improving and expanding educational facilities . . . it must concern itself with the full range of factors contributing to educational failure. . . .
We hope for an awareness of the size and scope of the danger confronting children born *of* and *into* poverty. We hope for a changed system of providing for those who cannot provide for themselves. (Furst 1970)

Furst also reported that the problem of decreased educational performance among children of the lower socioeconomic levels cannot be solved merely through school breakfast or lunch programs. The effort put into such programs should be determined by the severity and scope of malnutrition and by the influence of other factors, such as the home life of these children.

The most noxious of poverty's effects is malnutrition. Until the cycle of poverty is broken, the success of all efforts at compensatory education or remedial education will be limited if not doomed to failure.

Educational Components

Many children from low socioeconomic areas are placed in special education classes and the possible benefits of preschool for these children have been somewhat investigated. According to the President's Task Force on the Mentally Handicapped (1970), the greater part of those described as mentally retarded have suffered from developmental difficulties associated with social and environmental deprivation.

Mercer (1971) studied the "labeling process" of mental retardation in the public schools in California. She found that ethnic surveys conducted annually since 1966 by the California State Department of Education have consistently shown rates of placement for Mexican-Americans and black children in special education classes that were two to three times higher per 1,000 than rates for children from English-speaking, Caucasian homes (Anglos). The "labeling process" was investigated by reviewing and identifying the characteristics of all 1,234 children referred for any reason in a single school year to the Pupil Personnel Department for the Riverside Unified School District. Approximately 80 percent of the children in the school district were Anglos, 11 percent Mexican-American, and 8 percent black. Low-status or minority children were not referred at a higher rate than their percentage in the population nor were they tested by the psychologist at a higher rate. Of the 865 children tested by the psychologist, 82.9 percent were Anglo, 7.6 percent Mexican-American and 9.5 percent black. Among the children tested were 134 who received an IQ of 79 or below. Based on their test performance, they were eligible for placement in a special education class. There were approximately four times more Mexican-American children among those who failed than would be expected compared to their percentage in the tested population. There were twice as many black children and only about half as many Anglo children. There were 71 children who were actually placed as mentally retarded in this school district. Six times more Mexican-American children (45.3 percent) and two and a half times more black children (22.6 percent) were placed than would be expected from their proportion in the school district population. Mercer also found that children from ethnic minority groups were not only failing IQ tests at a higher rate, but selective factors operating in the "labeling process" resulted in disproportionately more minority children being recommended and placed as mental retardates from among all the children who were eligible for placement. She concluded that children from minority groups were more likely to be recommended for placement and placed as mental retardates than Anglo children, after they failed an IQ test.

Sabatino, Kelling, and Hayden (1973) specifically refer to linguistically different children such as Mexican-American and American Indian children who have been placed in special education classes because of low scores on standardized test instruments. The children discussed by Sabatino et al. seem to fit the authors' suggestions regarding disadvantaged children.

Specific recommendations are given by Sabatino and his co-authors to stress native language in early education programs and prepare children linguistically to live and be educated in the dominant culture. Thus, it is not the child alone *per se* with whom one must deal. The school curriculum must be modified to accept present linguistic functioning, and adequately prepare children to function away from home. This does not mean that linguistic and cultural background should be eliminated, but that these strengths should be used to prepare children to enter the school culture and function bilingually.

Classroom Characteristics

Many times in the classroom children exhibit some symptoms of learning disabilities; hyperactivity; disorders of attention; disorders of speech and hearing; specific learning disabilities in reading, arithmetic, writing, and spelling; impulsivity; and low test scores in the verbal or performance areas. Environment leads us to believe that they are deprived.

As a result of extreme poverty, children may be far from reaching the potential of their maturational ceiling. This may explain, in part, why children from deprived areas show poor performance on standardized tests of intelligence. These factors need to be taken into consideration in any appraisal of the ability levels of children. The range of stimuli offered children in many areas is very limited. They have little play space or few interesting things in the home. There may be a few pictures on the wall, but attractive objects are not the order of the day.

There is little doubt that deprived children typically work on academic problems in a slower manner. This is shown in many different ways; they require more examples before seeing a point, arriving at a conclusion, or forming a concept. They are unwilling to jump to conclusions or to generalize quickly (exceptions to the rule bother them). These students are slower readers, slower problem solvers, slower getting to work, and slower in taking tests. It is, on the other hand, important to note that in many areas of life the underprivileged are not at all slow. They are frequently remarkably quick in athletic activities, and in many games they function rapidly and seem to think quickly.

Often deprived children live on the level of basic psychological responses of love, anger, and sensual behavior. They express these directly while growing up in deprived areas. They follow the characteristic patterns of pleasures and ambitions of those about them. Not only are they allowed to fight when angry; they are expected to do so. They have learned to protect themselves rather than rely on authorities. Hence physical aggression is often regarded as the normal way of life.

Language in the lower class is not as flexible a means of communication as in the middle class. It is not as readily adapted to the subtleties of the particular situation, but consists more of a loosely patterned repertoire of the same phrases and expressions which are used without much effort to achieve a subtle correspondence between perception and verbal expression. Considerable lower-class language consists of a kind of incidental "emotional" accompaniment to here and now action.

The child from a disadvantaged environment may have missed some of the experiences necessary for developing verbal, conceptual, attentional, and learning skills. These skills play a vital role in understanding the language of the school and the teacher, in adapting to school routines, and in mastery of such a fundamental tool subject as reading. In this absence of these skills, there is a progressive alienation of teacher from child and child from teacher. Children may suffer from feelings of inferiority because of failure. They may withdraw or become hostile and find gratifications elsewhere.

One reason for the difficulties in the education of disadvantaged children is that many of them are relatively slow in performing intellectual tasks. In our society, speed is rewarded. In many intelligence tests, speed of reaction is an important factor in determining the level of mental ability. Slowness of response needs to be given attention in terms of the final learning outcome. Speed of reaction, although important, may have received more attention than it rightly deserves. Perhaps it is incorrect to associate speed of reaction with gifted children and slowness with dull children. There are values that can accrue from slowness of response if the student is persistent.

Linguistic Diversity

Foss and Hakes (1978) indicated that black English (BE) should not be considered substandard, but referred to as a linguistic system with a full range of expression. The history of black English is not clear, but it should not reflect a racist theory that black English is a degenerate form of standard English. Foss and Hakes state that black English probably has its development from pidgin and Creole. Pidgin is a language which has no native speakers. The language may have developed when speakers of different languages needed to communicate. Consequently, the input comes from many sources, and the cultural languages developed by many minorities in the U.S. reflect the influence of the Portuguese, West African, plantation Creole, West Indian, and many other languages.

Grammatical rules exist (Foss and Hakes) for black English and it has its own logic. Therefore, schools are faced with the decision to include black English as a primary language and consider standard English as a second dialect, or to encourage the use of standard English as the primary dialect (language). One approach leads to a public interpretation that may support the pride of minorities; the other to an interpretation that minorities are subjugated.

Educators should understand that language does not necessarily reflect intellectual strengths or weaknesses. Language reflects the culture in which a child lives. Each language has different perceptions which may or may not reflect cognitive development. Foss and Hakes quote Benjamin Lee Whorf's (1897–1941) statement that some children grow up speaking languages that enable them to develop more cognitive categories for different words simply because they know the languages. Other children, such as the Hopi Indian, may use a language that has a timeless verb that does not distinguish between present, past, or future. Such a child's cognition of and perception of time is based on language, not lack of intelligence.

We feel strongly, however, that children need the strength of standard English as a part of their curriculum. Each child should rise to the highest level of language that is compatible with that child's rate of growth. Obviously, the teacher's aspiration level and expectation for the student's growth must be realistic.

Motor and Visual Perception Difficulties
The culturally deprived child is more adequately described as a disadvantaged child. There is a culture, but an inferior one by the standards of the middle-class culture. Since it is the middle-class structure upon which the schools' expectations are built, the disadvantaged are often handicapped in school.

It is estimated that the disadvantaged child is functioning one to two years below the middle-class child in many areas of learning upon entering the first grade. This gap may widen through the school years.

Typically, gross motor skills are well developed, often superior in early life. It is probable that there is positive reinforcement for motor development. Parents may feel this shows superiority. They may feel the child will be less dependent on them, and so they encourage gross motor development. Less emphasis is placed on fine muscle coordination skills, and few stimuli are provided to encourage these skills.

Perceptual development, which emerges as a product of experience with an environment and with maturation shows widespread dysfunction among disadvantaged children. They are usually exposed to a minimal amount of stimuli to enhance normal perceptual development: bare beds and rooms, and few objects in their environment for exploration. The disadvantaged may also have overstimulation from noises—TV, radio, shouting, and fighting—which may cause withdrawal, and less exploration of their surroundings. Their limited environment, limited motivation, and lack of systematic interpretations can cause developmental retardation and limited generalizations.

Even though gross motor skills are usually well-developed, the disadvantaged usually have not learned to deal with their bodies in space, nor do they have a positive body image. They usually have poorly developed laterality, directionality, time sequencing, and chronological ordering abilities.

Whether learning disabilities derive from organic impairment, developmental lag, or genetic inheritance, remediation is largely the same. Areas of weakness must be determined and activities developed to provide the learning experiences needed for building the necessary concepts.

It has been suggested that enrichment, for the sake of enrichment, may fail for the disadvantaged; that they do not need additional or more varied stimulation, but experience to give stimuli a pattern of sequential meaning. The disadvantaged are often slower learners (not poorer or stupid learners), needing programming to insure readiness and success. They seem to profit from having the abstract associated with the immediate, the sensory, and the motor. They seem to succeed more easily in a structured environment, with rules, order, and organization; but they also need to learn by doing— by active participation. Because they tend to be physical learners, movement and action play important roles in their remediation.

Space concepts can be taught through motor activities. Body awareness, impulse control, serial memory, and identification of forms can be remediated through motor activities. Some visual perception activities are possible without motor activity, and some may be artificially paired with movement to aid the educational process. Many gross motor learnings can, by teaching the application, be transferred to fine motor activities. Both motor abilities and perception need to be trained until they are automatic.

Motor learnings are the earliest learnings. Kinesthetic experiences provide feedback about movement and the body parts. Motor information provides the base for organizing information from the senses. From reflex movements, the child differentiates body parts and the movement, recombines movements, integrates them and learns generalized movement patterns. A generalized pattern allows a child to focus on the goal of a movement, not the movement itself.

Laterality is the inner awareness that the body has two sides. Without this inner awareness, there is no left, right, up, and down. Laterality develops as it is associated with posture and the balance of the body. After learning about objects within arm's reach, the child begins to structure objects that fill space. As space is organized, information from it is matched to the motor base. Without this match, stimuli remain just stimulation.

To function adequately in school, children must learn to perceive form, organize information gained through vision, and perceive relationships of objects in space. They must be able to structure space and time. Without a time structure involving synchrony, rhythm, and sequence, they cannot follow directions.

After motor development, a motor perceptual level is reached whereby the eye follows the movement. This is followed by a perceptual motor level where the eye leads the hand, ultimately leading to the ability to learn perceptually—to organize incoming data without reference to motor activity. If a lack in these structures is creating a learning problem, activities to promote balance, posture, laterality, body image, eye-hand coordination, figure-ground, and form concepts must begin. Such perceptual-motor training helps children structure self-concept and the space-time-world in which they function.

Behavior of the Culturally Deprived
Children who fall into the category "culturally deprived" are typically ill at ease and uncertain in the classroom. These traits too frequently manifest themselves in aggressive, even hostile behavior.

The lack of self-esteem accounts for much of their hostility, their negative outlook on life, and their apparent lack of enthusiasm for learning. Because most of the parents of these children are so occupied with earning a living or so harassed by unemployment and financial pressures, they pay little, if any, attention to these children. By the time they are six or seven, they gravitate to the street to achieve a feeling of belonging. The gang code becomes a moral code; gang values become personal values. There is unwillingness and often fear of losing status in the gang hierarchy. If going to school, learning, and reading are considered a waste of time by the gang; a child adopts that attitude. The gang follows the leader. If the leader sleeps in class or provokes the teacher, the others do, too. The student's violently defensive reactions, developed as survival measures in the streets, are difficult to overcome.

In their environment, physical strength and cunning are admired as desirable traits. A boy grows up fighting for his place among his peers. At home, breaches of rules set up by the head of the house result in physical, punitive action. Authority seems to be designed more to keep the child "in line" than to help and protect. Thus, the teacher's task is made more difficult because it, also, represents authority.

Immediate reinforcement of sought-for behavior is particularly suited to the disadvantaged child. The learning style of the deprived child requires that considerable ego-enforcement be given, and encouragement or discouragement be given right away, for this is how his society operates. In the street-corner curriculum, if the child displays undesired behavior, the reprimands are immediate and forceful. The rewards for "right" behavior, too, are immediate.

Here is an example of one teacher's use of the principle of immediate reinforcement. The name of each child was printed on the chalkboard; immediately following any demonstration of good manners by any child, a star was drawn with colored chalk next to his name. The children soon "caught on" and made deliberate attempts to get rewards. Consistent use of this method resulted in a sharp increase in good manners in these children.

Another example is the technique of giving many spot quizzes from which feedback follows immediately. This should be done not so much to evaluate in terms of a grade as to allow the child to see problems immediately. In the case of testing, it has been found that instead of a letter grade, commercial trading stamps which can be cashed in for material goods seem to have more tangible meaning to "object-oriented" deprived children.

An individual photograph can be a very striking reward—especially a photo showing the child in a positive learning situation. In addition to displaying children's work on a bulletin board, photographs of them with their names clearly visible below them may be put next to their work. This not only fosters the image of the positive learning situation—the behavior one wants to encourage—it also gives the deprived child, who typically suffers from lack of a positive self-image, a great degree of ego-reinforcement.

Table 3.1 Identification of the Disadvantaged Gifted

Test	Author	Date	Emphasis	Comments
Alpha Biographical Inventory	Taylor, C.W. and Associates	1966/68	A 300-item life-experience inventory	No racial differences on creativity index and small differences on academic index
Relevant Aspects of Potential (RAP)	Grant, T. E.	1974	How students feel about self and reaction to everyday situations	Indicates high potential among minority group students
Torrance Tests of Creativity	Torrance, E. P.	1971	Creativity	Shows no difference or difference in favor of culturally different groups
Abbreviated Binet for Disadvantaged (ABDA)	Bruch, C. B.	1971	Selected items from Stanford-Binet	Shows bias toward disadvantaged
Stallings's Environmentally Based Screen (SEBS)	Stallings, C.	1972	Identification based on responses to environmental matters	For urban youths restricted to an area no larger than a ten-block radius
Test of Learning Abilities	Meeker, M. and Meeker, R.	1973	Based on the Structure of Intellect-specific strengths and weaknesses	Appropriate for black, chicano, and Anglo disadvantaged boys
System of Multicultural Pluralistic Assessment (SOMPA)	Mercer, J. B. and Lewis, J. G.	1978	Allows performance to be compared with one's own socioeconomic group	Provides for below normal, normal, or supranormal indications of performance

Source: Mary M. Frasier, "Rethinking the Issues Regarding the Culturally Disadvantaged Gifted," *Exceptional Children*, vol. 45, no. 7 (1979). © The Council for Exceptional Children.

Role playing is extremely successful with this "action-oriented" child. If a child walks in front of the teacher without saying "excuse me," the teacher immediately engages in role playing in order to dramatically drive home this breach of manners. The peer group itself might be asked to evaluate a role-playing situation. By inviting the classes' immediate analysis, there would be on-the-spot reinforcement by peers. Feelings of self-worth and hopefulness increase as a result of continuous daily exposure to challenging situations in an atmosphere of mutual acceptance.

The Disadvantaged Gifted

Past efforts have focused almost entirely on the learning deficits of the disadvantaged child. During the 1960s and particularly the 1970s, some studies indicated concerns relative to the learning styles of the disadvantaged gifted. An excellent review of literature regarding the identification of the disadvantaged gifted and programs for that population has been compiled by Fraiser (1979). At the outset, Fraiser indicated that too much emphasis was placed on the jargon for identifying the disadvantaged, such as the *culturally disadvantaged, culturally different, culturally deprived,* or *culturally diverse.* The real issue should simply involve a method of identifying the disadvantaged gifted, because many of these children have greater potential than was formerly thought possible.

Several test instruments have been designed to identify the disadvantaged gifted. These instruments have been the focus of recent studies of the proficiency of testing. Fraiser's thorough discussion of these instruments is presented in table 3.1.

Preschool Education

Kirk (1965) reported an experiment in preschool education based on the hypothesis that if education were started with very young children, (excluding extreme clinical types) training and experience could very possibly accelerate the rate of mental development and prevent some cases of mental retardation. The study involved groups of mentally retarded children below the age of six. Some children were offered preschool education while others were left without training. In follow-up studies after three or four years, it was found that preschool education had some effect on social and mental development.

Goldstein (1966) found that the real test of preschool education was its ability to increase the child's rate of social and intellectual development beyond that which would ordinarily occur with the first exposure to formal school, and to teach skills and abilities so meaningful that long-term retention takes place. Goldstein cites Jones (1954) who stated that one could expect gains in intelligence among children whose environment is changed from static and unstimulating to fresh and dynamic.

Strickland (1971) reported on the Milwaukee Project which was launched in 1964 when a multidisciplinary team from the University of Wisconsin under the direction of Dr. Rick Heber, Professor of Education and Child Psychology, began a series of surveys designed to learn more about the relationship of poverty to mental retardation. Surveys were taken in the residential section of Milwaukee which, according to census data, had the lowest median family income, the greatest population density per housing unit, and the most dilapidated housing in the city. This section of town also had a much higher rate of mental retardation among school children than any other area of the city. The first survey revealed that maternal intelligence was the most reliable single indicator of the level and character of intellectual development of the children. Even though mothers who had IQ's below 80 made up less than half of the total group of mothers in the study, they accounted for about four-fifths of the children with IQ's below 80. The data also indicated that the lower the mother's IQ, the greater the possibility that their children would score low on intelligence tests. The team observed in their repeated visits with hundreds of families that the mentally retarded mother created a social environment that was distinctly different from the environment created by her neighbor of normal intelligence. From this data, the team established an Infant Education Center in 1966 in the area where their surveys had been conducted. Their goal was to see if intellectual deficiency might be prevented—as opposed to cured or remediated later—by introducing an array of positive factors in the children's early lives, and displacing factors that appeared to be negative or adverse.

Forty mothers with IQ's of 70 or less, and their newborn children, participated in the Infant Education Center Project. The newborn babies of these mothers were divided into two groups. Two-thirds of the population was placed in the experimental program and the remaining one-third was placed in a control group. Shortly after the mother had given birth and returned from the hospital, the teachers began visiting the home for several hours each day. They focused most of their attention on the baby. Some weeks later, the mother and the child were admitted to programs at the Infant Education Center. The infant child, at approximately three to four months of age, was exposed to mental stimulation of a wide variety for many hours each day. Meanwhile, the mother was encouraged (but not required) to participate in a center program designed to teach her improved homemaking and baby-care techniques and in some cases to provide basic occupational training. At forty-two months of age, the children in the active stimulation program measured an average of 33 IQ points higher than the children in the control group. Some of the children measured IQ's as high as 135. Equally interesting was the fact that the children in the experimental program were learning at a rate that exceeded the norm for their age group.

A 1976 report indicated that the children in the Milwaukee Project had completed three years of school, and held the gains they showed in the preliminary report by Heber. The experimental children are still showing an advantage of more than 20 IQ points over the control group (Trotter, 1976).

Heber's study is referred to as a "shotgun" approach because he did not attempt to control the variables in the program. The early intervention and involvement with the mothers included so many variables that it is extremely difficult to account for the variables which were predominant in bringing about the performance changes.

The Milwaukee Project has been criticized, and one of the criticisms is directed at cost. However, the expenditure of approximately $30,000 per child for a period of six years seems to be a small price to pay for preventing mental retardation. In addition, all of the expenses which would have been involved for providing special services for these children later in their lives would surely have exceeded $30,000.

The trend of the data developed in the Milwaukee Project gives real hope that mental retardation in children whose parents are poor and of poor ability can be prevented. Longitudinal studies may eventually provide absolute conclusions about the effects of the environment on the attainment of learning and developmental skills. The approximately 85 percent of mental retardation which has unknown etiology may then be considerably reduced.

Overview

Evidence indicates that nutritional factors at a number of different levels contribute significantly to depressed intellectual level and to learning failure. These effects may be produced directly as the consequence of irreparable alterations of the nervous system or indirectly as a result of ways in which the learning experiences of the developing organism may be interfered with at critical points in the developmental course.

It is argued that a primary requirement for normal intellectual development and formal learning is the ability to process sensory information, and to integrate such information across sense systems. However, evidence indicates that both severe acute malnutrition in infancy as well as chronic subnutrition from birth into the school years results in defective information processing. Therefore, by inhibiting the development of a primary process essential for certain aspects of cognitive growth, malnutrition may interfere with the orderly development of experience and contribute to a suboptimal level of intellectual functioning.

Moreover, adequate nutrition is essential for good attention and for appropriate and sensitive responsiveness to the environment. One of the most obvious clinical manifestations of serious malnutrition in infancy is a dramatic combination of apathy and irritability. The infant is grossly unresponsive to his surroundings. This unresponsiveness characterizes relations to people as well as objects. Behavioral regression is profound, and the organization of functions is markedly infantilized.

Children who are subnourished also show a reduction in responsiveness and attentiveness. In addition, they are easily fatigued and unable to sustain either prolonged physical or mental efforts. Improvement in nutritional status is accompanied by improvements in these behaviors as well as in physical state.

It should not be forgotten that nutritional inadequacy may influence the child's learning opportunities by yet another route, namely, illness. Nutritional inadequacy increases the risk of infection, interferes with immune mechanisms, and results in illnesses which are both more generalized and more severe. The combination of subnutrition and illness reduces time available for instruction, which disrupts the orderly acquisition of knowledge and the course of intellectual growth.

Also pointed out in this discussion were intergenerational effects of nutrition upon mental development. The association between the mother's growth and the risk to her infant is very strong. Poor nutrition and poor health in the mother when she was a girl results in a woman with a significantly elevated level of reproductive risk. Her pregnancy is more frequently disturbed and her child more often of low birth-weight. Such a child has an increased risk of neurointegrative abnormality and of deficient IQ and school achievement.

Malnutrition never occurs alone. It occurs in conjunction with low income, poor housing, familial disorganization, a climate of apathy, ignorance, and despair. The simple act of improving the nutritional status of children and their families cannot of itself fully solve the problem of intellectual deficit and school failure. No single improvement in conditions will have this result. What must be recognized is that, in an overall effort to improve the condition of disadvantaged children, nutritional considerations must occupy a prominent place. Together with improvements in all other facets of life (including relevant and directed education), they contribute much to the improved intellectual growth and school achievement of disadvantaged children.

This writing has been concerned with the three-fourths of the mentally retarded and learning problem children in the United States who live in low socioeconomic areas. Their lives are plagued by prematurity, malnutrition, and inadequate educational experiences.

Maternal factors such as age, number of pregnancies, and economic circumstances are all related to the high incidence of premature births to poverty mothers. Low birth-weight has been correlated with low IQ and the long-term effects of premature births are seen as these children enter school. Prenatal and postnatal care should be available to all mothers in these areas as a positive preventive measure against premature birth and possible mental retardation.

As previously indicated, the first six months of life are the most crucial in terms of proper nutrition. The nutrition of the mother is an important variable related to the intellectual performance of her children. Positive steps must be taken to educate mothers and mothers-to-be in nutrition and child care. School breakfast and lunch programs do not reach the children who need them most. Again, free prenatal and postnatal clinics could partially provide the needed care and education in these low socioeconomic areas.

The "labeling process" of mental retardates in our educational system needs to be questioned. If a child is to be "labeled" mental retardate, adequate care and attention should be given to the process employed in labeling. Discrimination against minority groups on tests of intelligence and subsequent placement in classes for the mentally retarded should be investigated further. Dr. Heber and his Milwaukee Project give definite hope that through preschool and infant care centers, children from low socioeconomic areas can be helped and the high incidence of mental retardation in these areas can be reduced.

Study Questions

1. Report and reference recent studies relative to nutrition and its effect on learning.

   Author:

   Title:

   Source:

   Population and Setting:

   Study Conducted:

   Procedures:

   Results (effects on learning):

2. What behaviors distinguish the culturally disadvantaged child from the socioeconomically disadvantaged child?
3. How is prematurity associated with cognitive impairment?
4. Indicate how maternal factors relate to premature birth.
5. What types of appropriate school programs should be developed for linguistically different children?
6. Discuss the critical period of malnutrition and the effects upon the mother and the child.
7. For determining prematurity, why do pediatricians now use birth weight rather than the length of pregnancy?
8. What are the significances of IQ changes among the children included in Heber's study?
9. As a regular classroom teacher, how would you modify your program to serve the specifically different needs of a disadvantaged child?
10. Discuss the possible long-term effects of prematurity.

Bibliography

"Action Against Mental Disabilities." 1970. *The Report of the President's Task Force on the Mentally Handicapped.* (September).

Bakan, Rita. "Malnutrition and Learning." *Phi Delta Kappan* 51: 529 (June).

Cooke, Robert E., M. D. 1964. "Freedom from Handicap." *The Special Child in Century 21.* Edited by Jerome Hellmuth (Special Child Publications of the Seguin School, Inc.).

Cravioto, Janquin; De Lacardie, Elsa; and Birch, Herbert. 1966. "Nutrition, Growth, and Neurointegrative Development: An Experiment and Ecologic Study." *Pediatrics* 38, no. 2, Pt. 12 (August).

Department of Health, Education, and Welfare. 1970. "The Decisive Decade MR70." The President's Committee on Mental Retardation.

Foss, Donald J., and Hakes, David T. 1978. "Psycholinguistics—An Introduction to the Psychology of Language." Englewood Cliffs, N.J.: Prentice-Hall.

Frasier, Mary M. 1979. "Rethinking the Issues Regarding the Culturally Disadvantaged Gifted." *Exceptional Children* 45, no. 7.

Furst Caryn M. 1970. "Nutrition's Effect on Mental Development." *Forecast* 16:F-160.

Goldstein, Herbert. 1966. "Preschool Programs for the Retarded." *Prevention and Treatment of Mental Retardation,* ed. Irving Philips. New York: Basic Books.

Hardy, Janet B. 1965. "Perinatal Factors and Intelligence." *The Biosocial Basis of Mental Retardation,* ed. Sonia F. Osler and Robert E. Cooke. Baltimore: Johns Hopkins Press.

Inzer, Lenore C. 1970. "A Study of Nutrition in Pregnancy." *The Journal of School Health,* October.

Jordan, Thomas E. 1966. "Patterns of Development." *The Mentally Retarded.* 2d ed. Columbus, Ohio: Charles E. Merrill.

Kirk, Samuel A. 1965. "Diagnostic, Cultural and Remedial Factors in Mental Retardation." *The Biosocial Basis of Mental Retardation,* ed. Sonia F. Osler and Robert E. Cooke. Baltimore: Johns Hopkins Press.

Koch, Richard A. 1966. "Diagnosis in Infancy and Early Childhood." *Prevention and Treatment of Mental Retardation,* ed. Irving Philips. New York: Basic Books.

Maternal Nutrition and the Course of Pregnancy. 1970. Committee on Maternal Nutrition. Food and Nutrition Board. Washington, D.C.: National Research Council, National Academy of Sciences, p. 25.

Mercer, Jane R. 1971. "Sociocultural Factors in Labeling Mental Retardates," *Peabody Journal of Education* (April).

Pasamanick, Benjamin, M. D. 1971. "A Child is Being Beaten—The Effects of Hunger," *Vital Speeches* (May 15).

Perkins, Stanley, A. 1977. "Malnutrition and Mental Development," *Exceptional Children Journal* 43, no. 4.

Profiles of Children. 1970. White House Conference on Children. Washington, D.C.: U.S. Government Printing Office.

Robinson, H. B., and Robinson, N. M. 1965. *The Mentally Retarded Child, A Psychological Approach.* New York: McGraw-Hill. Citing B. Pasamanick. 1959. "Influence of Sociocultural Variables Upon Organic Factors in Mental Retardation." *American Journal of Mental Deficiency* 64.

Sabatino, David A.; Kelling, Kent; and Hayden, David L. 1973. "Special Education and the Culturally Different Child: Implications for Assessment and Intervention," *Exceptional Children* 39, no. 7 (April).

Strickland, Stephen P. 1971. "Can Slum Children Learn?" *American Education* (July).

Thompson, John D. 1968. "Protecting the Preemie," *Newsweek,* (January 29).

Trotter, Robert. 1976. "Intensive Intervention Program Prevents Retardation." *American Psychologist Association Monitor* 7 (September/October).

Waisman, Harry A. 1966. "Recent Advances in Mental Retardation." *Prevention and Treatment of Mental Retardation,* ed. Irving Philips. New York: Basic Books. Citing Lula O. Lubchenco, et al., 1963 "Sequelae of Premature Birth. Evaluation of Premature Infants of Low Birth Weights at Ten Years of Age." *American Journal of Diseases of Children.*

White, William F. 1971. *Tactics for Teaching the Disadvantaged.* New York: McGraw-Hill.

4

gifted and talented children

Definition and Estimates of Prevalence

Giftedness is becoming a popular topic for discussion, research, and action in the field of education, and particularly in special education within recent years. "Despite divergent opinions about what constitutes 'giftedness' or 'creativity' or 'talent', workable criteria must be established to provide for the young people we know are there" (U.S. Commissioner of Education, 1971). The same office also indicates that generally speaking, the following evidence would indicate special intellectual gifts or talent:

1. Consistently very superior scores on many appropriate standardized tests.
2. Judgment of teachers, pupil personnel specialists, administrators and supervisors familiar with the abilities and potentials of the individual.
3. Demonstration of advance skills, imaginative insight, and intense interest and involvement.
4. Judgment of specialized teachers, pupil personnel specialists and experts in the arts who are qualified to evaluate the pupil's demonstrated and/ or potential talent.

Gowan (1971) reported that giftedness has variously been defined as a cutoff point on the Standford-Binet Individual Intelligence Test. Terman used the cutoff point of 140 IQ and above. Recent researchers have used 130 IQ. The problem with many definitions appears to be that there is no real rationale for what constitutes a gifted child. If a definition doesn't have functional or operational implications it becomes a useless description. Gowan says, "A gifted child is one who has the potential to develop creativity. Giftedness, after all is potentiality, since it is an IQ." Creativity logically should be a product of intelligence, but evidence seems to support the fact that gifted children are no more creative than normal children. Therefore, if giftedness is creativity, then normal children may also be gifted. Some observation seems to show that there is a correlation between 120 IQ as a cutoff for creativity. Gowan also thinks that mental health helps a child's creativity, because mental health obviously increases the child's rate of mental development. An increase in the child's rate of mental development might mean an increase in the child's IQ. Consequently, a person in the 110–120 IQ range with a high degree of mental health should be able to push the measured IQ into the range that may be defined as potentially creative.

For the purpose of federal funding for educational projects, these definitions must be more specific. The federal government has defined "gifted and talented" for purposes of federal education programs by Public Law 91–230, Section 806, as follows:

Gifted and talented children are those identified by professionally qualified persons who by virtue of outstanding abilities, are capable of high performance. These are children who require differentiated educational programs and/or services beyond those normally provided by the regular school program in order to realize their contribution to self and society. Children capable of high performance include those with demonstrated achievement and/or potential ability in any of the following areas, singly or in combination:

1. general intellectual ability
2. specific academic aptitude
3. creative or productive thinking
4. leadership ability
5. visual and performing arts
6. psychomotor ability (U.S. Commissioner of Education 1971)

In 1978 the Elementary and Secondary Education Act was amended by the passage of Public Law 95–561. This law authorized the expenditure of 6.28 million dollars in 1980 for programs for the gifted. The states received 75 percent of this when plans were submitted indicating how the funds would be distributed to local education agencies. The remaining 25 percent was spent to support professional preparation, aid to the states for planning, direct aid to local education programs, support for model programs, and to develop a clearinghouse for information regarding programs (Sisk 1980). Under this law the definition of gifted and talented children remains the same as given above. However, the focus of programs no longer includes the visual arts and psychomotor ability (Sisk).

This definition is primarily applicable for federal program funding. Each state has the opportunity through state legislation to devise a definition for its own educational needs. However, in the early 1970s, there were only seventeen states that had legislative acknowledgment of these children and their educational needs.

In order to make funds available, an operating definition is required. There are, however, some pitfalls in describing giftedness too specifically. Gensley (1970) cited the Special Study Project for Gifted Children in Illinois as a case in point. From the beginning of the program in 1959, planners avoided a definition for "gifted children" in the legislation for two reasons. First, specification and description of human abilities were, they thought, a problem for behavioral scientists rather than legislators. Therefore, they reasoned that definitions at the operational level in schools should respond to new scientific findings and not be delayed by legal restrictions. Secondly, they recognized that allocation of funds usually requires a description of the special category; but they felt that description for giftedness should be made through administrative regulations, not by law. The Illinois definition does appear to be educationally functional: "Gifted children are those children whose mental development is accelerated beyond the average to the extent that they need and can profit from specially planned educational services" (U.S. Commissioner of Education 1971).

Another example is the state of Oklahoma, where no laws or specific programs for the gifted existed until 1969. At that time the legislature recognized that many gifted children and youth do not receive the kinds of educational programs necessary for development of their potentials. The Oklahoma definition designates gifted children as those who indicate creativity, leadership ability or high academic potential, and are not adequately provided for in the general program (Special Education, Oklahoma 1980).

Considering the difficulty in defining this group, it is not easy to sort out the number of gifted young people in our society. Many go unnoticed by teachers and administrators. Many cover their abilities in order to fit into the group. Many, moreover, do not find adequate systems for the application of their talent in the public schools.

There is no absolute procedure for finding the exact number of children in the schools who are gifted, although the socioeconomic level of the community does seem to be an important factor. Telford and Sawrey (1977) indicated that in an average community, 16–20 percent of the elementary school population can be expected to have an IQ above 115, but in a superior community 45–60 percent may be found above 115 IQ. They also point out that between three and five times as many children in the elementary schools in a superior community will have IQ's above 115–140, than in a school in an average area.

Thomas (1966) has shown that gifted and talented pupils may constitute 20–30 percent of the school population on a nationwide basis. These children should be making the "A's" in the average classroom, but this is not always the case because they are undiscovered genius and talent. The number of children presumed to be gifted has varied considerably in recent estimates. Before the 1960s, many research workers agreed that the gifted included those within the upper 2 to 3 percent of intellectual ability. Recently, however, more variables have been introduced, such as social, mechanical, and other aptitudes, which are important in an estimate of prevalence. The total census projection for the 1980s United States elementary-secondary school population is approximately 51,000,000. A reasonable estimate indicates that the gifted population is a minimum of 3 to 5 percent of that school population.

Methods of Identification

The way in which intelligence is defined is a partial determinant of the way in which the intellectually gifted will be identified. Uniformity of definition will not be found. A commonly used method of defining and identifying the gifted is in terms of scores on an intelligence test. The use of the IQ in identifying the gifted has the advantage of objectivity. It can also be applied relatively early in life (Telford and Sawrey 1977).

The IQ method of identification has been patterned after Terman's studies. Terman (1925–26) laid the basic groundwork for research of the gifted child as early as the 1920s. Jacobs (1970) indicated that Terman relied on teachers to nominate those children who might possibly be gifted, then those children were screened for their actual levels of mental ability. He indicated, though, that before the children nominated by the teachers were individually tested, they first had to survive the screening of a group intelligence test. The IQ method is still being used, but in most cases there are variable inclusions and this method of identification is being changed. Issacs (1970) reported that Peganto and Birch (1959) and Cornish (1968) concluded that when teachers nominate children as gifted, they miss half the gifted children. Hughes and Converse (1962) and Cornish concluded that the gifted are not the high scorers on group intelligence tests.

Renzulli and Smith (1977) suggested the case study approach as a method to identify the gifted. Their study compared the case study approach to the traditional approach (group screening and individual intelligence testing) in terms of time and cost factors, and the number of children screened, identified, and appropriately placed in programs for the gifted. The case study approach, as suggested by Renzulli and Smith, includes the following:

1. Aptitude and Achievement Testing
2. Past and present teacher reports
3. Cumulative Record evaluation
4. Parent Ratings
5. Self Ratings

In four school districts using the case study approach, 149 students were selected out of a total of 1,025 at an average cost per student of $40.78. This compares to 95 students selected out of a total of 666 students in three school districts using the traditional approach at an average cost per student of $119.79. The average number of hours per student selected for the case study approach was 7.57 as compared to 12.06 average hours using the traditional approach. Project teachers indicated that 92% of those students selected and placed using the case study approach were qualified to be in the program, and 79% of the students selected through the traditional approach were qualified.

These comparisons indicate that the case study approach is a very effective method of identifying and selecting students for programs for the gifted. Renzulli and Smith concluded that the use of individual intelligence testing should not be abandoned, but perhaps may have added to the effectiveness of their case study approach.

Kinds of Giftedness

The U.S. Office of Education specified many kinds of giftedness in 1972 and from this report Khatena (1977) described them for clarification and assistance in identifying gifted children. The following information has been abbreviated by the authors from Khatena's report.*

General Intellectual Ability

The gifted who have high intellectual ability usually obtain IQ's on the Wechsler Intelligence Scales of 130 or above. This test is preferred because of the verbal score, performance score, and full scale IQ. Additionally, several factors are provided within the verbal and performance tests to indicate that general intellectual ability is more than a single IQ score.

General intellectual functioning as multidimensional may be seen in Guilford's model which he refers to as the Structure of the Intellect. Guilford's (1967) model has five kinds of mental *operations*: cognition, memory, divergent production, convergent production, and evaluation. Four kinds of *contents* are also in the model: figural, symbolic, semantic, and behavioral. There are six *products*: units, classes, relations, systems, transformations, and implications. With the combination of operations, contents, and products there are 120 possible intellectual abilities. Several gifted programs throughout the U.S. use the Structure of Intellect (S.O.I.) model.

Creative or Productive Thinking

Guilford (1967) generally describes creative thinking as divergent production, redefinition, and transformational abilities. He gives major emphasis to four creative thinking abilities in his tests of creative thinking: fluency, flexibility, originality, and elaboration.

Torrance (1975) included the four abilities mentioned above in his tests of creativity and has added the areas of synthesis and closure. Torrance (1974) defined creative thinking as one's ability to become sensitive to problems, deficiencies (in problems), gaps in knowledge, and missing elements.

Specific Academic Aptitude

A gifted or talented individual may be superior in performance in one or more academic areas. A combination of IQ scores and achievement test scores in the specific areas gives the best indication of an individual's functioning or potential for functioning in this area.

*J. Khatena, "Gifted Children in the United States and Abroad," *Gifted Child Quarterly* 21 (Fall 1977). © National Association for Gifted Children.

Leadership Ability

Guilford's Structure of Intellect model has a behavioral component which best depicts leadership ability. This component relates to nonverbal information involving attitudes, needs, desires, moods, intentions, perceptions, and thoughts.

In order to assess leadership ability one should examine an individual's skills in relating to others, understanding others, and being sensitive to changes. Also, high general intellectual ability is necessary to be an effective leader.

Visual and Performing Arts Ability

Since the 1978 passage of Public Law 95–561, visual arts ability is no longer included in the kinds of giftedness; therefore, only the performing arts area will be discussed. Performing arts ability involves creativity in drama, music, dance, oratory, and other related areas. Assessment must be accomplished through observation since few, if any, standardized measurements are available. A child with high potential for performing arts ability will demonstrate creativity through being highly productive, innovative, and capable self-expression above a "normal" performance. Skills in performing arts ability require an in-depth background of knowledge and experience related to the specific area.

The factors involved in identifying the gifted child are much more intricate than the score of one group intelligence test. The U.S. Commissioner of Education's Office (1971) expressed that the factors of importance are as follows: (1) age of identification (research reveals early identification does not fight concealed giftedness for the purpose of peer group relations). (2) screening procedures and test accuracy; (3) the identification of children from a variety of ethnic groups and cultures; and (4) tests of creativity. The Commissioner of Education's Office also reports that Bloom, after an analysis of major longitudinal studies, concluded that general intelligence develops lawfully; that the greatest impact on IQ from environmental factors probably takes place between ages one and five, with relatively little impact after age eight. This observation is very similar to Hollingsworth's observation that methods of measuring intelligence had low predictive value when applied before seven or eight years of age.

A number of other studies cited by the Commissioner of Education's Office have shown that individual tests identify gifted children much more accurately than do group measures. There is possibly evidence that group test ratings tend to be higher for the below-average individual, while for the above average, group test scores are lower than those obtained on the individually administered IQ scales. Data seem to show that the discrepancies between group scores and individual scores increased as the intelligence level increased. The most highly gifted children were penalized most by group test scores; that is, the higher the ability the greater the probability that the group test would overlook such ability.

It is unsafe to assume that teachers will consistently identify even the highly gifted. Plowman (1969) reported that identification of the gifted must be acquired by multiple means, including measures of intelligence, achievement, talent, and creativity. Practice seems to indicate to us that one of the best methods, the individual intelligence test, is presently not being used in many states because of the cost involved. Plowman also feels that school personnel are important in identifying these children. The personnel valued as most critical are school psychologists, talent specialists, guidance counselors, teachers, and school administrators, (last because they lack direct contact with the children).

Identification of gifted children should be a continual process. The screening and search for these children must involve a battery of methods including individual tests, school staff observations, case studies, and class evaluations. It is important that after identification has been made, at least an annual reevaluation should be employed to be certain placement and educatiomal planning are appropriate.

An interesting type of identification worthy of notation is a supportive device called "A Diary of Learning" by Gensley (1969). It is a teacher, pupil, and parent approach to identification through communication and evaluation of learning by keeping a diary of daily achievements. It is a mutual evaluative technique which may prove especially good for the gifted underachiever.

Characteristics of the Gifted

Krippner (1967) indicated that the gifted person demonstrates consistently remarkable performance in any worthwhile line of endeavor. First of all, though, gifted children are children, and they have the same developmental needs for love, security, companionship, acceptance, challenge, self-determination, guidance, respect, and other support that offer optimum development in all children. Generally, these needs are satisfied until the child enters school.

Torrance (1970) related that gifted children need a rich and challenging program because they have broad and numerous interests, high abilities, curiosity, and an insatiable desire to learn. He indicated that from their earliest years bright children delight in examining details of their surroundings and in constantly asking adults questions. Generally, these children will express inquisitive and curious behavior as they grow older, unless they are inhibited by schools, adults, or other children.

Issacs (1970 b) reported that intellectually gifted children in the classroom are usually capable of abstract reasoning with little teacher help as long as they are guided properly, and that they have the capacity to perform numerous processes mentally that are considered laborious for average pupils. Issacs also agrees with Torrance that one of the attributes of the gifted is the ability to do several things at once. She indicated that these boys and girls are able to think in terms of symbols or group situations instead of specific data or concrete objects.

Krippner (1967) referring to Project Talent concluded after studies on the high school level that nonintellectual characteristics such as sex and emotional control are related to academic success. He related that the National Merit Scholarship program revealed that exceptional students are marked with continued academic success, are first born children, from small families, and are personally more independently oriented. Krippner reported a series of studies by M. J. Stern (1957) which indicate that the creative person is less authoritarian and less anxiety-ridden than the noncreative person.

Professional school personnel cannot assume that gifted and talented children live only in privileged environments. Gifted children have been found in many different environments and cultures. The number of gifted children, though, appears to be concentrated in particular ethnic, religious, socioeconomic, and occupational groups. This concentration is probably because of problems in identification rather than true prevalence.

Characteristically, gifted children are curious and explore different situations earlier than do their peers. They enjoy social association as other children do, but they seem to relate earlier to older companions and games which require higher degrees of skill and intellectual involvement. The U.S. Commissioner of Education (1971) reported that biographical data from studies of large populations reveal that gifted individuals excel in widely varied organizations and that the total impression is of people who perform superbly in many fields and do so with ease.

The U.S. Office continues by reporting that the composite impression from studies of gifted people ranging from childhood to adulthood shows a population which values independence, which prizes integrity and independent judgment in decision making, which rejects conformity for its own sake, and which possesses unusually high social ideals and values. Apparently, of all human groups, the gifted and talented are least likely to form stereotypes.

Groth's (1969) studies have somewhat characterized gifted children as separate entities, boys and girls. The results on a study of the hierarchical needs of gifted boys and girls concluded that girls seemed to have a narrower spectrum of needs than boys. The two highest categories of needs for gifted girls were love and belongingness, with self-actualization third. Gifted boys appeared less mature and more oriented toward a multiplicity of goals than girls. Their three most important needs were safety and security, love and belongingness, and self-esteem. This study supports Maslow (1954) and Gowan (1967 and 1968). Groth concluded that development in the cognitive domain is interdependent upon development in the affective domain. We wish to note that even though gifted children appear to be functioning at a higher level than average children, the former still are not free from emotional or affective problems.

Some of the creative positives indicated by Torrance (1970) which may be characteristic of gifted children are as follows:

1. Ability to express feelings.
2. Ability to improvise with commonplace materials.
3. Articulate in role playing, creative activities.
4. Enjoyment and ability in art.
5. Enjoyment and ability in creative dramatics.
6. Enjoyment and ability in music.
7. Expressiveness in speech.
8. Fluency and flexibility in nonverbal media.
9. Enjoyment and skills in group learning.
10. Responsiveness to the concrete.
11. Responsiveness to the kinesthetic.
12. Expressiveness of gestures.
13. Humor.
14. Richness of imagery in informal language.
15. Originality of ideas in problem-solving.
16. Problem centeredness.
17. Emotional responsiveness.
18. Quickness of warm up.

These creative positives do not necessarily fit a stereotyped homogenous group. Any teacher can observe data which may be characteristic of and correlated with the gifted child's performances.

Hershey (1976) outlined the characteristics of gifted children relative to problems and instructional suggestions. We believe this is one of the best condensed profiles which offers comprehensive information concerning gifted children. It is presented in table 4.1.

Lewis M. Terman (1925–26) was the pioneer in the education of gifted children. His project was longitudinal in that it began in 1921 and ended in 1955. During this period of time, Terman and his associates studied in excess

Table 4.1 Hershey's Characteristics of Gifted Children

Characteristic of Gifted Children	Concomitant Problems	Instructional and Guidance Suggestions
Verbal proficiency		
Large vocabulary	Inappropriate reading and resource material (especially at lower grades)	Access to multi-level and conceptually challenging material
Facility in expression	Escape into verbalism	"Verbosity" channeled into concrete ideas and concepts
Breadth of information	May appear "Know it all" and conceited to age mates	Opportunity for interaction with intellectual peers
Power of Abstraction		
Interest in inductive learning and problem-solving	Resistance to drill and repetition (may have gaps in basic skills)	Incorporate "basic skills" into a prerequisite for self-selected study projects
High level conceptualization	May omit details	Draw up mutually agreeable contracts that delineate important details
Pleasure in intellectual activity	Impatient with "busywork" assignments and uninspired teaching	Allow the student opportunity to suggest and set up alternative ways to learn concepts
Intellectual Curiosity		
Interested in a wide range of things	Stifled by a limited environment	Early stimuli-laden intervention in barren home/school/environments
Willingness for complexity	Bored by simplistic explanations	Opportunity to interact with gifted accepting adults
Persistent pursuit of goals	Often construed as stubbornness	Opportunity to analyze and redirect behavior
Retentiveness/Power of Concentration		
Intense attention	Resists interruptions	Discuss schedule realities; seek cooperation by lucid discussion
Long attention span	Frustrated by chopped up traditional school day	Set up blocks of time
Retains and uses information	Lack of exposure to appropriate information	Utilize mentors and special community resources to feed the hungry minds
Independent/Goal Directed		
Skepticism	May be too easily disillusioned by social injustices (in extreme cases drops out or escapes in unhealthy ways)	Give students bona fide opportunities to implement constructive suggestions for change
Self-criticism	May lead to overly critical (negativistic) attitude toward others	Utilize encounter group activities with people of diverse backgrounds
Adept in analyzing strengths and weaknesses	Frustration with inactivity and lack of progress	Give opportunities for students to assume various roles in group interaction. (simulation activities)
Sensitivity/Intuitiveness		
High level of awareness	Possible gullibility; super sensitive to criticism, low self-concept	Ample opportunity to earn success in areas important to him/her. (Gifted need as much positive reinforcement as slow learners)

Table 4.1 (Continued)

Characteristic of Gifted Children	Concomitant Problems	Instructional and Guidance Suggestions
Keenly observant	Vulnerable to peer group rejection (may compensate with behavior construed as conceited or dislike her own superiority especially true of girls)	Opportunity to discuss unique problems with intellectual peers and understanding adults
Emotional depth	May lack the necessary social support and peer acceptance	Leadership training and opportunity for value clarification with role models to help understand potential in relation to social responsibility
Potential for Creativity Inventiveness	Invention of own systems, sometimes conflicting with norm	Ample opportunity to "invent" without threat to instructors
Liking for new ways of doing things	Rejection of the traditional	Opportunity to study origins of traditions—particularly from a human interest standpoint (e.g., interview with elderly "sage types")
Interest in brainstorming, free wheeling	Lack of opportunity to take risks in a supportive environment—may lead to great frustration and avoidance of divergent thinking	Opportunities to explore in simulated problem-solving environment that is psychologically safe
Versatility / Virtuosity Diversity of interests and abilities	May hop from one interest to another and fail to build basic competencies	Early "career guidance" to build competencies in major interests
Many hobbies	May lack guidance in exploring and developing interests to full level of potential	Provide flexible and individualized instruction from earliest school years
Proficiency in art forms such as music and drawing	Lack of early training	Identify talent early and subsidize opportunities for early training

Source: Myrliss Hershey, "Characteristics of Gifted Children." Gifted Association Conference, Kansas City, Missouri, 1976.

of 1500 children who had IQs over 140 on the Stanford-Binet. Terman's study is reported in detail in *Genetic Studies of Genius* (five volumes). His findings, in general, are given below (Gallagher 1975).

1. Gifted children develop physically and intellectually earlier than normal children.
2. Gifted children tend to have less physical and emotional difficulties than normal children and maintain these differences over several years.

3. Gifted individuals tend to pursue a wider variety of extracurricular activities and pursue many different areas of interest.
4. Gifted individuals tend to excel in school and even perform much above average in college work and advanced studies beyond the bachelor's degree.
5. Gifted individuals tend to have less difficulties in marriage and tend to establish continuity in their home lives.

Gifted students, such as those included in Terman's study, do exceedingly well in all aspects of life. One must recognize, however, that the subjects of Terman's study came from an urban area of California, and all had superior environmental backgrounds. Terman's study did not include the disadvantaged gifted, gifted from minority groups, or the creatively gifted. Therefore, some assumptions regarding the gifted based on Terman's study may not be appropriate. His comprehensive study was a major and historical contribution, which demonstrated that the gifted do have a wide variety of superior abilities and many specialized areas of interest.

Services for the Gifted

The use of federal funds has markedly strengthened federal, state, and local programs for the handicapped through improved preparation of specialized personnel, quality of research, and understanding and support of the education profession and the public. These programs vividly demonstrate the social benefits from federal investment in the education of target populations with needs which cannot be met by general education (U.S. Commissioner of Education 1971).

Progress has been made in services available for the gifted and talented primarily because of the 1972 creation of the Office of Gifted and Talented within the U.S. Office of Education. Since 1974, Section 404 of Public Law 93–380 has provided an annual allocation of $2.5 million to assist the states in program development and the training of personnel (Mitchell and Erickson 1978).

Progress in services for the gifted and talented is indicated in a recent report by Mitchell and Erickson. Their findings (table 4.2) reflect information from the fifty states and the District of Columbia as of June 1, 1977.

The progress in services for the gifted and talented shows an increased interest in the area. The figures presented above reflect a tremendous growth in this area during the 1970s. With increased federal funding, as cited earlier, and continuing efforts on the parts of the states, more services will be available to the gifted and talented during the 1980s.

Too often in past years the gifted have been overlooked as a group in need of support. One of the most powerful ways to aid this group is through

Table 4.2 Services for the gifted

Item	Number
Number of states with some type of written policy	43
Number of states with no written policy or regulations	8
Estimate of the number of gifted and talented of public school age (3% estimate)	1,352,915
Estimate of the number of gifted and talented receiving services (32 states reporting)	437,618
Range in percentage of gifted and talented receiving services (32 states reporting)	.06% to 4.5%
Full-time persons by states who serve in programs for the gifted and talented at the state level.	27
States having at least one part-time person in the gifted area.	14
Of the total funds spent, the percentage provided by the states.	95%
States which have colleges or universities offering training for teachers of the gifted.	45
Total number of colleges or universities in the U.S. which offer one or more courses in the area of the gifted.	177
States which offered some type of in-service training in the gifted area during 1976–77.	42

Source: Patricia Bruce Mitchell and Donald K. Erikson, "The Education of Gifted and Talented Children: A Status Report," *Exceptional Children* no. 1, vol. 45 (1978). © The Council for Exceptional Children.

federal, state, and local programs. The U.S. Commissioner of Education (1971) related that the need for funding for the gifted and talented is critical. If funds can be devoted to program improvement, personnel preparation, improved and extended research, and general support and understanding, the educational opportunities and life possibilities for gifted children will improve.

Even though progress has been made in services for the gifted and talented, Gallagher (1980) indicated that, as a group, these children are still receiving less emphasis than they deserve. In comparison to their abilities, they still stand farthest from the norm in comparison to other children. Gallagher indicates that broader public support for gifted programs is required in order to combat negative attitudes toward gifted children.

The U.S. Commissioner's Office (1971) reported from a federal survey that the gifted children were losing to the competition of other problems. The survey (1970) revealed that 295 persons from diverse backgrounds gave oral testimony to the Regional Assistant Commissioners of Education on the perceived needs of the gifted child. The testimony analysis was divided into statements of specific needs and recommendations. One major theme mentioned was the need for curriculum flexibility to allow talented students to move forward on their own. A second strong need was for better prepared teachers. There was a consensus that teachers are currently not prepared and cannot handle the special educational issues presented by gifted youngsters. Under organizational needs, testimony stressed the need for partial separation of the educational program to allow gifted students to work with one another and to allow for necessary freedom to explore. There was a general rejection of a complete separation for the entire day in either special schools or special classes. There are many ways to provide for gifted children and some of these procedures will be discussed later.

The recommendations from the testimonial report to the U.S. Commissioner of Education generally supported the following suggestions:

1. A strong need was expressed for additional funds and higher priority for gifted programs.
2. Funds should be specifically earmarked for spending on the gifted.
3. Request for more teacher training help in both in-service and preservice programs, which could be made possible through fellowships and scholarships.

Issacs (1970 a) stated that the needs for the gifted are more specific than stated above because their needs are specific to their educational differences.

The learning styles and rates vary from those of the average child. Smaller teacher-pupil ratio are needed. Individualized and flexible programs are desirable. More freedom for self-initiated learning is required. There is a need for all boys and girls to learn to value and treasure the gifted. The emotional needs of the gifted must be met in order to insure mastery of academic and communicative skills.

Plowman (1969) stated that programming starts with an assessment of a child and proceeds to placement in environments and experiences. Characteristic rating sheets, screening and nomination forms, case study records, and child study programs may suggest that a gifted child needs access to intellectual peers, exemplary individuals, empathetic mentors, or special resource persons. He indicated further that programming is a continual process and as such must be based upon continual appraisal of development of interests, knowledge, intellectual skills, traits of creativity, attitudes, aspirations, and values.

With the increased emphasis on programs for the gifted, the question arises: Do programs for the gifted make a difference? Educators and lay persons tend to believe that special programs may or may not make a difference, and in some cases, special programs may cause gifted individuals to become snobbish. Tremaine (1979), compared gifted children who had participated in special programs with gifted children who had no special programs with respect to their achievements, accomplishments, and attitudes. Her findings indicate that those who had experienced special programs were different in the following areas:

1. Demonstrated significantly higher grade point averages.
2. Had higher test scores.
3. Received more honors and scholarships.
4. Expressed more favorable attitudes toward school and teachers.
5. Selected higher and more definite vocational goals.
6. Expressed more awareness of and respect for needs of society.
7. Had higher self-concepts.
8. Had personal cognitive growth which was more attributed to curriculum and teachers.

The two groups had similarities in the following areas:

1. Expressed similar attitudes toward peers.
2. Were equally comfortable with competition.
3. Indicated an equally wide range of friends.
4. Engaged in an equal number of school and community activities.

The special programs for the gifted did not lead, in this case, to snobbery, elitism, conceit, or any other negative qualities. Certainly Tremaine's study indicates that gifted students profit significantly from having experienced special programs, and that negative side effects were not present. When legislators, educators, administrators, or even parents contend that programs for the gifted make no differences, one should cite Tremaine's study.

Further evidence is given by Lytle and Campbell (1979) who studied the affects of special programming on the social status of the gifted. Contrary to the beliefs regarding negative affects, Lytle and Campbell suggest that peers perceive the gifted as class leaders and as desirable students to work with on class assignments.

Programs for the Gifted

Plowman (1969) said that enrichment in regular classes is often advocated for gifted children who may not be physically or socially mature enough for special classes or grade acceleration. In general, enrichment programs should provide greater breadth and depth of learning, more opportunities for developing creative behaviors, increased emphasis on rich social experiences, and ample freedom to pursue independent study.

Plowman also included private study as a method of instruction for gifted children. Private study includes correspondence courses and certain tutorial and independent study programs which are pursued most satisfactorily by children who require a minimum amount of direction from the teacher.

Acceleration is another program that has been used and is still being used. Plowman indicates that the acceleration program appears to work well with high-achieving gifted children who are emotionally and physically mature and seek opportunities to associate with older children and adults.

Torrance (1970) reported on a program for the gifted which is called the *open-ended* program. This simply means that it is a nongraded arrangement. School work is done inside and outside the school building. This type of program has been criticized because of a lack of structure. It is felt that these children need structure as much as the average child.

Gensley offered information on another service for gifted children which is called programmed learning. It uses machinery to stimulate and teach subject matter. The machine, though, cannot be asked questions, which presents a disadvantage. However, programmed learning used as a tool can help provide for creativity.

Many model programs have been introduced for the gifted. One such program was a special project by the Boston School System (1970) in which a trailer was used as a facility for twenty gifted children on a half-day basis. The program was focused on language arts, and all materials and equipment were selected to offer instruction in a particular field. When the program originated, ESEA Title III money funded it, but it is now locally financed. The project personnel felt that an important facet of the program was the focus on individual responsibility: children were accountable for their own work. The gifted students in this program manifested improvement in self-concept, behavior, and attendance, and their attitudes made them better students in their regular classes.

Torrance (1969) reported on another program, which was started by George Witt of New Haven. This program was called the Life Enrichment Activity Program; the objective was to discover unrecognized potential in low socioeconomic areas. This program was established because research revealed astounding numbers of unrecognized gifted and talented children. Joseph H. Douglass (1969) estimated 80,000 of the youth who drop out of school each year have IQs within the top 25 percent of the population.

Nash, Borman, and Colson (1980) reported that career education for the gifted and talented is essential. They developed a model program, which began during the school year 1976–77, for seniors in high school. Their program has three phases that require about two hours per school day, for which credit is given. The phases last about three months each and are titled

(1) Guidance Laboratory Experience, (2) Mentorship Laboratory Experience, and (3) Working Internship Experience.

The phases move from developing more self-awareness (Phase 1), to working with a community or nearby college mentor (Phase 2), to having an actual work experience in an internship capacity (Phase 3). Seminars are conducted throughout the phases for the purposes of sharing information. Based on the model developed by Nash, Borman, and Colson, one teacher can work effectively with fifteen to twenty-five students; therefore, the program is not expensive, particularly when compared to the long-term benefits.

Many other projects for the gifted have been organized. We list here a random selection of projects from the Fall, 1979, publication of the *Gifted Child Quarterly*.* These programs serve different groups of gifted individuals and emphasize different areas of development. The projects used a variety of techniques to identify their gifted populations and many different models to establish their programs. Brief descriptions of these projects, the age or grade ranges served, and the basic emphasis of each are presented with names and addresses for further information. The descriptions are not meant to be comprehensive but should be informative regarding the wide range of programs currently in existence.

1. *The Lighthouse Project* Barbara Le Rosa, Linda King, and Sally Greenwood, Racine, Wisconsin 53404.

   Age Group
   Elementary school age

   Emphasis
   A general systems approach involving participatory interaction for teaching children to think and to think creatively.

2. *Moral Education for the Gifted: A Confluent Model* Jonatha W. Vare, Vestavia Hills, Alabama.

   Age Group
   Not given

   Emphasis
   To develop moral autonomy which is dependent upon the simultaneous achievement of both cognitive and affective goals in the classroom.

3. *AP in PA—Advanced Programs in Palo Alto* Ruthe A. Lundy, 25 Churchill Avenue, Palo Alto, California 94306.

   Age Group
   Elementary, middle, and high school.

   Emphasis
   Elementary School Three teacher specialists to help teachers plan an instructional program which has qualitative differences (enrichment).

Gifted Child Quarterly, Fall 1979. © National Association for Gifted Children.

Middle School Honors classes for enrichment; special grouping in math, and individual contracts in other classes; independent study centers to pursue subjects of interest.

High School Honor classes and advanced placements which are joint ventures with colleges.

4. *A Cooperative University—High School Project for Talented Students* L. W. Glass, Department of Secondary Education, Iowa State University, Ames, Iowa 50011.

   Age Group
   High school juniors

   Emphasis
   A six week summer program which uses the enrichment and acceleration models and results in early high school completion and early entrance to college with earned college credits.

5. *A Model Summer Program for Gifted Children* Donna G. Wright and Claude H. Cunningham, Houston Independent School District, Houston, Texas.

   Age Group
   Gifted children in grades 2–5; a multi-ethnic group of children who are black, Mexican-American, and white.

   Emphasis
   A three week summer session which has a three-tier activity and the theme, 'A Look To the Future'. The three-tier activity is organized so that each child functions as an individual, as a small group member, and as a member of the whole group.

6. *The Alabama School of Fine Arts* James Nelson, 820 North 18th Street, Birmingham, Alabama 35202.

   Age Group
   Secondary school

   Emphasis
   A six-year program of general academic studies in harmony with special fine arts studies. Many activities are provided with symphony orchestras, ballet groups, etc.

7. *Mobile County Public Schools: Program for Academically Gifted Students* Mobile County Schools, P.O. Box 1327, Mobile, Alabama 36001.

   Age Group
   Grades 1–12

   Emphasis
   Provides a multidimensional teaching approach including special curricula, in-depth curricula, acceleration, and the systematic development of higher level cognitive and affective processes. The program uses resource centers, mobile (traveling) labs, and seminar settings.

8. *Program for Academically and Creatively Talented (PACT)* 4600 DeBarr Road, Anchorage, Alaska 99504.

Age Group
Grades K–8 as of school year 1979–80.

Emphasis
Program uses the Cognitive-Affective Interaction Model developed by Dr. Frank Williams. Grades 7 and 8 involve acceleration and enrichment for three hours per week in math, science, and humanities.

9. *Project Potential: A Program for Gifted-Talented Students* Bobbie Shoob Kraver, Washington Elementary School District No. 6, 8610 N. 19th Avenue, Phoenix, Arizona 85021.

Age Group
Grades K–8

Emphasis
Resource centers before, during, and after school hours.

10. *S.O.I. Demonstration Center* Janice Bennett, 11174 Westonhills Drive, San Diego, California 92024.

Age Group
Grades 2–6

Emphasis
The gifted underachiever and academically talented are in self-contained programs using the model of J. P. Guilford to emphasize development of learning styles. S. O. I. (Structure of Intellect) is taught as a separate subject with concentration on the thinking processes.

11. *East Whittier City Schools Gifted Program* 14536 East Whittier Blvd., Whittier, California 90605.

Age Group
Grades K–8

Emphasis
To develop divergent modes of thinking in mentally gifted minor children and also develop creative problem solving. Uses Guilford's model of divergent thinking production.

12. *The Mall Project* Richard L. Gonzales and Norma L. Vice, Fountain Elementary School, 916 Fountain, Pueblo, Colorado 81001.

Age Group
Grades K–5

Emphasis
MALL—Motivation Acceleration Learning Laboratory. Focuses on multiaged/multilevel team teaching situations with special consideration given to educationally disadvantaged gifted. Emphasizes the integration of academics, intellect development, and behavioral development.

13. *The Learning Lodge: A Rural Consortium for Elementary Academi-cally Gifted Students* Janet McCumsey, Area Education Agency 7, 3712 Cedar Heights Drive, Cedar Falls, Iowa 50613.

Age Group
Grades 1–6

Emphasis
Students travel to a half-day per week program which uses independent study and mentors to develop creativity and a strong self-concept.

14. *Coeur D'Alene, Idaho Planned Enrichment Program for Gifted/Tal-ented Students (PEP)* Coeur d'Alene District No. 271, Coeur d'Alene, Idaho 83814.

Age Group
Grades 1–7

Emphasis
A "pull-out" enrichment program (resource center) in which students are taught through independent study learning centers.

15. *T. A. G. S.* Alice Independent School District, 200 N. Reynolds, Alice, Texas 78332.

Age Group
Secondary—Grades 8–12

Emphasis
Based on Renzulli's *Enrichment Triad Model,* Frank E. Williams' *Classroom Ideas for Thinking and Feeling,* and Bloom's taxonomy. Works on leadership training, strengthening creativity and preparation for advanced placement and the study of occupational goals. Uses com-munity mentors.

16. *Horizons Enrichment* Toledo Public Schools Gifted Programs, Man-hattan and Elm Streets, Toledo, Ohio 43608.

Age Group
Grades 1–6

Emphasis
Enrichment opportunities, acceleration programs and encouragement to work independently on creative and productive projects.

17. *G–TIRA (Gifted and Talented in Rural America)* Big Spring School District, Box 98, Newville, Pennsylvania 17222.

Age Group
Grades 1–12.

Emphasis
Individual programming, leadership training, problem solving, inter-grade level group discussions, career education with internships at the secondary level, and active parent organizations.

18. *Exemplary Program* Guthrie Public Schools, Mrs. Zola Arnett, 802 East Villas, Guthrie, Oklahoma 73044.

Age Group

Grades K–12.

Emphasis

Self-contained program providing acceleration and personalized education programs. Enrichment activities are provided through developing plays, field trips, creative writing, special science labs, creative dramatics, film making, book publication, and individual study.

19. *WINGS (Widening Interests Through New Experiences For Gifted Students)* Jean Randall, Harold D. Fayette School, 1057 Merrick Avenue, Merrick, New York 11566.

Age Group

Grades 4–6.

Emphasis

Cluster groups within the regular class and attendance 1½ days per week in resource rooms in cross-grade groupings. Uses the *Enrichment Triad Model* of Renzulli.

20. *Gifted Child Center in Language Arts/Reading* Worcester State College, 486 Chandler Street, Worcester, Massachusetts 01742.

Age Group

Grades 2–8.

Emphasis

Students from the entire state come to college for fifteen Saturday mornings each semester. The students study creative writing and literature, and work on an optional area of interest related to language arts skills.

21. *SPARK* Calcasieu Parish School Board, 1120 W. 18th Street, Lake Charles, Louisiana 70601.

Age Group

Grades 1–12.

Emphasis

Resource room programs which provide differentiated learning experiences beyond the scope of regular class instruction.

22. *Acres of Diamonds Talented and Gifted Program* Portage Township Schools, 5894 Central Avenue, Portage, Indiana 46368.

Age Group

Grades K–6

Emphasis

Classroom challenge centers, creative writing, "pull out" independent study, and Talented and Gifted (TAG) classroom activities. Uses the multiple talent research of Dr. Calvin Taylor, which involves divergent thinking, areas of creativity, predicting, planning, communication, decision making. It also focuses on the works of Guilford, Renzulli, E. Paul Torrance, Frank Williams, and others.

23. *Diversified Educational Experiences Program (DEEP)* Jane Connett, Project DEEP, 640 North Emporia, Wichita, Kansas 67214.

Age Group
Grades 7–12

Emphasis
Alternative classroom management system that stresses self-directed learning, student developed goals and objectives, individual and small-group projects, decision making, analysis, planning, and problem-solving skills.

There are other programs, but the need for gifted classes exceeds the availability of classes. Not only are services needed for the school child, but community services should be made available to parents of these children. Programs may include seminars, work-study programs, remedial instruction, personal counseling, and cooperative programs with colleges.

Whatever type of program is developed, Bruch (1969) indicated that the following suggestions should be considered:

1. Provisions for the gifted should be available at every grade level for every gifted student.
2. Programs should be designed for the high achieving, the low achieving and the gifted with special needs in mind.
3. The students should be selected for the programs which best meet their educational needs.
4. Factors such as staff appraisal, achievement, interests, aptitudes, and individual intelligence test scores should be used in the selection process.

Recognition of Abilities in Early Childhood

The ever-increasing complexity of society and expanding horizons of scientific investigation have served to emphasize the necessity for early identification. It is theorized that early identification and training will help to bring about more complete use of the potential of these people (Telford and Sawrey 1977). Obviously giftedness does not manifest itself at a set time, and even though difficult to recognize, potential giftedness is present at birth. Therefore, evaluation of preschool children should receive serious consideration. Torrance (1969) reported that individuality is established largely in the early years of a child's life and therefore these years are critically important in the emergence of a healthy strong identity and realization of potentialities.

In view of what is speculated on the importance of early learning processes, adequate identification must be available. The U.S. Commissioner of Education (1971) reported that attempts to identify gifted children through tests at the preschool and kindergarten level have been successful with careful preliminary search and screening. Young gifted children can be individually tested and accurately identified more easily than can young mentally retarded children, who are similarly deviant from the norm.

A good example of early identification of gifted children as reported by Rellas (1969) is the method used by the Pasadena City Schools in California. They use the Weise Predictability Scale to screen children, who are labeled Potentially Academically Talented (P. A. T.). Later they are tested by an individual intelligence test such as the Binet or Wechsler. By this method all of the children are included in the appraisal and given the opportunity of being described as gifted.

One cannot deny that early identification would be an asset to educational planning. These children have specific needs that must be met before they become older and their potential becomes correspondingly more difficult to identify.

Parents of Gifted Children

J. C. Gowan, San Fernando Valley State College, Northridge, California and Helen Letlow, Psychologist, San Diego School System wrote "Suggestions for Parents of Able Children," which was distributed by The Louisiana Association for Gifted and Talented Students (1976), and reedited by the authors. These guidelines should be of value to parents of gifted children in situations and environments in which compatible application is possible.

1. Gifted children are still children. They need love, but controls; attention but discipline; parental involvement, yet training in self-dependence and responsibility.
2. Consonance of parental value systems is important for the gifted child's optimum development. This system means that there should not be wide disagreements over values between parents.
3. Parental involvement in early tasks demand training the children to perform tasks themselves, to count, tell time, use correct vocabulary and pronunciation, locate themselves and get around their neighborhood, do errands, and be responsible.
4. Emphasis on early verbal expression, reading, discussing ideas in the presence of children, poetry, and music are all valuable. Parents should read to children. Parents should emphasize doing well in school.
5. The lack of disruption of family life through divorce or separation, and the maintenance of a happy, healthy home is an important aspect in raising able children, as well as other children.

6. Gifted children may often have vague awarenesses of adult problems such as sex, death, sickness, finances, war, etc., because of lack of experience; therefore, they may need reassurance in these areas.

7. Parents should help the gifted child of age six or above to have a playmate who is talented, even if a child has to be "imported" from some distance.

8. Good books, magazines, encyclopedias, charts, collections, and other aids to home learning are important.

9. Parents should take gifted children to museums, art galleries, educational institutions, and other historical places which may enhance experiential learning.

10. Parents should be especially careful not to "shut up" gifted children who ask questions. In particular, they should not be scolded for asking, nor should it be implied that questions are improper or forbidden subjects. The parent may, however, insist that questions not be asked at inappropriate times, and may require the child to sharpen or rephrase a question to clarify it. Sometimes questions should not be answered, but the reply should be a question which sends the child searching. A parent who cannot answer a question, should direct the child to a resource which can. Sometimes questions call for clarification of concepts: one young child asked, "Why aren't all those rockets liable to shoot down God?"

11. There's a difference between pushing and intellectual stimulation. Parents should avoid "pushing" children into reading, "exhibiting" them before others, or courting undue publicity. On the other hand, parents should seek in every way to stimulate and widen the child's mind, through suitable experience in books, recreation, travel, and the arts.

12. The gifted child usually has a wide and versatile range of interests, but may be somewhat less able to concentrate on one area for a long time. Parents should encourage children who have hobbies to follow through on them, to plan and strive for creditable performance and for real mastery, rather than "going through" a lot of hobbies or collections in a short time.

13. Parents should avoid direct, indirect, or unspoken attitudes which indicate that fantasy, originality, unusual questions, imaginery playmates, or out-of ordinary mental processes are bad, "different," or to be discouraged. Instead of laughing at children, laugh with them and seek to develop their sense of humor.

14. Parents should avoid overstructuring children's lives. The child should have free time. Sometimes parents are concerned that gifted children spend too much time watching TV or reading comic books. They should not be expected to perform at top academic capacity at all times.

15. Respect the child and his knowledge, which at times may be better than your own and which is impatient of authority. Assume the child means to do right, and the deviations are not intentional. Do not presume on your authority as a parent except in crises. Allow liberty on unimportant issues. Try to give general instructions that allow some liberty, rather than specific commands to carry out your way.

16. Gifted children are sometimes impatient with conventional situations. Have a frank talk with your child about the importance of conventions, such as driving carefully, politeness, manners, courtesy, and regard for others, all of which have similar bases in experience that clarify social advantages.

17. Whenever possible talk things out where there has been a disciplinary lapse. Gifted children are much more amenable to rational argument than are many others, and they usually will have a well-developed sense of duty.

18. Give children the stimulation of private lessons in some skill in which they excel. Provide social membership in worthy groups. Foster special experiences outside the home (traveling alone, or visiting friends overnight). Try to facilitate chances to talk alone with an adult authority about personal interests.

19. Try to improve their sense of taste in mass media, TV, radio, cinema, newspapers, comics, reading, art, etc. Discuss the basis for taste and provide experience with new forms of expression in the arts—*don't force*.

20. Take time to be with them, to listen to what they have to say, to discuss ideas.

21. Be a good example, and try to provide worthy male and female adult models outside the family with whom the child can interact.

22. Support school efforts to plan for gifted children. Help to interest the PTA in the gifted. Support study groups on gifted children. Form with other parents into cooperative endeavors, and associations.

23. Investigate scholarship programs in your community for other gifted children and help provide them.

24. Work to provide better community understanding and appreciation of the role of the gifted child in society and the importance of community planning.

25. Support community action for gifted children, including bonds and school taxes for extra educational advantages. Advocate more guidance and special education for the gifted.

Of course, the gifted child is not a handicapped child, although without appropriate service, and appropriate intervention, he or she may become handicapped. In fact, Horwitz (1973) stated that the gifted child may be the most retarded within a school population when we compare their mental ages to their levels of achievement.

The parents of gifted children may recognize at a very early time that they are different. The parents may observe that the developmental sequence is accelerated—walking, talking, etc. This rapid development may be alarming to the parents because they really don't know how to manage this type of child. They see the potential developing in their child; perhaps age three or four, the child is beginning to read without instruction. The child may be able to pursue academic areas and the development of abstract concepts and his curiosity and talent may be well beyond his chronological age. The parents may become very frustrated because by the time the child reaches school age: few resources are available within the public schools or within their financial means to provide their child with an appropriate academic and school program.

The child enters the first grade already reading on the second, third, or fourth grade level, and the regular classroom teachers are frustrated because they do not know how or do not have the time to provide an appropriate instructional program. They are busy with twenty-five to thirty-five first-grade youngsters who are very curious and eager to learn the basics of school, and the gifted child has progressed well beyond that stage of development. Therefore, the gifted child may develop severe behavior problems because of boredom. The behavior is reported to the parents. Now, the parents are unable to understand why their child, who has progressed rapidly, has suddenly become a discipline problem. A resource that will help them cope with this difficulty is necessary, but often no resource is available. Schools are now beginning to develop programs for the gifted and talented; consequently, parents can now expect that certain modifications will be made for their gifted child. The continuous development of programs for gifted and talented children can keep these situations from happening, and efforts should be directed toward making appropriate modifications more possible for these children.

Bruch indicated that there is a gap in basic research on how gifted children develop and learn. Because of this inconsistency, resource material which is especially designed for the gifted child is limited. However, there are many books written about gifted children, and some of them are specifically for teachers of gifted children. The books and periodicals listed below may be of value for those who are involved with gifted children.

Resources

Gowan, J. C. *The Development of the Creative Individual.* San Diego, Calif.: Robert Knapp, 1971.

Gowan, J. C. and Bruch, C. B. *The Academically Talented Student and Guidance.* Boston: Houghton Mifflin, 1971.

Gowan, J. C. and Torrance, E. P. *Educating the Ablest.* Itasca, Ill.: F. E. Peacock Publishers, 1971.

Provisions for Talented Students: An Annotated Bibliography. Washington, D.C.: U.S. Dept. of HEW, Bureau of Research, 1966. (Document Catalog No. FS5235:35069.)

Purkey, W. A. *Self Concept and School Achievement.* Englewood Cliffs, N.J.: Prentice-Hall, 1970.

Rice, J. P. *The Gifted: Developing Total Talent.* Springfield, Ill.: Charles C Thomas, 1970.

Rosner, Stanley and Abt, L. E. *The Creative Experience.* New York: Grossman Pub., 1970.

The Exceptional Parent. 264 Beacon Street, Boston, Mass.

The Gifted Child Quarterly. National Association for Gifted Children. Cincinnati, Ohio.

Torrance, E. P. and Myers, R. E. *Creative Learning and Teaching.* New York: Dodd, Mead & Co., 1970.

Whitmore, Joanne Rand. *Giftedness, Conflict and Underachievement.* Boston, Mass.: Allyn and Bacon, 1980.

Overview

Concannon (1969) reported that the gifted child poses one of our greatest problems, beginning in the home and ultimately becoming a concern in the school. School staffs bear the responsibility for recognizing and planning for the needs of the gifted. The authors of this text agree with Concannon and also realize that programs for gifted children should obviously result in improvement for the total public school system.

Issacs (1970) indicated that the question whether enrichment, acceleration, or some other administrative form of organization best cares for the needs of the gifted has not yet been answered. We favor the enrichment program. The acceleration plan has definite social and maturity limitations. The young student who is accelerated to a higher class will eventually reach a level of incompatibility even though academic abilities are evident. The grouping plan appears to place gifted children into a disadvantaged culture, because they would not be integrated totally and functionally with the balance of the school program. The enrichment program enables children to embellish upon their present grade level, but allows them to remain with their peers. Therefore, the enrichment program should provide the teacher with the opportunity to make provisions for the gifted child within that child's own classroom.

Whatever gifted children may be, they are still children and must be able to enjoy and profit from the activities that are common to a youngster's world. They need a lot of play and need to be with other children of equal age. Gifted children should not be difficult to discover. They generally have a rich vocabulary, are curious, search for materials on a higher grade level, appear somewhat mature in conversation, and should be a delight to have in a classroom.

Gifted children do not fit the stereotyped picture of a physically deficient child with eye-glasses at the back of the room reading a book. Gifted children are usually physically well children, and they manifest activities in all parts of the school program.

Study Questions

1. In what ways will a gifted child differ from other children in learning?
2. Discuss and defend your choice of either grouping, acceleration, or an enrichment plan for the gifted child.
3. Discuss the appropriate procedures and methods for identifying gifted children.
4. Generally, how should a regular classroom teacher provide for gifted children?
5. Discuss guidelines which would be appropriate for the parents of a gifted child.
6. Indicate the most commonly defined characteristics of gifted children.
7. Discuss research which indicates a relationship between intelligence and creativity.
8. Discuss the early research of gifted children conducted by Terman.
9. Indicate the characteristic differences between gifted boys and gifted girls.
10. Select a recent journal article pertaining to gifted children and write an abstract using the following format:

   Author:

   Title:

   Source:

   Population and Setting:

   Study Conducted:

   Procedure:

   Results:

Bibliography

Boston Public Schools Learning Laboratories. 1970. "Model Programs: Childhood Education." Palo Alto, California: American Institutes for Research.

Bruch, Catherine. 1969. "Problems and Intentions in the Education of Gifted Students." *Gifted Child Quarterly* (Summer).

Concannon, S. Josephina. 1969. "The Gifted: A Major Concern." *Peabody Journal of Education* 46, no. 5 (March).

Gallagher, James J. 1975. *Teaching the Gifted Child.* 2d ed. Boston: Allyn and Bacon.

————. 1980. "On Educating the Gifted." *The Education Forum* 44 XLIV, no. 2 (January).

Gensley, Julian. 1970. "Programmed Learning for Gifted Children." *Gifted Child Quarterly.* (Summer).

Gensley, Juliana Townsend. 1969. "A New Method of Evaluation for Gifted Students." *Gifted Child Quarterly.* (Summer).

Gowan, J. C. 1971. "The Relationship Between Creativity and Giftedness." *Gifted Child Quarterly.* (Winter).

Gowan, J. C., and Letlow, Helen. 1976. "Suggestions for Parents of Able Children," Louisana Association for Gifted and Talented Students.

Groth, Norman Jean. 1969. "Hierarchial Needs of Gifted Boys and Girls in the Affective Domain." *Gifted Child Quarterly* (Summer).

Hershey, Myrliss. 1976. "Characteristics of Gifted Children." Gifted Association Conference, Kansas City, Missouri.

Horwitz, Elinor. 1973. "Gifted Children," *Children Today* (January–February).

Issacs, Anne F. 1970 a. "Listen Young Gifted Ones." *Gifted Child Quarterly* (Summer).

————. 1970 b. "Additional Observations and Recommendations Given During the Congressional Hearings of the Gifted." *Gifted Child Quarterly* (Winter).

Jacobs, John C. 1970. "Are We Being Misled by Fifty Years of Research on Our Gifted Children?" *Gifted Child Quarterly* (Summer).

Khatena, J. 1977. "Gifted Children in the United States and Abroad." *Gifted Child Quarterly* 21, (Fall).

Krippner, Stanley. 1967. "Characteristics of Gifted and Talented Youth." *Marmodes Medical Center* (January).

Lytle, William Grant, and Campbell, Norma Jo. 1979. "Do Special Programs Affect the Social Status of the Gifted?" *The Elementary School Journal* 80, no. 2 (November).

Mitchell, Patricia Bruce, and Erickson, Donald K. 1978. "The Education of Gifted and Talented Children: A Status Report," *Exceptional Children* 45, no. 1 (September).

Nash, William R.; Borman, Christopher; and Colson, Sharon. 1980. "Career Education for Gifted and Talented Students: A Senior High School Model." *Exceptional Children* 46, no. 5 (February).

Plowman, Paul B. 1969. "Programming for the Gifted Child." *Exceptional Children* 35 (March).

Rellas, A. 1969. "The Use of the Wechsler Preschool and Primary Scale WPPSI in Early Identification of Gifted Students." *California Journal of Educational Research* 20, no. 3 (May).

Renzulli, Joseph S., and Smith, Linda H. 1977. "Two Approaches to Identification of Gifted Students." *Exceptional Children* 43, no.8 (May).

Sisk, Dorothy. 1980. "Issues and Future Directions in Gifted Education." *Gifted Child Quarterly* 24, no. 1 (Winter)

Special Education System, Oklahoma State Department of Education. 1980. "Policies and Procedures Manual for Special Education in Oklahoma."

Telford, Charles W., and Sawrey, James M. 1977 *The Exceptional Individual.* 3rd ed. Englewood Cliffs, N.J.: Prentice-Hall.

Terman, Lewis M. 1925–26. *Genetic Studies of Genius.* Stanford, Calif.: Stanford Univ. Press.

Texas University Research and Development Center for Teacher Education. 1968. "Dimensions and Criteria of Talented Behavior: Final Report."

Thomas, George I. 1966. "Gifted Child." *Guiding the Gifted Child.* Candam Hse., New York: Joseph Crecimbeni.

Torrance, E. Paul. 1970. "Broadening Concepts of Giftedness in the 70's." *Gifted Child Quarterly* (Winter).

————. 1969. "Creative Positives of Disadvantaged Children and Youth." *Gifted Child Quarterly* (Summer).

Tremaine, Claire D. 1979. "Do Gifted Programs Make a Difference?" *The Gifted Child Quarterly* 23, no. 3 (Fall).

U.S. Commissioner of Education. 1971. *Education of the Gifted and Talented*, vols. 1 and 2. Report to the Congress of the United States.

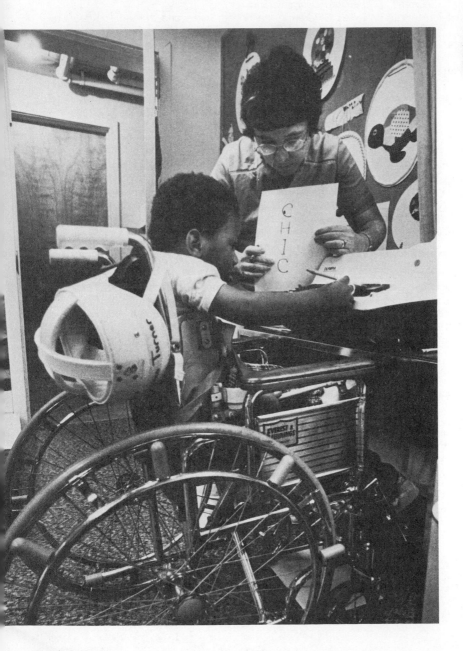

5

physically, chronically, multiply, and severely handicapped children

Physically Disabled and Chronically Ill Children

Physically disabled and chronically ill children are included in one chapter primarily because there has been less emphasis in recent years on providing special classroom programs for them. A large number of physically disabled children are now provided instructional programs in regular classrooms. Chronically ill children who need special provisions for their educational programs, may be offered homebound teaching, hospital teaching, or home-school telephone teaching, rather than special classes in the public school.

The trend toward not providing special program modifications *within the public schools* for the physically disabled or chronically ill does not mean that the regular or special class teacher should not be informed about these children. Information about the characteristics and needs of physically disabled and chronically ill children is essential if adequate provisions are to be available for their educational, emotional, physical, and adjustment needs.

This chapter is not a comprehensive presentation of the various conditions which cause physical disabilities or chronical illnesses. It does provide a basic understanding of the conditions of physical disabilities and chronic illnesses, and presents the more common problems encountered by these children. These common concerns include the psychological and emotional overlay, as well as the physical problems.

Program Changes

Physically disabled children are included within the regular class program to a greater extent than they were in the past, because the design of a majority of elementary and secondary school buildings of today has eliminated many of the architectural barriers. Older elementary and secondary schools are usually multistory buildings without elevators or ramps into the buildings. Disabled children cannot, in the majority of cases, attend these schools because they can not climb the stairs, doors are too narrow for a wheelchair, or there are many steps to climb prior to entering the building.

As a result, they were either placed in special self-contained classrooms on the first floor of the building, placed in groups in a special school modified for their use, or not provided a school program in the public schools. The modern architecture of schools usually involves one floor and eliminates the need for elevators. Federal legislation, followed by legislation in all fifty states, requires that all new public buildings be built so that they are accessible for the physically disabled or the chronically ill. This means that ramps must be built; wider doors or openings into buildings, classrooms, and restrooms must be provided. Special facilities in the restroom must be installed, and, when necessary, elevators must be provided for any person who is physically disabled or chronically ill to the extent that he or she could not otherwise use the facilities within the building.

Consideration for the problems of the physically disabled and the chronically ill have usually not included the problems created because the child is also mentally disabled. There are exceptions to this combination of handicaps when one considers the multiply disabled child, such as the mentally retarded child who has cerebral palsy. However, many physically disabled and chronically ill children have intellectual abilities well within the normal range. Their primary difficulties are often the result of being excluded from school because of architectural barriers. Thus, by the time a school program is provided they are one or more years behind their peer groups in academic achievement as well as general social adjustment. With the construction of schools which are accessible to physically disabled and chronically ill children, many of their learning problems should be minimized.

Definitions

Physically disabled and chronically ill children are those who are so disabled or so ill that they cannot profit from school without some special provisions or modifications. The category of children with physical disabilities who require special provisions or modifications in school programs includes conditions such as cerebral palsy, muscular dystrophy, multiple sclerosis, wry neck, congenital club foot, or poliomyelitis. A chronically ill child has an illness which is severe enough to require frequent intensive care services in a hospital setting or an instructional program in the home. Therefore, the student is prevented from attending classes in the public schools on a day-to-day basis. A chronically ill child is one who has such conditions as epilepsy, chronic and severe asthma, ulcers, cystic fibrosis, and rheumatic fever. The more common problems of cerebral palsy, muscular dystrophy, multiple sclerosis, epilepsy, and chronic asthma are presented in this chapter. For conditions such as bone imperfections, postural conditions, conditions because of infections, and other conditions, excellent reviews are provided in Cruickshank and Johnson (1975) and Kirk (1972).

An Interdisciplinary Approach

It is usually necessary to use an interdisciplinary approach if the needs of the crippled or chronically ill child are to be properly met. Whether psychology, physical therapy, education, or rehabilitation would play the leading role depends upon such factors as the age at onset of the condition, the severity of the problem, and the prognosis. Each profession must play a part in the interdisciplinary approach. Members of the cooperating disciplines must have, therefore, an understanding of the various orthopedic impairments and the problems that are often associated with them.

Various agencies such as schools, clinics, and rehabilitation centers are well aware of the need for united efforts. When properly staffed, they can do much to help crippled and chronically ill children become well-adjusted adult citizens.

Almost every disabled person can be helped. The whole process of helping the disabled to make the most of their possibilities is called rehabilitation. The first step is medical and surgical treatment. Transplanting bone from another part of the body causes a short, twisted leg to be straightened and even lengthened. The pain and swelling of arthritis may be relieved by the use of certain drugs. The doctor in physical medicine takes over after other specialists have done all they can. A program is then designed to include exercise and training for the patient, and the doctor may prescribe aids such as a brace or an artificial limb.

The nurse, physical therapist, speech therapist, occupational therapist, vocational counselor, social worker, and psychologist work with the specialist in physical medicine and rehabilitation. Social workers and psychologists are very important because the patient's feelings about the disability and the family's attitude can make the difference between success and failure.

Often clinics and rehabilitation centers are not available, and schools may lack the needed specialized personnel. It then becomes the responsibility of the school to devise some means for adequately serving crippled or chronically ill children.

Distinction of Disability versus Handicap

Children with physical disabilities or chronic illnesses may be considered together in a discussion of a disability as opposed to a handicap. These conditions, in the opinion of the authors and others, are disabling conditions and should be recognized by the classroom teacher as disabilities rather than handicaps. Hamilton (1950) made this distinction by describing a disability as a condition which may be either physical or mental and can be defined and described medically whereas a handicap refers to the way in which a person's disability interferes with the ability to function in accordance with one's capability. This means that a person who is disabled is not necessarily handicapped. The disability will depend upon the situation and the demands of the particular environment. Many people could find, if they have not already done so, a situation in which they would be handicapped according to a definition of handicapping conditions; however, a disability does not automatically limit all areas of one's functioning. Therefore, the important point seems to be that provisions should be made for an environment in which these children can function at their best. This will mean a structuring of the environment, psychologically as well as physically, in order to insure that they are able to function according to their abilities. In other words, without modifications in the environment, physically disabled or chronically ill children may not be able to perform adequately and may become grossly handicapped (Wright 1960).

Special Considerations

Although the physical environment may be modified, teachers and other school personnel who work with physically disabled or chronically ill children must modify the attitudes and the approaches they use with these children. If, because of a physical disability or chronic illness, one assumes that the child cannot perform certain tasks, and therefore provides nothing to do, then one may cause that disability to become a handicap. In other words, the teacher and parents should not approach the disabled child as a child who cannot perform. Developing a positive attitude toward the physically disabled and the chronically ill is not an easy task. Doing so will entail the use of one's ingenuity in order to modify the learning environment and the psychological environment so that the child can progress in learning. Learning to accept frequent absences and frequent interruptions because the child needs the services of a therapist or hospitalization will not be an easy adjustment for the classroom teacher. Factors such as these will require the teacher to be flexible—to plan an individualized instructional program for the child. Adjustments in attitudes and preparing instructional programs will be necessary if the physically disabled or chronically ill child is going to remain within the mainstream of education.

When a teacher has one or more children who are physically disabled or chronically ill, there may be a tendency to do too much for those children. For example, the teacher may want to pick up the child when the child is capable of walking; or to get something for the child when the child can do it without help. Several of these children may take a long time to accomplish a task such as moving from one part of a room to another, but the teacher must permit them to complete the task alone. A primary objective in working with children who have physical or medical problems is to help them build and maintain as much independence as possible. Fostering or encouraging dependency should be avoided at all times.

We have experienced several demonstrations of training programs which have enabled physically disabled children to promote their independence and physical activity. In one situation the children were in wheelchairs and all were multiply disabled. During the training demonstration, these children were required to remove themselves from their wheelchairs without assistance, move across a padded floor for a distance of approximately five to ten feet, return to their wheelchairs, and lift themselves into their wheelchairs. These exercises were not for mere demonstration. They were part of a program which focused on developing physical movement which was within the capabilities of the children.

It is not recommended that teachers of physically disabled or chronically ill children follow the procedures presented above without being certain that the activity is within the child's capability. Determining the child's capabilities for physical activity must be accomplished through consultation with the child's medical doctor, and never arbitrarily decided by the classroom teacher or other school personnel.

The ways in which teachers can promote independence and safety habits on the part of the physically disabled or chronically ill child are quite varied. The teachers should become a part of the total program provided for the child. They should also consistently check special equipment for the child to insure that it is safely operating. This safety awareness includes such things as checking crutches for breaks, for missing tips or screws, for defective wheelchairs which won't lock, for broken chin straps on helmets, and for safety features throughout the school area (Swack 1969). The teacher may also remind children to take medication, aid in the acceptance of the children in the classroom and in the total school, and insure that they are provided adequate rest periods.

School personnel who work with such children must consistently be aware of the child's current functioning. For example, the teacher, principal, school nurse, and school counselor will need to request and carefully read periodic reports from the child's medical doctor. These reports should provide answers or guidelines to such questions as:

1. Is the child presently taking medication?
2. Has the child's medication been increased or decreased recently, and if so, in what ways might this affect the child's behavior?
3. Is the child's physical or health problem improving or worsening?
4. Does the child's condition warrant any specific physical restrictions?
5. Does the child's present condition require any specific approaches or cautions on the part of school officials?
6. Can the child safely be removed from a wheelchair, or may braces be removed once or twice daily?
7. May certain pieces of equipment, such as standing tables, be provided to give the child a change from the wheelchair?
8. In what ways might the child's physical or health problem affect ability to perform tasks such as reading and writing?

9. If the child is to be confined temporarily at home or in a hospital setting, are visitors permitted?

10. Can and should the child, if confined at home or in a hospital for a temporary period of time, continue to perform school work?

11. What is the child's prognosis? Has the condition permanently stabilized? Will the condition improve or deteriorate?

12. To what extent should the school provide rest periods for the child? How often should the child rest and what type of rest period should be provided?

13. Does the child's condition require any modifications in diet? Should meals be light but frequent? Should any items be eliminated from meals?

14. If medication has to be administered at school, what procedure must school personnel have to follow?

15. Does the child need protective equipment, such as a helmet, in order to prevent injuries? If so, who will furnish this equipment?

16. If the child needs physical, occupational, or speech therapy, how often will these services be provided? Will these services be provided in school or will the child have to miss school?

17. Does the child need assistance in using restroom facilities? If so, how much assistance is needed?

These questions should serve as a sample of the modifications in the school program and the teacher's preparation which are essential for appropriate educational services for the physically disabled or chronically ill. Without current information regarding the conditions of the child, the teacher will not be sure about which procedures to use. Answers to questions such as those posed above may also provide a school counselor with appropriate information for counseling the children. As the children mature and become more aware of the limiting aspects of their conditions, they will need assistance, through counseling, in the continual process of developing self-concepts.

Physical Modifications for Physically Disabled or Chronically Ill Children

Although children who are physically disabled or chronically ill may not need a self-contained special classroom for instructional programs, many modifications will have to be made in the school building. These modifications may include the following:

1. Building ramps which will not be weather-slick at any time, to provide entry into the building.
2. Installing handrails throughout the hallways.
3. Lowering lavatories in the restrooms.

Stairways are among the most common architectural barriers.

4. Widening doors of and enclosing toilets, lowering toilets and providing handrails within the toilet stalls.

5. Provision within the children's classroom or the school building for physical facilities required for rest periods.

6. Permitting children the necessary time to move from one classroom to another.

7. Providing space for conducting physical, occupational, or speech therapy.

8. Providing children with the necessary time to complete assignments. They may write slower, read slower, or require brief periods of rest during the day.

9. Providing cars or buses with special equipment such as hydraulic lifts so children may get easily in and out.

10. A teacher's aid who can help care for the physical needs of children who need assistance.

11. Provision of special equipment in the classroom, such as a special typewriter for children who cannot write legibly.

12. Training the teacher in procedures to follow when a child has an epileptic seizure.

Of course, all children who are physically disabled or chronically ill will not require all these modifications. However, if the school system is planning to provide a program for the majority of the children in the community having physical or medical problems, these factors must be considered carefully and planned in advance. In the experience of one of the authors who assisted in planning and opening a school program for the physically disabled, all these factors were considered and careful planning was completed prior to beginning the program.

Architectural Barriers

The removal of architectural barriers is an appropriate concern for educators who provide services for the physically, chronically, multiply, and severely handicapped. Accessibility and the use of facilities should be available to any individual who can benefit from the services offered by a particular program.

In order to present pertinent information regarding this area the authors have chosen some guidelines as produced by the American Institute of Architects and the Rehabilitation Services Administration, HEW, (Kliment 1976).*

Suggested Accessibility Compliance Checklist

	Yes	No
A. Parking Lots		
1. Are accessible spaces approximate to the facility?	___	___
a. Are they identified as reserved for use by individuals with physical disabilities?	___	___
2. Are there parking spaces open on one side, allowing room (12 ft. minimum width) for individuals in wheelchairs or on braces and crutches to get in and out onto a level surface?	___	___
a. Do they allow people to get in or out on a level surface?	___	___
3. Is it unnecessary for individuals in wheelchairs or those using braces and crutches to wheel or walk behind parked cars?	___	___
4. Is distribution of spaces for use by the disabled in accordance with the frequency and persistency of parking needs?	___	___
B. Walks		
1. Are public walks at least 48″ wide?	___	___
a. Is the gradient not greater than 5%?	___	___
2. Are walks of a continuing common surface, not interrupted by steps or abrupt changes in level?	___	___

*Courtesy of Iowa Chapter AIA.

3. Wherever they cross other walks, driveways, or parking lots do walks blend to a common level?   ____   ____

4. Do walks have a level platform at the top which is (a) at least 5 feet by 5 feet if a door swings out onto the platform or toward the walk, or (b) 3 feet by 5 feet if door doesn't swing onto the platform?   ____   ____

5. Does the platform extend at least 1 foot beyond each side of the doorway?   ____   ____

C. Ramps

1. Do ramps have a slope no greater than 1 foot rise in 12 feet?   ____   ____

2. Do ramps have handrails on at least one side?   ____   ____
   a. Are they 32″ in height measured from the surfaces of the ramp?   ____   ____
   b. Are the surfaces smooth?   ____   ____
   c. Do they extend 1′ beyond the top and bottom of the ramp?   ____   ____

3. Do ramps have a surface that is nonslip?   ____   ____
   a. Do platforms comply with Questions B4 and B5?   ____   ____

4. Do ramps have at least 6 feet of straight clearance at the bottom?   ____   ____

5. Do ramps have level platforms at 30 foot intervals for purposes of rest and safety, and wherever they turn?   ____   ____

D. Entrances/exits

1. Is at least one primary entrance to each building usable by individuals in wheelchairs?   ____   ____
   (It is preferable that all or most entrances (exits) should be accessible to, and usable by, individuals in wheelchairs or other forms of physical disability).   ____   ____

2. Is at least one entrance usable by individuals in wheelchairs on a level that would make the elevators accessible?   ____   ____

E. Doors and Doorways

1. Do doors have a clear opening of no less than 32″ when open?   ____   ____
   a. Are they operable by a single effort? Note: Two-leaf doors are not usable by those with disabilities unless they operate by single effort, or unless one of the two leaves meets the 32″ width.   ____   ____

2. Are the doors operable with pressure or strength which could reasonably be expected from disabled persons? ____ ____

3. Is the floor on the inside and outside of each doorway level for a distance of 5 feet from the door in the direction the door swings? ____ ____

    a. Does it extend 1′ beyond each side of door? ____ ____

4. Are sharp inclines and abrupt changes in level avoided at doorsills? ____ ____

5. Do door closers allow the use of doors by the physically disabled persons? ____ ____

F. Stairs and steps

1. Do steps avoid abrupt nosing? ____ ____

2. Do stairs have handrails 32″ high as measured from the tread at the face of the riser? ____ ____

3. Do stairs have at least one handrail that extends at least 18″ beyond the top and bottom step? ____ ____

4. Do steps have risers 7 inches or less? ____ ____

G. Floors

1. Do floors have a nonslip surface? ____ ____

2. Are floors on each story at a common level or connected by a ramp? ____ ____

H. Restrooms

1. Is there an appropriate number of toilet rooms for each sex? ____ ____

    a. Are they accessible to physically handicapped persons? ____ ____

    b. Are they usable by physically handicapped persons? ____ ____

2. Do toilet rooms have turning space 60″ × 60″ to allow traffic of individuals in wheelchairs? ____ ____

3. Do toilet rooms have at least one toilet stall that:

    a. is three feet wide? ____ ____

    b. is at least 4′8″ (preferably 5 feet) deep? ____ ____

    c. has a door that is 32 inches wide and swings out? ____ ____

    d. has grab bars on each side, 33″ high and parallel to the floor, 1½ inches in diameter, with 1½ inches clearance between rail and wall, fastened securely to the wall at the ends and center? ____ ____

  e. has a width of at least 48″ between the wall
     and the front of the stall entrance.   ____ ____
  f. has water closet with seat 20″ from the floor?   ____ ____
4. Do toilet rooms have lavatories with narrow
   aprons, which when mounted at standard height
   are usable by individuals in wheelchairs?   ____ ____
5. Are drain pipes and hot water pipes covered or
   insulated?   ____ ____
6. Are some mirrors and shelves at a height as low
   as possible and no higher than 40 inches above the
   floor?   ____ ____
7. Do toilet rooms for men have wall mounted urinals
   with the opening of the basin 19″ from the floor,
   or have floor mounted urinals that are level with
   the main floor of the toilet room?   ____ ____
8. Do toilet rooms have towel racks mounted no
   higher than 40″ from the floor?   ____ ____
   a. are towel dispensers mounted no higher than
      40″ from floor?   ____ ____
   b. are other dispensers mounted no higher than
      40″ from the floor?   ____ ____
   c. are disposal units mounted no higher than 40″
      from floor?   ____ ____
9. Are racks, dispensers and disposal units located to
   the side of the lavatory rather than directly above?   ____ ____

I. Water fountains

1. Is there an appropriate number of water fountains?   ____ ____
   a. Are they accessible to physically handicapped
      persons?   ____ ____
   b. Are they usable by physically handicapped per-
      sons?   ____ ____
2. Do water fountains or coolers have up-front spouts
   and controls?   ____ ____
3. Are they hand operated?   ____ ____
4. Are they hand and foot operated?   ____ ____
5. If coolers are wall mounted, are they hand oper-
   ated, with basins 36 inches or less from the floor?   ____ ____
6. If there are floor mounted fountains, are spouts no
   higher than 30 inches?   ____ ____
7. Are these fountains accessible to people in wheelchairs?   ____ ____

J. Public telephones
1. Is there an appropriate number of public telephones accessible to physically handicapped persons?   ___ ___
2. Type: booth ___ wall mount ___
3. Is height of dial from floor 48 inches or less?   ___ ___
4. Is coin slot located 48 inches or less from the floor?   ___ ___
5. a. Are there telephones equipped for persons with hearing disabilities?   ___ ___
   b. Are these telephones identified as such?   ___ ___

K. Elevators
1. If more than a 1 story building, are elevators available to physically handicapped?   ___ ___
   a. Are they usable by physically handicapped?   ___ ___
2. Are all of the controls 48″ or less from floor?   ___ ___
3. Are the buttons labeled with raised (or indented) letters beside them?   ___ ___
4. Are they easy to push or touch-sensitive?   ___ ___
5. Is the cab at least 5 feet × 5 feet?   ___ ___

L. Controls
1. Are switches and controls for light, heat, ventilation, windows draperies, fire alarms, and all similar controls of frequent or essential use, within the reach of individuals in wheelchairs?   ___ ___

M. Identification
1. Are raised (or recessed) letters or numbers used to identify rooms or offices?   ___ ___
2. Is identification placed on the wall, to the right or left of the door?   ___ ___
   a. Are they at a height between 4′6″ and 5′6″, measured from floor?   ___ ___
3. Are doors not intended for normal use, that might prove dangerous if a blind person were to exit or enter by them, made quickly identifiable to the touch by knurling the door handle or knob?   ___ ___

N. Warning signals
1. Are audible warning signals accompanied by simultaneous visual signals for the benefit of those with hearing or sight disabilities?   ___ ___

O. Hazards

1. When manholes or access panels are open and in use, or when an open excavation exists on a site, when it is approximate to normal pedestrian traffic, are barricades placed on all open sides at least 8′ from the hazard, and warning devices installed?   ____ ____

2. Are there no low-hanging door closers that remain within the opening of a doorway, or that protrude hazardously into regular corridors or traffic ways?   ____ ____

3. Are there no low-hanging signs, ceiling lights, fixtures or similar objects that protrude into regular corridors or traffic ways? (A minimum height of 7′, measured from floor is recommended.)   ____ ____

4. Is lighting on ramps adequate?   ____ ____

5. Are exit signs easily identifiable to all disabled persons?   ____ ____

Psychological Aspects of Physical Disability or Chronic Illness

The psychological aspects of physical disabilities or chronic illnesses are important for school personnel to consider. Children who are or become disabled by reason of a physical difficulty or a chronic illness will have to make several adjustments. As they grow older, the effects of their problems will have more impact upon their functioning. For example, when they reach the teenage years they may not be as mobile or physically active as the normal peer group, and may often be excluded from school activities such as dances, plays, and clubs. They will not be able to participate in physical education programs or engage in athletics. These restrictions will cause them to recognize time and again that, in some ways, they are different from their peers. Then they may feel isolated and very inadequate. Counseling services will be required periodically throughout the lives of these youngsters to help them maintain adjustment to these situations. Classroom teachers will also have to focus on helping them to develop appropriate hobbies so that their leisure hours can be meaningful and constructive.

Teachers should carefully plan activities such as field trips to insure that physically disabled or chronically ill children may actively participate. The physical plant of the school should be constructed to provide these children with recreational and sporting activities and for possible development of interests as spectators. Class parties should also be planned thoroughly enough to include all children who have a physical or medical problem. In brief, school programs need to include these children in as many activities as possible in order to help them become an integral part of the program and school.

Selected Physical Disabilities and Chronic Illnesses

Medical descriptions of physically disabling conditions or chronic illnesses are not essential information for school personnel. However, descriptions of the ways in which physical functioning is affected are important. Medical doctors will generally provide this information upon request. Therefore, school personnel can become knowledgeable about specific circumstances of a particular condition that a child may have. With this thought in mind, we have selected a few conditions which are more common among children.

Muscular Dystrophy

Muscular dystrophy is generally a progressive disease which causes the muscles to be replaced by fatty tissue. As the disease progresses, a child will become more disabled and lose the use of the voluntary or skeletal muscles. The progressiveness of muscular dystrophy is often referred to as a wasting away of the muscles. The child becomes progressively worse, eventually must be confined to a wheelchair, and will usually die before reaching adulthood.

There is no cure for muscular dystrophy at the present time; however research is being conducted by the National Institute of Neurological Diseases and Blindness in an effort to control and find a cure for this disease. Muscular dystrophy does not affect large numbers of children, but school personnel may have one or more children with this condition in the school program.

Children with muscular dystrophy will require special provisions, because of confinement to a wheelchair. They often miss school and need homebound instruction. As the condition progresses they will require periodic counseling, physical therapy, and frequent rest periods during the school day (*Muscular Dystrophy: Hope Through Research* 1968).

There are presently over one hundred clinics in the United States which provide no-cost services such as diagnostic services, follow-up care, and medical services. These clinics have been established through the efforts of the Muscular Dystrophy Association of America, Inc. (1972). The services provided through these clinics include: medical management, physical therapy, genetic counseling, education, and guidance in using community resources.

Deaf-Blind Children

Deaf-blind children's auditory and visual handicaps cause severe communication, developmental, and educational problems. They need services different from those provided in a program for the hearing or the visually impaired.

Children become deaf-blind because of rubella, encephalitis, meningitis, improper use of drugs during pregnancy, exposure to radiation, and genetic anomalies. Obviously, these visual and auditory problems cannot be corrected, although the children can be trained to become contributing members of society.

The many problems of a deaf-blind child should be obvious. When the combination of severe visual and hearing problems exists, a child will have extreme difficulties in learning from environmental experiences, language development, cognitive development, mobility, dressing and feeding skills, personal grooming, development of any form of meaningful communication, and the simple recognition of others. The child with these problems will not learn spatial or temporal concepts easily, and will have severe problems in establishing relationships with others. It is very difficult to teach this child safety precautions.

The small number of children who are deaf-blind and the seriousness of their problems caused congress to establish ten regional centers to serve them. Since 1969, these centers have provided a wide variety of services to 5,050 children which is estimated to be nearly 80 percent of the known deaf-blind children. The regional centers have served as a resource to all states and territories which are now providing a program for deaf-blind children. Through the cooperative efforts of the regional centers, the states and territories, and the federal government, plans are being implemented to improve diagnostic methods, formulate prevocational and vocational programs, expand community based programs, increase basic and applied research, and improve technical assistance from the centers (Dantona 1976).

Multiple Sclerosis

Multiple sclerosis is a disease which is also progressive, and generally does not afflict people until they are twenty years of age or older; however, cases have been reported in children who are under fifteen. This disease affects the central nervous system through the destruction of myelin which serves as a protective, insulating sheath around nerve fibers. As the disease progresses, the individual becomes more disabled, although, at times, the condition may appear to be improving (*NINDB Research Profile: No. 6, Multiple Sclerosis* 1967).

School personnel on the secondary level should be aware of this condition and the symptoms involved. Symptoms include difficulties in coordination, speech, and vision. Children who consistently have symptoms of this type may not have multiple sclerosis, but their parents should be notified so they may seek appropriate medical consultation (Dunn 1973).

Cerebral Palsy

Cerebral palsy is one of the most common physical disabilities. It involves multiple handicaps such as impairments in hearing, vision, speech, and intellectual functioning. Cerebral palsy is not a progressive disease, but it does cause problems in motor coordination. Many children with this disorder will, therefore, have difficulty in mastering skills which involve fine or even gross motor abilities. This will include writing ability and motor skills for carrying, sorting, and manipulating objects (Dunn).

According to Hopkins, Bice, and Colton (1954) the most common types of cerebral palsy are spastic and athetoid. They estimate that over two-thirds of cerebral palsied children will have one of these two types. The other types, less common, are ataxia, rigidity, and tremor.

Dunn describes the motor involvement of the spastic child as follows:

Involuntary contraction of affected muscles when they are suddenly stretched—called stretch reflex—resulting in tenseness and difficult, inaccurate voluntary motion.

The child with athetosis will have the following motor difficulties:

Involuntary contraction of successive muscles resulting in marked incoordination and almost constant motion of the extremities. (Dunn, 1973)

School personnel should be aware of the extreme difficulties these children have in performing motor skills. Working with these children requires patience, understanding, and special modifications in learning tasks in order to provide appropriately for their instructional programs. For example, instead of requiring handwritten work, the teacher may permit the child with cerebral palsy to recite lessons orally, or provide the child with a typewriter.

Children who have cerebral palsy require many modifications in a school program if they are to have success. Of course, some children with this disability are so grossly limited that they cannot speak intelligibly, cannot move in a meaningful way, and are confined to a wheelchair. They may also be blind or deaf. For such children a public school is usually not feasible, and a residential facility will be required for their care and training. If children with cerebral palsy can attend public school, they may require the services of a speech, physical, or occupational therapist. If fact, many of these children can progress if they are provided services from one or all of the therapists mentioned above during their early childhood years. Teachers will also have to modify their programs because of the children's motor problems. The children may also drool excessively when speaking, and special equipment will be required in order to preserve their classroom work (Robinson and Robinson 1976).

Epilepsy

Epilepsy is among the many disorders about which volumes have been written. It has been frequently misunderstood, and a person with epilepsy has often been plagued with adverse social attitudes. Prior to drug therapy, which has been responsible for improvements by way of partially or completely controlling one's seizures, many persons with epilepsy were prevented from participating in numerous events. For example, children with epilepsy were often excluded from school because of their seizures. If permitted to attend, they were not given the opportunity to participate in many of the school's activity programs. Persons with epilepsy have been feared, shunned, and treated very cruelly. Surprisingly, even in an enlightened society such as the United States, many of these attitudes are still prevalent today.

According to Robinson and Robinson epilepsy is characterized by the following:

. . . recurrent attacks of unconsciousness, convulsions, stereotyped movement, and other miscellaneous symptoms. The types of attacks can be classified into several groups, but the patterns are not always distinct; numerous children show mixtures of symptoms. It is important to note that epilepsy in many children can be controlled medically with a high degree of success.

It is essential that classroom teachers know that a child has epilepsy. They also need to know what medication the child is taking, how often the medication is required, and to what extent the child's seizures are controlled by the medication. Even if teachers receive reports that a child's epileptic seizures are controlled by medication, they still need to be prepared for the possibility of a child having a seizure in the classroom. The teacher must know what can be done for the child, and how to help the other children in the room understand the child's seizures. Most importantly, the teacher must provide for the safety of a child during a seizure. A seizure which manifests severe activity is commonly referred to as grand mal. This is the type of seizure for which the teacher must be prepared to protect the child.

A grand mal seizure involves convulsions in which there is rigidity of the muscles. This activity immediately precedes the convulsive state in which the child will begin jerking. This stage is commonly referred to as the seizure. Many persons with epilepsy will have some type of warning prior to their seizure. The warning, referred to as an aura, may be in the form of a motor, visual, hearing, olfactory, or psychic process which actually forewarns the individual of an impending seizure. The seizure may start immediately after the aura or may be delayed long enough for the person to prepare somewhat. Grand mal seizures seldom last long (possibly thirty seconds) and may vary in their frequency during any one day. The longer the duration, the more likely there will be a period of deep sleep which is usually followed by disorientation and confusion. The grand mal is the most common type of epileptic seizure and may usually be controlled by proper medication (Kirk 1972).

If a child has a grand mal seizure, the teacher should not try to restrain the activity, but instead help the child in the process of falling to the floor to prevent injury. Then turn the head to one side, and try to provide comfort. Remove any sharp objects or classroom equipment that is near so the child will not hit them during the seizure. Even though a majority of grand mal seizures are controlled by proper medication, the teacher should still be aware of the condition in the event the child forgets the medication, or needs new medication.

Other types of seizures include the petit mal, psychomotor, and Jacksonian. None of these are as severe as the grand mal. However, the teacher does need to be aware of the child with petit mal seizures. Children with this type of seizure may have brief periods of time during which they are inactive, may stare into space, hesitate in speech, or temporarily stop a motor activity. Seizures of the petit mal type may go unrecognized if teachers are not alert to the different behavior. Teachers may think the child is not paying attention, daydreaming, or just slow. One of the authors worked with a child who had petit mal seizures characterized by brief periods of inactivity during which the child stared into space. The seizures were as frequent as one or two every ten minutes and would last as long as ten to fifteen seconds per seizure. Without detection, this child would have consistently missed many aspects of the instructional program. Additional information regarding epilepsy is available in many special education publications.

The *National Spokesman* (December 1979), published by the Epilepsy Foundation of America, reports that new terms are being adopted regarding the different types of epilepsy. In order to improve communication about epileptic seizures, the grand mal seizure is called a *generalized tonic clonic seizure*. These terms indicate that the seizure activity is generalized throughout the brain. The petit mal seizure is also generalized throughout the brain; the term used is a *generalized absence seizure*. Focal and psychomotor seizures are referred to as complex partial seizures since they begin in one part of the brain.

Severe, Chronic Asthma

Asthma affects many children. The more severe the asthma, the more likely it is that the child will need some type of special provisions in the school program. Asthma becomes more severe during specific seasons, such as the spring when many plants are blooming and there is pollen in the air. The condition of asthma, "is a disease of the bronchial tubes of the lungs marked by attacks of difficult breathing" (Kirk 1972).

The main concern of educators with respect to asthma is that the child may miss school frequently or require hospitalization and have to receive an educational program in the hospital setting. Educators should also be alert to situations which may bring on an asthmatic attack, such as taking a group of children on a field trip to a location where ragweed is growing. An asthmatic attack is seldom very dangerous. Teachers should know about a child's medication for controlling it and should also be informed about any restrictions on a child who has asthma and adjust the program accordingly.

Many individuals may assume that the extent of such problems as asthma are comparatively small. It may also be assumed that problems such as asthma have very little effect on daily living. Greer and Christian (1976) quote several sources which report that nearly 8.6 million Americans have asthma. Also, asthma causes the death of approximately 4,000 people annually. Considering bronchitis and emphysema as well, over 31,000 persons died from these problems in a recent year.

Asthma and other allergic conditions also require large expenditures of a family's income and considerable lost time from work and school. Greer and Christian cite a report which indicates that almost 9 million school days were lost in a recent year because of asthma.

Other Conditions

As mentioned previously, we did not intend to be comprehensive in this discussion of chronic illnesses and physically disabling conditions. However, for the reader's individual research, a list is provided of several conditions which have not been discussed in this chapter (Van Osdol 1977).

Arnold Chiari A hernial protrusion on the spine due to fusion failure. Causes elongation, swelling and spinal protruding through the brain stem.

Arthritis Inflammation of the joints; may be caused by infection, trauma, et al.

Ataxia A loss of the power of muscular coordination—cerebral palsy.

Athetoid A type of cerebral palsy characterized by involuntary movement of the muscles and usually accompanied by a speech handicap.

Buerger's Disease Condition in which the main arteries and vessels in the legs are inflamed and clogged, usually resulting in amputation.

Buphthalmia Congenital glaucoma; vitreous humor of the eye cannot drain and therefore becomes hardened and opaque; blindness.

Choreiform Disease affecting children aged five to fifteen, characterized by irregular, involuntary movements of limbs and face.

Cyclopia A congenital disorder consisting of severe defects of the facial skeleton and brain.

Diabetes Many different symptoms and kinds; general to all is the inability of the pancreas to secrete adequate insulin.

Diplegia Paralysis of corresponding parts on both sides of the body.

Dysdiadokokinesia Impairment of the power of alternately moving a limb in alternate directions as of flexion and extension.

Hemiplegia Palsy affecting but one side of the body.

Hepatitis Liver infection, may cause jaundice or liver enlargement. Need to be aware of the different types of hepatitis.

Heterotopia The displacement of an organ or part in the body.

Hydrocephalus A common skull malformation; an increased volume of cerebrospinal fluid within the skull ordinarily produces an enlargement of the cranium.

Hypoplasia A condition of decreased or arrested growth of an organ or tissue of the body.

Kernicterus A jaundice which is the yellow skin color due to the presence of erythrocyte breakdown products in the bloodstream. Anemia and enlargement of the liver and spleen are often present.

Kuf's Disease Late juvenile form of Tay-Sachs disease which has its onset at fifteen to twenty-five years of age; characterized by mental and physical deterioration.

Leukemia Blood cell proliferation; may affect bone marrow, spleen, lymph nodes; chronic to fatal.

Microphthalmia Condition in which the eyeball is abnormally small.

Myelodysplasia Defective development of the spinal cord, lumbosacral portion.

Myositis Inflammation of the muscles; may be caused by infection, trauma, etc.

Nephritis Kidney infection; may be chronic or cause death.

Neurosyphilis Syphilitic infection of the nervous system.

Niemann-Pick Disease An infantile inherited disorder very similar in symptoms to Tay-Sachs disease, but also involving the enlargement of liver and spleen.

Osteomyelitis Inflammation of the bone marrow.

Otosclerosis A disorder in which the oval window and the ossicles become hardened and do not carry vibrations.

Paraplegia Motor and sensory paralysis of the entire lower half of the body.

Phocomelia Describes the absence of arms or legs in newborn infants.

Poliomyelitis Inflammation of the gray matter of the spinal cord; often causes infantile paralysis.

Polydactylism Congenital defect in which newborn has extra fingers or toes.

Porencephaly Congenital defect in which holes are present in the cerebral cortex and gray matter of the brain.

Rheumatic Fever Respiratory infection, fever, pain; usually followed by heart disease.

Spastic Cerebral palsy manifestation of hypertension and rigidity of muscles

Spielmeyer-Vogt Disease The juvenile form of Tay-Sachs disease which has its onset between the ages of three and ten years, with blindness, impairment of balance, and coordination, and convulsions in the early stages.

Spina Bifida A defect in the closure of the spinal column which is associated with retardation or epilepsy.

Syndactylism Webbing of the fingers or toes—grown together.

Tay-Sachs A rapidly progressing infantile disease which is transmitted by a single autosomal recessive gene and characterized by hypersensitivity to light and sound, otherwise apathetic and weak, blindness, spastic paralysis, convulsions, and early death.

Tonus A slight, steady contraction of all muscles due to the influence of the cerebellum. Impairment results in either flaccidity or spasticity.

Torticollis Contraction of the neck muscles which draws the head to one side; various causes.

Trachoma A disease of the eye in which the eyelids develop a sandy crust on the bottom lid, causing the cornea to be scratched. This is caused by a germ attacking the mucous membrane; usually found in areas of poor sanitation.

School Provisions

Homebound instruction and hospital teaching services are authorized through the majority of state departments of education, and may be administered through the state agency for education or a local public school system. Both programs are essential for children with physical disabilities or chronic illnesses because of frequent absence from school, or lengthy intervals between their classroom sessions.

Homebound Instruction

Homebound instruction is provided for a child who is confined at home for a period of time. The absence from school must be over an extended period of time and cannot be because of some minor disability. Before a child can be placed on homebound instruction, a physician's report concerning the child's health is required and the local school system must usually apply for approval to have the child receive this type of service (Policies and Procedures Manual for Special Education in Oklahoma 1981).

Larger school districts generally have homebound instructors who are regular members of the teaching staff. Homebound instructors are similar to itinerant teachers, except that they travel from home to home providing instruction to children for whom services have been approved. The number of children a homebound instructor can serve is usually limited by law. The number of hours the child must be instructed is also specified. Homebound instructors must serve as a liaison between the child and the regular classroom teacher. In this manner, the homebound instructor may help such children to progress in a manner similar to their classmates, and may also prepare the regular classroom teacher for the time when they will return to the class program.

Hospital Teaching

Hospital teaching is somewhat different from homebound instruction; however, children with similar problems may be found in both settings. The hospital teacher is generally on the staff of the hospital. If the hospital teaching program is quite large, the program may operate as an independent school system.

Hospital teachers must plan the instructional program around the medical services and treatment scheduled for the child. If at all possible, teachers who serve in hospital settings must be strong-willed and convince hospital staff that the child's continuing education is important and should also be scheduled. A child who must remain in the hospital setting for a long period of time and is not provided with appropriate educational services may lose a year or more of school.

A teacher in a hospital setting must be prepared to teach all subjects and all age ranges. In many instances, this person may be the only teacher in the hospital, which will require a highly skilled person if the children are going to receive adequate instructional programs. Hospital teachers must also be innovative and knowledgeable in obtaining any special equipment that will be required in teaching children from a variety of backgrounds, grade levels, and age ranges.

Teacher Characteristics

Teachers of physically disabled or chronically ill children must have certain characteristics if they are to be successful. From the descriptions of children and program modifications given previously it should be obvious that the teacher must be extremely patient, innovative, and capable of developing meaningful working relationships with other professional personnel. Teachers of these children must also be capable of discussing the children's problems with medical doctors and obtaining information from other professionals that will benefit the children.

Teachers of physically disabled or chronically ill children must be firm and sensitive. Because of the child's current problems and the possibility of overprotection from parents and family, the teacher has to know what is realistically expected of the child relative to performing tasks and caring for physical needs. The teacher must also have the ability to work effectively with children who may have terminal conditions. Children who are rapidly becoming totally disabled may want to cease trying, often become discouraged, and may be overwhelmed with despair. The teacher will have to be aware of these conditions and have the training and sensitivity to handle these emotional situations. To accomplish these tasks and to avoid being discouraged in providing a meaningful program is a most difficult challenge.

Parent Counseling

The parents of children who are physically disabled or chronically ill will need periodic counseling services similar to those provided to the parents of other exceptional children. School personnel must be prepared to provide this counseling service to help parents gain a better acceptance and improved understanding of their child. School personnel, including the principal and counselor, should also recognize that these parents have been to many doctors, spent considerable periods of time in hospital wards, and sacrificed many material things in order to provide for the special needs of their child. The particular condition of their child may be such that the parents are in serious financial difficulties and are emotionally drained. Sensitivity to the needs and emotional state of the parents is essential if school personnel are to provide appropriate counseling services. Educators should also be knowledgeable about community resources which can provide services to children or their parents. Knowledge of sources which can and will provide counseling services, special programs for the children, and possibly financial assistance will save parents considerable time in searching for facilities, and considerable frustration from not knowing where they may turn next.

Organizations like the Shriner's have been most influential in making facilities available for children who are physically disabled. Other fraternal organizations provide services, and there are also government agencies which can be helpful to these families. For example, although the program may not help their child, parents will be interested in knowing about the research which is being conducted by the National Institutes for Neurological Diseases and Blindness, and other service organizations.

Counseling services for parents can help them improve their family relationships. Recognizing that parents may be restricted in their own social

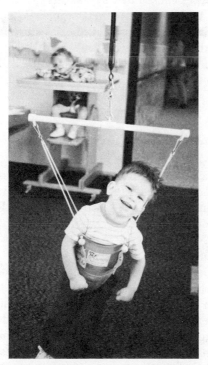
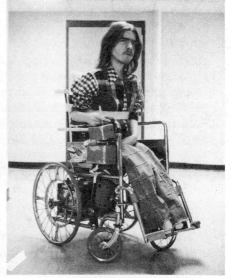

For many of the severely handicapped, special provisions will be part of their entire educational career.

activities because of the care required for their child may help counselors to understand family tensions.

Services for the physically disabled or chronically ill must be comprehensive and meaningful and should include all the members of the family. These children must be given every opportunity to develop their skills, interests, and their lives to the fullest extent possible.

The problems of the crippled child are always multifaceted and have varying effects on parents. Thompson (1979), who is the mother of a daughter who became paralyzed from the waist down at seventeen months of age, reports some of these effects and how she responded. The daughter progressed normally until seventeen months; then, because of a malformation of her spinal cord, she became paralyzed from the waist down. The parents were told that Janice would be confined to a wheelchair for her entire life. However, in 1974, surgery was performed. By the time Janice was five and a half years old, she was walking with braces that fit from the knees down.

Mr. and Mrs. Thompson had difficulties discussing their daughter's condition. Misunderstanding on the part of friends led to more confusion. In school, the Thompsons experienced distress in communicating Janice's mobility problems. The teacher did not include Janice in some activities and could not accept her frequent absences caused by colds, surgery, etc.

The Thompsons moved and Janice entered a new school. When this change occurred, Mrs. Thompson wrote a complete medical history in lay terms regarding Janice, distributed it to the school's staff, and had a copy placed in Janice's school folder. This effort toward communicating Janice's problems was received very favorably and her school program improved considerably.

Communication Devices

Many communication devices have been made to serve as nonverbal communication alternatives for the handicapped. These devices improve teaching and serve as a means for communication which was not possible previously. The following series of pictures and descriptions (figs. 5.1–5.11) are reprinted with the permission of Prentke Romich Company (Electronics Center, R. D. 2, Box 191–B, Shreve, Ohio 44676).

Alphabet Message Scanner AMS–3

The Alphabet Message Scanner (fig. 5.1) has a white plastic panel with six rows and eight columns, including the alphabet and numerals. The characters are organized approximately such that the easiest to select are most frequently used in English literary text. A blank display mask is provided to cover the panel and permit the use of words, pictures, Bliss or other symbols. Extra masks can be ordered. A small lamp and an audible tone correspond to each character. The scanning rate is adjustable, and the tone can be

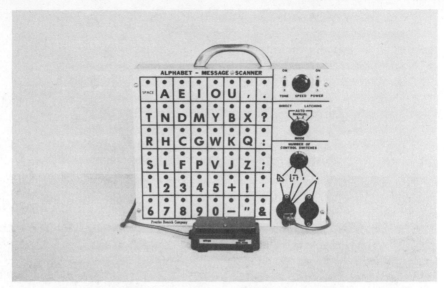

Figure 5.1 Alphabet Message Scanner AMS-3. (Courtesy of the Prentke Romich Company.)

switched off. Either one, two, or four control switches can be used. With the Arm Slot control, or the Joystick, the user can scan diagonally as well as up, down, left, and right. The RL–2M switch is supplied, but another control switch can be specified. Both direct and latching modes are provided. The AMS–3 can be ordered as an AMS–3M with a built-in memory that permits storing up to 64 entries for rapid sequential display; or the memory can be built into the AMS–3 at a later time. The same control switch that is used for scanning can be used for entering messages in the memory, or a separate switch can be used for this purpose.

Bliss Symbol Scanners
The Bliss Symbol Scanner BSS–200(M) (fig. 5.2) uses the standard 200 vocabulary with an additional blank column added on the right edge. It has twelve rows and twenty-two columns with a lamp in the upper right corner of each location. A blank white plastic coated display mask is included with each unit, and extra masks can be ordered.

The Bliss Symbol Scanner BSS–512(M) (fig. 5.3) has a full BCF size white grid on a dark background. Behind each of the 512 locations is a lamp. Since each vocabulary at this level is designed for the specific user, we provide the equivalent of the 512 level symbol stamps in the form of white symbols on clear adhesive backed film. These can be applied to sheets of clear film for conveniently changing from one symbol set to another. White transfer letters of different sizes are also provided.

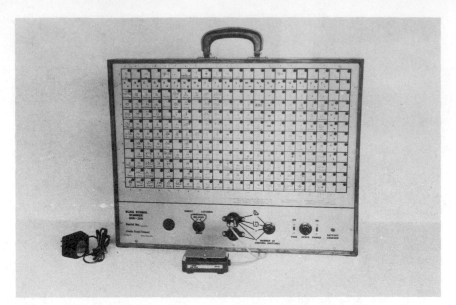

Figure 5.2 Bliss Symbol Scanner BSS–200(M). (Courtesy of the Prentke Romich Company.)

Figure 5.3 Bliss Symbol Scanner BSS–512(M). (Courtesy of the Prentke Romich Company.)

Figure 5.4 Bliss Symbol Wall Display. (Courtesy of the Prentke Romich Company.)

Bliss Symbol Wall Display

The Bliss Symbol Wall Display (fig. 5.4) permits an entire class to view messages on a four foot by eight foot panel. Each of its 512 locations has an incandescent lamp that can be replaced from the front of the panel. An individual Bliss Symbol 512 Scanner is provided for each student, and a control unit permits the teacher to connect any one of the individual units to the larger display. The system can accommodate up to eight student scanners. Bliss symbol flash cards can be used with the display.

Scanning Strip Printer SSP-2

The Scanning Strip Printer (fig. 5.5) has a black anodized panel with silver colored characters, utilizes row-column scanning, and has ten rows and eight columns. Provision is made for using one, two, or four control switches. With the Arm Slot Control, or the Joystick, the user can scan diagonally as well as up, down, left, and right. The RL–2M is supplied, but any other switch can be specified. Both direct and latching modes are provided. A small lamp and audible tone correspond to each character, and in one position a call signal is activated. The scanning rate is adjustable, and the tone can be switched off.

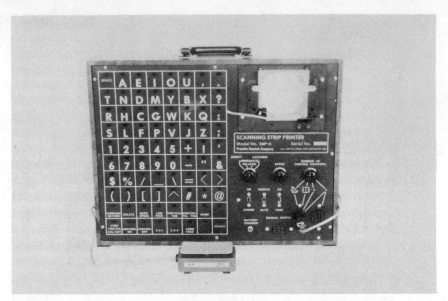

Figure 5.5 Scanning Strip Printer SSP–2. (Courtesy of the Prentke Romich Company.)

Figure 5.6 Keyboard Strip Printer KSP–1. (Courtesy of the Prentke Romich Company.)

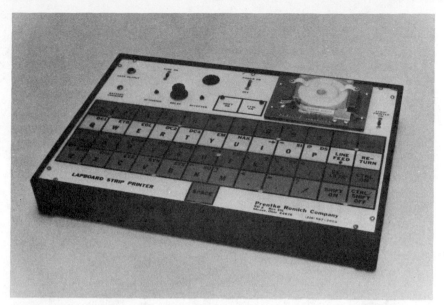

Figure 5.7 Lapboard Strip Printer LSP–1. (Courtesy of the Prentke Romich Company.)

Keyboard Strip Printer KSP–1
The Keyboard Strip Printer, smaller than a portable typewriter, has a forty-nine button keyboard that requires a force of only sixty-eight grams (three oz.) (fig. 5.6). Typing can be done with a finger, mouth stick, or head stick. An adjustable delay requires that a key be depressed for a period of time so that accidentally touching the wrong key will not print an incorrect character. Operation is also inhibited if more than one key is pressed at the same time. An optional key guard prevents activation of undesired keys.

Lapboard Strip Printer LSP–1
The Lapboard Strip Printer (fig. 5.7) features a magnetically actuated keyboard with large color coded characters in one and three-eighths inch square spaces, with one and one-half inch spacing. Printing is accomplished by placing or sliding a small magnet to the desired character. The magnet is mounted in a hand held plastic tube, with several slide-together parts, to permit the use of various positions of the hand. The magnet can be attached to a mouth stick, head stick, or foot. An adjustable delay requires that the magnet be held on a character for a period of time, so that incorrect characters won't be printed during the time the magnet is over an unwanted character.

Figure 5.8 Optical Headpointer Strip Printer OHSP–1. (Courtesy of the Prentke Romich Company.)

Optical Headpointer Strip Printer

The Optical Headpointer Strip Printer OHSP–1 (fig. 5.8) is a communication aid for persons with head position control and spelling skills. It is a portable, independent device utilizing the direct selection technique. The basic approach was developed at the University of Tennessee Rehabilitation Engineering Center in Memphis and has been incorporated into a commercially available aid by Prentke Romich Company.

Express I

Express I (fig. 5.9) is the first of a series of microprocessor based communication aids available from Prentke Romich Company for the nonverbal physically handicapped. At the heart of Express I is a computer that can be programmed to make the aid behave in a manner best suiting the application. The physical configuration of Express I permits utilization of a wide range of user capabilities including good, moderate and poor manual pointing skills, head position control and other body movements.

Express I should be considered for persons with high potential for achievement. The full capabilities of the system can be realized only by spelling persons, but it can be valuable for symbol and picture users also.

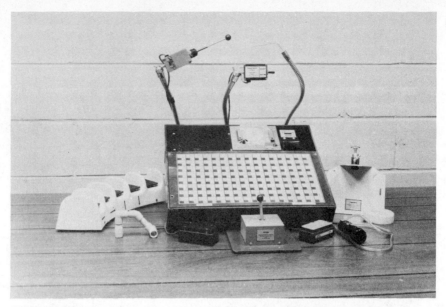

Figure 5.9   Express I. (Courtesy of the Prentke Romich Company.)

The strength of Express I lies in the fact that the program can be easily changed. This is important to accommodate a changing user. For an evaluation setting, it can be used to simulate other more specialized aids. With a single Express I, a wide range of user capabilities can be assessed.

System 80 Interface

The Borg-Warner System 80 (fig. 5.10) has gained wide acceptance as a diagnostic and prescriptive audio-visual learning system. A projected picture and an audio message constitute a frame of instruction. Five response buttons are located below the screen on which the picture is shown. The user is expected to press the button indicating his response. Due to physical limitations, many severely handicapped persons have not been able to use System 80. Dr. Eugene McDonald of the Pennsylvania State University developed a scanning interface that has been used at the Home of the Merciful Saviour for Crippled Children in Philadelphia. The Rehabilitation Engineering Center of the Children's Hospital at Stanford developed a direct selection interface. Prentke Romich Company is now offering System 80 Interface which incorporates both the scanning and direct selection techniques as well as a call signal.

The System 80 Interface is a device that permits the use of the Borg-Warner System 80 instructional machine by the severely handicapped. A variety of standard and special control switches is available, permitting chil-

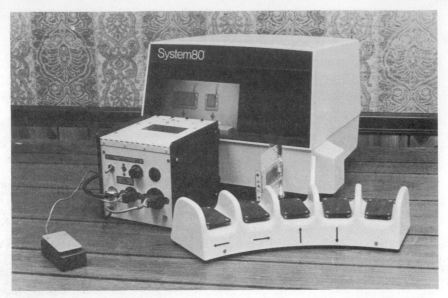

Figure 5.10 System 80 Interface. (Courtesy of the Prentke Romich Company.)

dren to use the device in either scanning of direct selection mode, including activation of a call signal. The interface can quickly be added to or removed from the System 80 machine without tools.

Environmental Control Systems

Today technology can do much to improve the quality of life and productivity of the severely handicapped. For high level spinal cord injured quadriplegics and others with nearly total paralysis, environmental control systems permit operation of many of the electrical devices in one's surroundings (fig. 5.11).

In addition to the commercially made communication devices pictured in this chapter, teachers may make communication boards. The boards may be used for the physically handicapped, language impaired, or the severely mentally retarded. The use of the communication board requires the child to point to a desired word or picture and say or sign (manual language) the word. Such adaptations of teaching communication have been used successfully at the Wilson-Pacific School in Seattle, Washington. Although verbal communication is the most desirable form of language, the use of communication boards enables the more severely handicapped child to have alternatives to language (Detamore and Lippke 1980).

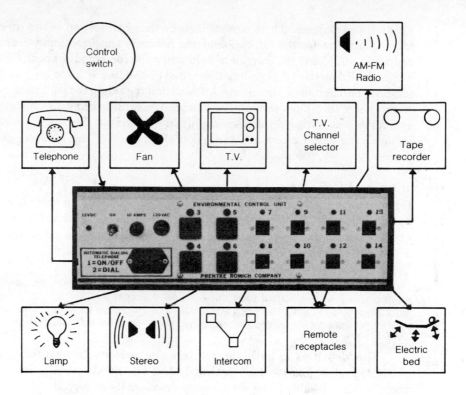

*One control switch can operate many devices.

Figure 5.11 Environmental Control System for the severely handicapped. (Courtesy of the Prentke Romich Company.)

Multiply and Severely Handicapped Children

Children who have multiple and severe handicaps have been served traditionally in residential centers or have received no services at all. Since 1972, these children began to receive services in their communities, including public school classrooms. According to Sontag, Burke, and York (1973), the provision of community services for multiply and severely handicapped children has been the direct result of court decisions. The first lawsuit demanding public school programs for the mentally retarded was brought by the Pennsylvania Association for Retarded Children. A lawsuit that created a greater impact for all handicapped children was Mills vs. Board of Education of the District of Columbia (1972). Many court decisions rendered since 1972 have required public schools to provide services for multiply and severely handicapped children. Professionals should find it interesting that most of these court decisions were the direct result of parental pressure.

Stainback, Stainback, and Maurer (1976), discuss the reasons why there is an increasing concern for the education of multiply and severely handicapped children. These reasons include the organization of the American Association for the Education of the Severely and Profoundly Handicapped in 1975, and the Bureau of Education for the Handicapped (Office of Special Education) designating this group of children as a top priority for services. Through these two efforts, information regarding the education and training of multiply and severely handicapped children is being disseminated, and funds are being provided for exemplary programs. These efforts will influence the improvement and expansion of services for this group of children.

Definition and Incidence

Definitions of the multiply and severely handicapped vary to some extent; however, because of the serious and obvious problems of these children, the definitions tend to be similar. We have selected a definition presented by Thompson (1976):

Those children who because of the intensity of their physical, mental, or emotional problems, or a combination of such problems, need educational, social, psychological, and medical services which will make it possible for them to maximize their full potential for meaningful participation in society and for self-fulfillment.

This definition includes the severely and profoundly retarded, deaf-blind, deaf-blind and mentally retarded, deaf-blind and mentally retarded and physically disabled, and the severely emotionally disturbed.

Professionals have assumed that the incidence of these problems has been insignificant in comparison to other exceptional children. A task force appointed by the Bureau of Education for the Handicapped (Office of Special Education) determined the number of severely handicapped children at approximately 1.5 million. Of this number, about 60 percent are severely emotionally disturbed, and 30 percent are severely and profoundly mentally retarded. The remaining 10 percent are severely multihandicapped children (Thompson 1976).

Public School Programs

As a result of the litigation regarding free public education for *all* children, public schools are providing programs for multiply and severely handicapped children. Including these children in public school programs is a tremendous challenge, not only to existing school programs, but also to the university training of future special education teachers.

Including *all* children within the public school program means that schools will be working with children who cannot feed themselves, dress themselves, walk or sit unassisted, or speak intelligibly. Also included will be children who are not toilet trained, those who do not respond to verbal controls, self-mutilating children, extremely aggressive children, and those children whose seizures are not controlled or are only partially controlled (Sontag, Burke, and York 1973).

How can the public schools provide the comprehensive services required for these children? Many professionals are advocating that there should not be standard services. Encouragement is given for a variety of services in many different settings. However, the establishment of a community special school is discouraged, because the special school is a continuation of segregation similar to that of institutions. There is no doubt that the planning of public school programs for the severely and multiply handicapped child will require the cooperative efforts of an interdisciplinary team.

Special classes must be small and the teacher must be very well trained, because of the severe problems manifested by multiply and severely handicapped children. The number of these children who can be served adequately by one teacher will range probably from two to seven. This range will have to remain flexible depending upon the severity of the childrens' problems and the training of the teacher. Individual and thorough assessment of each child is required in order to determine how many children may be included in a specific class. Also, the supportive services available to the teacher must be considered before deciding upon the student-teacher ratio.

Some of the problems relevant to serving multiply and severely handicapped children in the public schools cannot be solved easily. For example, with smaller pupil-teacher ratios, the initial costs of educating and training these children increases significantly. Obviously the range of the children's problems will necessitate the hiring of a paraprofessional (teacher-aide). In addition to the professional teaching staff, there is a need for specialized transportation; services from supportive personnel such as physical, speech, and occupational therapists; modifications of the physical environment; supportive medical services, and specialized teaching materials and equipment. Behavior modification specialists and personnel from residential centers are required to conduct on-going in-service training and assist school personnel with evaluation of the children's progress. Continual contacts and counseling with the parents of the children are essential. In many cases, parents will become an extension of the training program. All factors are important in the provision of services for multiply and severely handicapped children; the neglect of any could result in an inadequate program. These services increase the need for additional school funding and school planning that must be considered in the implementation of a program for the multiply and severely handicapped.

Regardless of the cost, Public Law 94–142 and numerous court decisions require that we provide services for the multiply and severely handicapped in public school programs. Any argument that funds are not available for these services is not sufficient. Weintraub and Abeson (1974) report that the court decision against the schools of the District of Columbia ruled that funds must be redistributed, if necessary, and that no child can be eliminated from a school program on the basis of a lack of funds. From various interpretations of court decisions and Public Law 94–142, these services will be provided.

Teacher Training

Training is separated from the section on teacher characteristics because of the uniqueness of the training required. Many physically disabled and chronically ill children will receive a substantial portion of their education and training in the regular classroom. The multiply and severely handicapped child will require the services of a specially trained teacher. When appropriate, regular class teachers may provide a supportive role.

Many teachers are needed for this area because of the small pupil-teacher ratios and the provision of services from birth through adulthood. Early intervention and a continuum of services through adulthood are required for multiply and severely handicapped children if they are to reach their potentials. Based upon the wide range of services needed by these children and the lack of teachers, colleges and universities will have to establish training programs for this area.

The training required for the special class teacher of multiply and severely handicapped children is stated very succinctly by Haring (1975):

The training given to most special educators has concentrated on refining their skills for teaching primarily school-age children—and on teaching rather traditional academic subjects. When, as now, special education is confronted with teaching children from the first days after birth through adulthood; and when, as now, special education finds as its subject matter such skills as self-feeding, toileting, sitting without aid, or walking with prosthetic devices—the discipline finds itself in a whole new realm.

Training programs for these teachers must be very comprehensive. Teachers must be prepared to sequence instructional objectives through the use of task analysis, use continuous evaluation of the daily performance of children, and be able to select or construct instructional materials that emphasize developmental sequence. They must learn how to make close evaluations of diagnostic instruments and have a thorough knowledge of early human growth and development. They must be sophisticated in the use of behavior modification techniques, particularly in the specification of target behaviors and the precise measurement of behavior. The specification of target behaviors identifies behaviors of primary concern. Precise measurement indicates progress and gives clues for the next direction of instruction. Applying meaningful group and individual reinforcement contingencies, learning how to elicit appropriate responses, and modifying severe behavioral difficulties such as extreme aggressiveness, headbanging, and feces smearing are a definite part of the training program for teachers (Stainback, Stainback, and Maurer 1976; Haring 1975).

Communicating and working effectively with an interdisciplinary team is more important for the teacher of multiply and severely handicapped children than for any other teacher. The teacher must know the various specialists and how their efforts relate to the total program. Allaying the fears and misinformation among school administrators, school counselors, and regular class teachers is an additional responsibility of the special class teacher, and training must be provided for this. The importance of developing oneself as a contributing team member cannot be overstressed.

Parents of multiply and severely handicapped children are a vital part of the program. They can profit from training to assist them in working with their child in the home. They are also a vital source of information for the team. As a part of their training, teachers must learn to work effectively with parents and be able to train them to work with their own child. Such parent training is a new dimension for most special education teachers and should be part of the total training program.

Prosthetic aids are needed by many multiply and severely handicapped children and youth. Specially designed tools for eating, lifts for entering buses, wheelchairs, standing tables, walkers, etc., are examples of the equipment they use. The practical use of these prosthetic aids and the necessary safety precautions in their use must be a part of the teacher's training. The training program might also emphasize ways in which prosthetic aids can be made or modified for use by the severely handicapped child.

Typewriters designed to assist disabled individuals are now available through The Typewriting Institute for the Handicapped, 3102 W. Augusta Ave., Phoenix, Arizona 85201. One is designed for those who can use only one hand. An easily read manual is available for this typewriter. Another typewriter has a shield over the keyboard with a hole directly over each letter so that the individual who has a muscle control problem can type one letter at a time and not type a letter by accident. This typewriter is especially useful for the child with cerebral palsy. A recent model has a light which flashes when the typist reaches the end of a line instead of the usual bell. A complete brochure is available from the Institute.

An essential aspect of the training program is field experience with the multiply and severely handicapped. Through this experience future teachers have opportunities to practice the skills they have learned. Field experiences also allow future teachers to explore their own attitudes and abilities for this type of work.

Through the combination of all aspects of training mentioned above, teachers of multiply and severely handicapped children will be prepared to fulfill their responsibilities. Many preservice and in-service programs are needed in order to fill the present gap in providing services to multiply and severely handicapped children. In addition to the resources mentioned above, the following may be useful to those pursuing this area of study.

Resources

Anderson, Robert M. and Greer, John G. *Educating the Severely and Profoundly Retarded.* Baltimore, Maryland: University Park Press, 1976.

Baker, Bruce L.; Brightman, Alan J.; Heifetz, Louis J.; and Murphy, Diane M. *Steps to Independence: A Skills Training Series for Children with Special Needs.* Champaign, Ill.: Research Press.

Donlon, Edward T. and Burton, Louise F. *The Severely and Profoundly Handicapped: A Practical Approach to Teaching.* New York: Grune and Stratton, 1976.

Haring, Norris G. and Brown, Louis J., eds. *Teaching the Severely Handicapped.* New York: Grune and Stratton, 1976.

Paraprofessionals

According to Frith and Lindsey (1980) paraprofessionals can be an invaluable resource in providing services for multihandicapped children. In order to be effective, the paraprofessional needs preservice as well as inservice education. The preservice training should include areas such as the following:

1. Behavioral and learning characteristics of the exceptional children to be served.
2. Subject content such as academics, adaptive physical education, music, and art.
3. Basic skills pertaining to the physical environment such as feeding, use and maintenance of equipment, and toilet training.

With appropriate preservice and ongoing in-service training, the paraprofessional should be able to assist in administering informal tests and screening instruments; prepare instructional tasks which are individualized; obtain specialized equipment and materials; modify the instructional program, equipment, and materials; support team teaching efforts; help students enter buildings and change classes; and assist teachers in home-school coordination of special support services such as physical therapy.

Reverse Mainstreaming

Poorman (1980) indicated that mainstreaming the severely and profoundly handicapped may not be a realistic plan. This includes those children who are severely and profoundly handicapped by reason of mental retardation, physical handicaps or emotional disturbance. As an alternative to mainstreaming in regular classes, the teachers and staff in a Central Pennsylvania Community provided mainstreaming in reverse. They brought normal children from regular classes to the special classroom to work with the handicapped children.

The staff prepared the children to understand the nature and complexity of the problems experienced by the severely and profoundly handicapped. Films and slides were used, and special and regular teachers worked together to instruct the regular class children before their visit. Guidelines were presented to inform the children how they could assist the handicapped children. Only children who volunteered participated in the program. Initially the volunteers worked for short periods (five to ten minutes) in play activities. Participation never exceeded a total of thirty minutes in one day. After this introduction, the volunteers were prepared to engage in short sitting activities. They were always given opportunities to discuss their participation.

Project Special Friend helped the special children become more socially aware, and a positive attitude among the regular class children and school staff evolved from the project. We suggest that schools attempt this type of program.

Study Questions

1. Discuss the psychological impact of physical disabilities and chronic illnesses on the child.
2. Discuss the psychological impact of physical disabilities and chronic illnesses on the parents and family.
3. Discuss the psychological impact of physical disabilities and chronic illnesses on school personnel.
4. What resources are available to the regular classroom teacher to improve classroom services for the chronically and physically disabled child?
5. Determine the differences between a disability and a handicap.
6. From resource materials, discuss architectural barriers.
7. What are your state department of education guidelines for homebound instruction?
8. What rehabilitative services are available in your city or state for the chronically or physically disabled child?
9. Why should the regular classroom teacher be aware of the hidden symptoms of the chronically or physically disabled child?
10. Choose one condition which is physically disabling or a chronic illness and describe this condition using the following format:
   Name or condition
   Physical symptoms
   Effect on physical performance
   Effect on learning performance
   Ways in which this condition can be prevented, controlled or improved

Bibliography

Cruickshank, William M. and Johnson, Orville G. eds. 1975. *Education of Exceptional Children and Youth.* 3rd ed. Englewood Cliffs, N.J.: Prentice-Hall.

Dantona, Robert. 1976. "Services for Deaf-Blind Children." *Exceptional Children* 43, no. 3 (November).

Detamore, Kristie L., and Lippke, Barbara A. 1980. "Handicapped Students Learn Language Skills with Communication Boards." *Teaching Exceptional Children* 12, no. 3 (Spring).

Dunn, Lloyd M., ed. 1973. *Exceptional Children in the Schools: Special Education in Transition.* 2d ed. New York: Holt, Rinehart & Winston.

Frith, Greg H., and Lindsey, Jimmy D. 1980. "Paraprofessionals Roles in Mainstreaming Multihandicapped Students." *Education Unlimited* 2, no. 2 (March).

Greer, Thomas L., and Christian, Walter P. 1976. *Chronically Ill and Handicapped Children: Their Management and Rehabilitation.* Research Press Co.

Hamilton, K. W. 1950. *Counseling the Handicapped in the Rehabilitation Process.* New York: Ronald Press Co.

Haring, Norris G. 1975. *Special Education for the Severely Handicapped: The State of the Art in 1975.* Reston, Va.: The Council for Exceptional Children.

Hopkins, T. W.; Bice, H. V.; and Colton, Kathryn C. 1954. *Evaluation and Education of the Cerebral Palsied Child.* Washington, D.C.: Council for Exceptional Children.

Kirk, Samuel A. 1972. *Educating Exceptional Children.* 2d ed. Boston: Houghton Mifflin Co.

Kliment, Stephen A. 1976. "Into the Mainstream, a Syllabus for a Barrier-Free Environment." The American Institute of Architects and the Rehabilitation Services Administration, HEW, printed by the Superintendent of Documents. Washington, D.C.: U.S. Government Printing Office.

Lyght, Charles E., ed. 1964. *The Merck Manual,* 10th ed., Rahway, N.J.: Merch Sharp and Dohme Research Laboratories.

"Muscular Dystrophy Association of America, Inc." 1972. *The Exceptional Parent* 1, no. 6 (April/May).

Muscular Dystrophy: Hope Through Research. 1968. National Institute of Neurological Diseases and Blindness, National Institutes of Health, Bethesda, Md. Distributed through Washington, D.C.: U.S. Government Printing Office.

NINDB Research Profile: No. 6 Multiple Sclerosis. 1967. U.S. Department of Health, Education, and Welfare, Public Health Service, rev.

Policies and Procedures Manual for Special Education in Oklahoma. 1981. Oklahoma City: The Oklahoma State Department of Education.

Poorman, Christine. 1980. "Mainstreaming in Reverse with a Special Friend." *Teaching Exceptional Children* 12, no. 4 (Summer).

Robinson, Halbert B., and Robinson, Nancy M. 1976. *The Mentally Retarded Child.* New York: McGraw-Hill.

Scherer, Ann, ed. 1979. "Good-bye Grand mal." *National Spokesman* 12, no. 10 (December).

Sontag, Ed; Burke, Philip J.; and York, Robert. 1973. "Considerations for Serving the Severely Handicapped in the Public Schools." *Education and Training of the Mentally Retarded* 8, no. 2 (April).

Stainback, Susan; Stainback, William; and Maurer, Steven. 1976. "Training Teachers for the Severely and Profoundly Handicapped: A New Frontier." *Exceptional Children* 42, no. 4 (January).

Swack, Myron. 1969. "Therapeutic Role of the Teacher of Physically Handicapped Children." *Exceptional Children* 35, no. 5 (January).

Telford, Charles, W., and Sawrey, James M. 1977. *The Exceptional Individual*. 3rd ed. Englewood Cliffs, N.J.: Prentice-Hall.

Thompson, R. Paul. 1976. "The Severely Handicapped: A New Horizon." *Exceptional Children* 43, no. 3 (November).

Thompson, Susan M. 1979. "Lifeline for Janice: A Personalized Medical History." *Exceptional Parent* 9, no. 5 (October).

Van Osdol, Bob. 1977. *Vocabulary in Special Education*. 2nd ed. Dubuque, Iowa: Kendall/Hunt.

Weintraub, Frederick J., and Abeson, Alan. 1974. "New Education Policies for the Handicapped: The Quiet Revolution." *Phi Delta Kappan,* 55, no. 8.

Wright, Beatrice A. 1960. *Physical Disability—A Psychological Approach*. New York: Harper and Brothers.

6

visually and hearing impaired children

The Visually Impaired

For sensorially impaired children, educational as well as other legal procedures are determined by definitions specifically adopted for such purposes. Deviations from that which is considered normal vary. In order to meet the needs of children who are visually impaired, certain criteria for exceptionality have been determined.

Definitions and Estimates of Prevalence

According to Telford and Sawrey (1977), blindness is usually defined as follows: "Visual acuity of 20/200 or less in the better eye with proper correction, or a limitation in the fields of vision such that the widest diameter or the visual field subtends an angular distance no greater than 20 degrees." Criteria within this definition were established by the American Foundation for the Blind. This definition means that a person with this impairment must be at a distance of twenty feet in order to read the standard type which a person with normal vision can read at a distance of 200 feet. A restriction in the field of vision means that a person may have normal vision for a specific area of focus, but the field of vision is so restricted that only a limited area can be seen at one time. This is usually referred to as "tunnel vision."

Another definition of blindness is based on the degree of useful vision that is retained or the media that can be read. Dunn (1973) reported that blind children include those who have little remaining useful vision; therefore, they must use Braille for purposes of reading.

The determination of eligibility for services available for blind persons through agencies or states is usually based on two characteristics of vision—visual acuity and field of vision. If corrected vision in the better eye is 20/200 or less the person is considered blind. The second characteristic for determining blindness pertains to the condition in which a person's visual field is restricted to an angle no greater than 20 degrees at the widest diameter (Dunn 1973). These conditions are defined as legal blindness or economic blindness.

Educators have also used these definitions for placement of children in special classes. Children with 20/200 vision or less are placed in self-contained classes for the blind. Children with vision of 20/200 and upwards but less than 20/70 are eligible for placement in classes for the partially sighted, which are seldom found today. However, such definitions are not practical in terms of all education, because children with limited visual acuity make different uses of their abilities.

One of the most generally accepted characteristics for the partially sighted child is a visual acuity of between 20/70 and 20/200 in the better eye after maximum correction. Further stipulations are made regarding the methods used to educate children with this visual problem. These children retain relatively little residual vision and can read only very large print or possibly regular print under very special conditions.

Abel (1958) as reported by Cruickshank and Johnson (1975) described five categories or degrees of visual acuity:

1. Total blindness, or light perception, or visual acuity up to but not including 2/200: would be unable to perceive motion or hand movements at a distance of three feet.

2. Motion or form perception or visual acuity 5/200: would be unable to count fingers at a distance of three feet.

3. Visual acuity up to 10/200: would be unable to read larger headlines of a newspaper, but would be expected to have some travel vision.

4. Visual acuity up to 20/200: would be unable to read 14-point or smaller type but would be expected to read large headlines of a newspaper.

5. Visual acuity of 20/200: would be able to read 10-point type, but insufficient vision for those daily activities for which vision is essential.

The state of Oklahoma (Policies and Procedures Manual for Special Education in Oklahoma 1981) accepts students as legally blind for special services whose best corrected vision is 20/200 or less. A child is eligible for special class placement with a corrected visual acuity of 20/70 or less in the better eye.

It seems to be generally accepted that the incidence of blind and partially sighted individuals is one of the lowest among the different exceptionalities. However, the incidence of mild visual defects is very high. We estimate that one-fourth of all school children have some visual defects. A majority of these defects are easily correctable and do not require special educational or vocational considerations.

Statistics on the prevalence of blindness and partial sightedness tend to be undependable. Part of the difficulty in collecting reliable data in this area, as reported by Hoover (1964), may be ascribed to a lack of uniform definition of blindness or visual impairment, and part to the fact that visual acuity is not determined by standardized methods.

The prevalence of blindness often depends on the characteristics of the culture involved. The rate may be higher in some areas, such as Asia or Africa, because of poor medical care and malnutrition. As medical services improve, incidence may go down for children and up for the aged, because average life spans are increasing. Therefore, the types of visual difficulties would also be reflected in the ages of those involved, because older people are most susceptible to varying types of visual difficulties.

The means most widely accepted for estimating the prevalence of blindness in the United States is the Hurlin method, which was based on studies of blindness in North Carolina and included the criterion of legal blindness presented above. Race and age factors in the various state populations served as a guide for Hurlin's estimates of blindness. The rate of prevalence for different states varies from slightly over one per 1,000 to almost four per 1,000 population. Using these estimates, more than 200,000 persons in the United States were blind in 1965 (Hurlin 1953 and 1962). Current estimates of blindness in the United States approach 700,000 (Wilson 1965).

According to Dalton (1943) mild visual defects affected approximately one-fourth of the school population. A survey taken in California involved over 5,000 children and indicated that 22 percent of the elementary children and 31 percent of the high school students had visual defects. The majority of these problems were so mild, though, that they required no special services because the defects were corrected.

Assuming that the criterion for blindness is a corrected vision of 20/200 or less in the better eye, it is estimated that there is one blind child in every 3,000 school-age children. The partially sighted population, using the criterion of a visual acuity of between 20/70 and 20/200, is estimated to be one in 500. As a total group, a conservative estimate is that approximately .0009 of all school-age children need special educational facilities for the visually impaired. Two-thirds of them are educationally partially sighted and the remaining one-third are educationally blind. Based on a current estimate of more than 53 million school children, there would be approximately 16,000 educationally blind and 32,000 partially sighted children who could benefit from special education services (Telford and Sawrey 1977; Dunn 1973).

Methods of Identification

Identifying children with gross visual defects is much easier than identifying those with less obvious difficulties. The child who is partially sighted is often not identified until some time during the elementary school years when visual acuity becomes important in order to accomplish certain academic tasks.

In many instances, observation of behaviors may cause a teacher to suspect visual difficulty. Some of the more common symptoms associated with visual impairment are listed below. These symptoms were selected from Winebrenner (1952), and are still current.

1. Has chronic eye irritations as indicated by watery eye or by red-rimmed, encrusted, or swollen eyelids
2. Experiences nausea, double vision, or blurring during or following reading
3. Rubs eyes, frowns, or screws up the face when looking at distant objects
4. Is overcautious in walking, runs infrequently, and falters for no apparent reason
5. Is abnormally inattentive during chalkboard, wall chart, or map work
6. Complains of visual blurring and attempts to brush away the visual impediments
7. Is excessively restless, irritable, or nervous following prolonged close visual work
8. Blinks excessively, especially while reading
9. Habitually holds the book very close, very far away, or in other unusual positions when reading
10. Tilts the head to one side when reading
11. Can read only for short periods of time
12. Shuts or covers one eye when reading

The following similar and additional aids for identification of visual problems are offered by the National Society for the Prevention of Blindness, Inc. (1980):

Behavior
1. Rubs eyes excessively
2. Shuts or covers one eye, tilts head or thrusts head forward
3. Has difficulty in reading or in other work requiring close use of the eyes
4. Blinks more than usual or is irritable when doing close work
5. Holds books close to eyes
6. Is unable to see distant things clearly
7. Squints eyelids together or frowns

Appearance
8. Crossed eyes
9. Red-rimmed, encrusted, or swollen eyelids
10. Inflamed or watery eyes
11. Recurring styes

Complaints

12. Eyes itch, burn or feel scratchy
13. Cannot see well
14. Dizziness, headaches, or nausea following close eye work
15. Blurred or double vision

Testing Instruments

Of the various formal tests used to screen visual impairment, the Snellen Test is the most widely used because it can be easily administered. The test consists of a chart with rows of E's printed in different sizes and placed in various positions. A distance designation is assigned to rows of letters of a specific size. For example, at a distance of 20 feet, persons with normal vision can read the 20 feet row. One who can read correctly the letters on this row at this distance, has 20/20 vision. Deviations from an ability to read correctly the letters at specified distances provide an indication of visual impairment.

The Snellen E Chart should be used as a screening device for the possibility of visual problems with all school age children. However, this test is not appropriate for attempting to determine all visual impairments. For example, a telebinocular is a measuring instrument that is easy to use. It assesses visual skills in the areas of depth perception, vertical imbalance, lateral imbalance, and distant and near point fusion. It can be very helpful in determining a child's visual skills for reading and other close work. Another means of identifying children with visual impairments is the Massachusetts Vision Tests, which consist of a monocular vision acuity test, plus a sphere test, and the Maddox Rod Test. The Massachusetts Vision Tests are generally considered to be more effective in measuring visual difficulties than the Snellen E Chart.

Children suspected of having a visual difficulty should be referred to an ophthalmologist or other eye specialists. Schools or other agencies that work with children may do limited screening of vision, but specific diagnosis should be made by a professional eye specialist. If a child has a visual impairment, recommendations should be made to the parents to return the child to the eye specialist frequently for periodic checks for possible progressive disorders.

Characteristics of the Visually Impaired

The National Society for the Prevention of Blindness, Inc. (1980) describes the characteristics of certain common conditions that cause visual impairment:

Amblyopia Dimness of vision without any apparent disease of the eye; usually the result of not using an eye ("lazy eye") in order to avoid the discomfort of double vision caused by a muscle problem.

Astigmatism An eye problem in which there is blurred vision because of irregularities in the shape of the cornea, the transparent covering of the eye, or of the lens. Light rays cannot focus on the retina, so it is difficult to see far and near objects.

Color Deficiency An inherited vision defect, not a disease, characterized by the inability to recognize colors—usually red or green but sometimes blue or yellow.

Hyperopia (farsightedness) In farsighted eyes, the eyeball is too short from front to back. Farsighted people see distant objects well, but things that are close are blurry.

Myopia (nearsightedness) In myopia, the eyeball is too long from front to back. Nearsighted people see nearby objects well but distant objects are blurred.

Strabismus (squint, crossed eyes) One or more muscles of the eye is out of balance; one or both eyes turn in toward the nose or outward away from the nose, making it impossible for the eyes to focus on the same object at the same time.

Totally blind children often lack animated facial expression, often having blank looking or disfigured eyes. They display a general awkwardness in the ability to move. Children who are partially sighted wear thick lenses or hold objects unusually close to the eyes in order to see.

However, using general physical appearances to differentiate between the sighted child and the visually impaired child is not always appropriate. The visually impaired child may have organic impairments in addition to visual problems; however, the incidence of multiply handicapped, visually impaired children is infrequent. Visually normal children may also have organic impairments similar to those of children with visually limited ability. These impairments may result from prematurity, malnutrition, or German measles.

Motor Skills—Mobility Training
A common difficulty found among blind or partially sighted children is related to gross motor performance. Obviously, they may have difficulty in areas such as mobility. Buell (1950) indicated that these children tend to be deficient in physical skills and general physical coordination. Environmental conditions may be the primary factor in difficulties in gross motor performance, because the visually limited child is seldom encouraged to participate in physical activities.

Visually impaired children will be deficient in imitation of skills, skipping, running, and other childhood activities. They may not be encouraged or desire to explore their environments; thus, the development of physical skills will be limited. As the children grow older, they may prefer to sit

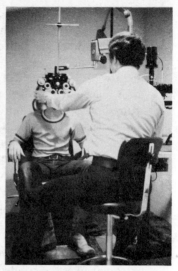

School children must receive adequate vision care. (Courtesy of Dr. Curtis Roberson, Yukon, Oklahoma.)

Visual training enables students to have easier access to public schools.

rather than participate in physical activities because they have been consistently warned of the dangers in their environment. They need to be encouraged and assured that any normal activities will be beneficial.

Fine motor skill development may be deficient in the visually impaired. Deficiencies in this area of functioning will usually be evident because the children may have had limited practice in the manipulation of small objects, such as playing with building blocks, reaching and grasping objects for visual inspection, and learning the use of their hands. The inability to see objects limits the practice needed for the development of fine muscles.

Independent travel will also be an area in which visually limited children will be restricted. Consistently bumping into sharp objects or falling over objects will cause less desire to move about. Mobility of visually impaired children may be affected by other handicaps which may involve the other senses. The importance of the auditory sense is apparent. When the visual sense is limited, there is more dependence upon the auditory sense to provide clues about the environment. Other senses may also become important in providing the necessary motivation for these children. In some instances, persons close to visually impaired children may be overprotective, which tends to increase anxieties relative to mobility problems.

Early mobility training is essential for young children as well as adolescents and adults. Only recently has cane training been promoted for young children. The primary purposes of providing cane training for young children is to enhance their independence, safe movement, and peer acceptance. A study conducted by Dickstein (1976) involved children from eight to twelve years of age from the Los Angeles area. All of the parents had to agree to the training; however, the final decision to participate was made by each individual child. The children were trained in familiar environments and were given training in safety precautions, climbing stairs, cane techniques, traveling in their neighborhoods, and using their hearing and other senses to greater advantage.

The cane training was so successful that it is now a permanent part of the training at the Braille Institute of America. The children gained independence, confidence, and travel abilities and learned the cane method faster than older individuals. Early cane training is beneficial for young children and should be included in all training programs serving them.

Visual Cue Limitations

Being hampered somewhat in the ability to learn through visual imitation may cause visually impaired children to suffer some major restrictions in the acquisition of knowledge. They cannot learn through simple imitation of visual cues as does the normally sighted child. Parents and teachers must patiently teach simple childhood skills. They must also be taught how to use other senses to the best advantages.

Visually impaired children experience many difficulties in the normal educational environment. They may have extreme problems in reproducing or interpreting written communications. Their limited early childhood experiences with concrete objects, which aid the children's learning skills for discrimination of sizes, shapes, and colors probably will cause difficulties with abstract ideas. Some of the problems encountered with abstract ideas will involve distance, height, speed, and applying appropriate language to a complex problem.

The emotional needs of visually impaired children do not differ from those of sighted children. However, because of the problems mentioned previously, emotional growth and developmental processes may be severely affected. Anxious parents may often overprotect their child because of visual defects, which restricts the normal desire for independence. Special help and counseling may be necessary to help parents cope with the special problems their child will encounter. Of course, parents also encounter many problems themselves in learning to care for their child, and counseling services will be periodically needed for them.

The inability to participate in physical activities, such as playing sports, going on school field trips with classmates, or learning to dance may cause visually impaired children and their families to be faced with periods of serious emotional stress and anxiety. Experiences that result in stresses of this type will vary considerably among the visually impaired. The inner resources of the children and families will determine how well these periods of stress are handled. The extent to which emotional stresses and anxieties are met successfully will depend upon how successfully previous encounters have been met, and how well children and families have been prepared to cope with problems of this type.

Experiences which result in emotional stress and anxiety may also depend upon when the child became visually impaired. For example, a child visually impaired from birth may have less difficulty in adjusting to the disability than the child who becomes seriously visually impaired later in life. The child who was born with good vision will have to adjust perception of self from one who was capable of certain activities to one who is less capable. This process may require more time and patience on the part of the child and family. For the visually impaired child who once had good vision, adjustment will involve accepting a certain amount of dependence on others.

Differences in the emotional adjustment of visually impaired children based on the time of onset of the impairment cannot be determined by hard and fast rules. For example, a child who is born blind or with a serious visual impairment will have difficulties in skills such as learning to eat, playing with toys, dressing, exploring the environment, and caring for personal needs. Parents may become discouraged and quite exasperated in their attempts to teach the child. During their efforts, the child will not respond to them with visual recognition, bright smiles, or other facial expressions, and the parents may unavoidably resent the lack of emotional responses. Thus, they may do everything for the child, or neglect and cease trying to help the child. During the child's stages of early development, the parents should seek training and counseling to guide them in caring for, understanding, and teaching their child. Otherwise, the child may be overly dependent or neglected and become, for all practical purposes, helpless.

Restrictions in physical activities and overprotection of blind children may result in the development of certain characteristics which have no social or functional purpose. These children may rock, roll their heads, move hands before their eyes, or poke fingers in their eyes so often that these behaviors become a part of their characteristics. Other handicapped children may also exhibit these same characteristics, which are not limited solely to visually handicapping conditions. Blind children who develop these characteristics will generally require training to eliminate them. With appropriate guidance about activities which such children can perform, teachers and parents can provide an environment which will help them develop more functional characteristics (Cruickshank and Johnson 1975).

If blind children or seriously visually impaired children learn to use their other senses appropriately, they can become very sensitive to small cues for information and guidance. However, in comparison to normally sighted children, visually impaired children are usually not superior in the use of their senses. Blind children can be taught to listen closely to environmental stimuli and learn how to use these sounds for determining distances and sensing possible obstructions. Abilities such as these are not, however, innately superior in visually limited children (Telford and Sawrey 1977).

Indications of significant educational retardation may be evident when one compares blind children to children with normal vision of the same chronological or mental age. This difference is not necessarily a lower general intellectual functioning among visually impaired children. It may be the result of a lack of appropriate educational services. Children with severe visual problems will have more difficulty learning abstract concepts and learning through the use of Braille, large print type; or audition will tend to cause these children to learn at a slower rate. Visually impaired children may have medical problems which cause them to miss school frequently and they may not start school at the age of six. All of these factors contribute to problems in learning. Thus, one may conclude that the significant educational retardation of visually impaired children is multidetermined (Dunn 1973). Of course, this does not mean that blind children cannot be mentally retarded, emotionally disturbed, or below average in general intellectual functioning. Genetic factors may influence intellectual functioning and environmental situations may contribute to the development of severe emotional problems. We have worked with several children who were blind, deaf, and mentally retarded. Several instances of multiple handicaps among the visually impaired have also been reported in the professional literature.

Education of the Visually Impaired

Educational objectives for visually impaired children do not differ from the objectives for normally sighted children. Obviously, there are some who may require special vocational training, teachers who are specially trained, and special equipment within the classroom (Telford and Sawrey 1977).

Classrooms for visually impaired children must be equipped with various tools that provide other than visual cues. Emphasis is usually placed on learning through listening. Children also must be trained to use tactile skills, and encouraged to engage in appropriate physical activities, all of which offer the opportunity to develop needed social skills.

It must be decided as soon as possible whether a visually handicapped child is to use Braille as the primary means of learning, or if the child is to use both Braille and large print books. The child who is not totally blind must be encouraged to use residual vision as much as possible.

Training in the use of a Braille typewriter is also essential for the visually handicapped. In some cases, where the visual deficit is less severe, the child may be taught a minimum usage of pen and pencil.

Additional special equipment and other resources necessary for visually impaired children include such items as the following:

1. Tape recorders
2. Record players
3. Special resource or itinerant teachers
4. Braille typewriters
5. Special calculators
6. Rulers and slide rules
7. Compasses and protractors
8. Relief maps and globes
9. Special large print books
10. Magnifying devices

Classrooms for blind children must also be carefully designed and advantageously located. Special care should be taken to arrange each room to facilitate movement which in some cases makes possible a sight-saving program. Correct illumination, either natural or artificial, becomes an essential factor. The classroom must have ample space for special materials, which are usually larger and more cumbersome than those found in regular classrooms. Care should also be taken in the selection of furniture to be used in a special classroom.

When a sight-saving program is being used, special considerations should be given to the placement of the teacher's desk and other pieces of equipment. Chalkboards should be of a lighter color so as to reflect light. It should be noted that sight-saving classes are older concepts of education. Today's curriculum should require children to use their residual sight. Sight activities are not harmful to the sight-defective child. In fact, maximum use of one's residual sight is recommended for educational growth.

Partially sighted children usually should be encouraged to remain in the regular classroom as much as possible. They are also educated and prepared for life in much the same way as the normally sighted individual.

They are encouraged to use vision to its maximum, learn to read and write, and acquire as much education as possible by normal means. In some cases there is a need for a slight adjustment in curriculum and the use of special equipment. Otherwise, education for partially sighted children may follow that of normally sighted children.

If partially sighted children remain in the regular classroom, one special provision should be the seating arrangement. Allocations must be made to place these children closer to information centers such as the chalkboard. They also must have the freedom to move around the classroom to get closer to special equipment and materials. In general, partially sighted children should be included in as many of the activities provided for normal children as possible.

Residential Facilities

Residential schools for the blind involve an intensive care program, which should provide a homelike environment. In many facilities the children are encouraged to go home as much as possible; and arrangements are made for special students to get broader educations by taking courses that are not regularly offered in the residential schools. One of the primary concerns of residential schools is maintaining the student's contact with the general community, because they need to be able to live in a sighted-society also. Presently, nearly all states make special provisions for educating visually handicapped children. Either special schools are provided by the state, or arrangements are made to have these children educated by other agencies (Cruickshank and Johnson 1975).

Community Services

Barnett (1955) indicated that the vocational services for the visually handicapped are usually not adequate. Even though visually impaired people may be vocationally trained, they still have difficulty in finding appropriate employment. It is estimated that less than half of the blind who could work are doing so, and only about 20 percent of those who could function in a sheltered workshop are doing so.

Training programs to prepare the blind with employment skills are usually not available. In most cases, the blind learn employment skills in the same situations as the sighted. However trained, though, the blind or partially sighted person must compete with sighted persons for jobs, and combat the prejudices of some employers.

Sheltered workshops probably employ more visually handicapped people than other facilities do. The employment outlook is not totally bleak, because many companies accept visually handicapped employees and integrate them into jobs with sighted people (Telford and Sawrey 1977).

Although many advances have been made in the vocational training and employment of the blind and visually impaired, this is still an area of major concern to the American Foundation for the Blind (AFB). In September, 1979, the AFB held a four-day institute to focus on this concern. The audience consisted primarily of rehabilitation personnel who were trained to help employers improve the employment of the blind and visually impaired. The institute focused on the hiring and retention of those with severe loss of vision. The need for continuing efforts to improve the vocational training and employment of blind and visually impaired individuals was emphasized by a report given at the institute which stated that the 2,000 blind and visually impaired individuals who graduate annually from college have severely limited career opportunities in industry and commerce. The findings and recommendations of the institute should be available now to help local rehabilitation personnel improve the employment outlook for these people.

Special Training for Teachers

Generally many of the same requirements necessary for the normal classroom teacher apply to the teacher of the visually handicapped. The ability to get along with people and, in some cases, to counsel with parents is important. The special class teacher must also be able to withstand the physical and mental trauma that may be present in working with exceptional children.

In addition, the special teacher should have a broad general educational background and courses in special techniques and procedures for teaching the visually handicapped. Coursework should include study in the behavioral sciences, developmental psychology, and practicum experience with exceptional children. Teachers should continue their education by maintaining an awareness of methods, procedures, and materials that are being developed.

Blind children were the first handicapped group for whom special provisions, such as residential centers and day school classes, were available, although blindness is less common than other handicapping conditions. Visually handicapped children do not differ significantly from normal sighted children in physical appearance, although they may display certain characteristics often associated with anxious or mentally retarded children. They also tend to fall behind in certain areas of cognitive learning and in arithmetic.

Visually handicapped children may have some difficulty in social adjustments, but they do not usually exhibit special characteristics or personality types. The difficulties they encounter are related to their desires for independence and their needs for a certain degree of dependence because of their disabilities; and to their feelings of anxiety about moving around in an unfamiliar environment which is full of potential hazards.

The overall intelligence levels of visually impaired children do not differ significantly from that of children with normal vision. Intellectual deficits that do occur may often be associated with another handicap. Generally, the basic intellectual capacity of blind children can be compared to that of the general population.

The Hearing Impaired

The ability to communicate is established through verbal language. Although non-verbal feedback is important to hearing people, non-verbal cues are even more important to the hearing impaired. Without verbal language abilities children's developmental progress will be slowed. Speech development, therefore, is extremely important to children with hearing impairments.

Hearing deficiencies seem to create more ego concerns than many other disabilities. People wear glasses, use crutches, ride wheelchairs, and speak with articulatory or stuttering problems but when they must depend on hearing aids, they often become defensive and pretend to hear. Consequently, emotional adjustment is a serious adaption to a hearing impairment.

Educators and parents should be aware of signs of undetected hearing losses. For example, if children consistently position themselves close to televisions or in the front of the classrooms in order to hear better, parents and teachers may gradually accept the behavior and not realize that these children cannot hear well.

Definitions

The term *deafness* is commonly used to refer to either total or partial loss of hearing. However, more recently, the term *hard-of-hearing* has replaced the phrase *partially deaf*.

The problems faced by partially hearing or hard-of-hearing children may be completely different from those encountered by children with complete hearing losses. Therefore, careful considerations must be made in discriminating between the two groups.

Social, educational, and medical factors are the criteria used to determine the extent to which deafness is a problem. For example, the social criteria involve adequate communication skills; without these skills deaf children will have serious problems. Communication problems usually exist if the hearing loss exceeds 80 decibels. If the decibel loss is less than 80; there may still be severe communication problems; however, they may learn communication skills to the extent that they are considered hard-of-hearing. Determining whether children are deaf or hard-of-hearing will also depend upon the ability to learn how to use a hearing aid. The medical criteria for determining the effects of a hearing loss are based on the decibel loss which the child suffers (Davis and Silverman 1970).

In making a distinction between *deaf* and *hard-of-hearing*, it is necessary to point out that very seldom does someone have *complete* loss of hearing. Many people show some degree of residual hearing as measured on an audiometer; however, the ability to use residual hearing is a primary factor in discriminating between deafness and hard-of-hearing.

Proposed definitions for the hearing impaired were prepared in 1937 by the Committee on Nomenclature of the Conference of Executives of American Schools for the Deaf. These definitions are still valid and are reported by Davis and Silverman (1970) as follows:

1. The deaf: those in whom the sense of hearing is nonfunctional for the ordinary purposes of life. This general group may be divided into two smaller groups which are determined by when the loss of hearing occurred.
   a. The congenitally deaf: those who were born deaf.
   b. The adventitiously deaf: those who were born with normal hearing but in whom the sense of hearing became nonfunctional later through illness or accident.
   c. The hard-of-hearing: those in whom the sense of hearing, although defective, is functional with or without a hearing aid.

Pauls and Hardy (1953) indicated that the following classification of hearing loss is based on the necessary intensity (loudness) in decibels (db) before an individual is capable of detecting the pressure of sound.

20–40 db loss = Mild
40–60 db loss = Moderate
60–75 db loss = Severe
75–100 db loss = Profound

An intensity of about 70 decibels, or about 48 decibels above the normal speech-reception threshold, is indicative of average intensity for conversational speech. According to Newby (1964) this means that people with a loss of 30 decibels who use hearing aids would be able to hear conversational speech. The students would, of course, miss much of what is said because many speech sounds would be made below the threshold for speech.

Telford and Sawrey (1977) indicated that a definition of deafness or hard-of-hearing also takes into consideration the quantitative aspects of the loss. This factor typically differentiates hearing loss as it is measured audiometrically in decibels. Such a loss refers to the deficit in the better ear for the frequencies in the speech range. The White House Conference on Child Health and Protection (1931) used the age of onset of the hearing loss as the main criterion for distinguishing between the deaf and the hard-of-hearing. This conference defined deaf children as those born with a hearing loss which prevents the maturational acquisition of speech; those who acquire deafness before language and speech develop; and those who become deaf shortly after speech develops, and consequently, lose their language skills. Even though these definitions are old, they still seem to be applicable to children who are hearing impaired.

Hard-of-hearing children have hearing losses which have not prevented the acquisition of speech and language in the normal manner, which may be described as imitating sounds (Policies and Procedures Manual for Special Education in Oklahoma 1980). However, we realize that children with this type of hearing loss experience difficulty in auditory reception. Therefore, they may not hear all speech sounds distinctly and may confuse, substitute, or omit sounds. They are, though, still capable of oral communication and able to master language to some degree.

Most audiometers use standards that were set by the American National Standards Institute (ANSI) in 1969. Such instruments are used to classify the degree of hearing loss.

Group A—Mild hearing loss: 25–40 db (ANSI 1969) in the better ear across the speech range. Those who have a hearing loss in this range usually learn speech spontaneously in the normal manner and are considered to be on the borderline between normal hearing and significant hearing impairment. They are unable to hear certain speech sounds, and what they hear is slightly diminished in volume. Children with a mild hearing loss require special help so that they can maintain the speech and language skills they have learned.

Group B—Hard-of-hearing: 45–70 db (ANSI 1969) in the better ear across the speech range. Such a loss is distinctly a handicap. Children may be able to learn language with the help of amplified sound, but will encounter difficulty in following group conversations. They may have a limited vocabulary and may be easily confused by words with more than one meaning. What they hear is more diminished in volume. Their speech will reflect distorted hearing and will be characterized by numerous articulation problems, consisting of distortion, omissions, and substitution of consonant sounds. For example, they would not be able to distinguish between the k-t-p or b-d-g. Special help would be required in order to establish good speech patterns and full language development.

Group C—Borderline severely hard-of-hearing—severely deaf: 75–85 db (ANSI) above 500 (Hz) frequency range in the better ear across the speech range. Adequate language and intelligible speech will not be spontaneously developed by children with this range of hearing loss. They may make numerous grammatical errors and tend to use a more concrete vocabulary. As in the previous group, they will have some difficulty in comprehending words with more than one meaning. They also show much distortion in their articulation. Amplification and intensive special training is necessary for these children.

Group D—Severely deaf: 90–105 db (ANSI) in the better ear across the speech range. Children in this range of hearing loss do not develop speech spontaneously. They hear mainly speech pitch patterns and the vowel sounds. Even with amplification, these children hear conversa-

Audiometric screening is a necessary service which should be provided by all schools.

tions as a whisper. They need amplification and an educational program specifically planned for deaf children.

Group E—Profoundly deaf: 105 db—no response (ANSI) above 500 Hz in the better ear across the speech range. Even with amplification, these children hear only noise. They require intensive training and special education teachers who are trained to teach deaf children. Education must start during the preschool years if they are to learn speech and language adequately. Without special aids, these children are unaware that someone is talking.

One may go beyond these classification systems in order to gain a fuller understanding of the impact of a deaf child's language problems. At a conference (1970) on Vocational Education for Handicapped, Howard Wyks who was the vocational principal of the Marie Katzenback School for the Deaf in Trenton, New Jersey, proposed that deaf children should be considered part of the disadvantaged population. His proposal was based on the premise that English for deaf children may be considered as a second language. As severely hearing-impaired children progress through school, language becomes more difficult. They must have educational experiences which relate communication and computational skills to pertinent areas of employment.

Estimates of Prevalence

Davis and Silverman reported a Silverman and Lane (1970) estimate that 5 percent of school-age children have hearing levels outside the range of normal, and that one or two out of every ten in this group (of the 5 percent) require special educational attention. A percentage estimate for today would reflect a more accurate count, but according to O'Neill (1964) there were approximately 300,000 children and 2,300,000 adults in the United States who were considered hard-of-hearing. Also, because of the aging process, the incidence of hearing difficulties tends to increase each year if the age of the population is considered.

The Oklahoma *Policies and Procedures Manual* (1976) suggests that because of confusion in arriving at an acceptable definition and an adequate criterion for assessment, it is difficult to estimate accurately the number of children with auditory problems. However, most current surveys show that 1.5 percent of the total population have some type of hearing impairment. Estimates for the 1980s may run as high as 4 to 5 percent of the population.

Deafness or hearing impairment may be found in any subpopulation group within the United States. There is no particular group in which deafness is more prevalent, and severe hearing impairments may be the result of a variety of factors such as genetic causes, rubella, prenatal influences, or injuries.

Methods of Identification

In more severe cases where a child is auditorially handicapped, it is possible to identify the handicap by behavioral symptoms alone. A research report (Curry 1954) indicated that teachers do only slightly better than chance in selecting students in their rooms with some type of hearing loss. Therefore, in a minority of cases involving children with mild to moderate hearing losses, it is necessary to use more formal means of identification.

Several tests have been devised to assess hearing losses. Many were devised prior to the development and sophistication of the pure-tone audiometer. Although no longer widely used, a few of these older methods employed such devices as tuning forks; one's ability to hear conversational speech; the tick of a watch at specified distances; and the use of noisemakers, such as bells or wood blocks. These methods only provided rough estimates of the possibility of a hearing loss because of variances such as outside noise factors, the lack of appropriate acoustics, the shape and size of the testing room, and even the extent to which the tester had normal hearing (Newby 1964).

The most frequently used electronic device is the pure-tone audiometer. The audiometer produces tones of varying frequency (pitch) and intensity (volume), which cover a wide range. This machine is carefully calibrated to give out "pure" tones at each frequency, ranging from 125 cycles per second (cps) to 8,000 cps. The volume is controlled by an attenuator which is usually calibrated in 5 db steps. The test consists of systematically presenting a series of tones that vary in pitch and volume. The person being tested hears the tones through a set of earphones, one ear being tested at a time. The subject is asked to respond verbally, by hand signals, or by pressing a buzzer upon hearing the tone that is being presented. The results are plotted on an audiogram, giving an indication of the individual's ability to hear a tone at each of the frequencies presented (see figure 6.1).

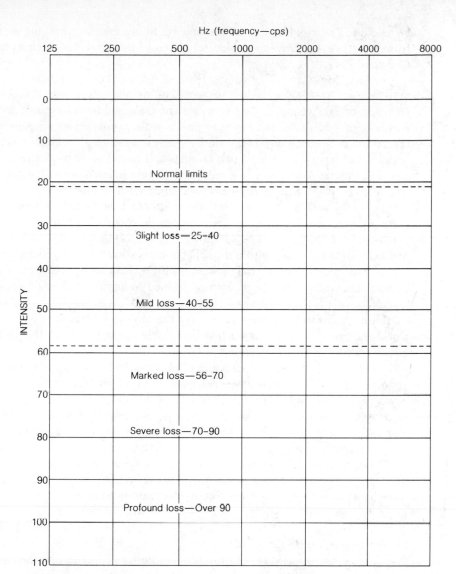

Figure 6.1 Audiogram.

The pure-tone audiometer is commonly used in the public schools to screen children in order to find those who may have a hearing impairment. Another type of audiometer can test from ten to forty children at one time. This special device is a phonographic audiometer which will accommodate up to forty headphone receivers. Special recordings using both male and female voices are played through the headphones. One ear is tested at a time. The voices, reading digits or words, grow gradually less distinct until only those with normal or superior hearing acuity are able to hear what is being said. The children are to respond by filling blanks, checking words from a list, or by drawing a picture of the object that has been named (Newby 1964).

Moss, Moss, and Tizard (1961) reported another special test which may be used to test an individual suspected of malingering or who is severely retarded, or very young. Such a test uses the Galvanic Skin Response as an indicator of whether or not a person has heard a presented sound. Initially the person is conditioned to respond by pairing a tone with a small electric shock. The responses are indicated on a special machine. If proper learning has taken place, the person responds in the same manner when the tone is presented by itself. Such a device is used under special circumstances.

A child with a hearing impairment should be referred to a medical specialist who can determine if the loss can be corrected by surgery or by the use of a hearing aid. The specialist trained in the anatomy of the ear and hearing is the otologist. Public schools may also have an audiologist on the staff who can appropriately assess a child's hearing by using an audiometer. The audiologist should also be trained to know the special types of assistance or training which will benefit the child. The audiologist should establish good working relationships with the otologist, since they will often work as a team in diagnosing a hearing problem, working with the child's parents, and specifying a training program.

Simmons (1980) reported some interesting findings regarding the diagnostic and rehabilitation processes used at Stanford University for deaf newborns. The babies were given the Crib-o-gram hearing test which detects responses by a motion-sensitive transducer placed under the child's mattress. The Crib-o-gram is sensitive to changes in respiration as well as almost any motor movement except eye blinks. If a hearing loss is detected through use of the Crib-o-gram, the babies are referred for a follow-up evaluation, which takes place within seven months of the first evaluation.

The intent of Stanford's screening program is to provide early habilitation for deaf children. In spite of the staff's efforts, babies identified as deaf went an average of 13.5 months before a hearing aid was purchased. The three primary reasons for this delay are not new, according to Simmons, and most professionals working with the hearing impaired babies and their parents are aware of them. The three reasons are as follows:

1. Referral back to the physician for hearing evaluation and then long, silent periods in the records.
2. Babies with multiple handicaps whose hearing loss is only a part of their total problems.
3. Parents refusing to accept or ignoring the report that their child has a serious hearing impairment.

Simmons reports that other advances have been made in determining hearing losses among babies. These are a brainstem-evoked response evaluation (BSER) and a Cochleography (ECoG). Both of these techniques lessen the "wait-and-see" attitude on the part of some professionals and parents and provide earlier habilitation procedures.

Simmons gives conclusions which have been learned or reinforced as a result of the Stanford studies:

1. Most handicapping sensorineural deafness is present at or shortly after birth, at least during the first three years of life.
2. Deaf babies can systematically be identified and diagnosed early, but the effort is wasted unless the follow-up is of equal enthusiasm and firmness. Considerable valuable time is lost both between identification and final confirmation, and between hearing aid recommendation and acquisition.
3. Contrary to popular opinion, milder hearing losses are just as easy to confirm as profound losses. However, parental suspicions and acceptance of more moderate losses is more difficult.
4. Contrary to what one might expect, establishing the presence of a hearing loss in babies with mild to severe developmental motor retardation requires a diagnostic test time interval no longer than that for normal babies.
5. About 40% of babies had important threshold sensitivity difference between ears and many of these were fitted with binaural aids of the same model.
6. Probably 33% of babies have progressive hearing losses.
7. BSER is a valuable and reliable tool when early behavioral audiometry is in question and in establishing the symmetry of a hearing loss.

Characteristics of the Hearing Impaired

All children at birth, whether deaf or normal, go through the same steps of language development. They experience emotion, cry, gurgle, and laugh. However, the child with a severe hearing loss or profoundly deaf child will eventually slow down in the area of speech development referred to as babbling. This is the stage of speech development when children with normal hearing concentrate on reproducing sounds personally made or sounds they heard others make. Normal children gain a sense of satisfaction in hearing themselves make funny noises. They also gain pleasure from the way some sounds feel as they are made, as in the "m" sound, and from the reactions they receive from significant adults around them. For deaf children, much of this experience is missing. If children are unable to hear the sounds that they or others make, they may lose interest in making sounds. Rather than repeating favorite sounds, they utter random concoctions of sounds. In some cases, they may be self-stimulated to reproduce sounds that are kinesthetically pleasing as in the "m" sound. However, for deaf or hard-of-hearing children, speech development will suffer at this point. They may also become handicapped in other areas of development because they are unable to respond to or react to sounds in the environment.

For children with less severe hearing losses, speech may be slower in developing, but a hearing loss may often go unnoticed until the child has entered school. Then, poor articulation, chronic inattention, failure to respond when spoken to, confusion when given directions, or other common symptoms of a hearing loss become more apparent. If a child has other handicaps, such as a physical disability or mental retardation, hearing losses may also often go undetected because of the primary problems or symptoms of the other handicaps.

Symptoms of a Conductive Loss

It is not possible to specify with accuracy the symptoms that are always associated with a conductive hearing loss. However, certain generalizations can be made. For example, if there is a conductive hearing loss, children may not be aware of external noises. They are generally able to hear themselves well through bone conduction. Therefore, they may speak consistently in relatively quiet voices, omit some inflections in speaking patterns, and make it difficult for others to hear them.

Children with a conductive hearing loss usually have no impairments in speech discrimination skills. In a noisy environment where normally hearing individuals tend to raise their voices, these people will be able to hear the loud voices and perhaps not hear the surrounding noises. They can tolerate loud voices of an intensity that would be uncomfortable for people with normal hearing. The conductive hearing loss acts as an earplug, thus protecting the inner ear. They also tend to have about the same degree of loss for all frequencies. However, they may hear the higher frequencies better than lower ones.

A person with a conductive hearing loss may frequently complain about subjective head noises. These noises may be focused in one or both ears, or throughout the head. This is usually caused by increased awareness of sounds caused by normal bodily processes. The person with normal hearing is more aware of sounds from the environment (Newby 1964).

Symptoms of a Sensori-Neural Loss

Newby relates that people with sensori-neural hearing losses may not be able to hear themselves speak. They may speak in very loud voices when such intensity is inappropriate. Because of this inability to hear their own voices, they cannot judge how loudly they speak. It should be pointed out, however, that many children with either type of hearing loss can learn how to regulate their voices using other cues from their environment.

Difficulty with speech discrimination is much more common among those with a sensori-neural hearing loss. Primary problems are in discriminating high frequency sounds, particularly if these sounds are produced with weak intensity. Words which sound similar but have different meanings may be very difficult to discriminate. They may hear normal speech, but find it

Noise pollution is a serious problem that has direct effects on hearing.

difficult to understand what was said. Part of this difficulty may be because of failure to hear initial or final sounds of a word and hearing only the vowel sounds. These children experience great difficulty in noisy surroundings. External noises interfere with the ability to perceive normal conversations or other types of verbal productions. The person with a sensori-neural hearing loss may also complain of consistent buzzing noises in one or both ears and the head. Obviously, these hearing problems will be more intense than those of the person with a conduction type loss (Newby 1964).

Current Hearing Problems and Concerns

The following information (Bradley 1976) describes problems and concerns as they relate to contemporary life-styles. The article is not specifically directed toward special education, but it does reflect many preventive and awareness concepts that will be of value to anyone who has a concern to prevent hearing problems. Dr. Bradley's interview is presented verbatim.*

How Modern Life Can Damage Your Hearing

Interview with Dr. Wesley H. Bradley, a leading medical authority

Just how dangerous is "noise pollution"? What else causes hearing loss—and what can be done to cope? For answers to questions affecting millions, the magazine invited Dr. Bradley to its conference room.

Q Dr. Bradley, is it indisputably true that today's "noise pollution" is causing many people to lose hearing?

A Yes, we do feel there is a definite increased incidence in hearing loss due to the amount of noise that's in our environment. Factory machines, diesel trucks, jet airplanes—all are examples of noise that can cause hearing loss, especially if a person is exposed to it repeatedly and over prolonged periods.

   If you get enough rest away from the noise, the effect on your hearing is usually reversible. But if you go beyond a certain intensity level and the exposure to the noise is long enough, then permanent damage to hearing can result.

Q What other kinds of noises can cause loss of hearing?

A Surprisingly, many possible sources of noise-induced hearing loss may be in your own home. I'm talking about noise from power lawn mowers, chain saws—even some garbage disposals, dishwashers and vacuum cleaners. Most people don't realize how loud these devices can get.

---

*Dr. Wesley H. Bradley, 53, heads a special program on communicative disorders at the National Institutes of Health. He was a practicing otolaryngologist—dealing with disorders of ear, nose and throat—for two decades as well as a clinical professor at State University of New York in Syracuse before coming to NIH in 1975. He has served as president of the American Otological Society. His article is reprinted from *U.S. News and World Report*, May 3, 1976.

Q Parents are continually warning their children that they'll hurt their hearing by listening to loud rock music. Are they right?

A Yes. Rock music can very definitely be a cause of hearing loss, and the practice of young people in amplifying it excessively is particularly bad. It can really damage your ears. As a matter of fact, the Institute [National Institute of Neurological and Communicative Disorders and Stroke] recently supported an interesting study in this area. Researchers took some chinchillas—small animals often used in experiments on noise exposure—and put them in a discotheque where they were exposed to the same amount of music that people listen to for a number of nights.

When the inner ears of the chinchillas were examined, one could see definite changes indicating permanent damage that would be consistent with noise-induced loss of hearing.

We have found, incidentally, that the most frequent victims of this type of hearing loss are the musicians themselves, as they are exposed to the noise over long periods and often in confined areas.

Q How many people in this country suffer from hearing problems?

A Between 14 and 15 million people have a significant hearing handicap—one that interferes with everyday communication.

Of this number, nearly half a million are profoundly deaf. They cannot hear even with the most powerful hearing aid, and have to resort entirely to speech reading or other aids to communication.

Q Can hearing problems be inherited?

A Yes. There are many different types of hearing loss with a heredity factor involved. One example is a condition called "otosclerosis." This affects the bone structure of the ear and tends to be passed down through families, sometimes entirely skipping a generation. It is more common in females, though we don't know why.

Q Do you find more women than men suffer from hearing trouble?

A It's the other way around, in fact. Slightly more men than women have hearing loss, but the difference is not significantly great.

Q Is age a factor in hearing loss?

A Yes, indeed. The age factor is most important. What most people don't realize is that the effect of aging on our hearing often starts earlier than we think.

We used to believe that hearing loss due to age didn't begin until we got into our sixties. That's not true. It starts much sooner than that. Most of us are showing some hearing loss that can be clinically measured by the time we are in our forties—certainly by our early fifties.

Q What sounds do we miss first?

A Usually the high-frequency sounds are the first ones lost as we grow older. For this reason, people forty-five or older who are so concerned about getting a high-fidelity record player to reproduce the very highest frequencies might as well forget it. They probably aren't going to be able to hear those sounds anyway.

For the same reason, wives of men in this age bracket should have patience if their husbands occasionally fail to hear them talking. The wife's higher-pitched voice is simply more difficult for the husband to hear.

Q Besides noise, what are some of the other common causes of hearing loss?

A Accidents and injuries frequently damage the hearing system. Any type of blow on the head, for instance, can result in a loss of hearing. It can be permanent, too.

Children who are slapped on the ear can suffer a ruptured eardrum. Fortunately, such an injury will often mend itself or can be surgically repaired.

Q What about diseases?

A Certain diseases do result in hearing loss. If a pregnant woman contracts rubella—German measles—in her first three months of pregnancy, the hearing of the unborn child may be affected.

Mumps also can cause hearing loss, and almost any of the viral diseases can affect the inner ear.

Q We've heard about a disease called "Meniere's syndrome." What is its connection with impaired hearing?

A Meniere's disease is an imbalance of fluids in the inner ear that can affect both hearing and the sense of balance. It's a disorder that usually occurs in early adult to middle life. Often it will be accompanied by a ringing in the ears—what we call "tinnitus."

As a result of overaccumulation of inner-ear fluid, the patient will experience a loss of hearing that comes and goes. Most often the disease is progressive and involves imbalance or dizziness that can be almost disabling.

We don't know exactly what causes Meniere's disease, although it's generally felt that, in many instances, the overall metabolic system of the body is involved. In some cases, however, it can start from problems within the ear itself.

The usual treatment is a medical program aimed at preventing a build-up of inner-ear fluid. In those cases where such medical treatment is not effective, surgical procedures can be used.

Q What are the early symptoms of hearing loss?

A Very often the first indication is that a person notices that he's missing parts of conversations. It is most evident when there is some sort of distracting background noise—talking, music or whatever.

Q Is ringing in the ears a sign of hearing problems?

A Usually, yes. In fact, many people will be aware of the ringing in their ears before they are aware of the fact that they are losing some sense of hearing. With individuals who develop a loss in the nerve part of the ear, there almost always is a ringing sensation.

Q Does the ringing go on constantly?

A It often is a constant thing, but it will fluctuate as the individual fluctuates. When the patient is working hard and under tension, he'll notice it more. If he relaxes and plays golf or something he especially enjoys, it may be less apparent to him. But if he stops and listens, the ringing is still there.

We don't usually realize it, but there is a certain noise level or sound in our ears all the time. If we get into a quiet enough place, we can hear it.

I often use this analogy with my patients: If you're driving along in your car and the engine is well tuned, you hear the engine and yet you don't hear it. But if something goes wrong and you suddenly develop a knock in that engine, then all you hear is the knock. The same thing happens when the functioning of the inner ear changes.

Q Does this ringing sensation bother people much?

A Oh, yes.

In most cases, no matter how loud the sound is in a person's ear, only they can hear it. I've had patients tell me: "Put your ear up against my ear. You've got to be able to hear that ringing." Well, ordinarily you can't hear it, and in some ways that bothers the person even more.

The ringing sensation is *very* disconcerting to people who don't realize what is happening. It can be quite frightening. Some people worry that it may mean an impending stroke or a brain tumor.

In fact, it usually means none of these things. But, most important, it serves to bring people to a doctor, who can give them a careful examination to determine the cause of the ringing and advise them accordingly.

Q Discovering that your hearing is going bad can be a pretty severe psychological shock—

A It can. And it can affect not only the person concerned but his entire family. Take the child who has been born deaf. This inflicts a total change on the life of that child's family. Say that they've had two other normal children, and suddenly they have a child who is totally deaf. Often the parents either direct all their attention to the deaf child, or they shun him completely.

It can be just as tragic at the other end of the calendar. Some of the hardest things we see are what happens psychologically to older people as they begin to lose their hearing. Take a person who has been very vigorous and active. All of a sudden he finds that he's not hearing as well. He's afraid that he's going to make mistakes, so he begins to pull away from people. Pretty soon he's not certain of himself, and as time goes on he may withdraw completely from contact with others.

Or we'll see the opposite. An older person with hearing loss may overcompensate. He'll hide behind bravado and conceal the fact that he's not hearing. He can make a fool of himself in many situations.

All these people need counseling, support and understanding.

Q Can deafness be faked, or perhaps originate from mental instead of physical causes?

A Yes. Most ear doctors will see some of these patients, although not a large number.

In today's society, the potential of financial gain can be the basis for pretending to have hearing loss. We always have to be aware of that possibility. Usually, though, we soon become suspicious, and proper testing can uncover a faker.

At the other extreme are the so-called functional losses of hearing that are not done intentionally. I have seen many of these. Very often it will be a child whose teachers think he has a hearing problem. At first, tests seem to indicate that there is a hearing loss. But everything isn't quite right, and as you get into it, you can pretty well demonstrate that something else is going on.

It may be a child who feels that he's been neglected—that another member of the family is getting all the attention. This is his way of getting people to notice him.

Once recognized, these types of cases are reversible, although it isn't always easy to handle the psychological problems.

Q While we're on children: Is hearing loss among them much of a problem?

A It's a very major problem if it is not recognized early in the child's educational process. Poor hearing immediately puts a child at a disadvantage. Fortunately, most schools today have screening procedures that are quite effective in picking out the youngsters with problems.

Why Some Babies May Be Born Deaf

Q Can newborn infants be tested for hearing trouble?

A We're beginning to learn techniques which can screen babies in hospital nurseries. It's not a matter of routine yet, but I think eventually it will be in most hospitals.

Already, though, the high-risk infants are being checked in many hospitals for possible hearing loss. These are the babies whose mothers have had problems during pregnancy, whose parents may have incompatible Rh blood factors, or a child who experienced a difficult delivery. Any premature infant—one born a month or six weeks early—is definitely a high-risk child so far as hearing is concerned.

If the hearing problem is mechanical—that is, in the outer ear—there is a very good probability that something can be done for him at the proper time. It may have to wait a few years while the child grows, but it usually can be helped. But if the trouble is in the nerve part of the ear of a newborn infant, unfortunately at the present time we can't do much to correct the hearing loss. A program of special education should be started as early as practical for such a child.

Q Are there different kinds of hearing loss, Doctor?

A Yes, there are two main types of hearing loss. They are very different, and the medical approach to treating them also is different. It's important to understand this, so I'll take a minute to explain:

Think of the ear as a two-part system. The outer part is primarily a mechanical system which picks up and conducts sound waves through the ear canal to the eardrum, causing the eardrum to vibrate. The drum is attached to three little bones—the hammer, anvil and stirrup—which transmit the sound to the interface of the inner ear. So we have the transmission of sound energy from outside the body to the inner ear with an increase in intensity but without distortion.

Then we have the inner part, or the nerve system. At the junction of the two systems there is the transfer of sound energy from an air medium in the outer ear to a fluid medium in the inner ear. Inside the inner ear, the sound creates a wave in the fluid that stimulates thousands of sensory cells called hair cells. These are very specialized cells which convert the mechanical energy into electrical energy—nerve impulses—by means of a biochemical process. Precisely how this process works is still not completely known, and it may hold the answer to many of our as-yet-unanswered questions about the ear.

The resulting nerve impulses are transmitted along the hearing nerve into the brain for interpretation, processing, storage, recall, and so on. This remarkable process takes place every time we "hear" something.

Q And there are different types of hearing loss that affect the outer and inner ear—

A Exactly. Some types of hearing loss occur entirely in the mechanical part of the ear, some only in the nerve part of the ear, or we can have a combination of both.

Q What sort of loss happens in the outer ear?

A One of the simplest kinds is a blockage of the ear canal, say by a plug of wax. Or it could be a hole in the eardrum caused by poking something into your ear. It might be an infection that ruptures that eardrum, which then fails to heal. The condition I mentioned before—otosclerosis—produces a growth of bone around the stirrup, and blocks its movement.

Almost all of these mechanical problems can be treated medically or surgically with an excellent chance of improving or restoring hearing.

Q What about hearing loss in the inner ear?

A That's where the serious problems come in. Most types of hearing loss that occur in the inner ear cannot be restored. These include noise-induced loss and the hearing loss that occurs with advancing age.

These hearing losses due to problems in the inner ear, unfortunately, are the more common kinds of hearing problems.

Q Can hearing loss in the inner ear due to age be improved?

A Not by medical or surgical means. However, the hearing ability can very often be improved with use of a properly fitted hearing aid. Usually hearing loss caused by age comes on very slowly, and we tend to adapt to it quite well. But, no, it can't be reversed.

A Caution on Use of Medicines

Q What else besides noise and age can lead to hearing problems?

A Many people aren't aware of it, but certain medications can cause hearing loss. These medications can destroy the hair cells we talked about in the inner ear. Some of the antibiotics can have this effect. Streptomycins, for instance, are known hazards in this area. Diuretic agents—the water pills—have the potential to damage hearing. Quinine, which fortunately isn't used much any more, has long been known to cause hearing loss.

Now, remember that doctors know about the side effects of the drugs that we're talking about. Often these drugs are essential, even life-saving. That's why it's so important for people not to take drugs without consulting with their physician, and then to follow the directions carefully as to dosage, etc. Any change in hearing or ringing in the ears while a patient is on a medication should be reported to the physician.

Q What are the common treatments for loss of hearing?

A For losses in the mechanical part of the ear, where surgery is possible, most people prefer surgery to using a hearing aid. But some people will say that they don't want an operation, that they'd rather wear a hearing aid. Fine. This should be the patient's choice once the situation is explained and clearly understood.

By and large, however, most people prefer to have surgery. Some of the most grateful patients I have been involved with are individuals who have worn a hearing aid for a long time and found that they could have an operation and get rid of it. The hearing quality is different when you hear naturally through your ear than the artificial sound coming through a hearing aid.

As far as people with a loss in the nerve part of the ear, they don't have much choice. If they're going to do anything, they have to use the hearing aid. We just don't have medical or surgical means to improve their hearing at the present time.

Q Are surgery and hearing aids the only two choices? What about drugs?

A There are not many cases where drugs are particularly helpful in restoring lost hearing. A few exceptions do exist.

One example is the person with a hypothyroid condition. One of the symptoms of that is impaired hearing, and it can be reversed in some cases by medication. Again, this is why it's so important for anyone with a hearing problem to get a thorough physical examination. Sometimes the ear may be only an indicator of a problem elsewhere in the body.

Q What about antibiotics for earaches?

A These are very effective, when properly prescribed by a physician, in controlling ear infections. They certainly prevent a lot of hearing loss that occurred in days gone by.

You may remember that mastoid operations were very common years ago. This was simply a surgical drainage of an infected ear to prevent further spread of infection. Sometimes the patient was in a hospital for six weeks and ended up with a large depressed area behind his ear. Antibiotics help avoid this, and we rarely see that type of a mastoidectomy today.

Other types of mastoid surgery are still required today, however.

Q You have mentioned hearing aids. Are they always helpful if surgery or other remedies are impossible?

A Not always—but in many cases, yes. There may be a few instances where a person should not wear a hearing aid. If a person needs help with his hearing and it can't be done by medical or surgical treatment, then a hearing aid certainly should be considered and proper evaluation done in an attempt to determine its usefulness.

Pitfalls in Getting a Hearing Aid

Q Can you just walk into a store and buy a hearing aid?

A You can, but I don't think this is the wisest policy for most people to follow. That doesn't mean that some people don't just shop around and find a hearing aid with which they are happy. But generally a person with a loss of hearing should initially be examined by an ear doctor.

In certain cases the doctor may recommend additional hearing evaluation by an audiologist. The hearing problem may originate from trouble other than in the ear, and just wearing a hearing aid could divert attention from the real trouble.

Q What's the biggest drawback with hearing aids?

A The biggest problem is that people don't understand what a hearing aid is and what it isn't. They don't understand what it can do and what it can't do.

A hearing aid, no matter what anyone tells you, is one thing—and one thing only: It's a mechanical amplifier. It's going to bring sound into your ear. A hearing aid of better quality will not distort that sound, and it may amplify some parts more than others. But essentially it is still primarily an amplifier.

Our natural hearing is more than that. It has a factor of intensity—bringing the sound in and getting it into the ear at a loud-enough level so we can appreciate it. In addition, there is the factor of discrimination—the ability to separate sounds and make possible the understanding of words.

There are some types of hearing problems where the individual has lost so much ability to discriminate that he's going to have a lot of trouble in understanding, no matter how carefully you amplify it. But too many people don't know this. An individual will pay a good price for a hearing aid and afterward report: "I can hear everything twice as loud, but I can't understand the words any better."

You have to demonstrate to such a person how he can use a hearing aid to maximum effect and what its limitations are. But most important, he must know two things: (1) that no hearing aid available will allow him to hear like he used to, and (2) if he works with the aid and accepts it for what it can do, time will help in its usefulness to him.

Q Dr. Bradley, are there any promising developments in prevention and treatment of hearing loss?

A Yes, in several areas. Modern vaccines for rubella, mumps and other viral infections now help reduce incidence of diseases which lead to hearing loss. Research in genetics could eliminate a great many hearing problems that now are inherited.

A great deal depends on what we discover about the workings of the inner ear—the still-unsolved parts of the basic process of transmitting mechanical energy into nerve impulses through biochemical changes. Once we get a better understanding of this, we will have a base to work from that, hopefully, will lead to therapy on the inner ear.

Outlook for Ear Implants

Q What are you looking for?

A One thing we're trying to learn is how the ear "encodes" messages to the brain. It's like getting a photograph from a satellite circling Mars. The satellite doesn't send a picture—just a lot of shades of gray dots that you put together into a picture. We feel that the ear sends something like that in the nerve impulse.

Much attention has been called to work under way involving the possibility of implanting a device within the ear to electrically stimulate the nerve endings of the ear. Such a system, if found feasible, would be *only* for those individuals with a profound or total loss of hearing who retain sufficient functioning nerve endings within the ear.

So far, trials with such a system have demonstrated no ability to transmit words or speech meaning as we know it. Electrical stimulation does produce a sensation—not true hearing—which, after a long period of practice and relearning, some individuals have been able to use as an alerting mechanism to help communication.

Further research in this area is ongoing, but at this time it is not yet a solution for restoring hearing to the many millions afflicted with a serious hearing loss.

Q Is much research going on related to hearing, and how is it supported?

A The major source of support for research on the ear and hearing in this country is through the communicative-disorders program of the National Institute of Neurological and Communicative Disorders and Stroke. Such work is ongoing both in the laboratories at NIH and institutions distributed throughout the country. We're still learning about the ear, and there is a lot of work yet to be done.*

Education of the Hearing Impaired

Ewing (1960) indicated that because of the problems involved, it is preferable to educate deaf and hard-of-hearing children in separate rooms or by different means. The differentiation between deaf and hard-of-hearing children is usually based upon the ability to learn and understand speech. Totally deaf children must depend almost entirely on visual and other cues. Children with some residual hearing need auditory training in order to make maximum use of their hearing. The mixing of hard-of-hearing children with deaf children may cause the hard-of-hearing children to manifest deaf characteristics and fail to use their residual hearing.

Some deaf children need special devices which offer amplification systems. The classroom should be designed to reduce sounds which interfere with amplification of desired sounds. Walls, ceiling, floors, and other openings must be specially designed or treated for this purpose. The location of the room is also important in reducing or eliminating extraneous, distracting noises. Special soundproofing materials should be used on the walls and ceilings. Lighting is another consideration in the special class, because deaf or hard-of-hearing children must depend on visual cues for much of their learning. The Oklahoma *Policies and Procedures Manual* (1976) recommended the following equipment for classroom use with deaf or hard-of-hearing children:

1. All the equipment provided in the regular classroom
2. Sense training equipment: Montessori equipment or a suitable substitute; colored yarn, balls, or ribbon for matching color; children's jigsaw puzzles

3. Equipment used in teaching speech reading; small table and chair so the teacher may sit with her lips on eye level with the child

4. Equipment for instruction in reading and other visual subject matter; chart racks for picture and word charts, picture cards; picture dictionaries; textbooks with simple language and large print; opaque projector; slide or film projector; 16mm projector; bulletin boards on children's eye levels

5. Piano

6. Records for acoustic training

7. Instruments for rhythms; bells, drums, cymbals, horn, tambourines, etc.

8. Television

9. Work books

10. Audiometer—pure-tone

Hard-of-hearing children in the regular classroom should have a learning aid if necessary and should be seated close to the teacher so that they can use lipreading skills. The use of concrete objects whenever possible helps the hard-of-hearing child grasp abstract ideas. Pictures may also be used to illustrate the meanings of words, especially if they are similar in sound.

A classroom that consists only of hearing-impaired children may use a group hearing aid which stimulates both ears. Also, tape recorders and record players with which intensity level can be controlled may be beneficial in auditory training. Although there are special visual aids designed for use with the aurally handicapped, the teacher can also make materials based on the needs of the children.

At Oralingua School in Whittier, California (Duffield 1980), hearing-impaired children receive specific training in social survival skills. This training provides competencies necessary for group participation. According to Duffield, all of these skills are written into every instructional plan. The skills are essential for successful mainstreaming at any level. The skills and emphasis for their development are briefly discussed below.

1. *Attending Skills* Learning to receive and use input from the environment is essential. An example is learning to attend to a speaker in a group situation. This level is the foundation for all other skill development. It requires the child to watch and listen as well as attend to all facets of the environment including verbal and nonverbal stimuli.

2. *Spontaneous Interaction Skills* This area of skill development focuses on training the child to initiate interactions. Learning communication skills, listening to their peers' contributions, and learning to become comfortable in contributing ideas to discussions are stressed.

3. *Communication Clarification Skills* The training in this area helps the child to ask freely for repetition of specific parts of any misunderstood

communication. Hearing-impaired children do not learn this skill automatically and must be taught to ask such questions as, "Where did you say to put our papers when we are finished?" In other words, such children need training in asking for repetition of a specific idea rather than for a total repeat of the idea or direction given.

4. *Social Skills* The skills developed in this area include learning how to converse skillfully, which includes making eye contact, waiting for a response, and responding appropriately. Social skill development also provides specific training in learning to take one's turn, gaining permission to speak, sharing personal belongings, helping others, and giving compliments.

The emphasis on skill development should assist the hearing impaired to become more proficient in communication skills as well as improving adjustment to life.

How effective are hearing aids in the schools? In a sample of 102 hearing aids which were evaluated according to ANSI standards, 38 percent were functioning inappropriately and 4 percent were missing entirely. The 102 hearing aids were worn by 98 children in the Detroit metropolitan area, and 38 percent of these children were reported to wear them in school only.

As a result of this survey conducted by Robinson and Sterling (1980), one may question the orientation programs that should assist hearing-impaired children to wear their hearing aids.

The study of Robinson and Sterling also presented data regarding parental ratings of their child's progress in school and the actual progress of the children. The findings indicated that 91 percent of the parents were satisfied with the progress being made even though over 40 percent of the hearing aids were malfunctioning and 20 percent of the children had failed at least one grade. In addition 30 percent of the malfunctioning aids were worn by children who had failed in school.

Robinson and Sterling recommend that educational audiologists should play an active role in hearing aid orientation and parent counseling. In addition, hearing aids should be evaluated on site periodically. Caution should be used in mainstreaming hearing-impaired children because of the high incidence of malfunctioning hearing aids, the distortion received through hearing aids in regular class settings, and because only less-than-maximum speech discrimination is possible with hearing aids in the regular classroom.

There have been many approaches used in the education of hearing-impaired children. The basic principles of human learning include various inputs such as visual, auditory, and motor stimuli and communication through verbal expression and many forms of nonverbal expression such as body language, facial gestures, and hand movements. The hearing impaired should also be permitted to learn and express themselves through a variety of approaches or methods. However, some approaches have stressed the auditory method of instruction and excluded other approaches. The auditory method requires that the child learn primarily through the development of listening skills. Another program might stress the oral method of instruction. This method requires that the child learn through speech reading, amplification of sound, and expression through speech. According to Moores, Weiss, and Goodman (1973) the Total Communication Method is the best approach for the education of the hearing-impaired child. This approach includes the simultaneous use of residual hearing, speech reading, amplification of sound, and the use of fingerspelling and signs. It also emphasizes verbal expression. In essence, this approach involves presenting learning in a variety of ways and permits the hearing impaired to use verbal and manual expression as a means of communication. A very comprehensive approach to the education of these children may be found in Lowenbraun, Appelman, and Callahan (1980).

Residential Facilities
The residential school was one of the first facilities for educating deaf children. Several residential schools are in operation, but there has been a decrease in the number of children being sent to such special schools. Deaf children, like other children, need contact with the hearing environment.

There are advantages and disadvantages associated with special programs and the needs of each child must always be considered. The trend today, however, is for the aurally impaired child to remain in the community and attend the public schools.

Community Services
Lunde and Bogman (1959) indicated that the aurally handicapped are employed in almost all major occupational areas. However, there are usually fewer in the higher professional, managerial, and clerical and sales areas, which may be because of the greater demand for communication skills in those occupations. A larger proportion of this group is employed in the crafts or in semiskilled employment, and a smaller proportion work as unskilled laborers. There are indications that approximately 85 percent of deaf workers have successful vocational careers.

Every state has a vocational division responsible for training or working with the hearing handicapped to prepare them to become self-supporting. A list of occupations for which these people can train may be obtained from the United States Office of Education, Vocational Division. Similar information may also be obtained by inquiring at local state offices of rehabilitation.

Special Training for Teachers
Once again, teachers who work with deaf or hard-of-hearing children must have a good general educational background. In addition, they should be competent in the areas of parent education, special techniques, methods and

materials necessary in educating the hearing impaired, and in cooperating with other professionals involved in the educational program. They must be aware of the physical and emotional demands often present when working with exceptional children.

Teachers who work in special schools may be required to meet the state's certification requirements for special education. Special training in methods and techniques for teaching the aurally impaired, as well as experience in working with exceptional children, may be required.

Because many hard-of-hearing children are enrolled in the regular public classroom, the regular teacher may be called upon to become oriented to their needs. Certain suggestions are found in Cruickshank and Johnson:

1. Handicapped children should be placed close to the teacher with their backs to the light so they can use visual clues.
2. The teacher must make sure of the child's attention before giving assignments or directions.
3. The teacher may need to rephrase a new idea in several different ways when it is first presented.
4. Other children should be helped to understand the handicap.
5. Handicapped children should be included in as many extracurricular activities as their classmates so that they feel that they belong to the group.

Study Questions

1. Discuss how contemporary living conditions influence hearing.
2. Discuss the most common types of visual impairments.
3. Contact your local or state agency or association which serves the visually impaired and discuss the services offered and how a person qualifies for them.
4. Among children who are visually impaired or hearing impaired, which group is the most educationally deprived? Discuss and defend your position.
5. What are the differences in the services provided by an optometrist, an opthalmologist, and an optician?
6. What are the differences in the services provided by an audiologist and an otologist?
7. Discuss the services and equipment available to assist the visually impaired in mobility, reading, and daily living.
8. List the types of modifications of educational services and resource materials for the blind or partially sighted child.

9. From library research, discuss the problems parents of the newborn deaf child will encounter and the types of services required for them.
10. Discuss ways a regular classroom teacher may become aware of hearing or sight problems which are undetected or not diagnosed.

Bibliography

"A Program of Education for the Exceptional Children in Oklahoma." 1976. S.E. Bulletin no. 10, prepared by the Special Education Section and the Oklahoma Curriculum Commission.

Barnett, M. R. 1955. "Current Problems of the Blind." *Special Education for the Exceptional,* vol. 2, ed. M. E. Frampton and E. D. Gall. Boston: Porter Sargent Publishers.

Bradley, Wesley H. 1976. "How Modern Life Can Damage Your Hearing." *U.S. News and World Report,* (May 3).

Buell, Charles. 1950. "Motor Performance of Visually Handicapped Children." *Journal of Exceptional Children* 17 (December).

Cruickshank, William M., and Johnson, G. Orville, eds. 1975. *Education of Exceptional Children and Youth.* 3rd ed. Englewood Cliffs, N.J.: Prentice-Hall.

Curry, E. T. 1954. "Are Teachers Good Judges of Pupils' Hearing?" *Journal of Exceptional Children* 21.

Dalton, M. M. 1943. "A Visual Survey of 5,000 School Children." *Journal of Educational Research* 37.

Davis, Hallowell, and Silverman, R. Richard, eds. 1970. *Hearing and Deafness.* 3rd ed. New York: Holt, Rinehart & Winston.

Dickstein, Cynthia. 1976. "Mobility for the Blind Child." *The Exceptional Parent* 6, no. 2.

Duffield, Janice. 1980. "Skills and Strategies for Preparing a Hearing Impaired Child for Participation in a Group." *Volta Review* 82, no. 1 (January).

Dunn, Lloyd M., ed. 1973. *Exceptional Children in the Schools: Special Education in Transition.* 2d ed. New York: Holt, Rinehart & Winston.

Ewing, A. G., ed. 1960. *The Modern Educational Treatment of Deafness.* Washington, D.C.: The Volta Bureau.

Hoover, Richard E. 1964. "Toward a New Definition of Blindness." *Blindness.*

Lowenbraun, Sheila; Appelman, Karen I.; and Callahan, Judy Lee. 1980. *Teaching the Hearing Impaired.* Columbus, Ohio: Charles E. Merrill.

Lunde, A. S., and Bogman, S. K. 1959. *Occupational Conditions among the Deaf.* Washington, D.C.: Gallaudet College Press.

Moores, Donald F.; Weiss, Karen L.; and Goodwin, Marilyn W. 1973. "Receptive Abilities of Deaf Children across Five Modes of Communication." *Exceptional Children* 40, no. 1 (September).

Moss, J. W.; Moss, M.; and Tizard, J. 1961. "Electrodermal Response Audiometry with Mentally Defective Children." *Journal of Speech and Hearing Research* 4.

Mulvihill, John F., Jr., ed. 1979. "New Directions in Employment Opportunities." *Newsletter of the American Foundation for the Blind* 14, no. 3 (October).

Newby, Hayes A. 1964. *Audiology.* 2d ed. New York: Appleton-Century-Crofts.

O'Neill, John J. 1964. *The Hard of Hearing.* Englewood Cliffs, N.J.: Prentice-Hall.

Pauls, Miriam D., and Hardy, William G. 1953. "Hearing Impairment in Preschool-Age Children." *Laryngoscope* 63 (June).

Policies and Procedures Manual for Special Education in Oklahoma. 1981. Oklahoma City: The Oklahoma State Department of Education.

Robinson, Dale O., and Sterling, Gail R. 1980 "Hearing Aids and Children in School: A Follow-Up Study." *Volta Review* 82, no. 4 (May).

Simmons, F. Blair. 1980. "Diagnosis and Rehabilitation of Deaf Newborns: Part II." *Journal of the American Speech-Language-Hearing Association* 22, no. 7 (July).

Telford, Charles W., and Sawrey, James M. 1977. *The Exceptional Individual.* 3rd ed. Englewood Cliffs, N.J.: Prentice-Hall.

Wilson, John. 1965. "The Blind in a Changing World: The Extent, Causes, and Distribution of Blindness." *Blindness.*

Winebrenner, D. K. 1952. "Finding the Visually Inadequate Child." *Visual Digest* 16.

Wyks, Howard. 1970. "Deaf Children are Disadvantaged." Paper read at Vocational Special Education Workshop at Texas Tech University (June).

speech and language disorders

Definitions of Speech Impairment

"Speech is defective when it deviates so far from the speech of other people that it calls attention to itself, interferes with communication, or causes its possessor to be maladjusted" (Van Riper 1978). In order for speech to be defective, there must be a listener who makes such a judgment. Speech that is conspicuous may depend on the age of the individual involved. Young children, when learning how to talk, make many types of speech errors such as, "wabbit" instead of "rabbit." If the same types of errors were made consistently by older children or adults, their speech would be considered defective. Adults suffering certain types of mental or physical shock following a severe accident, or war action, may develop speech impairments. Thus, it is possible for a speech defect to arise at any time in life.

If the way a person speaks (such as using a peculiar vocal quality, hestitations, or distortions) causes a lack of communication, that speech may be unintelligible or defective. Facial contortions, often seen in the child who stutters or the person with cerebral palsy, may also be considered defects. The listener may be paying more attention to the facial distortions than to what is being said. In cerebral palsy, the inability to control facial muscles may interfere with articulation, which may cause several problems that impede communication. The individual who is unable to talk may develop systems or gestures to replace words. However, if another person were not in constant contact with this type or gesturing, it would be very difficult to interpret this method of communication. Therefore, the impaired person's effective communication is limited.

Speech is also considered defective when speakers become so self-conscious that they become handicapped socially or vocationally. Emotions can greatly affect the flow of speech and the ability to communicate. Children who stutter often become so concerned about their speech problems that they avoid situations where they must speak. This often creates another emotional problem, and a vicious cycle is set in motion. Similar reactions may be observed in those with other speech difficulties.

Another definition cited by Telford and Sawrey (1977) offered similar implications regarding defective speech. "Speech is considered to be defective when the manner of speaking interferes with communication, when the manner of speaking distracts attention from what is said, or when speech is such that the speaker is unduly self-conscious or apprehensive about speaking." Once again the listener's interpretation plays an important part in determining whether or not speech is defective, except in the instance where the speaker is too concerned to be able to communicate.

Estimates of Prevalence

It is difficult to pinpoint the prevalence of speech disorders, usually because of the different criteria used by investigators, the areas sampled, and the interpretation of what constitutes defective speech. In general, however, we estimate that from 5 to 10 percent of all school children have some type of speech impairment.

Telford and Sawrey (1977) cited findings by two committees of the American Speech and Hearing Association (1952, 1959) which independently estimated that a minimum of 5 percent of school-age children have defects sufficiently serious to warrant speech correction or therapy, and that an additional 5 percent suffer from noticeable but less serious defects. We do not believe that a percentage breakdown of the different types of defects would be pertinent because of the rapidly changing population and the availability of services for handicapped children.

Methods of Identification

Many indications of speech defects may be discussed by parents or classroom teachers. These cases should be referred to speech and hearing clinics or other professional people. Systematic speech screening procedures are used in most public schools, but thorough diagnostic evaluations are usually made when a more severe type of speech defect is involved. A battery of tests, including a complete physical and dental examination, an assessment of intellectual level, an audiometric evaluation of hearing, and, in some cases, a psychiatric examination should be given.

Telford and Sawrey (1977) reported that there are several scales and tests used to screen speech or aid in assessment. Some of these are the Wood Index of Defective Articulation, The Templin-Darley Screening and Diagnostic Tests of Articulation, and the Boston University Speech Sound Discrimination Picture Test. There are also specially scaled phonographic recordings of defective speech available. These are graded in terms of severity and the individual's speech may be compared with the samples.

Characteristics of the Speech Impaired

In some cases, those with speech defects have other disabilities. Children with more severe speech problems include the mentally retarded, brain-damaged, or those with structural deformities such as cleft palate or cleft lip.

However, there is another group of children whose only problems are their speech impairments. They are otherwise physically and intellectually normal.

Although most people with a speech defect are found to be physically normal, generally 10–15 percent of those with the more serious speech defects also have other physical disabilities. On tests of motor proficiency, children with a speech impairment perform slightly below normal children (Jenkins and Lohr 1964).

The incidence of speech defects is higher for children who are either visually or aurally handicapped. Children with speech defects generally seem to have difficulty in the area of language proficiency, which may affect their overall intelligence. Some evidence possibly shows that these children frequently fall below the norm in measured intelligence, because speech defects are more commonly associated with mental retardation. A person must have a certain intellectual capacity to be able to learn proficient speech.

Speech disorders are often accompanied by emotional problems. In a society that values oral communication, the child with a noticeable speech defect is sometimes heavily penalized or rejected. The one group that is most markedly affected is the stutterer. Children with other types of speech disorders are sometimes ridiculed by those who do not understand the problems. It should be noted that children with speech problems resulting from emotional trauma should receive emotional therapy primarily, and speech therapy secondarily.

We believe that readers should be aware of normal speech developmental patterns and the different characteristics of defective speech. Therefore, the following descriptions are offered only as introductions to impaired speech. Further study in these areas may be pursued in speech and hearing courses.

Speech Development

Speech development begins with the birth cry. In the early months of life, the baby begins to experiment with sounds, producing a majority of vowel sounds. This also is a time when the muscles, as well as the lungs, needed for later speech are exercised and strengthened. Swallowing is also used to develop the skills necessary for the production of certain speech sounds, such as *k* and the *g.*

The stage of babbling begins early, usually around the eighth week. This stage consists of the production of various vowel sounds and consonant sounds such as the *g, b,* and *m.* These sounds are fairly easy to produce and are a part of the gurgling and other sounds made by the baby. This vocal play is easily reinforced by attention from others. Babbling continues until about the fifth to sixth month when vocal play begins to become more purposive. Sound production is also pleasing to the child, although a majority of the speech sounds uttered are randomly selected. The child doesn't need to be able to hear in order to enter this stage of speech development.

During the second six months of life the child begins to repeat heard sounds, and the lalling stage in speech development is begun. Sound production is associated with hearing, and by producing sound a child is beginning to learn how to control the environment through speech.

The echolalia stage usually begins during the ninth or tenth month. During the lalling stage children are inclined to repeat sounds that they have heard themselves make. During the echolalia stage, they begin to imitate sounds they have heard others make. Their repertoire is increasing and they are able to form more sound combinations. Hearing acuity is vital to this stage of development, because children must be able to hear sounds produced by others in order to develop speech.

True speech generally appears around twelve to eighteen months. Children are able to make certain sound combinations at will and do so for a purpose. They are also able to comprehend certain speech such as "no-no," and will respond motorically. Beginning vocabulary usually consists of nouns which are important to the child. Later, verbs enter the vocabulary, followed by adjectives and adverbs. Pronouns are next with articles and prepositions coming last. Parts of speech, though, are often omitted or used incorrectly as the child begins to learn language. By the age of one year, the child should have a vocabulary consisting of two to three words. By age two the vocabulary should contain nearly 300 words, and the child should be able to put together simple two- or three-word sentences. The acquisition of vocabulary then increases rapidly. The three-year-old child should have a vocabulary of approximately 800–900 words. At age six, growth in vocabulary generally slows down.

Articulatory Defects

Defects in articulation are the most prevalent of the speech disorders. Errors in articulation are characterized by omissions, substitutions, distortions, and additions of speech sounds. Although many such errors are common among children who are just learning to talk, speech is considered defective if errors persist at a later age. It is felt that a child should be capable of producing all the speech sounds (consonant and vowel sounds, including blends, diphthongs, etc.) accurately by the age of seven to seven and one-half, unless there is some physiological or psychological cause, such as defects in the articulators (larynx, teeth, tongue, lips, hard palate, soft palate, jaws, or nasal cavity) or a fear of communicating with others.

Omission of speech sounds occur when a child leaves out a sound in a word, such as pay for play, or pease for please. Such errors are very common in young children who are not yet capable of blending two consonant sounds. Certain sounds may also be omitted from the beginning, middle, or end of words.

Substitutions of speech sounds involve the replacement of one consonant sound for another. For example, children may substitute the *w* for the *r* sound in the word *rabbit*. Some children may be able to produce a sound in one word, yet substitute another sound for the same sound in another word. For example, children may be able to say the word, *yes,* correctly, but substitute the *l* for the *y* sound in the word *yellow*. They may substitute the *f* for the *th* in the word, *tooth,* and the *p* for the *f* in the word, *fork*. Such errors are often inconsistent in that the child may be able to produce the sound, but has not stabilized the use of the sound in speaking.

Distortions of sounds are probably most noticeable in children who are said to have a lisp. The sibilant sounds, *s* and *z,* usually take on a mushy characteristic. In a frontal lisp, the voiced or unvoiced *th* sound is also substituted for the *s* or *z* sounds. In the lateral lisp, air is forced out the sides of the mouth and the *s* and *z* take on the characteristics of the *sh* or *zh* sounds.

Another type of distortion is referred to as lalling. In this case the *r* and the *l* sounds are usually affected, because of misplacement of the tongue. However, the *t* and *d* sounds may also be affected. Distorted sounds are often caused by improper manipulation of the articulators, possibly caused by poor learning.

Some children may attempt to add a sound to a word. For example, the word, *please,* may become *puhlease,* the word, *hanger,* may become *hangger*. This type of error frequently occurs in words that have blends.

Be aware that omissions, substitutions, distortions, or additions of speech sounds may occur in either the initial, medial, or final position in a word, or may occur consistently in all three positions. Errors in articulation often may appear to be very inconsistent.

Some of the causes of articulatory defects may be attributed to poor speech models in the home or environment, mental retardation, poor muscle coordination or control, emotional conflicts, organic anomalies, structural defects involving the articulators, or hearing impairments and auditory perception difficulties.

Winitz (1977) provided a discussion of the complications in describing and treating articulation disorders. Disciplines which have contributed to the study of articulation disorders include modern phonological theory, models of the speech motor control system, and behavioral analysis. There is some evidence that articulation disorders are not merely an inability to produce sounds; rather, they reflect a deficiency in the learning process. The areas of learning emphasized in the treatment of articulation disorders are discrimination training, production practice, generalization training, and retention.

In discrimination training the emphasis is placed on auditory experience. In production practice, those who study articulation disorders need to recognize that producing speech sounds in isolation may have no direct relationship to conversational speech. Generalization is, of course, a serious concern, and the speech therapist must provide training so that the current production of speech sounds is used outside the clinical situation. Retention of learned speech sounds, the last area discussed by Wintz, should focus on memory theory. Whether or not the person has learned the speech sounds is not the main concern. The important question is whether the person can retrieve the newly learned sound production. All of these treatments require that the speech therapist have training in the techniques of behavioral analysis.

Voice Defects

Defects which involve the voice usually include deviations of pitch, quality, or intensity. When pitch is involved, the person may speak in a voice that is too high, too low, a monotone, or has the pitch breaks often associated with the onset of puberty. When a teenage girl speaks in a voice so low that she attracts attention to herself, she is using an inappropriate pitch level for her age and sex.

Some children speak so softly that they are difficult to hear. Others may speak too loudly. In either case, a hearing impairment may be suspected. It is also possible that the child has learned to speak loudly in order to be heard over the noise of other sounds in the environment, such as those made by several brothers and sisters, TV, or radio.

Defects in voice quality include hypernasality, denasality, breathiness, or hoarseness and huskiness. In normal speech, a certain amount of nasality is required, for example in the proper production of *m, n,* and *ng* sounds. For other speech sounds, it is necessary to close the nasal passage to prevent excessive nasal resonance. The person who seems to "talk through his nose" has hypernasal speech. This is often characteristic of the child with a cleft palate, or the child who has some paralysis of the soft palate and is unable to effect the necessary closure of the nasal passage. In some cases, improper speech may be caused by a poor speech model.

In denasal speech, the person may sound like someone with a head cold. There is a complete lack of the nasal resonance necessary for certain speech sounds. In such cases, the cause of denasal speech may be attributed to occlusions to the nasal passages, as when the adenoids are swollen or infected in some way.

In some children, an unusual amount of hoarseness may be noticed. If this condition appears to be persistent, the throat should be examined, because this voice defect may be caused by the growths of nodules or polyps on the vocal cords. These growths, caused by improper use of the voice or by straining the cords, pose a difficulty common to those who use their voices a great deal. With help, though, they may be retrained in the proper use of the voice.

The person who appears to be out of breath when speaking may also be retrained to speak more effectively. Breathiness involves both tension and quality difficulties.

An overview of the history of voice disorder description and treatment has been compiled by Moore (1977). He reports on four outstanding features regarding voice disorders:

1. Greater detail has been provided in describing voice disorders which improves understanding of the basic problems, but the problems have not changed.
2. More attention is given to conditions such as laryngectomy.
3. More therapeutic techniques are in use.
4. The major emphases in therapy have not changed. They include listening training, articulatory adjustments, breath control training when appropriate, specialized techniques, and training in relaxation and reduction of laryngeal tension.

Moore indicates that systematic behavior modification has improved voice disorder therapy; however, more research and study are needed to further improve the effectiveness of treatment methods. Voice therapy will be enhanced by such technological advances as the development of computer models of laryngeal behavior, which give three-dimensional manipulable displays, and by the further exploration of nerve cell development and function, which will contribute to learning theory and practice and to vocal training and remediation.

Defects in Rhythm—Stuttering

The most common difficulty in speech rhythm is stuttering. Stuttering is characterized by blocking, repetition, or prolongation of speech sounds, words, phrases, or syllables. Physical tension or facial or other types of bodily distortion may also be observable.

Although difficulties in the rhythm of speech are fairly common under various circumstances, the stutterer becomes more emotionally involved because of nonfluency. Many children experience such nonfluency during the process of developing speech. However, as they become more proficient, such nonfluencies disappear. If they do not, the child may be regarded as a primary stutterer. This usually means that there is a certain amount of nonfluency in speech. Still, the child is not yet concerned about speech and has not yet adopted any gestures to help initiate speech, or avoidance reactions to speech. With some help from a speech therapist, the child may often be helped to overcome these periods of nonfluency.

However, as more people begin to notice nonfluent speech and call attention to it, the person may experience tension and anxiety toward speaking, and then adopt various means of initiating speech such as stamping the floor, hitting a table, or moving some other part of the body. Facial grimaces may become apparent, as may other signs of physical strain and tension. In some cases the person may attempt to avoid speaking situations, thus jeopardizing social and vocational or educational opportunities.

It is fairly safe to say that no two people who stutter are alike in their patterns of stuttering. There are many instances when stutterers may go for long periods with fluent speech. At other times they are unable to communicate at all. In many cases stutterers are able to sing or recite poetry without a single period of nonfluency. They may be able to speak to certain people freely, with little stuttering, yet unable to talk to other people without becoming hopelessly involved in nonfluent speech.

The emotions are deeply involved. It is important for those who are in contact with a child who stutters to become informed about the various aspects of this speech disorder. After such children begin to think of themselves as stutterers, the anxiety surrounding speech becomes self-perpetuating and a vicious cycle is established. There are several theories regarding the cause of stuttering. However, no one has yet discovered a satisfactory answer to this relatively unique phenomenon.

According to Cooper (1973) most studies pertaining to stuttering indicate that two out of three persons who have the problem of stuttering will recover spontaneously. Cooper has developed "The Cooper Chronicity Prediction Checklist for School Age Stutterers: An Inventory for Research," which is one approach to use in predicting recovery from stuttering. He also reported that his inventory may assist a speech clinician in identifying variables which have a cause-effect relationship to stuttering. These include chronicity and family history, chronicity and severity, chronicity and duration of stuttering, and chronicity and stutterer's attitudes. Further research with this inventory may prove very beneficial to speech clinicians.

A variety of problems such as interpersonal communication and functioning in the environment exist for the person who has the problem of stuttering. Therefore, according to Silverman (1980), the remediation of stuttering should focus on more than speech fluency. In order to study the dimensions of stuttering, Silverman collected 288 statements regarding improvements from 108 adult stutterers (age range fifteen to fifty-one). These dimensions included four primary areas:

1. Modification of speaking behavior—reduction in frequency or severity of stuttering.
2. Reduced avoidance of words or of speaking situations—increased verbal output and a willingness to enter into previously avoided speaking situations.
3. Modifications and attitudes and feelings related to the stuttering problem—areas such as embarrassment associated with speaking.
4. Modifications in the personal-social area-modifications of behavior in personal-social situations, i.e., interacting with others.

The statements regarding improvement were analyzed by twenty-six clinicians in speech therapy. The results indicated the degree of improvement not only in speech fluency, but in many dimensions of behavior associated with the problem of stuttering.

The study has enabled Silverman to compile a *Stuttering Problem Profile* (in press) which consists of 86 statements. The study and Silverman's profile will have direct applications in such areas as defining the boundaries of the stuttering problem. They should also provide areas to be screened in the evaluation of the stutterer; provide a way to establish goals for stuttering therapy, in that stutterers may choose areas in which they desire to improve before beginning therapy; and provide guidelines for determining specific degrees of improvement.

Many methods are used to treat stuttering. They include delayed auditory feedback, speaking with time out as a contingency for each stuttering, being told "wrong" contingent upon stuttering, speaking with a white noise masking, and rhythmic speaking to the beat of a metronome. Martin and Haroldson (1979) conducted a study using all of these methods with twenty subjects who had the problem of stuttering. For each method, the subjects had a twenty-minute baseline and then thirty minutes of treatment. During the treatment phase the percent of stuttering time decreased significantly, and stuttering duration decreased significantly in all but the white noise method. In comparison of the methods, a positive relationship was shown in the change scores of percent of stuttering in time out, delayed auditory feedback and the metronome. The change scores of stuttering duration were positively related for the time out and delayed auditory feedback and with the metronome and delayed auditory feedback method.

It is interesting to note that at the completion of each method there was at least a two-day rest period, and when the subjects entered a new baseline condition prior to the next treatment, the percent and duration of stuttering returned to the original baseline behavior. The lack of sustained improvement may have been due to the short period of time during which treatment took place. Other findings are reported by Martin and Haroldson which are too detailed to include. However, it is important that the simultaneous use of different techniques may have implications for improving the reduction of percent and duration of stuttering if these methods are used over a longer period of time.

Language Disorders

Language disorders have received recent emphasis and may be a large percent (up to 60 percent) of a speech therapist's caseload (Bankson 1978). Language disorders refer to the ability to comprehend, express, and functionally use spoken language. The four components of language as presented by Bankson follow:

1. Phonemes—a sound within a language.
2. Morpheme—the minimal meaningful unity of language.

3. Syntax—rules for placing words together in a meaningful sequence or sentence.
4. Semantics—the meaning given to arbitrary linguistic symbols used in language (vocabulary, concepts, and word associations).

Determining the extent of a language disorder requires the speech or language therapist to use a battery of tests. The tests should provide information regarding the way in which a child comprehends and expresses semantic knowledge, the use of grammatical rules, and sentence formations.

Therapy must focus on the aspect of language which is deficient and may vary from an environment providing informal language stimulation to a formal, programmed instructional program. The primary objective of language therapy is to improve verbal expression and provide generalization and maintenance of the improvements in everyday situations.

There is a difference between language disorders and speech impairments. A child with a language disorder could be already diagnosed as mentally retarded, learning disabled, emotionally disturbed, or come from a culturally diverse background. Seriously considered, this means that the speech or language therapist who serves children with language disorders must have a broader training background than the training generally provided for a speech therapist.

Delayed Speech

Delayed speech usually refers to a marked retardation in the ability to use language or to communicate. Children may frequently substitute or omit sounds. They usually use simple words and phrases rather than sentences and may use a vocabulary that consists primarily of nouns and verbs. In some cases they show no interest in speech at all and not only will not attempt to speak, but will often not listen to speech. Such children may attempt to communicate by the use of gestures.

If children have not acquired small vocabularies by the time they are eighteen to twenty-four months old, there may be reason to suspect some degree of speech retardation. If they are not using simple two- or three-word phrases by the time they reach thirty months, they should be referred to a physician or to some other type of specialist to determine if there is some physical cause for the delay in language development. Of course, if a child has been ill frequently throughout infancy, such a rule may not apply. Retardation in speech may be related to the child's illness.

There are several possible causes of delayed language. One is mental retardation. The retarded child is usually slower in developing in all areas of physical activity. Coordination is often poor, especially in areas that require fine motor skills, such as speech. These children have difficulty in articulation, and in higher level aspects of speech, such as perceiving, thinking, and remembering.

Another cause is emotional disturbance. In some cases, a child may develop a fear of communicating with others. For some children, the act of not speaking is a powerful means of controlling the behavior of others. The child who becomes voluntarily mute may be considered as speech defective. In such emotionally involved cases, a child may have gone through the normal stages of speech and language development and then suddenly stopped talking. Such cases may often be related to some event that has caused regressive speech. Small children also may go through negative stages in which they do not respond well to communication. As they grow, there are so many demands placed upon them that the pressures become momentarily unbearable, and they may learn to react by not speaking. In this way they can maintain some control of the situation.

Autistic children also are under this category. These children are often so sensitive to their surroundings that speech or communication is threatening to them. This type of speech problem is very complex and usually involves a child who does not desire to relate to people in any way. Although such children may be taught to speak through good therapeutic assistance, they usually exhibit other marked differences that place them in a category by themselves.

Delayed speech may also be caused by a lack of appropriate stimulation. Children must be able to hear speech and have a reason to communicate before they can be stimulated or motivated to speak. If their needs are met without using speech, they will not develop it as quickly as others. In some environments, children are often discouraged from speaking for various reasons. Demands may be made on children regarding speech that are impossible for them to meet. Demands place pressure on children. Then they may associate speech with unpleasant experience.

Brain injuries may also be responsible for a delay in language development. Certain areas of the brain are responsible for the proper development of speech skills. If any of these areas are damaged, such as that responsible for the movement of the articulators, speech may be more difficult to acquire.

Finally, another cause for a delay in speech is hearing impairment. If physically unable to hear speech, children will not feel motivated to speak. They may also have difficulty in perceiving speech, which may be caused by other types of auditory problems.

Delayed Language

Many of the causes assigned to delayed speech may affect children in the area of language. When brain damage is present, they may have difficulty in understanding speech, performing the motor act of speaking, or learning how to read and write. They may also have similar difficulties if a brain lesion occurs after language has been learned. The degree of difficulty the child experiences is dependent upon the extent of the brain damage. Milder forms can often be observed in the child who has great difficulty in learning how to read, commonly known as dyslexia and alexia. Some children experience a primary handicap as an inability to express thoughts, although they are capable of comprehending what is said. Still another child may experience difficulty in several areas, which make communication a very arduous task.

Aphasia

Many definitions of the term *aphasia* exist in the literature. However, most agree that aphasia is an interference with the comprehension and use of language. Researchers have emphasized that aphasia is a disorder of symbolization of language rather than speech.

The aphasic has difficulty in (1) formulating, (2) comprehending, or (3) expressing *meanings*. Often there is some impairment in all of these functions. Along with these difficulties there may be associated problems of defective articulation, inability to produce voice, and broken fluency; but the basic problem in aphasia lies in handling symbolic *behavior*. (Van Riper 1978)

There are four main classifications of aphasia: receptive aphasia (also called sensory or auditory), expressive aphasia (also called motor or verbal), mixed receptive-expressive aphasia, and central aphasia. With children the term often used is developmental aphasia (sometimes called congenital aphasia). This refers to a condition in which either poor endowment or brain injury occurring before, during, or after birth prevents the child from acquiring language.

Predominantly expressive aphasia is indicated by four characteristics: (1) intelligence within normal range, (2) normal hearing and understanding of language, (3) inability to imitate words, and (4) inability or limited ability to imitate individual speech sounds. Expressive aphasia is common in children and is fairly easy to identify.

Predominantly sensory aphasia refers to the incapacity to understand the speech of others. Comprehension of speech is the problem, not the ability to hear. A child with sensory aphasia may ignore all sounds and may be considered peripherally deaf. Sometimes the child with sensory aphasia will comprehend a word intermittently and unexpectedly. This child will also have normal intelligence, usually normal hearing, an inability to name objects, an inability or partial ability to associate spoken names of objects, and poor recall of names the child has repeated.

The most common type of aphasia seen clinically in children is the mixed receptive-expressive classification. This child cannot understand or produce speech because of deficiencies of symbolization in both respects. The behavior of the child with mixed receptive-expressive aphasia is similar to the behavior of the child with receptive aphasia.

Central aphasia is a severe language disorder including defects in both receptive and expressive capacities. The primary disorder is an inner language problem which, of course, makes remediation much more difficult.

Some of the characteristics of children with aphasia may be confused with other disorders. The following behavioral characteristics may assist in differentiating this child from other children with disorders such as mental retardation, deafness, autism, and delayed speech. Children with mixed receptive-expressive aphasia do not acquire language. They speak a meaningless jargon which has good tonal quality in contrast to the child with a hearing impairment. They neither gesture nor use verbal expression to call others. Their responses to sounds are inconsistent and erratic. Children with receptive aphasia have retarded motor development and coordination. Their social perception is also deficient and they may have uncontrollable crying, screaming, or laughing when confronted with tasks which require greater integrative capacities than they possess. The aphasic child may have disturbances of visual perception, exhibit perseveration, distractibility, and disinhibition. All of these difficulties make aphasia a serious disorder which requires the intervention of a well-trained speech therapist.

Cleft Palate Speech

Cleft palate speech is usually characterized by a very nasal quality. It often includes mild to severe distortion of certain speech sounds, such as the plosives, which require the buildup of a certain amount of air pressure in the mouth before the sound can be produced. Other speech sounds may also be affected in different ways.

A cleft or opening may occur in several places in the mouth or nasal passages. A cleft may involve the hard palate, the soft palate, the hard and soft palate, the lips, the jaws, or the nose. These openings are generally caused by the failure of these areas of the mouth to close completely during growth and development in the early stages of pregnancy. There may be no visible signs of an opening, yet a child may exhibit the same type of cleft palate speech. In such a case, the cleft may be just under the skin covering of the hard or soft palate, where it involves the bony structure between the oral and the nasal cavity.

The peculiar nasal quality characteristics of cleft palate speech is caused by the fact that air cannot be blocked off from the nasal cavity as is necessary for most of the sounds in normal speech. In most cases, these clefts can be surgically repaired. However, the child may continue to have some difficulty with speech.

Cerebral Palsy Speech

In speech associated with cerebral palsy, brain damage may cause extreme difficulty in the control of the muscles necessary for the production of speech. A majority of children with cerebral palsy do experience a handicap in this area. The child is usually unable to control such things as speech rate or rhythm, and the accurate production of consonant sounds. Speech is often jerky, or very labored, and slow. The voice is also affected because the child may not be able to control the pitch and quality of the sounds.

Speech Defects Associated with Hearing Impairment

Children unable to hear speech clearly may exhibit speech defects, usually in articulation, but sometimes in voice production as well. Their voices may be either too loud, or too soft, or show a lack of inflection, which gives a monotonal quality. Depending on the type of hearing impairment present, children may have mild articulation defects, may show retardation in the development of speech and language skills, or may not be able to develop speech at all without special training. The type of articulation problem that exists is generally determined by the type of hearing loss.

The Provision of Services

A project emphasizing the serious concern regarding provisions for speech services to the hearing impaired was conducted by Hochberg, Levitt, and Osberger (1980) for three years. The results indicated that hearing-impaired children were not reaching their potential in speech communication. Some of the reasons contributing to this lack of development included the following:

1. Poorly trained teachers.
2. Lack of emphasis on speech in preservice training programs.
3. An emphasis on language skills instead of speech skills for hearing-impaired children.
4. An anticipation of limited results in development even after years of speech training.

These authors designed a model intended to improve the provision of speech services to hearing-impaired children. This model has been applied in workshops for preservice teacher trainers and for professionals in the field. It involves developing cooperation and interaction of preservice teacher training programs and professional personnel serving in programs. The model focuses on upgrading preservice training and emphasizing in-service training for professionals to improve their competence to deliver speech services to hearing-impaired children.

Education of the Speech Impaired

In most public schools, a speech correctionist is available to work with children who have relatively mild speech defects. Those with more serious speech difficulties are usually referred to special speech clinics. Speech therapists generally do not work in regular classrooms. Rather, they use small rooms equipped with mirrors to accommodate anywhere from one to six

Most public schools provide therapy for children with mild speech defects.

children at a time. Special equipment is generally carried from one school to another, and usually includes materials prepared specifically to suit the needs of children involved in a speech therapy program.

A relatively comfortable room with pleasant surroundings is essential. In some cases, special equipment, such as a tape recorder, may be desirable. Other commonly used items may be obtained from the school, such as tongue blades, speech improvement cards, blowing equipment, practice devices, and educational toys and games. A place to keep therapy case records is also important.

The speech therapist or speech pathologist is also involved in the implementation of Public Law 94–142. If a child needs the services of a speech therapist and has no other disabilities, then the speech therapist is responsible for the implementation of the child's Individual Education Plan (IEP). Of course, the speech therapist should also be a member of the IEP team and play a primary role in the development of the IEP. If the child's only difficulty is a speech impairment, the speech therapist will be the primary person to select appropriate assessment instruments to determine the type of speech impairment and the extent of the disability. Additional testing may also be required, such as an intellectual assessment and a hearing evaluation. The speech therapist may have to coordinate the arrangements for these evaluations. In addition, the speech therapist may have to assume a primary role obtaining parental permission for administering the test batteries. Since an average caseload is seventy-five to one hundred, these involvements may require a large portion of the speech therapist's time.

If a child needs the services of a speech therapist and has one or more other disabilities, the speech therapist should still be a member of the IEP team, but primary responsibility for the development of the IEP will rest with other school personnel. The goals of the IEP which are related to speech therapy should, however, be developed by the speech therapist. In addition to the development of the IEP, all other aspects of Public Law 94–142 must be considered for the child who has a speech impairment. For example, the child has a right to appropriate and free speech therapy services. If this service is not provided by the local school system, the parents have the right to due process just as they would if their child had some other type of disability.

In the implementation of services for children with a speech impairment without other disabilities, the speech therapist must become a consultant to regular classroom teachers. This involves assisting teachers to recognize improvement in the child's disability; assisting, if possible, in the child's individual speech improvement program, and helping teachers to work around their instructional schedules to prevent punishing the child for absences while receiving speech therapy. The speech therapist has several different schools to serve, or, if in one building, several different children to serve. Therefore, the services needed by the various children should be scheduled as conveniently as possible for all concerned. If the regularly assigned teacher is concentrating on an essential area of instruction while the child is receiving speech therapy, the teacher must find a way for the child to receive that instruction before or after speech therapy. To do otherwise is penalizing the child for receiving speech therapy, which would tend to lessen the child's willingness to participate in the needed therapy.

The speech therapist must also be an accurate record keeper. Records must indicate when the child entered therapy, the amount of therapy provided, and the improvements made by the child. These records, like other school records, may be requested by the parents of the child. Therefore, they must reflect accurately the services provided and how those services are associated with the objectives established on the child's IEP.

Needless to say, the position of a speech therapist in today's schools is not an easy task, nor should it be assigned to someone who is not trained appropriately. The speech therapist should be a professional in the area of speech pathology.

Resources

Bloom, L., and Lahay, M. *Language Development and Language Disorders.* New York: John Wiley, 1978.

Gottsleben, Bob, and Tyack, Dee. *Golden Gate Reading and Spelling Series.* Palo Alto, Calif.: Consulting Psychologists Press, 1979.

Hain, Rosalind and Lainer, Harriet. *Language Rehabilitation Program.* Hingham, Mass.: Teaching Resources, 1980.

Mowery, Charlane and Replogle, Anne. *Developmental Language Lessons.* Hingham, Mass.: Teaching Resources, 1980.

Ryan, Bruce P. *Programmed Therapy for Stuttering in Children and Adults.* Springfield, Ill.: Charles C Thomas, 1980.

Study Questions

1. List the types of modifications of educational services and resource materials for the speech-impaired child.
2. Contact a practicing speech therapist and provide a list of the various materials used in his or her practice.
3. From library research, discuss recent trends in therapy provided for children with language disorders.
4. Distinguish the differences in articulation disorders and language disorders.
5. In what ways can a regular or special classroom teacher support and enhance the services provided by a speech therapist?
6. Discuss ways a regular or special classroom teacher may become aware of speech problems that require the services of a speech or language therapist.
7. In what ways might a speech impairment be related to the problem of mental retardation?
8. Distinguish the differences in language therapy and speech therapy.
9. What services might be required to help the hearing-impaired child develop speech and language skills?
10. Discuss the variety of problems which may be encountered by the child who stutters.

Bibliography

Bankson, Nicholas W. 1978. "The Speech and Language Impaired." *Exceptional Children and Youth: An Introduction,* ed. Edward L. Meyen. Denver: Love Publishing Co.

Cooper, Eugene B. 1973. "The Development of a Stuttering Chronicity Prediction Checklist: A Preliminary Report." *Journal of Speech and Hearing Disorders* 38, no. 2 (May).

Dunn, Lloyd M., ed. 1973. *Exceptional Children in the Schools: Special Education in Transition.* 2d ed. New York: Holt, Einehart & Winston.

Hochberg, Irving; Levitt, Harry; and Osberger, Mary Joe. 1980 "Improving Speech Services to Hearing-Impaired Children." *Journal of the American Speech-Language-Hearing Association* 22, no. 7 (July).

Jenkins, E., and Lohr, F. E. 1964. "Severe Articulation Disorders and Motor Ability." *Journal of Speech and Hearing Disorders 29.*

Martin, Richard, and Haroldson, Samuel K. 1979. "Effects of Five Experimental Treatments on Stuttering." *Journal of Speech and Hearing Research* 22, no. 1 (March).

Moore, G. Paul. 1977. "Have the Major Issues in Voice Disorders Been Answered by Research in Speech Science? A 50-Year Retrospective." *Journal of Speech and Hearing Disorders* 42, no. 2.

Silverman, Franklin H. 1980. "Dimensions of Improvement in Stuttering." *Journal of Speech and Hearing Research* 23, no. 1 (March).

Telford, Charles W., and Sawrey, James M. 1977. *The Exceptional Individual.* 3d ed. Englewood Cliffs, N.J.: Prentice-Hall.

Van Riper, Charles. 1978. *Speech Correction: Principles and Methods.* 6th ed. Englewood Cliffs, N.J.: Prentice-Hall.

Winitz, Harris. 1977. "Articulation Disorders: From Prescription to Description." *Journal of Speech and Hearing Disorders* 42.

children with learning disabilities

Definition

Learning disabilities is a term that is compatible with the educational system. Through the years during which this term has become popular, educators have seen a number of different nomenclatures attached to this specific area of disabilities. One will read terms such as minimal brain dysfunction, specific learning disabilities, perceptually handicapped, perceptually immature, dyslexia, word blindness, hyperkinetic syndrome, hypokinetic syndrome, attention syndrome, clumsy child syndrome, aphasia, and dysgraphia. We do not believe that there is a specific equation between any one of these terms and the term *learning disabilities*. Children may have dyslexic symptoms, but this does not necessarily mean they are categorized as learning disabled. Also, if a child is categorized as learning disabled, it doesn't necessarily mean that all of these particular handicaps are evident.

Learning disabled children may have difficulties in some areas of reading, arithmetic, and writing, or demonstrate behavioral problems. They are not mentally retarded. They do not have severe hearing, or sight problems, or severe motor involvement. A severe motor involvement reflects such limits as indicated by a cerebral palsy child. Learning disabled children have average or above average mental ability, but are probably performing academically below their mental abilities. They may have secondary emotional, social, or cultural kinds of problems that disrupt the classroom and home.

The field of learning disabilities is relatively new. This is exemplified by the diffuse number of definitions used to describe these children. A few of these definitions will be referred to in this chapter to illustrate different views of learning disabilities. It is not our purpose to indicate a single preferred definition. Minskoff (1969) cited the following definition from the National Advisory Committee on Handicapped Children:

Children with learning disabilities means those children who have a disorder in one or more of the basic psychological processes involved in understanding or in using language, spoken or written, which disorder may manifest itself in imperfect ability to listen, think, speak, read, write, spell or do mathematical calculations. Such disorders include such conditions as perceptual handicaps, brain injury, minimal brain dysfunction, dyslexia, and developmental aphasia. Such terms do not include children who have learning problems which are primarily the result of visual, hearing, or motor handicaps, of mental retardation, of emotional disturbance, or of environmental disadvantage.

Whittlesey's (1969) definition also includes children with certain specific motor problems, defects in coordination, and visual-motor difficulties. Thus, the defect may lie in the perceptual, integrative, or expressive areas. His definition *excludes* children with obvious defects such as cerebral palsy, mental retardation, emotional disturbance, defects in vision, or decreased hearing.

Cruickshank (1966) indicated that irrespective of the terminology, some children experience a disturbance of some sort in normal cephalocaudal neural maturation in different stages of development, either perinatally, prenatally, or postnatally. This disturbance may result in an inability to progress normally in various sensory modalities, which causes these children to exhibit visual-motor, audiomotor, and tactual-motor deficiencies. It appears that the great majority of children with brain injury manifest coordination problems in gross-motor and fine-motor movements. Therefore, they appear to be clumsy at cutting with scissors, cutting while using a knife and fork, lacing shoes, or writing with a pencil.

Learning disabilities usually refer to one or more significant deficits in the essential learning processes and require special education techniques for remediation. Kass and Myklebust (1969) also indicated that children with learning disabilities generally manifest discrepancies between academic expectations and actual achievement in one or more areas, such as language, mathematics, and spatial orientation.

In the Kansas Association for Children with Learning Disabilities pamphlet (Morrison 1971), Hellmuth (1971) indicated that the learning disabled child may be a student, usually a boy, who performs significantly below grade placement and general intelligence level in reading and spelling. This child does not exhibit measurable neurological defects or loss of visual or auditory acuity. This child also is not mentally retarded, cerebral palsied, and has no other obvious defects. Academically this child is unable to acquire at a normal rate, through the general curriculum, a proficiency in reading and spelling which corresponds to general ability. This is true even when good instructional procedures are used. This child may show minimal neurological signs commonly known to special education professionals, such as right-left disorientation, impaired motor control, perseveration, time disorientation, perceptual-motor and visual-motor problems, hyperkinesis, impulsive actions, short or no attention span, mixed laterality, directionality problems, unusual reading and writing posture, impaired two-point discrimination. Hellmuth indicated, too, that behavioral or emotional problems will exist by late grade three. He also indicates that psychometric testing yields a typical wide scattering of subtest scores, even though the student's IQ score is in the normal or above normal range. We have also noted the spread in the subtest scores of many children tested for learning disability classes, although that spread should not be considered as a conclusive criterion for diagnosis.

There has been considerable pressure from certain disadvantaged socioeconomic groups to define the culturally, socioeconomically deprived youngster as learning disabled. We do not agree with this inclusion, because there has to be an educational objective for learning disabilities that is meaningful and functional. If the gates are opened to include many different educational-socioeconomic problem areas, the training objectives would not be consistent with present learning disability definitions. Moreover, it appears that the learning disability category of education would be expanded to such an extent that learning disability school programs would become a dumping-ground for all educational problems. Like it or not, professionals have categories of exceptionalities, and these categorical concepts can be functional if schools maintain an educational guideline structure which is consistent with the total school program.

The following article (Hammill 1976) is reprinted entirely as written, which gives the reader a continuous reflection of Dr. Hammill's perspective on defining the learning-disabled child. Dr. Hammill's definition and incidence figures are somewhat different from those previously presented. Different ideas offer the reader a broad perspective on the various contemporary theories and research in the learning disability area. One will not get closure on controversial areas of exceptional children, but one must realize that controversy does stimulate concern, study, and research. Therefore, Dr. Hammill's information is offered in this spirit.*

Defining "LD" for Programmatic Purposes
Donald D. Hammill (1976)

As a result of recent parental and professional pressure on educators, legislators, and congressmen, public school programs for "learning-disabled" students have been implemented in staggeringly large numbers. When asked to state specifically the kinds of students who are to be served in these new programs, responsible individuals usually quote a definition for "children with learning disabilities." More likely than not, it will be the one offered by the National Advisory Committee on Handicapped Children.

Children with special learning disabilities exhibit a disorder in one or more of the basic psychological processes involved in understanding or in using spoken or written languages. These may be manifested in writing, spelling, or arithmetic. They include conditions which have been referred to as perceptual handicaps, brain injury, minimal brain dysfunction, dyslexia, developmental aphasia, etc. They do not include learning problems which are due primarily to visual, hearing, or motor handicaps, to mental retardation, emotional disturbance or to environmental disadvantage. [1]

*The article on pages 251–258 is from Donald D. Hammill, "Defining 'L.D.' for Programmatic Purposes," *Academic Therapy* 12, no. 1 (1976). Reprinted by permission of Academic Therapy Publications. Novato, Calif.

While definitions like this one allow students to be described in broad, general terms, they are much too obscure, open-ended, and subjective to be used as actual criteria for selecting individual students. Many of the words used in these definitions do not have any precise meanings and several of the ideas expressed or implied are currently surrounded by professional controversy. For example, what is a basic psychological process, a perceptual handicap, dyslexia, or minimal cerebral dysfunction? Professionals in psychology and education dispute hotly the existence, nature, and importance of the so-called "psychological processes."[2] In addition, experts in reading have never been able to reach a general agreement on the definition of dyslexia, much less on its diagnosis and treatment.[3] And speech pathologists still argue about the concept of developmental aphasia.[4] To this confusion may be added the observation that many of today's physicians consider terms like "minimal cerebral dysfunction" and "brain injury" to be ill-defined, wastebasket categories.[5]

Because the definitions are not very definitive, and therefore cannot be used to identify precisely the populations to be served, state education agencies have had to design regulations in which the exact criteria to be used in operationalizing the definition are set forth in specific detail. For example, the intelligence quotient (IQ) restrictions, the degree of educational or linguistic deficiency, the kinds of tests to be used, the formula to be applied, etc., are usually specified in the regulations. These are then used by local education agencies for the purpose of identifying those students whose education will be supported financially under the "learning disabilities" label. Therefore, in any particular state, the nature of the students diagnosed as having a learning disability is actually a function of the regulations used to identify them rather than the definition used to describe them. For example, two states might adhere to the same definition but employ considerably divergent sets of regulations; in these instances, the characteristics of students identified as being learning disabled in one state might differ markedly from those identified in the other state. Since these regulations, rather than a particular definition, are of such importance in identifying students as learning disabled, the remainder of this paper is devoted to discussing certain pitfalls often incorporated in existing regulations and to presenting an approach that looks somewhat promising.

Permit me to make one assumption at the onset—at this point in time, I believe that a specific learning disability is a true handicap; and as such, its consequences are regrettably serious but fortunately relatively rare. From my experience and study, I would estimate that the incidence of the condition is approximately three percent of the school-age population. This figure is essentially in agreement with that offered by Samuel Kirk and with the overall opinion of the "experts" surveyed by J. F. Wissink.[6]

Yet, many professionals believe that the incidence is much higher and include in their concept of learning disabilities almost every child in school who is not doing well and who is not obviously blind, deaf, mentally retarded, or disturbed. This wholesale "diagnosis" of 10, 15, or even 30 percent of the school enrollment as LD has brought the field to near disaster and the schools into severe financial difficulties. Understandably, public reaction to this point of view has not been slow in taking form. The excessive labeling of essentially normal children as "handicapped" has been "exposed" in the popular press by A. Silverman and D. Divoky among others.[7] They suggest that learning disabilities have become little more than an educational fad. In response to these kinds of articles, to the urging of some professionals, and to the fears of some school personnel that there is not enough money to handle the numbers of children being diagnosed, governmental agencies have moved to place a lid on the number of children who can be served under the learning disabilities label (e.g., the recently passed Public Law 94–142 specifies a two-percent limit). Since I believe that the real incidence of learning disabilities is low and since we are to be held to a two-percent maximum, it seems reasonable that well designed regulations should result in the identification of approximately two to three percent of our students as learning disabled.

This can be done using irrelevant criteria which would invite a legal challenge to the regulations; or preferably, it can be accomplished by applying validated guidelines which will result in locating truly disabled learners. There are several irrelevant regulations which, if used, will no doubt result in the identification of an acceptable number of children, but with which I take particular objection. For the most part, I fear that their use leads to the inclusion of students who are not handicapped. For example:

Any procedure which uses the mental age (MA) concept: In many states, the MA is used in formulas to determine the discrepancy between a student's estimated intellectual ability and his actual performance. If the gap is sufficiently wide, the child may qualify for placement in a learning disabilities program. The idea here is sound basically; it is the use of MA, rather than IQ, that causes my concern.

First, usually bright students can be achieving in school several years below their MA; but this level frequently is above the mean of their school district and nowhere near a handicapped performance level. For example, the MA of a student whose chronological age (CA) is 15, with an IQ of 130, is 19½:

$$MA = \frac{CA \times IQ}{100}$$

This youngster could be reading at the level of a 12½ year old, i.e., at grade level 7.5, and thereby evidence a seven-year lag between his MA and his Achievement Age. Since the average reading achievement of adults in this country does not exceed sixth-grade level, how can he seriously be considered "handicapped"? He may be poorly taught, disinterested, unmotivated, turned on or turned off, but not handicapped. If these children are to be diagnosed as such, then school personnel must be prepared to label most bright youngsters as handicapped (i.e., "learning disabled"), because most of them tend to underachieve to a surprising degree.

Second, the idea of MA may have some value when applied to very young children, but its use with older students can be ludicrous. For example, a fifteen-year-old educable mentally retarded (EMR) student with an IQ of 70 has an estimated MA of 10.6. If this were a true indication of his mental ability, then he would likely be achieving at the fifth-grade level and in no way could he be considered either EMR or handicapped in reading. The ultimate example of the limitation of the MA concept is when it is applied to adults, a fifty-year-old trainable mentally retarded individual with an IQ of 50 has an MA of 25!

Any procedure which makes eligibility dependent on failing process tests: Students who do poorly in academics and/or language are often administered process tests (i.e., tests that measure modality preferences, memory, perception, closure, etc.). If they fail sufficiently, it is said that they suffer from one or more process deficits and therefore satisfy the "psychological process" phrase in the definition. The inference being made is that the process deficit is related somehow to the school program.

In light of the current state of the science regarding the use of process tests for predicting performance in academics or for differentiating between good and poor readers, spellers, etc., this would appear to be a most hazardous assumption to make. The results of a considerable body of recent research raises serious questions concerning the relationship between process tests and academic failure.[8]

Any procedure which ties identification of learning disabled students to the presence of positive neurological findings: A few states still require that a physician certify a child as showing signs of neurological disturbance before he can qualify for learning disability services. The validity of this requirement rests on the reasoning that: if all learning disabilities are caused by brain dysfunction (an assumption not yet proved), then children who evidence both educational difficulties and signs of brain dysfunction must be learning disabled (a conclusion that is not necessarily true). Such thinking is fallacious, is without experimental support, and more likely than not is articulated by educators and psychologists rather than by physicians.

H. R. Myklebust and B. Boshes have done a creditable piece of research on this topic.[9] They studied the neurological status of large samples of learning-disabled and achieving children and reported that, while the two groups differed markedly in the presence of hard neurological signs (e.g., paralysis, seizures, etc.), no real differences were noted between the groups on the soft signs (e.g., distractibility, awkwardness impaired spatial orientation). In fact, not one of the 137 items on the neurological evaluation differentiated significantly between the groups. The findings relative to the soft signs is particularly noteworthy because it is the soft signs that are supposed to be associated most frequently with learning disabilities.[10]

After reviewing approximately 50 studies relating to the electro-encephalogram (EEG), an indicator of brain dysfunction which is used commonly with LD referrals, R. D. Freeman concluded that EEG results simply do not relate conclusively to educational failure, psychiatric conditions, hyperactivity, etc.[11] In general, these conclusions are supported by those of R. S. Paine, J. S. Werry, and H. C. Quay, who studied 83 children with diagnosed minimal cerebral dysfunction, and of numerous other investigators.[12]

While the results of neurological examination might be interesting on occasion, and while a state might want to require one for all children being considered for special education placement, there is no reason based upon the current research for regulations to specify positive findings as a requisite for diagnosing learning disabilities in children.

With these irrelevancies deleted from the regulations, I believe that only three conditions need to be met in order to identify the cases to be served under the learning disabilities label: (1) the minimum intellectual level; (2) the degree of educational or language deficit; and (3) the categories of youngsters to be excluded:

Only students with average or near average mental ability should qualify:
To qualify, students should have measured IQs of 90. This quotient can be based on either group- or individually-administered tests. Children who have IQs less than the set figure should be given the *Wechsler Intelligence Scale for Children* (WISC) or *Wechsler Adult Intelligence Scale* (WAIS), because they are comprised of a verbal (VQ) and a performance (PQ) component. These children can still qualify if they score above 90 on either the VQ or the PQ. Many professionals don't care for IQ testing or are not permitted to give such tests. In such cases they should use whatever procedures they may choose; the important point is to identify children who are average or near average in intellectual ability.

Let me be the first to say that this and the other criteria about to be discussed are arbitrary in the sense that all regulations must be arbitrary, and that their use may well keep some children who do have learning disabilities from being labeled as such for "record keeping" purposes (e.g., many mentally retarded children also have learning disabilities). In these cases, however, they are identified, for programatic purposes, according to their major handicap (i.e., mental retardation), and qualify for special services provided under that label.

Only students with serious problems should qualify: The term *handicapped* is too stigmatizing to be applied capriciously; therefore, it should be used infrequently and then only in relation to those students who evidence *significant* difficulties. Therefore, only children who underachieve in reading, math, spelling, written expression (not penmanship), or spoken language (not articulation, stuttering, cleft palate, etc.) by the following amounts should qualify for the learning disabilities category.

1. Preschool and kindergarten: performance of minus 1.5 standard deviations on tests of readiness or language.

2. First and second grade: performance of minus 1.5 standard deviations on tests of readiness, language, or achievement.

3. Third through seventh grades: estimate the grade that the child should be in according to his CA; divide the grade level by two; if his measured performance in an academic area is below that figure, he qualifies. For example, if he should be grade level 6.4 and is achieving in reading at 3.2 or below, he would qualify for learning-disabled services.

4. Eighth grade and above: students must perform at 4.5 or below (presumably, students who score higher have already reached or are approaching a functional mastery of that skill).

Exceptions may apply in instances where a child was identified as learning disabled early in his school career and, because of continued specialized teaching and support, is now learning at a level above the minimum specified in these criteria. There may be solid reasons for retaining such a child in the program.

Children to be excluded: The purpose of this restriction is to avoid a needless overlapping of professional responsibilities and to ensure that handicapped children are assigned according to their major problem. Therefore, students with significant hearing losses especially if in the speech range, with visual acuity of less than 20/70 in the better eye after correction, with diagnosed mental retardation, and/or with psychologically- or psychiatrically-defined emotional disturbance, are not usually labeled as learning disabled. There are exceptions, however, which might be considered on occasion (e.g., when a child meets the other two criteria for eligibility and when his learning difficulty is apparently not the result of the major handicap).

More than usual caution is necessary when applying these criteria to children who have had extended periods of school absence because of truancy, illness, or family mobility. Their discrepancies may well be due to insufficient instruction rather than to learning disabilities. Caution is also needed in qualifying students who speak foreign languages or dialects because most of the criteria depend on test results which are administered in English.

It should be pointed out that the particular values mentioned with regard to the intellectual and academic criteria were intended to serve as demonstrations rather than as recommendations. For example, even though 90 was used as the minimum IQ that a child could have to qualify as "learning disabled," a school might prefer 85 or 100. In selecting a cut-off for the academic criterion, I referred to minus 1.5 standard deviations, though minus 1 or 2 might be better. It is to be hoped that figures which are actually used will be chosen on the basis of the results of applied research and not merely on speculation.

Personally, I have some philosophic difficulty with these criteria. If it were left entirely to me, I would identify the children using clinical judgment derived from direct observation and diagnostic teaching; but realistically, I know that that is not the way it is going to be done. Like it or not, state education agencies and local education agencies are going to be required to set up criteria which are "objective" and which can be converted into numbers. Sitting idly by in the ivory tower hoping for a day when labels will be unnecessary and when funding patterns will be different is "pie in the sky" thinking, and will not help those who must face today's problems today.

To conclude, the eligibility criteria just described are offered for discussion purposes and should be used on a trial basis only. *They may not work at all!* Even if they do prove to be successful, they will have to be refined and adapted to meet local situations before being adopted into regulations. The criteria should be field tested in several schools that utilize a cross section of the enrollment to determine answers to the following: (1) How many children are identified as learning disabled? (2) What are the socioeconomic and ethnic characteristics of those identified? (3) Are the children selected actually those we sought to identify? (4) What types of learning disabilities do they have?

Notes

1. National Advisory Committee on Handicapped Children. *First Annual Report, Special Education for Handicapped Children* (Washington, D.C.: U.S. Office of Education, Department of Health, Education, and Welfare, 1968).
2. P. Newcomber and D. Hammill, *Psycholinguistics in the Schools* (Columbus, Ohio: Charles E. Merrill, 1976); L. Mann, *Marianne Frostig Developmental Test of Visual Perception,* in O. K. Buros (ed.), *The Seventh Yearbook of Mental Measurements* (Highland Park, New Jersey: Gryphon, 1972); J. Chalfant and F. King, "An Approach to Operationalizing

the Definition of Learning Disabilities" (unpublished manuscript; Department of Special Education, University of Arizona, Tucson, 1975); S. A. Kirk and W. Kirk, *Psycholinguistic Learning Disabilities: Diagnosis and Remediation* (Urbana, Illinois: University of Illinois Press, 1971); M. Frostig and P. Maslow, *Learning Problems in the Classroom* (New York: Grune & Stratton, 1973).

3. J. Money (ed.), *Reading Disability* (Baltimore: The Johns Hopkins Press, 1962).

4. C. Van Riper, *Speech Correction: Principles and Methods* (5th ed.) (Englewood Cliffs, New Jersey: Prentice-Hall, 1972).

5. M. R. Gomez, "Minimal Cerebral Dysfunction (Maximal Neurological Confusion)," *Clinical Pediatrics* 6 (1967): 589–591.

6. S. A. Kirk, *Educating Exceptional Children* (2nd ed.) (Boston: Houghton Mifflin, 1972); J. F. Wissink, "A Procedure for the Identification of Children with Learning Disabilities" (unpublished doctoral dissertation; The University of Arizona, Tucson, 1972).

7. A. Silverman, "If They Say Your Child Can't Learn," *McCalls* 103 (1976): 76–81; D. Divoky, "Learning Disability 'Epidemic'," *New York Times* (January 15, 1975); P. Schrag and D. Divoky, *The Myth of the Hyperactive Child* (New York: Pantheon, 1975).

8. Newcomer and Hammill, *op. cit.;* D. Hammill and S. Larsen, "The Relationship of Selected Auditory-Perceptual Skills to Reading Ability," *Journal of Learning Disabilities* 7 (1974): 429–436; S. Larsen and D. Hammill, "The Relationship of Selected Visual-Perceptual Abilities to School Learning," *Journal of Special Education* 9 (1975): 281–291; R. Colarusso, H. Martin, and J. Hartung, "Specific Visual-Perceptual Skills as Long-Term Predictors of Academic Success," *Journal of Learning Disabilities* 8 (1975): 651–655; S. Larsen, D. Rogers, and V. Sowell, "The Use of Selected Perceptual Tests in Differentiating between Normal and Learning-Disabled Children," *Journal of Learning Disabilities* 9 (1976): 85–90.

9. H. R. Myklebust and B. Boshes, *Minimal Brain Damage in Children, Final Report* (Washington, D.C.: U.S. Department of Health, Education, and Welfare, June, 1969).

10. S. D. Clements, *Minimal Brain Dysfunction in Children* (Washington, D.C.: Cosponsored by the Easter Seal Research Foundation of the National Society for Crippled Children and Adults and the National Institute of Neurological Diseases and Blindness Public Health Service, 1966).

11. R. D. Freeman, "Special Education and the Electroencephalogram: Marriage of Convenience," *The Journal of Special Education* 2 (1967): 61–73.

12. R. S. Paine, J. S. Werry, and H. C. Quay, "A Study of Minimal Cerebral Dysfunction," *Developmental Medicine and Child Neurology* 10 (1968): 505–520.

HEW Proposed Rules

The *Federal Register* (1976) listed the following proposed rules as a criteria for determining the existence of a specific learning disability. These rules were not mandated to the states, but most states by 1980 had incorporated similar eligibility criteria.

(a) The team may not identify a child as having a specific learning disability if the severe academic discrepancy is primarily the result of:
　(1) A visual, hearing, or motor handicap;
　(2) Mental retardation;
　(3) Emotional disturbance; or
　(4) Environmental, cultural or economic disadvantage.

(b) A team may determine that a child has a specific learning disability if:
    (1) The child does not achieve commensurate with his or her age and ability levels in one or more of the areas listed in paragraph (b)(2) of this section, when provided with learning experiences appropriate for the child's age and ability levels.
    (2) The team finds that a child has a severe discrepancy between academic achievement and intellectual ability in one or more of the following areas:
        (i)   Oral expression;
        (ii)   Listening comprehension;
        (iii) Written expression;
        (iv) Basic reading skill;
        (v)   Reading comprehension:
        (vi) Mathematics calculation;
        (vii) Mathematics reasoning; or
        (viii) Spelling
(c) A severe discrepancy between achievement and intellectual ability means achievement in one or more of the areas listed in paragraph (b)(2) of this section which falls at or below 50 percent of the child's expected achievement level, when intellectual ability, age, and previous educational experiences are considered.
(d) The team shall use the following method to determine whether the severe discrepancy exists:

$$\text{C.A.} \left(\frac{IQ}{300} + 0.17 \right) - 2.5 = \text{severe discrepancy level}$$

Example: Child age 10, with 90 IQ, fifth grade

$$\text{Age } 10 \left(\frac{IQ\ 90}{300} + 0.17 \right) - 2.5$$

$$10 \left(300\overline{)90.00}^{\ .30} + 0.17 \right) - 2.5$$

$$10 \, (.30 + 0.17) - 2.5$$
$$10 \, (.47) - 2.5$$
$$10 \times .47 - 2.5$$
$$4.7 - 2.5 = 2.2$$

Therefore, this child has to be functioning at or below a 2.2 grade level in one or more of the above listed areas. Any area with a grade level above 2.2 is not considered to be a severe discrepancy. The child would not qualify for an LD class in those areas in which the grade level is above 2.2

Example: Child Age 10, with 100 IQ, fifth grade

$$\text{Age } 10 \left(\frac{IQ\ 100}{300} + 0.17 \right) - 2.5$$

$$10 \left(300\overline{)100.00}^{\ .33} + 0.17 \right) - 2.5$$

$$10 \, (.33 + 0.17) - 2.5$$
$$10 \, (.50) - 2.5$$
$$10 \times .50 - 2.5$$
$$5.0 - 2.5 = 2.5$$

This child age ten with an IQ of 100 will have to function at or below second grade, fifth month (2.5) in one or more of the above listed areas to qualify for an LD class.

Example: Child Age 10, with IQ 150, fifth grade

$$\text{Age } 10 \left(\frac{\text{IQ } 150}{300} + 0.17 \right) - 2.5$$

$$10 \left(300 \overline{) 150.00}^{.50} + 0.17 \right) - 2.5$$
$$10 \left(.50 + 0.17 \right) - 2.5$$
$$10 \left(.67 \right) - 2.5$$
$$10 \times .67 - 2.5$$
$$6.7 - 2.5 = 4.2$$

This child age ten with an IQ of 150 will have to function at or below fourth grade, second month (4.2) in one or more of the above listed areas to qualify for an LD class.

Obviously, one can understand the different discrepancy levels of these three children, all of whom are age ten, which is fifth-grade level. The discrepancy level is based upon the child's chronological age and IQ.

Child, Age 10, IQ 90 must function at or below grade 2.2

Child, Age 10, IQ 100 must function at or below grade 2.5

Child, Age 10, IQ 150 must function at or below grade 4.2

All three children are in the fifth grade, have different IQ scores and must measure different levels of discrepancies.

CANHC-GRAM (1977) reported a validity study by Berman and Denhoff which indicates that the most serious problem with this formula is that the final subtracted constant is the same for all ages. Subtracting 2.5 grades makes the formula nearly unworkable for young children. However, there is a good argument for the fact that 2.5 grades is too much to subtract in *all* cases, since only at age eleven was the current formula able to predict above 50 percent accuracy. This information was obtained from a study completed by Berman and Denhoff involving a total of 82 children who had been previously identified as learning disabled.

Therefore there are two significant problems with the formula:

1. It demonstrates poor accuracy in predicting correctly a group of known learning-disabled children.
2. It discriminates most against the youngest children. This seems to run contrary to all current theorists and workers in the field who feel that accuracy at young ages is the most critical for effective treatment.

Estimates of Prevalence

Estimates of prevalence depend on the criteria and cutoff points used, whether reflected in the form of learning quotients, or achievement level discrepancies. The prevalence range suggested by Kass and Myklebust is from 3 to 5 percent of the school population. There may be overlapping among different areas of the handicapped in which some of these children are currently being serviced in other special education programs.

There are controversy and difficulty in defining learning disabilities because the minimal brain dysfunction category is not popular with many pediatric-neurologists, and since brain injury is not an accountable ailment, no exact figures exist on the number of these children. A general estimate seems to indicate that at least 5 percent of United States school children have learning disabilities. Major interest in the learning disability area is recent, and there is still confusion among professionals as to terminology and identification. Therefore, estimates of incidence seem to depend on individual interpretations of the scope of the category and may vary from 5 to 20 percent of the total school population. As indicated, though, by PL 94–142 only 2 percent of the school population may be federally funded for learning disability programs.

Methods of Identification

Identifying children with specific learning disabilities should be accomplished as early as possible. It is vital that preschool and first-grade teachers be aware of the major signs and symptoms and have information concerning referral sources where extensive evaluations can be made.

The preschool and first-grade teachers can use an individual record sheet for each child. This record sheet should contain a list of characteristics which may be indicative of learning problems. An example by Slingerland (1969) is as follows:

1. Attention span
2. Behavior and social relations
3. Indications of mental growth and general maturity
4. How crayon or pencil is held
5. Family pattern of handedness or language difficulties, if known
6. Language
7. Preferred and avoided activities
8. Coordination
9. Writing of name
10. Handedness

In parent conferences the teacher can learn when the child began to talk, to walk, to develop hand preference (if indicated), how directions are understood and followed at home, if the child is at ease with verbal expression or is frustrated by inadequate expressive efforts. The regular class teacher will have a number of children with learning disabilities in a classroom and the teacher will be valued as a part of the identification process. It is suggested that all teachers become aware of the identification procedure for such children. Some clues are easily recognized, and the regular class teacher, if aware of these clues, will be a referring agent.

Standardized tests can be administered to aid in the evaluation of general abilities. Such tests as readiness tests, perceptual tests, IQ tests, and achievement tests are suggested evaluative techniques.

Continued experience with learning disabilities in children may reveal identifiable symptom complexes. Kirk and Bateman (1962) suggested three common symptoms that could be used to identify learning disabled children:

1. All are retarded or disordered in school subjects, speech or language, and/or manifest behavior problems.
2. None are assignable to major categories of exceptionality such as mental retardation or deafness.
3. All have some presumed neurologic basis (cerebral dysfunction) for their manifested disability or disabilities.

In some schools it is common practice to use group screening for children who are likely to have learning problems. Each child's learning characteristics are described, and the information is produced for the necessary intervention-instructional programs aimed at prevention of learning disabilities.

Rice (1970) indicated (from Dunn 1968) that there are three facets of an effective evaluation process:

1. Make a study of the child to find behaviors acquired along the dimension being considered (language, cognitive skill development, motor skill, etc.).
2. Develop samples of a sequential program designed to move the child forward from that point.
3. Demonstrate the method by which the child can best be taught.

An important thing to remember in diagnosis is that one needs to estimate realistically how much each child can learn, under what circumstances, and with what materials. Each child must be programmed on an individual level of functioning.

Characteristics

A number of characteristics are observable by classroom teachers and by parents which may suggest the presence of a learning disability or perceptual problem. These children have a tendency to reverse numbers or letters, such as *b*'s and *d*'s, *p*'s and *q*'s. They also may invert numbers, such as writing 17 for 71. Some of these children mirror write. They may write words or numbers upside-down-backwards; hold a mirror up and you can see perfect writing.

There may be some coordination problems. A child may appear awkward, may frequently trip, or bump into things. One should be careful to distinguish this child from the child who may be acting-out and has no learning problem. Learning-disabled children may have problems in audio-discrimination with such sound-alike words as dime and diamond. This situation is not a hearing problem, but it is an auditory inability to discriminate certain sounds and categorize these sounds.

These children may have a perseveration problem. Perseveration does not mean the same thing as persevering. Persevering is great. Persevering is to work on a task until it is completed. The child who perseverates will do a task, and then do it over and over again. There is no end to the task. Many times the child will start a task; erase it, and start over, erase and start over, get mad, tear up the paper, break the pencil, and never complete a satisfactory task.

These children may also be hyperactive. Hyperactive children may have difficulty in screening out the stimuli surrounding them. You may be sitting in a room while you read this chapter. You can hear the air conditioning or heating system. Somebody is making noise in the other room, but it isn't distracting to you. You are able to screen out these extra stimuli. Some learning disabled children cannot screen out excessive stimuli. Consequently, they have a very short attention span. This is a serious academic problem. If students are unable to sit at their desks and do arithmetic, reading, writing, or other school tasks because of the bombarding stimuli, they then become problems to themselves and to the teacher.

Learning-disabled children sometimes have very poor handwriting, art work, and drawing. The inability to coordinate eye-hand movements means that these children have trouble performing on group tests of intelligence or achievement. Of course, it should be obvious that if these children have reading problems, they will not do well on a group-administered test. Therefore, adequate assessment of the child's learning strengths and deficits will require an individual test battery.

Something that may be quite noticeable with learning-disabled children is their general performance. In their general environment they will appear brighter than tests show them to be, and teachers get indications that these children are not retarded, but that there is something missing. The teachers know the students can do these things if they have the right kinds of opportunities. This feeling is also evident with the child, who has a kind of confusion which says, "Well, I know I can do this, I'm just as smart as the other kids, I know I can do it. But something is wrong and for some reason I can't do it." These children also have poor perception of time and space. They may get lost easily and might not be able to tell time. They get confused in physical locations and can't understand directions.

Teachers and parents should make concrete kinds of demands upon these children, or even singular kinds of demands. A parent might say, "Get out of bed and come to breakfast," rather than, "Get up from bed, put on your shoes and your clothes, and go brush your teeth, and wash your hands, hang the towel up, make your bed, pick up your clothes, come in and eat breakfast." By the time such children receive all these orders they are so busy trying to sort them out, they get confused and probably end up unable to do any of them. Sometimes children may look at the teacher in a very confused manner after receiving a long list of orders, because they are having problems trying to sort out all of the information.

Poor perception causes problems in categorizing and associating. For example, the teacher may show four flying objects such as a bird, helicopter, airplane, and kite and then toss in a turtle, automobile, and baseball. Now if the teacher asks the child to put together the objects that are similar, the child may not be able to sort out the four flying objects. The child may toss in the ball or the turtle.

These inconsistencies can be tragic in the academic setting. LD children may recognize a word today and not recognize it the next day. Teachers may not use consistent teaching methods, and this is very important for these children because they lack perceptual consistency, which is an inability to perceive an object as having different qualities or varying properties such as size, position, and shape. They may look at a capital *A* and a small *a* and just not recognize them as the same letter. Pictures of a fire truck from the back, from the front, or from the side, may not be recognized as the same fire truck. This inability to recognize an object from any view causes problems when this child goes to school, because books have different size print, different colored letters, and other kinds of varying qualities.

Emotional-affective characteristics are also observable by teachers and parents in learning-disabled children. Such children are unable to control affect. In other words, they overreact to stimuli. They may have inadequate impulse control. As an example: a child may work for a period of time on a school task, maybe a picture, a painting, or writing assignment. At the end of this task the student loses control and becomes quite emotional, with crying outbursts and ridicule of self and others. The child simply does not have the ability to control the affective tones involved with the completion of tasks.

This child embellishes the task at hand whether reading a story out loud, telling a story, or adding details to pictures. It's something like the perseveration mentioned earlier in this chapter. It just seems that the child cannot stop. Such children may start a story and then keep it going, going, and going. Suggestions for teachers and parents at this point would be that one should not appear interested and agree with the embellished story and continue listening; nor should one reject them and tell them to shut up and stop adding to the story. Instead of either agreeing or rejecting, one should try to detour them down another avenue of conversation.

Learning-disabled children may have a very low frustration tolerance. Many times if they don't get immediate success on a task, or if they don't get the results they desire immediately, they may react like paranoids. They will attack the object or the person they feel is hindering the situation. As an example, a boy doesn't get the immediate success he wants from drawing a picture. He may attack the picture and rip it up or break the pencil. He may attack the teacher, because the teacher didn't give him the grade he needed or wanted on this particular assignment. The emotional procedure for avoiding failure is to attack the failing situation. The teacher may attempt to help a child or correct an assignment, and the child will try to avoid this situation by attacking the teacher with such language as, "You're stupid and everybody's stupid and I don't want you to look at my paper."

A child may not respond to the demands that the parent or teacher makes in order to upset and thus get even with them. Parents and teachers should maintain or at least try to control this situation simply by being aware of the child's tensions. The adult should be alerted to the emotional buildup within the child and realize that the child is beginning to reach the limit of toleration. Parents and teachers should learn to recognize clues before an explosion; then they would naturally avoid having a lot of trouble with the child.

Children with learning disabilities come to the attention of the schools by way of a number of characteristics. Clements (1966) selected ten of the most frequently cited characteristics of learning-disabled children. They are listed in order of frequency:

1. Hyperactivity
2. Perceptual-motor impairments
3. Emotional lability
4. General orientation defects
5. Disorders of attention (e.g., short attention span, distractibility, perseveration)
6. Impulsivity

7. Disorders of memory and thinking
8. Specific learning disabilities in reading, arithmetic, writing, and spelling
9. Disorders of speech and hearing
10. Equivocal neurological signs and electroencephalographic irregularities.

Myers and Hammill (1969) stated that the characteristics observed in children with specific learning disorders may be divided arbitrarily into at least six categories:

1. Motor activity: hyperactivity, hypoactivity, incoordination, and perseveration
2. Disorders of emotionality
3. Disorders of perception
4. Disorders of symbolization: receptive-auditory, receptive-visual, expressive-vocal, and expressive-motor
5. Disorders of attention: excessive attention and insufficient attention
6. Disorders of memory.

Cruickshank and Johnson (1975) indicated that Rappaport lists three major response patterns of brain-injured children, each of which he subdivides. His grouping includes the following:

1. Inadequate impulse control or regulation
   a. Hyperactivity
   b. Hyperdistractibility
   c. Disinhibition
   d. Impulsivity
   e. Perseveration
   f. Lability of affect
   g. Motor dysfunctions
2. Inadequate integrative functions
   a. Perceptual difficulties
   b. Conceptual difficulties
3. Defective self-concept and narcissistic hypersensitivity
   a. Low frustration tolerance
   b. Flight from challenge
   c. Overcompensation
   d. Control and manipulation of others
   e. Negativism or power struggle

Morrison (1971) presented Hellmuth's outline of the characteristics of children with learning disabilities as follows:*

I. Behavioral
   A. Mixed laterality—The child is dominantly neither right nor left sided. This includes hands, feet, and eyes.
   B. Delayed responses—There is a noticeable and unusual time lag in responding to questions or stimuli.
   C. Inconsistency—The child tends to respond to the same stimulus one way one time and a different way another time.
   D. Distractibility
      1. An abnormal fixation to unimportant details while disregarding the essentials.
      2. A blurring or inversion of background and foreground, where the main subject may blend with the background or the background itself may become the focus of attention.
   E. Hyperactivity—A forced, undirected response to stimuli. A drive that compels the child to act, to flit from one thing to another, that makes him unable to withstand countless stimuli which the normal child disregards.
   F. Quiet, daydreaming, phlegmatic behavior—This is the opposite extreme from the hyperactive child. Sometimes referred to as hypoactive.
   G. Emotional lability—The child may be "highstrung" irritable or aggressive, but change quickly from high temper to manageability and remorse. He may be panicked by what would appear to others as a minimally stressful situation; however, some of these children are of sweet disposition and even-tempered even in the presence of a frustrating inability to perform academically.
   H. Disinhibition—Lack of emotional control, easy laughing or crying which may persist beyond reasonable limits.
   I. Catastrophic reaction—Extreme helplessness, despair or anxiety experienced when a child is confronted with a task beyond his ability, usually accompanied by intense crying.
   J. Extreme irritability and intolerance of discipline.
   K. Aggressive, antisocial, or uncontrolled behavior.
   L. Aimless, random movements—May "paw the air," wave arms, shuffle feet, etc.
   M. Impulsiveness—Cannot keep from touching and handling objects, particularly in a strange or overstimulating environment.

*Kansas Association for Children with Learning Disabilities

N. Short attention span.

O. Perseveration—The persistent repetition or continuance of an activity once begun, especially if the child has experienced success or pleasure. This may be characterized by difficulty in shifting from one activity to another, or the inability to start or stop a series; also, the persistent repetition of questions over and over even though they have been carefully answered.

P. Meticulosity—An exactitude demanded by the child who must have everything "just so."

Q. Abnormal clumsiness or general lack of coordination, either gross or fine movements, or both.

II. Speech

A. Transformation of syllables—As "aminal" for animal.

B. Reversals of syllables—As "Jofe" for "Joseph."

III. Language or Reading

A. Jumbled language or disturbed syntax—As "Mother, me to the store" for "Mother and I went to the store."

B. Word-finding difficulty—The child just cannot "call up" a word to use. Similar to "having a word on the tip of the tongue, but can't say it."

C. Inability to separate a whole into parts or to combine parts into meaningful whole. The child may recognize the word "bus" as a whole but cannot put "b" with "us" to form the word. Likewise, he/she may be able to recognize the letters or syllables, but cannot break the word down into its component parts.

D. Letter substitutions
1. Inversions—as V for A
2. Reversals—as b for d, ma for am
3. Similar letters—as he for h
4. Random substitutions—as ro for m

E. Word substitutions—Was for saw, top for pot, etc.

F. Distracted reading—Skipping, jumping words.

G. Slow recognition of words.

H. Omission of words, phrases, and sentences.

I. Definite deficiency or retardation in reading—Two or more years behind age-grade placement is significant for most elementary school pupils.

IV. Writing and Drawing

A. Inability to form letters or digits correctly—Starts at wrong direction in marking, forms in segments, etc.

B. Difficulty in staying on or between the lines.

C. Difficulty in judging how long or how tall a letter is.

D. Disturbance in spatial relationships—Difficulty in identification or matching of shapes—rotation or distortion of drawings of geometric designs. To compensate for poor performance the child may make innumerable and meticulous tiny strokes of the pencil when drawing.

E. Reversal of letters or digits.

V. Intelligence

A. Apparently of normal, potentially normal, or superior intellect.

B. The child who "is bright enough but just can't learn."

C. Verbal intelligence appears to be better than performance intelligence. May have a good vocabulary and can readily learn things read to him. Has difficulty "figuring out things."

Each of these learning-disabled children is unique. The child who is afflicted with just some of these characteristics may have a very difficult time conforming to the demands of home and school. When provided with understanding, compatible instruction, and attention, many of these children are able to fit naturally into regular public school classes and develop their potentials as happy, productive citizens.

Hyperactive Children

The following article is by Dr. Mark Stewart*

"The hyperactive child" is a broad category covering children who have four main problems: overactivity, distractibility, impulsiveness, and excitability. The degree of a hyperactive child's problem varies greatly; at one end of the spectrum there are boys who don't do school work up to the expected standard because they can't concentrate, and at the other there are boys who are aggressively antisocial and cannot be kept in a regular class-room. Most children who are called "hyperactive" are somewhere in-between these two extremes.

The problem is a common one: probably about 5 percent of all grade school children have difficulties of this kind. Many more boys than girls are hyperactive. The origin of the problem is not known at present. For most of these children the difficulty is probably that they are at one end of the normal range of activity level; in other words they are like children who are unusually tall or heavy. In a small minority of cases (about one out of ten) there is evidence that the child had an injury or an illness which affected his brain and which is probably related to the onset of this difficulty. There is no evidence at all that lack of love, absence of parents from the home, or other unfortunate experiences, cause children to be overactive, though these things might make a hyperactive child's problems worse.

*The article on pages 269-278 are reprinted by permission of *Expectations*, vol. 2, no. 4, September/October, 1972, from an article, *For Parents of Hyperactive Children*, by Mark A. Stewart, M.D.

Symptoms

Overactivity is a term used to cover the following kinds of behavior: unusual energy, needing less sleep than other children, inability to sit still in the classroom or at meal times, talking a great deal, talking out of turn in class, being unusually loud, wearing out clothes and shoes faster than other children, inability to keep from touching other children in class and interfering with them, disrupting classes by clowning, etc.

Distractibility refers to not getting work done in school, not being able to persevere with homework, daydreaming, being easily distracted from projects by outside stimuli, being unable to listen to stories or attend to TV programs, leaving projects unfinished, tuning out teachers and parents when they try to give directions, being unable to play card games or games such as Monopoly through to the end.

Impulsiveness covers: running out in the street or riding a bicycle in front of cars, jumping into the deep end of the pool without knowing how to swim, being unable to save up money for something that is badly wanted, letting out secrets or saying things that are known to be rude, saying "sassy" things to the teacher to show off, doing dangerous things on the spur of the moment, etc.

Excitability means such things as being easily upset, having a low frustration tolerance, not being able to take "no" for an answer or to accept delay, having a "short fuse" and getting into fights over little things, getting wound up and excited around other children, and crying more than other children.

Other important difficulties for the hyperactive child are: having a low opinion of himself, being unpopular with other children, fighting, rebelliousness, and learning problems.

Hyperactive children often do not get along well with other children of their own age. This may be because they are silly and immature in their behavior, or because their behavior in class turns the other children off. As a result hyperactive children may develop a "chip on the shoulder" attitude; this leads to further trouble because of a vicious circle. Other kinds of behavior which stem from this difficulty with other children are clowning in class to impress other children, trying to buy friendship with money or candy, telling boastful stories, and fighting and bullying.

Because of their impulsiveness, hyperactive children may get involved in lying, stealing, playing with matches or setting fires, vandalism, and sometimes such things as running away from home or truancy.

Treatment

There are some very important things that parents can do which will help their hyperactive child to be happier and to behave better. There are also some specific treatments which doctors may give children with this problem. Commonly physicians treat hyperactive children with stimulant drugs, such as Ritalin or Dexedrine. Paradoxically these drugs make children calmer, less active, and better able to concentrate. Successful drug treatment also shows the child that he can succeed in school. It is important for parents to understand that the prime target of drug treatment is their child's difficulty in school, and that another approach is best for changing behavior at home. The person who can best tell whether the treatment is doing any good is the child's teacher, and direct reports from the teacher are the basis on which the physician can judge whether his treatment is doing any good.

What Can Parents Do to Help? The Most Important Job for the Parents Is to See That Their Child Doesn't Get Discouraged and Begin to Think of Himself as a Permanent Failure. At the Same Time They Must Keep up a Firm Discipline.

For Parents
The principles of raising a hyperactive child aren't different from those for a normal child, but the frustrations and disappointments are much greater. Naturally parents blame themselves for their child's misbehavior, and grandparents, neighbors, and teachers often help to make parents feel inadequate and guilty. These feelings may in turn lead to arguments and quarrels between the father and mother of the child, and unhappiness of the other children in the family. Again, Children Are Not Hyperactive Because Their Parents Haven't Loved Them or Disciplined Them Enough. Probably they were born that way, for reasons we don't understand. Parents also feel guilty when they lose their tempers and beat their hyperactive child severely. This isn't the right thing to do but it is forgivable because few parents have been taught how to raise normal children, let alone hyperactive. Try Not to Feel Guilty About the Way Your Child Is.

Principles of Raising a Hyperactive Child
1. You have to love and accept your child as he is. Perhaps you can change some of his behavior for the better, or perhaps he can, but he needs to be accepted for what he is, and loved in spite of his faults. Some aspects of his behavior are so much a part of his nature that it is fruitless to try to change them. Restlessness, fidgeting, and talking all the time can be contained for short periods, but they will find an outlet. It is better to accept this kind of behavior and channel it, rather than to try to stop it. Similarly you should work around his short fuse, his impatience, and his lack of perseverance rather than clash with him over these shortcomings.

The problems of hyperactive children seem never ending in the grade school age, but there is no need to be gloomy about the future. As these children grow into their teens they do become less active and better able to concentrate and stay with things. It seems likely that they may always be somewhat more restless, impulsive and so forth, but these qualities, which give them so much trouble in school, may have advantages in adult life. An abundance of energy, a desire for action, an outgoing attitude toward people, and an ability to make up your mind quickly are real assets in some walks of life. Many successful businessmen, engineers, physicians, salesmen, and so on have been hyperactive children. If your child grows up in a stable and well-organized home, the chances are very good that your hyperactive child will be a happy and successful adult. Much of the behavior that gets a hyperactive child into trouble during his grade school years would not be a problem were it not for the pressures and restrictions of our urban life, and the failure of our schools to come to grips with the fact that children come to school with different kinds of temperament as well as different levels of intelligence.

2. Hyperactive children need to be treated with a firm but kindly discipline, first as normal children do, only more so. One of the major difficulties of a hyperactive child is that he is more impulsive and impatient than a normal child, and it takes him longer to acquire self-control. He therefore has a greater tendency to get into mischief and this may lead him into serious misbehavior. At the same time he is high-spirited, curious, active, and perhaps aggressive; you can therefore expect him to be pushing at the limits of what his parents and teachers will allow all the time. Unless these limits are clearly defined, and firmly enforced, he will often be getting away with things and learning to flout authority.

On the other hand when parents try to apply the usual rules to their hyperactive child, they may find that they spend their entire time scolding him, thereby making life miserable both for him and themselves. It seems best to ration the rules for the hyperactive child, and to tell your other children openly that you are doing this because the hyperactive one has a problem. This should not involve giving up any important rules (always letting parents know where he is, coming straight home from school, doing homework promptly), but should be relaxing on less important rules, (keeping his room tidy, being neat with his clothes, and good table manners). Father and mother should get together and agree upon the really important rules; these should be as few and as general as possible, and should allow some flexibility; and these rules should be firmly enforced.

Hyperactive children need closer supervision because of their inability to control their behavior. Partly this can be achieved by companionship with a child; the father can share activities with the child and through his presence keep him out of mischief. Using the same principle a child can be kept out of mischief by having him in organized activities that will appeal to him, such as athletic programs at the YMCA. This supervision cannot be maintained all the time, and there will be times when the child has to be punished for breaking rules. Punishment should take the form of being deprived of a treat or a privilege (TV programs, candy, riding his bicycle) and to be effective it should be given out as soon after the offense as possible. When children become very upset and angry in your company, they should be given a choice of shaping up or of going to their room for a period; this time away from the family or their friends is the most effective way to treat outbursts of temper. On the whole punishment is a weak way to influence a child's behavior, and it may even backfire by reinforcing behavior. Some children, misbehave persistently knowing that they are going to be punished, the reason being that they would rather have their parents angry and upset than have no attention from them. Rewarding good behavior is the strongest way to influence a child's behavior, but parents and teachers tend to take good behavior for granted and show an active interest only in bad behavior. We need to catch children being good, particularly hyperactive children who seldom get rewarded for good behavior in the ordinary course of things. It is also important to reward children for beginning to do things right, rather than waiting for them to do things exactly the way you asked them to do. Love and praise are great rewards; little presents or treats can make your love more concrete. Keep a supply of dime store toys for this purpose, or take time to play a game with your child.

3. Your child's opinion of himself. He always feels trouble at home and at school; often disliked by other children, his teachers, and even you at times. The hyperactive child is likely to have a very low opinion of himself, and to react with resentment, or silly bids for attention that only make matters worse. Building up his morale is a crucial job for the hyperactive child's parents.

Parents can find other areas of success to compensate for the difficulties that a child has in school. Hyperactive children may be particularly good at working with their hands, selling things such as Boy Scout candy, handling animals, or at sports. *Parents must do everything they can to involve their hyperactive child in activities in which he can succeed.*

Team sports are usually difficult for hyperactive children because of the complicated rules and the necessity for waiting your turn. Sports such as swimming, gym, or wrestling are more likely to capture the hyperactive child's interest. Boy Scout activities and YMCA activities are very helpful, and as the child grows older he should be given the opportunity to meet physical and social challenges such as are required in camp counselors. Preparation for being junior camp counselors (lifesaving courses at the "Y" for example) is an excellent way to boost a boy's morale.

It may be difficult to involve children in outside activities because they tend to give up easily and because they've experienced failure and rejection before. The way around this is for the child's father to be involved in the same activity, and for him to do it with his son as a recreation.

The most basic and important factor in preserving a child's morale is that parents should enjoy being with their hyperactive child and doing things with him. No child will ever think more highly of himself than his parents do: if they're not interested enough to spend time with him, or if they spend their time scolding him and never seem to enjoy being with him, he is going to think poorly of himself.

Hyperactive children have a tough time in school because they are called on to do the things that are hardest for them, namely sitting still and paying attention to the teacher or working on assignments. They are criticized or disciplined for these problems though they have little or no control over them. A common judgment made on hyperactive children in school is that they could do better if they would only try. Remember not to be too hard on your son when he comes home from school; it is likely to have been a long hard day for him. Do not push the issues of good grades and his school performance. Some parents find it hard to accept anything less than the best school performance from their children; they forget that success in school is not the only thing that determines success in adult life.

4. Specific Problems. *Overactivity.* There should be definite limits set on the amount of boisterous and loud behavior that you are prepared to accept within your house. When your child goes beyond these limits he should be told that he must either calm down or go and do his thing outside or in the basement, or in some place that is acceptable to you. Besides this and having reasonable standards for behavior at the dinner table and in company, there is not much point in trying to control activity; you should live with the restlessness in front of the TV set, or the continual squirming while your child reads a book. On the other hand you and he will be much happier if his activity can be channeled into constructive outlets. When he plays iceless hockey, trampolines, goes out running with his dog, or wrestles at the Y he is enjoying being active, and probably building up his self-confidence; meanwhile he is not irritating you with aimless fiddling around.

Short attention span and inability to persevere. Whether your child is working on building a model or doing a homework assignment, he will do much better if the work is divided up into small units. In other words he can do a few of his problems, or put a few pieces of a model together; bring what he has done to you for your approval; stretch his legs, and go back in a few minutes and start over again. It is best that he not work on his own, because he will be subject to all sorts of distraction and have nobody to bring him back to the work in hand. If he works in your presence, you can encourage him, bring him back to the short piece of work he has to complete, and reward him with praise and recognition when he has finished each unit. You should always insist that he finish any project for the simple reason that completing a model or finishing a game, rewards him for persistence. If he never finishes anything, he will never experience the reward of seeing something through and he simply won't learn this habit.

Unfortunately much schoolwork is boring and repetitive, but there are some ways that parents can help to increase children's interest. A number of teaching machines are available for helping children to learn grade school arithmetic and language skills, and these are designed in ways that appeal to children who have short attention spans. In a more general way parents can help to promote their children's interest in school by cultivating shared interests. For example, an interest in the history of frontiersmen can become a joint interest of a boy and his father, and can be encouraged by visits to museums, old houses of pioneers, forts, Indian mounds, and so forth. Father and son can watch TV programs related to this interest together, and perhaps plan related games or build models together. In this way a father draws his child into an interest which will give reading and social sciences more meaning.

Written work is probably the child's greatest hang-up in school. The understanding teacher will reduce written assignments for a hyperactive child to the absolute minimum, and not fuss about the neatness of the work turned in. Parents should follow this example, but do what they can to encourage the child to make frequent use of his writing skill. For example, they should encourage him to write short letters to a favorite relative, or to a pen pal; he should also write off for catalogues, maps, tourist guides and so on. Whatever he writes and brings home from school should be recognized and praised, not taken for granted. He is likely to try to do his writing in a great hurry, and therefore to make a number of careless mistakes. Usually he will then get upset and want to throw the whole thing away. For this reason a parent should be around when he is doing this work, and try to slow him down and encourage him. He should use strong paper which will take a lot of erasing, and parents need a stock of the kinds of erasers used by typists. When a child is not too sure about his spelling it may be best to have him check words with parents before he writes them down. During this kind of work parents have a golden opportunity to gently brainwash the child with the idea that he should check his work at least once after he has finished. Probably nothing will prevent hyperactive children from making careless mistakes in arithmetic and writing, so that it is important that they learn to check their work.

Getting upset or wound up easily. Prevention is the art here, rather than treatment. Hyperactive children do get very wound up around a group of other children, and this has a number of implications. For example, birthday parties had better be out of doors, or in some place like the basement where it won't matter to you that things get a bit out of hand. It is a mistake to take a hyperactive child on a long shopping trip with your other children because when he gets bored he is likely to start stirring them up. One of the most important preventive measures you can take is to school your other children not to respond to the hyperactive child's irritability, teasing, and bickering. This is asking a lot of your other children, and you should be sure to let them know how grateful you are when they manage to keep the peace in face of provocation.

When your child begins to be upset you should take him out of whatever situation he is in and try to get him back to the situation and help him. Leaving him to go on trying to handle the situation on his own, and telling him to shape up or calm down, usually results only in his getting more and more frustrated. When your child has gotten beyond himself in being upset he should be taken to his room, or some other room where he can be on his own, and told to wait there until he feels he can behave in an acceptable way again. He should never be allowed to win his way in a dispute with you by having a temper tantrum, even when you are in some public place and it is mortifying to have him screaming and acting up. Buying peace by giving in to a child reinforces his tendency to have a tantrum the next time that he wants something and you don't want to give it to him.

Impulsiveness. This is a very difficult problem to work on, but it can be influenced through close supervision and the direct teaching of self-control. Riding a bicycle recklessly in the streets, and guessing wildly at words that he doesn't know when he is reading, are two good examples of impulsive behavior. The one can be handled best by very close supervision of the child's first trips around streets in the neighborhood, stern instruction in the rules of traffic, and rehearsing the natural consequences of his ignoring these rules. This means that when a child is first riding his bicycle, his father should ride with him and see that he stops properly at stop signs, stays on the right hand side of the road, gives signals and so forth. Whenever the child fails to observe these rules the father should patiently go over what are the likely consequences of his ignoring the rules when a car happens to come along. The first few times that the child rides his bicycle on his own he should be asked to recite what are the most important points he has to remember when he is riding in the streets; for example what he does when he comes to a stop sign. The idea behind this is to get him to instruct himself about the rules, and build a system for self-control. The same method can be applied to reading. The difficulty is that the child doesn't take the time to figure out a word, and because of his hurry tends to guess. At school and at home he can be coached gently in the idea of slowing down, stopping to think about a word that he does not recognize, and sounding it out to himself until he hits on the right word for the context. This can be made into a sort of game where the child is induced to say to himself . . . stop, think, look . . . or some similar short message. Again the idea is that he should learn to instruct himself in order to regulate his behavior.

Whenever this doesn't involve physical danger children should be allowed to face the consequences of their impulsive behavior. For example, if a child dashes out to school on a very cold day without a coat on he should be left to face the consequences of getting cold. He may learn something from this experience himself, but will not get anything from having his mother chase after him with his coat. Some kinds of impulsive behavior are best prevented altogether. Money should never be left lying around on the kitchen table or on top of father's dresser where it may be picked up by the child without the parent being sure that anything has happened. Each time the child does this and gets away with it, the habit is reinforced. The answer then is that all money should be put away in safe places; this includes your other children's savings banks, purses and wallets. The same kind of preventive measure should be applied to matches, gasoline for the lawn mower

What will help—vitamins, good teachers, classes, materials, or all of them?

and so forth. Lying cannot be handled in this way, but can be discouraged if parents emphasize to the child that owning up to having been in mischief will not be followed by punishment for the mischief. In other words self-incrimination will be recognized, and the act of telling the truth will be rewarded by forgiving the original sin.

Aggressiveness. This is best handled by the parents setting an example of calmness, and particularly by their avoiding physical punishment, and by encouraging the child to have normal friendly activities. The more he can find friends who are like himself and enjoy physical activity and competitiveness, the less he will resent other children and pick fights with them. Within the house your child should be rewarded when he has a peaceful day and does not bug his siblings, and his brothers and sisters should be rewarded for not responding to his trouble making. When he does get into fights he should be left to face the consequences, whether this is being beaten up by another or having an angry parent complain about his bullying a smaller boy.

Summary. Your hyperactive child will have the best chance of growing up happily if you accept him for what he is, believe in his future, help him as best you can with his specific problems, set firm limits to his behavior, and most of all if you enjoy his company. This is a difficult undertaking for you, and you should feel no shame if you need help and encouragement for yourself. On the contrary it is important that you let your physician know your own difficulties, and unburden yourself about your disappointments and frustrations. That is what he is there for.

The authors agree with the text of Dr. Stewart's statements, and believe that he has offered some valuable information relative to hyperactive children. This information should be quite helpful to parents and teachers.

Research with Hyperactive Children

As the years pass, teachers, educators, psychologists, and others have noticed considerable changes in the theories of and practice with hyperactive children—stimulation, nonstimulation; medication, nonmedication; mega-vitamins, allergies, food additives, etc. Information published by Wiederholt (1976) indicated some interesting research which expresses different causative factors relative to hyperactive children. A radical change in the treatment of hyperactive children—increasing stimulation rather than reducing it—has been suggested by observation of them in learning situations.

At one time it was thought best to provide the hyperactive child with as little stimuli as possible. In the classroom, this meant nothing on bulletin boards or walls near the child, and cubicles were suggested for work. This went along with the theory that hyperactivity was caused by an inability of the brain to filter out irrelevant stimuli. Empirical research that this lack of stimuli actually improved performance, however, was lacking.

Contrary to this theory, researchers noticed that hyperactive children were invariably attracted by moving stimuli, that moving playthings, an auto ride or a motion picture would "successfully hold the attention of even the most distractible child."

It was also noticed that holding or touching the child tended to reduce hyperactivity—another observation which did not agree with stimulus reduction theory—and isolated hyperactive children tended to "create" their own stimulus by playing with desks, screens, materials, etc.

Teachers in regular classrooms observed that hyperactive children were most active waiting their turns in groups—not at recess, free time, or at most seat work. Tasks involving little movement appeared to create more activity in hyperactive than normal children. It is now being theorized that hyperactive behavior may have a functional value for the hyperactive child—perhaps helping to maintain a focus on stimuli—a sort of homeostatic response, a kind of self-regulation.

Perhaps the hyperactive child would benefit from optimum stimuli. This theory is further supported by the fact that they behave quite like other children when exposed to a novel environment—high in stimulus value—and by a variety of classroom studies that show hyperactive children are not distracted by environmental stimuli, visual or auditory, any more than their classmates.

Amphetamine drug therapy, for all its controversial aspects, also seems to support the optimum stimuli theory. Wiederholt (1976) also reported a study in which the behavior of hyperactive children who were placed on a diet without artificial flavors and colors improved significantly. Teachers who observed the children for twelve weeks noted about a 15 percent reduction in symptoms of hyperactivity. The teachers did not know when a child began a new diet or whether the child was on the control or experimental diet.

The study by Dr. C. Keith Connors of the University of Pittsburg was the first controlled study of the effect of food additives on hyperactive children and tends to confirm the controversial findings of Dr. Benjamin Feingold.

However, a NIE staff review suggests that because of methodological problems, the Connors' study is not conclusive. Feingold, a leading California allergist, charged that food additives cause hyperactivity, but he was widely criticized for the quality and objectivity of his research.

Hyperactive children are characterized by their constant, unorganized activity, short attention spans, and unusually aggressive behavior. An estimated five million children in the United States are hyperactive.

Both diets used in the Connors' study—the control and the experimental—were similarly high in nutrition. The experimental diet eliminated fruits with natural salicylates and all food with artificial coloring, flavors, preservatives, or other additives. For example, soda pop, frankfurters, cake mixes, many breakfast cereals and aspirin were among the foods eliminated. Natural salicylates, contained in fruits such as apples, berries, and peaches, were also eliminated because of a suspected reaction with food additives.

NIE urges caution in interpreting the results of this study. Connors' research was very small; only fifteen children completed the study. In addition, parents noticed only slight differences in the children's behavior. The study also does not isolate a culprit. As Connors admits, "We cannot say whether the natural salicylates, food colors, food flavors—or indeed some unsuspected nutritional factors—might not be responsible for the results." Nevertheless, the changes in behavior observed by the teachers are significant, Connors argued, because the differences in behavior ratings could only occur by chance five times in one thousand. Senator Edward Kennedy, D-Mass. requested the Food and Drug Administration (FDA) to conduct further research into the relationship between food additives and hyperactivity.

The Neuropsychiatric Bulletin (CANHC-GRAM) reported additional interesting information relative to the etiology of hyperactivity. Carbon monoxide has become a prevalent toxic influence in this society. The symptoms of carbon monoxide toxicity (prior to headache and coma) include restlessness, sleeping difficulty, short attention span, and other irritable brain phenomena. The cause-effect relationship was established in a number of children seen at the Southern California Neurological Institute where carbon monoxide levels of 7–20 percent resulted in a syndrome presented as "hyperactivity." The symptoms resolved once the source of the carbon monoxide was identified and eliminated, and the patients returned to normal. (Toxic levels are given as 0.5–2.0 in nonsmokers in a rural area, up to 5 percent for nonsmokers in urban areas; heavy smokers may have up to 9 percent.)

The major sources of carbon monoxide are faulty gas heaters in the home and faulty mufflers in the family car. Also, in almost epidemic proportions, a major source is the decrepit school bus typically driven around town with its windows closed and loaded with children. Concerned parents, physicians and environmentalists should demand careful monitoring of the exhaust systems of school buses.

Pinworm infection is a frequently overlooked cause of hyperactivity in children. Its influence on behavior relates to the fact that the gravid worms lay their eggs outside the bowel in the anal and perianal region, causing severe itching and sleep disturbance. These in turn, cause daytime irritability, poor attention span, and other stigmata of hyperactivity (often including anorexia and weight loss) and can, understandably, lead to chronic emotional problems.

Of those seen at this Institute, girls were more frequent victims of hyperactivity secondary to pinworm infections. The speculation is that irrational fears may be greater for them because of anatomical differences.

Infected patients may suggest the diagnosis in a manner of ways. They may have scratch marks in the rectal area. Their complaints may specifically include itching and sleep disturbance. Often, however, none of the above clues are present. Only after finding pinworm ova, treating the infection and seeing the child's behavior dramatically return to normal that the cause of the problem is demonstrated.

Suggested Guidelines for Dealing with Hyperactivity, Distractibility, Short Attention Span, and Rigidity

1. Redirect the child: "Go back and do this." Redirecting will usually elicit a more favorable reaction from the child than stopping an activity.
2. Limit work periods so that the child can achieve success before tiring.
3. Use some physical contact with the child, which may be a hand on the shoulder, or directing arm and hand movements.
4. Avoid teaching at a frustration level. Teach at a tolerance level at which children can apply themselves easily and at a level which is challenging.
5. Help the child structure tasks which allow step-by-step sequence.
6. Counsel the child to provide insight into hyperactivity. Children of this nature feel out of place; they know life is falling apart for them and they do not understand that they have a bigger task than do other children whose bodies work normally.
7. Reduce distractions. Seat the child in a front side row, thus reducing the number of close contacts.
8. Be sure the child completely understands what is being taught.
9. Relate new situations to those the child already knows well.
10. Teach when the child is well motivated and ready to work.
11. Present the lesson in a vivid manner so that it stands out from background activities.
12. Keep the work area neat. Provide only the task on which the child is working.
13. Be calm. Show no anger, irritation, or *rejection* toward the child.
14. Speak softly so that the child must listen carefully.
15. Be firm. Do not allow the child to escape a task that you know can be performed.
16. Be consistent. Don't alternate between giving in to the child and being firm about completing a goal.
17. Use simple commands and directions. Don't talk too much.
18. Never ask, "Do you want to do this?" Say, "Do this." You must structure the situation.
19. Be respectful of the child as an individual. Realize limitations, be kind, but don't gush, overpraise, or overdo your concern.

Educational Provisions

There are numerous methods and procedures suggested for working with these children. However, education is still somewhat experimental concerning these children. There is very little evidence of research which indicates static procedures or techniques for learning-disabled children. Only a few years ago, authorities thought these children could not stand the stimuli in the classroom and recommended discarding bulletin boards, distractible objects, and bright curtains. In other words, keep a bland room, keep the toys out of sight, because these children can not tolerate these stimuli. We have noticed recently in visiting classrooms and talking with teachers that these forms of stimuli aren't necessarily disturbing the children. We have gone into classrooms which appear to be total chaos, not as a result of the bombarding of the stimuli, but because of the teacher's inability to tolerate the situation. We have also gone into classrooms which teachers had beautifully decorated. There were all kinds of stimuli and the children were performing very well, which indicates that the most important factor may be the teacher's ability to maintain the class, rather than how much stimuli were coming in from the outside.

Presently we believe that there are varying success factors in the learning disability area. A suggestion to parents and teachers would be for them to do what is advantageous to them and their children. The main thing to realize is that all methods and procedures indicated for a learning-disabled child are not appropriate for all learning disability children. Some will need specific things that will not work with other children. Therefore, one should not be conclusive and say that there is a specific panacea for learning-disabled children.

No single or best approach to teaching the learning disabled child is recognized today. General practice in their education in the public school has not followed systematic methodologies or specific practices of teaching to overcome specific disabilities. Modification has been in terms of what is taught rather than how it is taught.

Some good educational practices to use may be to influence the environment of learning, to realize a concept of individual differences and differentiated education, to develop techniques and methods for remediation of the faulty learning process, to realize an experiential framework, to experiment with and manipulate ways of learning, and to manifest a concept of education for total life adjustment.

Heckrel and Webb (1969) indicated that if a school is setting up a program for the learning-disabled child there are three basic steps that must be followed:

1. It involves the identification of those children who are not learning by normal techniques.
2. The diagnostic orientation must be integrated with treatment procedures.
3. Educators have the task of developing an effective school program that serves the learning-disabled child by providing special help and curriculum adjustments for as long as the child requires them.

After the teacher knows children well enough to set realistic goals for their accomplishment, a daily plan of activities may be devised. The activity schedule should not be rigid. The class needs a variety of activities throughout the day. The day's first activities should focus on the area of greatest difficulty. Effective supervision is mandatory.

Because the learning-disabled child may have faced constant failure, more attention must be directed toward developing self-motivation than would be necessary for other children. The goals must be simple and concrete, rather than abstract and complex.

Provisions for helping disabled children may or may not include the establishment of a self-contained classroom in which children receive all instruction from a special teacher. Special tutoring may be necessary for some children. The remaining part of their school time may be spent in the regular classroom or in a part-time special class with emphasis placed on specific learning problems.

Secondary School Programs—Learning Disabilities

During the initial development of school programs for children with learning disabilities, the emphasis was entirely at the elementary school level. Many educators and other professionals believed that secondary school programs were not needed. These beliefs were based primarily on the premise that early identification and good elementary school programs were sufficient for the remediation of learning disabilities.

Field experiences with elementary school children who had one or more learning disabilities have demonstrated that some learning disabilities cannot be remediated. Present research continues to indicate that some children may have learning disabilities throughout their lives. Acceptance of this possibility should influence the further development of secondary school programs and the structure and content of programs at both elementary and secondary schools. Instructional evidence supports the fact that most learning disabilities can be corrected or improved to the extent that a child may return to the regular class program on a full-time basis. Consequently, parents and educators should not consider their efforts or those of the child to be a failure when the child's learning disabilities do not improve immediately or extensively.

Children in secondary school who have significant learning disabilities will be achieving well below their expected grade level. The frustrating consequences of low achievement are compounded by the fact that they appear very capable. They have learned to perform quite well in some areas, but certain areas cause undue frustration. These factors may cause teachers to view them as lazy people who do not apply academic abilities appropriately. The typical adult solution may be to apply more pressure for achievement or punishment for nonachievement. In reaction to this pressure, the youngster may attempt initially to comply. However, after several unsuccessful attempts to achieve in the particular subject area(s), the youngster becomes very aggressive, hostile, severely withdrawn, or a school dropout.

High school students need learning disability classes also.

According to Marsh and Price (1980) assessment of adolescents who have learning disabilities is not a well-defined procedure, nor is there an appropriate definition to serve as a guideline for assessment. The basic premise is one of an underachievement model with primary emphasis on reading disability. Too many adolescents are included in this model. Tests which attempt to measure the processing of information do not suffice because the constructs are suspect, the tests are not reliable, and many of them are not appropriate for older students.

If psychoeducational tests are used, school personnel should select them on the basis of their appropriateness, recognize the limitations of the tests, give proper consideration to their statistical properties, and give no importance to differences that are not statistically significant. Marsh and Price are supporters of the use of criterion-referenced tests and ecological assessment. However, they recognize that psychoeducational tests will continue to be used because of the demand to support classification of students.

One of the primary concerns regarding the adolescent with a significant learning disability is the development of self-concept. Their inability to perform well in particular areas and awareness of normal or above-normal intelligence tends to make them feel less worthy. Parents, siblings, peers, and school people may add to their poor self-concept because they view them negatively, degrade them because of their problems, or consistently apply unrealistic pressure. Peer rejection and adult pressures added to the normal confrontations and frustrations of adolescence may do severe harm to their self-concept development. Good self-concept development will require counseling and also some meaningful attitudinal changes by those people with whom they have daily contact.

According to Wiederholt (1975), adolescents with learning disabilities do not exhibit all of the characteristics cited as being the most common for younger children with learning disabilities. Some of the characteristics are similar, but marked differences may appear at the adolescent age. The adolescent, in addition to being hyperactive, having perceptual difficulties, and a short attention span, may exhibit problems in modifying behavior, generalizing to new areas, and deciding upon alternative forms of behavior. These and other characteristics cited by Wiederholt have not been substantiated through research, but have been formulated from observation. Good research is needed to clarify common characteristics among adolescents who have learning disabilities. Research is also necessary to describe learning strengths and weaknesses which may have importance for the development of instruction.

Observation of and research with the adolescent who has a learning disability indicates many academic and social problems. In the secondary school, the ability to modify one's behavior is extremely important. The student must be able to adjust to the rules of the system, behave in appropriate ways, and learn behaviors which are acceptable to others. Also, the ability to decide upon alternative forms of behavior is essential for learning different types of problem solving.

The problems of adolescents who have learning disabilities are usually long-standing, since they have been attempting to cope for several years. Educators must consider this problem when working with them. Without sensitivity to long-term problems, teachers may inadvertently add to the difficulties. An adolescent with a learning disability may attempt to hide the learning problem. Generally, adolescents do not like to be recognized as being different, especially when that difference might be viewed negatively. Of course, students won't be able to hide low academic performance, but personal defenses may lead them to demonstrate to others that they don't care about learning or school. They may do this by becoming hostile and aggressive toward the teacher or toward school in general or by becoming show-offs in the classroom. In short, they may become severe discipline problems. In contrast to this type of development, students might become severely withdrawn and stop all relationships with their peers. This withdrawal may cause them to stress self-blame for their problems. Consequently, serious personality disorders may develop.

The academic problems of adolescents may include several subjects or, at least have an effect on several subjects. For example, their primary problems may be in reading, which would affect all subjects at the secondary school level. However, if they can perform at an average or above-average level in speaking and listening skills, perhaps their programs could be modified through the use of tapes, videotapes, and small group discussions. If these types of modifications are feasible, the youngster could be integrated into many regular classes.

Implementation of modifications must cooperatively involve the regular class teacher and learning disabilities teacher. Also, assessment information must be examined carefully, and the school counselor should play a vital role in the planning of the program. The size of the regular secondary class may add many complications to the development of meaningful modifications, and should always be considered when integration is planned. Appropriate modifications in the regular secondary program may require that the learning disabilities teacher provide supportive services. These may include tutoring, selecting or preparing modified instructional programs, close liaison work with the regular class teacher, and providing counseling services for the adolescents and their parents.

Assessment of the adolescent's learning and behavioral strengths and weaknesses may indicate that modifications in the regular class program are not necessary. Certainly, if the educational needs of the adolescent are to be served, some self-contained classrooms will be required. This suggestion is not in agreement with the current stress on mainstreaming, but all adolescents with learning disabilities cannot profit from being integrated into regular class programs. To assume that all secondary school programs for learning disability children should be on the format of the resource room or the lab class is not providing adequately for their individual differences. Professionals have stated frequently that schools must provide diversity in programs for the adolescent. However, in practice, one does not find a range of different services at the secondary level. When the various learning styles and the strengths and weaknesses of adolescents are examined carefully, the need for some self-contained programs becomes evident. If the only alternatives offered are a lab class or the regular class, then school programs are inadequately designed for this group.

In several situations known to us, adolescents are offered the special services of a learning disabilities lab teacher who serves primarily as a tutor for regular class subjects. The supportive services of the learning disabilities teacher are essential. However, how many regular class subjects can one teacher provide within each fifty-minute class period? It is not acceptable to require one regular class teacher to be proficient in American History,

World History, Psychology, Chemistry, English Literature, and Vocational Education. Some school administrators, however, require the secondary learning disabilities teacher to provide tutoring in all or several of these subjects in one class period. Such programming probably is frustrating to the learning disabilities teacher; and probably provides inadequate instruction for the adolescent.

In addition to academic progress and remedial education programs, career development for adolescents with learning disabilities must be explored. Career development must be a part of the secondary program and should be included through the development of work-study programs. After a thorough study of learning and behavioral characteristics and an evaluation of abilities and interests, school personnel should work with adolescents in the development of career education. Many vocational areas of study are available. However, they will need direct assistance in making realistic choices for career development. Career development from the elementary to the secondary level is an essential inclusion for an effective, comprehensive program.

The development of work-study programs at the secondary school level may follow many of the guidelines already prepared for the educable mentally retarded. The program will emphasize the development of practical living skills, the continued improvement of academic skills, on-the-job training opportunities, and a thorough exploration of vocational development and opportunities. Suggesting work-study programs for the adolescent with learning disabilities does not close the opportunity for college training. Some will be able to pursue college training as a viable alternative. However, because of the many areas of functioning which can be affected by learning disabilities, vocational exploration and development cannot be neglected.

Programs for adolescents with learning disabilities must differ from programs offered in elementary school. For example, Alley and Deshler (1979) indicated that making the same assumptions about secondary students as are made about elementary children is to totally ignore the developmental processes and the curricular and situational differences at the secondary school level.

Alley and Deshler propose that a learning strategies approach would meet the needs of many learning-disabled adolescents. Such an approach would enable them to acquire, organize, store, and retrieve information. With skill development in these areas, adolescents would be able to cope with the secondary school and society.

Models being used in secondary schools are reported by Deshler, Lowrey, and Alley (1979) as a result of a nationwide survey. These models are presented below.

1. The Basic Skills Remediation Model—51 percent of programs surveyed.
   a. Remediation of basic skills with emphasis on reading and mathematics.

2. The Functional Curriculum Model—17 percent of programs surveyed.
   a. Academic skills are developed in relation to career concepts such as banking, consumer education, and applying for employment.
3. The Tutorial Model—24 percent of programs surveyed.
   a. Tutoring in subject areas in which students are experiencing difficulty or failure.
4. The Work-Study Model—5 percent of programs surveyed.
   a. Job- and career-related skill development with on-the-job experiences provided.
5. The Learning Strategies Approach Model—Limited implementation.
   a. Cooperative endeavors of many school personnel to promote the development of learning strategies across settings and situations.

Deshler, Lowrey, and Alley reported that there is no evidence to support one model as opposed to another. In all probability, most programs for learning-disabled adolescents use a combination of models.

The staff of a school system or individual school may be concerned about the scheduling of services for learning-disabled adolescents. In many cases, one may find a self-contained program or a resource room program and no other modification of the regular school program. Marsh and Price (1980) presented several possible models for programming in the secondary school. It should be noted that their suggestions apply to students who are mentally retarded, learning disabled, or emotionally disturbed. These suggestions are presented in a modified form for the reader's perusal.

Schedule	Primary Emphasis
Study Hall Time	Compensatory and/or remedial instruction. Can result in too many students at one time, and one period per day may not suffice.
Release Time	Course Supplantation: Student attends the resource room for special instruction in a subject in lieu of attending the regular class.
	Shared Instruction: Student spends some time in the regular class with shared time in the resource room for individualized instruction.
Assigned Period	Specific time periods are assigned for resource room instruction just as is found for History, English, etc.
Reduced Load	A student reduces the academic year load in order to receive individual instruction and increases total time in school by one or more years.
Extra Time Arrangement	The resource room is open before and after school and during the noon hour for additional individual instruction. Adds important time but this schedule should *never* be the only program offered.
Interaction Model	Combines one or more of the approaches mentioned above. In addition, learning centers or resource rooms may provide individual instruction on an "as needed" basis.

Secondary programs for adolescents need more extensive development. As career education improves in general education, the offering and improvement of secondary learning disabilities programs will increase. As research adds to our knowledge regarding adolescents and appropriate programs which can serve their needs, school systems will begin to provide services which are more meaningful to this group.

College Programs

College programs designed especially for learning-disabled adults are few. Many of the programs offer services such as tutoring, taped lessons, counseling, and oral examinations. California, by state law, provides for the educational rights and privileges of learning-disabled adults. The program at Ventura Community College as described by Barsch (1980) is worthy of mention. The structure of the program includes five special courses:

1. Improving Learning Potential—A perceptual motor training approach to improve posture, bilaterality, rhythm, and muscular strength.
2. Advances in Perception—Designed to develop individual learning styles.
3. Self-Adjustment to College—Counseling services to improve self-image, assertiveness, social interaction, etc.
4. Maximizing Occupational Potential—A study of vocational potential in several areas such as plumbing and office machines.
5. Advanced Perceptual Motor Training—To be taken after completion of the first four courses. Use of the metronome to increase verbal expression, reading rate, and develop spelling proficiency.

This program provides an ongoing assessment of learning-disabled adults based on performance in the five courses and reports successful experiences with the students.

Objectives

The educational objectives for children with learning disabilities, indicated by Rappaport (1969), are as follows:

1. View this child as a total, integrated organism that needs a total, integrated program in order to have the most effective opportunity for learning.
2. Insure the consideration of all aspects of developmental growth and performance within the education program.

3. Acknowledge learning opportunities to be present both before and after school hours, so that more than classroom conditions are considered, and so that the teacher is not charged with the sole responsibility for the child's habilitation.
4. See this child not only as a pupil, but also as a member of a family and of society, with the result that the home and the community assume their responsibilities in providing adequate and appropriate learning environments.

Morrison (1971) presented Hellmuth's (1971) indication of the following goals and objectives:

1. Provide special educational programs which will bring *each child with learning disabilities* back into the mainstream of the regular educational system at the earliest possible time.
2. Provide for early detection of learning difficulties on the kindergarten and preschool level, so that children with learning problems may be channeled into a program best designed for their individual needs.
3. Implement special education programs for children with learning disabilities in every school district within the state.
4. Develop consistency in quality of programs and facilities throughout the state for education of children with learning disabilities.
5. Educate the public to understand and support better care for these children.
6. Help parents to understand and accept such children.
7. Stimulate research in the areas of learning disabilities.
8. Aid both state and national legislative processes to obtain funding for special education.

Long-term educational objectives for children with learning disabilities should be to assist them in actualizing their potential and help them become effective members of society. Short-term objectives should be directed toward enabling them to achieve academically, to attain social maturity, to be able to communicate, to care for themselves, and to function emotionally in a way acceptable to the public schools and their environment.

The ultimate goal is to provide these children with opportunities for total self-realization, to enable them to achieve dignity through their abilities and accomplishments. Also, the ultimate objective for these children is to remediate their problems and return them totally to the regular school program. Presently there seems to be a general opinion that many will return to a regular pattern of schooling. It should be noted, though, that parents and teachers should not set a time limit on the return schedule. Some may remediate in six months, others in one, two, or three years, and on. Do not plan a single schedule for all children's remediation. Consider each child separately.

An overall educational structure should include careful planning and control of time, space, materials, and techniques relative to the developmental needs of each youngster. This comprehensive planning should enable children to experience opportunities to succeed and overcome their previous failures.

Services for Learning-Disabled Children

If the concept of individualization is accepted, several major elements must be incorporated into the educational program. Research presented by Cruickshank and Johnson (1975) offered the following suggestions:

1. Rappaport's relationship structure—the ability of the teacher to understand the child sufficiently well at any given moment, through verbal and nonverbal communications, to relate in a way which aids the child's development of impulse control and other ego functions.
2. Environmental structure—the classroom must be a nonstimulating environment. The room should be smaller than the standard classroom because as space increases, so stimuli increase; as space decreases, the stimulus value of space also decreases.
3. Program structure—consistency is very important. The daily program must be structured with sufficient similarity from day to day to provide a pattern for adjustment and a setting wherein satisfying prediction can be practiced by the child.
4. Structured teaching materials—it is in the structure of the teaching materials that the child's peculiar needs can be met directly.
5. Motor training—there should be daily motor training, usually accomplished on an individual basis, for approximately thirty minutes. This child usually demonstrates incoordination of gross-motor and fine-motor movements.
6. Language development and speech therapy—daily speech and language development, under the supervision of a skilled speech therapist who understands the problems of speech in neurologically handicapped children, is a requisite.

These children need to be provided with immediate psychological, educational, neurological, and other determined evaluations. Space and facilities at each school should provide flexibility for special programs. There should be mobile partitions, audio-visual equipment, and other teacher desired materials. Teacher's aides should be available for service as special education teachers so that each child may receive the needed individual instruction. It is suggested that there should be one teacher per six students in programs for children with learning disabilities without a teacher's aide, and one teacher per ten students with a teacher's aide. In no case should there be more than ten students in one self-contained classroom. Many states have school laws that control class enrollment, and these controls usually maintain a maximum of ten students in each class.

The Multidisciplinary Approach

A multidisciplinary team of specialists more nearly matches a comprehensive theory of learning disabilities than does a single specialist or group of specialists working in isolation. Problems related to severe learning disabilities are many and tend to reveal themselves in interrelated clusters. Landreth (1969) suggested, "Research has indicated that certain physical deviations, brain injuries and defects, speech and hearing defects, emotional problems, and reading difficulties all frequently occur concomitantly in the learning-disabled child."

While the causality or exact sequence of occurrence for many children has never been satisfactorily established, it is recognized that the possible combinations of specific deficits are numerous. A multifaceted disability presents a complexity which must be matched with nothing less than multifaceted remediation, the kind of remediation that only a team approach can provide. Theoretically speaking, therefore, the team approach is an attempt to match the dynamic team structure.

Landreth (1969) also indicated that success of team cohesiveness depends upon a number of factors: a common commitment to similar professional beliefs, personal factors of openness and security, presessions, and adequate time.

Referrals are usually made by a school counselor or a classroom teacher. Sometimes parents refer their child. After children are referred, they should be given a comprehensive battery of tests to determine problems in intellectual development, emotional development, reading, speech, and hearing. The parents are interviewed. The information gained should be assembled and evaluated at a joint staff meeting. The team members then make recommendations which seem most beneficial for each child. Records of evaluation and recommendations are sent to the child's school and are discussed with parents.

Pediatric Examination

It is essential for the pediatrician to communicate directly with school personnel. School personnel, and particularly the classroom teacher, can often provide the pediatrician with valuable information about the child—areas of strengths and weaknesses behaviorally, academically, and socially. Direct preliminary communication in seeking school observations as part of the child's total evaluation enables a better understanding of the physician's findings and recommendations.

Clements (1966) indicated that the basic role of the pediatrician includes the following areas: (1) to detect any disease process, physical handicap, or sensory impairment which might deter the learning process; (2) to insure that all necessary studies and consultations are obtained, and to coordinate them in a meaningful and organized manner; (3) to provide interpretation of the findings to the parents and the schools, when necessary; (4) to assess development status periodically and to provide anticipatory counseling for the parents so adequate plans for appropriate school placement can be made to help avoid prolonged frustration, disappointment, and the secondary emotional problems resulting from prolonged school failure; (5) to provide periodic reevaluation, ongoing support, and medical management for the child, and appropriate counseling for the parents.

We suggest the following guideline for a comprehensive report on a child with suspected learning disability. This guideline is not recommended as a static profile. The different needs of each child, school, teacher, and other professionals may call for additions or deletions.

Pediatrician Report

I. Family Information
  A. Parent-family review
    1. Socioeconomic history
    2. Domestic-emotional stability
    3. Age and health of parents
    4. Intellectual functioning of parents
    5. Sibling information
  B. Parents' previous concern and referral history
  C. Parents' acknowledgement and understanding of the problem
II. Physical Examination
  A. Gestation period
  B. Prenatal, neonatal, perinatal and postnatal period conditions
  C. Maturational history (sat, walked, talked)
  D. Specific unusual accident or illness situations
  E. Pediatrician's observations of child's examination behavior
  F. Results of physical examination should reflect all areas of vision, perception, and coordination that may cause potential learning problems
  G. Electroencephalogram (if needed)

III. Educational Information (if available, may be added)
    A. School achievement and behavior records
    B. Present functioning level
    C. Intelligence Quotient Range
IV. Summary
    A. Relative diagnosis and prognosis
    B. Treatment recommendations for the child, parents, teachers, and siblings

Psychological Examination

The psychological examination should consider many aspects and levels of functioning. The examination will consist of a comprehensive evaluation. No single test should determine the fate of the child. Each psychologist has favorite evaluation techniques, and the results of this testing will be only as good as the ability to test and interpret. Therefore, one must realize that many degrees of testing exist. The following list contains some of the tests commonly used with children suspected of having learning disabilities:

I. Testing Instruments
    A. Wechsler Intelligence Scale
    B. The Raven Progressive Matrices
    C. The Peabody Picture Vocabulary Test
    D. The Bender Visual Motor Gestalt Test
    E. The Berry Development Test of Visual Motor Integration
    F. The Horst Reversals Test
    G. The Wepman Auditory Discrimination Test
    H. Wide Range Achievement Test
    I. The Frostig Developmental Test of Visual Perception
    J. Illinois Test of Psycholinguistic Abilities

Social History

It is recommended that the task of collecting domestic information should be the responsibility of a social worker.

I. Social-Economic History
    A. What is the cultural socioeconomic performance of the family?
    B. Is this child accepted into the family structure?
    C. What level of marriage and emotional stability exists?
    D. Do the family relationships reflect a functional environment?
    E. What community standards and educational aspirations does this family have?
    F. Indicate the intellectual functioning range of the family.
    G. How involved have the parents been in home-school communication?
    H. Indicate the educational level of achievement of the parents and siblings.
    I. Do the parents realize or reflect a problem?

Teacher's Report

The following areas of information should be the teacher's responsibility. We believe that a good teacher will be aware of many of the behavioral and educational manifestations of the child's performance. Therefore, the teacher is the one person who should be able to report accurately the children's performance levels.

I. Teacher communication to school and parent
   A. State what you see as the child's learning problem.
   B. Don't postpone or magnify the problem.
   C. Don't give false hope, be positive as well as negative relative to the child's level of growth. Don't mislead the parents, help them to understand what is said.
   D. Don't use a "brain-injury" vocabulary. Speak toward education remediation.
   E. Don't be defensive; the parents will supply you with information if you give them the opportunity.

II. Teacher's educational evaluation
   The teacher needs to be aware of the characteristics of the learning-disabled child in order to report the following information:
   A. The academic areas of learning problems.
   B. The degree of perceptual, conceptual, categorization, visual and audio discrimination, and symbolization involvement.
   C. The degree of aphasia or communication deficiency (speaking, listening, writing).
   D. The effect that the learning problem has upon the child's total education program.
   E. The effect that the learning problem has on the emotional and social growth of the child.

III. Teacher's observation of child's physical condition and hygiene
   A. Is the child obese?
   B. Does the child appear to be malnourished?
   C. Does the child appear to have eaten before school?
   D. Is the child clean and well groomed?
   E. Does the child appear to be fatigued?
   F. Does the child have visual problems?
   G. Does the child have auditory problems?
   H. Are speech or language problems evident?
   I. Does the child indicate confused left-right body dominance?
   J. Does the child have coordination problems?
   K. Are there other noticeable physical problems?
   L. Is attendance regular?
   M. What appears to be the child's general maturational level?

IV. Teacher's observation of attitude and behavior
   A. Is the child distracted easily by visual or audio stimuli?
   B. Is the child destructive, hostile, belligerent, or cruel?
   C. Is the child hyperactive or hypoactive?
   D. Is frustration tolerance low?
   E. Is the child stubborn, uncooperative, or undependable?
   F. Is the child emotionally in control of general behavior?
   G. Is school a pleasant situation?
   H. Is task application evident?
   I. Does the child distract other children?
   J. Is time utilized well?
   K. Does the child complete work? (on time, late, not at all)
   L. Does the child consistently leave an assigned position or desk?
   M. Is a short attention span evident?
   N. Is there a demand for attention from the teacher or from other children?
   O. Does the student appear to be in fantasy land (dreamworld)?
   P. Does the student relate to peer and teachers adequately?
   Q. Does the student have a poor self-concept or self-image?
   R. Is this a sad and unhappy child?
V. Teacher's observations of the educational history
   A. Is the home-school communication desirable?
   B. Is there a consistent school problem?
   C. Has the child repeated a school grade?
   D. Is there a history of individual tutoring?
   E. Is there a general interest and motivation lag?
   F. Does the student receive speech therapy?
   G. Is reading comprehension confused?
   H. Are there jerky eye movements when reading?
   I. Does the student attack reading through basic phonics and word analysis?
   J. Are reading, math, and spelling deficient?
   K. Is the student's vocabulary compatible with sex and age range?
   L. Is there difficulty in defining words?
   M. Does the child have a history of reversal problems?
   N. Does the child invert numbers and confuse letters?
   O. Does the child appear confused when given directions?
   P. Does the child call objects by the wrong names?
   Q. Does the child have proficiencies in other school areas?

The team approach should enable the teacher to have the advantages of many different disciplines. The multidisciplinary approach should include an optometrist or ophthalmologist, a reading specialist, a child psychiatrist, a speech and hearing therapist, a dentist, a social worker, a pediatric-neurologist, the parents, and the school personnel.

Degree and Certification Programs for Teachers

There is a general consensus that the teacher of learning-disabled children should be a master teacher. The McCarthys (1969) indicated that it has not been demonstrated that years in school or number of degrees increase one's success in teaching children with learning disabilities. They believe that what is acquired during training, not how long training takes, is the critical variable. We agree with their statement that it is the proficiency of training that is important, but the different trends should be interesting to note.

Cruickshank (1966) reported the following information relative to certification trends:

Certification requirements for school personnel in the United States have been published biennially since 1951. In 1964, one state, California, required five years of preparation for beginning elementary teachers. The fifth year had to be completed within the first five years of employment. Forty-five states required the bachelor's degree; five states required two, but less than three years of college work; and one state required less than two years. Nine states mandated the completion of a fifth year for secondary school teachers, thus indicating a trend in requirements which in time will probably be expected also of elementary teachers.

Another important trend is the effort to overhaul and improve the "approved-program" approach in which a specific number of course credits will be required in specified subject areas. This approach is now in use in forty states.

A third trend among the states is toward the strengthening of the academic preparation of teachers in the areas of general education requirements. In some states this is done by increasing the academic requirements in general, while reducing the course credit required in professional education courses. In other states the trend is toward requiring concentration in one field for an academic major and a minor in education.

Cruickshank continued by indicating that still another significant trend is toward the use of the National Teachers Examinations as a qualifying hurdle. Generally this exam would be in addition to the approved teacher education program for certification or as a supplement to accreditation. Cruickshank also indicated that there is an increase in the trend toward state acceptance of the certification standards proposed by the National Council for Accreditation of Teacher Education, and also for reciprocity of certification among states.

Good programs for the preparation of teachers for learning disabilities seem to plan a diversity of experiences, including training in assessment, remediation and research, participation in public school classrooms and clinical settings, and contact with a variety of children with learning problems, and their families as well. Adelman (1970) demonstrated that the forms these experiences take can be categorized into five types: (1) academic—including lecturers, seminars, and readings; (2) individual participation and supervision; (3) sensitivity training groups; (4) meetings; and (5) demonstrations.

In general, these programs have been prepared from the standpoint of achieving a positive commitment toward meeting the needs of the individuals in the program, the needs of the field of education, and the needs of society. Such a programmatic commitment and such experiences tend to produce an atmosphere wherein the trainee learns to appreciate and accept the full responsibility of a professional role. Specifically, the professional should accept the following responsibilities: (1) to participate in service (e.g., training, teaching, consultation) activities which will have a direct impact on improving the educational opportunities for children with learning disabilities; (2) to participate in research activities designed both to evaluate and improve such service and, more generally, to increase our understanding of the etiology; (3) to relate such understanding to the basic theories of instruction and learning, so that trainees become effectively and creatively involved in service, training, and research; (4) to increase our understanding of the diagnosis, remediation, and prevention of learning disabilities (Adelman 1970).

Adelman continues by indicating the need for a core program or unit divided into seven areas, as follows: (1) the developmental and learning processes and the relationship of these processes to instruction—here the focus would be on the interrelationship between instruction, development, and learning of both normal and abnormal individuals, emphasizing the pertinent facets of sensory, perceptual, motoric, linguistic, cognitive, social, and emotional development; (2) a conceptual model of the assessment procedures; (3) basic theories of instruction—including emphasis on principles related to effecting motivational and attitudinal changes; (4) the effective use of other human resources—clarifying both the potential value and limitations of such resources; (5) the development of the skills necessary for understanding and carrying out research; (6) the development of personal skills required for professional effectiveness; and (7) a systems analysis of the key variables involved in classrooms, schools, and their environments.

After completing the core program, graduate students who want to specialize in learning disabilities would be required to take courses which develop necessary on-the-job skills. These might include assessment techniques, curriculum development, general principles and techniques of remedial instruction; special principles and techniques related to teaching learning-disabled children, research design, and techniques of supervision and consultation.

The teachers of learning-disabled children may be taught by a three-step training program: (1) introduction of a concept or technique, that is, teaching a specific idea or skill through discussion and demonstration; (2) supervised practice; and (3) follow-up feedback and consultation.

Requirements for Teachers

In selecting a teacher for the learning-disabled child there are basic guidelines which can be followed by observing certain characteristics of elementary teachers who are to become specialized education teachers. Cruickshank (1966) suggested the following guidelines:

1. Identify those teachers from kindergarten through third grade who everyone agrees are outstanding teachers.

2. Watch them work with children—in formal planned visits, in informal drop-in observations, and in marginal day-to-day contacts.

3. Select from among them those who really enjoy teaching.

4. From the outstanding primary teachers who enjoy teaching, select those in whose classrooms the following conditions prevail: (a) the children all understand what they are doing and why; (b) all children feel reasonably sure that they will succeed at the task assigned; (c) the children know what instructional aids, materials, and resources are available and can use them correctly and independently without interrupting the teacher or class; (d) possible behavior problems are anticipated and prevented by redirecting a situation which could lead to trouble; (e) children move individually and as groups from one activity to another without confusion or loss of purpose; (f) the interest and efforts of the children are invested in the achievement of a task rather than in pleasing the teacher; (g) when the teacher makes a mistake, the children call attention to it and help to rectify the situation with the same good humor and tolerance which they enjoy when they are found in error; and (h) children with special problems know what their problems are and know that the teacher and class understand and are willing to help, and even though they still "goof" sometimes they feel certain that they are improving.

5. Select those who: (a) are secure in their dealings with principals, supervisors, psychologists, medical consultants, and parents; (b) are interested in and willing to try new ways of dealing with old problems; (c) are enthusiastic about experimentation and (d) are highly motivated to work with children who have special problems.

Teachers who meet those requirements can be somewhat assured of success after they have received adequate specialized training, provided that during the initial phase of their adjustment to meeting new requirements they maintain good health, have no major family crisis, and do not feel pressured to take courses to meet certification requirements in an area not directly related to their new assignment.

Characteristics of Teachers

Some of the characteristics of a good teacher are true self-respect, maturity, proper sensitivity, a well-integrated identity, and abundant frustration tolerance. Teachers should be trained both in specific techniques and skills, and also how to use their own behavior to aid in the children's growth.

Cruickshank expressed that a good teacher must possess the following attributes: (1) be successful in small group instruction; (2) be skilled in one-to-one teaching situations; (3) have much patience; (4) have an experimental point of view and a willingness to try new methods; (5) be able to accept slow progress of children; (6) be able to establish warm relationships between self and children; (7) feel comfortable in a structured teaching situation; (8) be verbally able to maintain strong relationships with representatives of related disciplines.

Parent Counseling

Many times parents are consistently aware of all the negative aspects of their learning-disabilities child and fail to open the door to positive growth. It should be noted, then, that the counseling of the parents must be concerned with the total life implications of the child's learning disabilities problem.

If teachers are counseling agents, they must be aware of all the ramifications of the different disciplines concerned with the child. If a school counselor is the counseling agent, that person must likewise become an integrative part of the team approach and be aware of the idiosyncratic behaviors common to a child and the family.

The parents should be given the opportunity to share information about the child's problems. The counseling session should not communicate a secretive, avoiding, detached atmosphere. The session should be a time of affective-intellectual sharing.

Rappaport (1969) expressed the need for the following conditions:

In the counseling session focus should be on the needs of the parents. Parents also need the opportunity to air their anxieties and to raise questions. In attempting to explain why their child has problems, the counselor should share neurological, medical, and all other information factually, but in a fashion that makes sense to the parents. Parents must know that if the professionals have not as yet identified all the causes of brain dysfunction, they cannot blame themselves for their child's problems. Parents should also be helped to realize that etiology is important only as a means of defining the appropriate habilitative program. Identifying the etiology is not meant to stigmatize or to indict them as being biologically or in any other way inferior.

Parents must be helped to become aware of their aspirations for the child and whether these aspirations are compatible with the level of growth of the child. Many times parents feel the pressures of the traditional school program and are unable to rid themselves of the anxieties brought about by their child's failing. Consequently, more pressure is applied to the child to get back into the normal academic and social world. This additional pressure causes the child to deteriorate even more rapidly.

Parents hold back many frustrations in their attempts to create a successful functioning level for their child. The relief of these frustrating situations should be the common goal shared by parents, school, and counselor. The counselor must be able to help parents structure a world for their child that is pleasant and comfortable. The counseling session must provide clues to the child's behavior and the kinds of reactions and feedback to the child that foster acceptance in the family and school.

Rappaport related that parents should want their child to be a person in his or her own right rather than an extension of themselves. Also, parents should not feel uncomfortable with their child's learning and behavioral disorders. They should recognize their child's need for structure and consistency, which would enable them as parents to conduct their lives and household in a manner that is organized, but not rigidly compulsive.

Parent counseling may be a time-consuming program; therefore the counselor needs to provide situations to meet the individual needs of parents. Some parents are knowledgeable about the learning disabilities problem and could work well in a group counseling session. Information could be shared directly with other parents, and each could lend emotional support to the other. They would be able to express themselves in a nonjudging, noncensoring, and nonblaming environment. The counselor, of course, would have to be skilled enough to lead the group toward a desired goal. Certain members of the group should not dominate the session. The counselor must assert some direct control at times.

Individual sessions may be the need of other parents, and must be provided if they are to achieve an adequate level of home-school growth. Many different problems will be mentioned by the parents, and the counselor must not seek closure on these problems until they have been thoroughly defined and discussed. All potential ramifications of subsequent problems must be explored. The parent is not in need of additional confusion. The counselor should not create problems by introducing areas of discussion which are wholly unrelated to learning disabilities and academic-social remediation.

Quite likely, one of the most important aspects of the counselor's role is merely to be available to the parents and to be aware of the problem. False hope or false information would be the epitome of poor counseling.

There are many materials that can be used in teaching the learning-disabled child. The following is a list of companies where various materials and tests can be obtained to aid the teacher.

Resources

Materials
AAHPHER Youth Fitness Test Manual (1967 revised edition). President's Council on Physical Fitness, 1201 16th St., N.W., Washington, D.C. 20036.
Autokinetic, Inc., Box 2010, Amarillo, Texas 79105. Various reading and penmanship materials.

Bell & Howell Company, 7100 McCormick Road, Chicago, Illinois 60654. The Language Master and various other materials.

Better Reading Foundation, 52 Vanderbilt Ave., New York, N.Y. 10017. *Children's Digest* and *Humpty Dumpty,* periodicals.

Burns Record Company, 755 Chickadee Lane, Stratford, Conn. 06497. *Square Dances—Album D,* and other records.

Colgate Palmolive Co., Professional Services Dept., 740 N. Rush St., Chicago, Illinois 60611.

Continental Press, Elizabethtown, Pa. 17022. *Instructional Materials for Exceptional Children* by Eichler and Snyder (1958) and other materials.

Cuisenaire Corporation of America, 12 Church St., New Rochelle, N.Y. 10805. Cuisenaire Rods (1958).

Dev. Learning Readiness, Western Division, McGraw-Hill Book Co., Manchester Road, Manchester, Mo. 63011.

Eye Gate House, Inc., 146–01 Archer Avenue, Jamaica, N.Y. 14435. Various filmstrips.

Garrard Publishing Co., Champaign, Ill. 61820. "The Happy Bears" story reading pad by E. W. Dolch (1956) and other materials.

Highlights for Children, 2300 W. 5th Ave., Columbus, Ohio 43212. A periodical.

Ideal School Supply Co., 11018 South Lavergne Ave., Oak Lawn, Illinois 60453. Magic Cards and other materials.

The Judy Company, 310 N. 2nd St., Minneapolis, Minnesota 55401. Judy-See Ques.

Lyons and Carnahan, c/o Rand McNally & Company, P.O. Box 7600, Chicago, Illinois 60680. Auditory and visual discrimination.

Milton Bradley Co., Springfield, Mass. Link Letters, Uncle Wiggley Game, and other materials.

Puzzles and Patterns, Matt G. Glauach and Donovan Stoner, Steck-Vaughn Co., Austin, Texas.

Science Research Associates, 259 East Erie St., Chicago, Illinois 60611. *Basic Reading Skills Workbook* (1963) and other materials. Reading Laboratory and Kindergarten Math.

Scott, Foresman and Co., East Lake Ave., Glenview, Illinois 60025. *Basic Reading Skills Workbook* and other materials.

Steps in Teaching Language for the Deaf, Volta Bureau, 1537 35th St., N.W., Washington, D.C.

Teaching Aids and Toys for Handicapped Children by Barbara Dorward, Copyright 1960 by the Council for Exceptional Children, NEA, 1201 16th St., N.W., Washington 6, D.C.

Teaching Resources Corp., 100 Boylston St., Boston, Mass. 02116.

Tiny Tots Publishing House, Inc., 5483 N. Northwest Highway, Chicago, Illinois 60630. Various materials.

Whitman Publishing Co., Racine, Wisconsin. *Picture Word Book, Simple Objects to Color,* and other materials.

Tests

American Guidance Services, Inc., 720 Washington Ave., S.E., Minneapolis, Minn. 55414.
Minnesota Pre-school Scale (Goodenough, Maurer & Van Wagenen)
Peabody Language Development Kit (Dunn & Smith)
Peabody Picture Vocabulary Test
Verbal Language Development Scale (Mecham)
Vineland Social Maturity Scale

Consulting Psychologists Press, 577 College Ave., Palo Alto, California 94306. Marianne Frostig Developmental Test of Visual Perception.

Language Research Associates, 175 E. Delaware, Chicago, Illinois 60611. Wepman Auditory Discrimination Test.

Illinois Medical Book Company, 215 West Chicago Ave., Chicago Illinois 60610. Illinois Test of Psycholinguistic Abilities (McCarthy & Kirk).

Bureau of Educational Research and Services, Extension Div., State University of Iowa, Iowa City, Iowa. Templin-Darley Articulation Test.

The Psychological Corporation, 304 East 45th St., New York, New York 10017

Arthur Point Scale of Performance Tests, Revised Form II

Bender Visual Motor Gestalt Test

Benton Revised Visual Retention Test

Eisenson's Examining for Aphasia (2nd Edition)

Goodenough-Harris Drawing Test

Harris Tests of Lateral Dominance

Minnesota Test for Differential Diagnosis of Aphasia (Hildred Schuell)

Vineland Social Maturity Scale, Revised (Doll)

Psychological Test Specialists, Box 1441, Missoula, Montana 59801

Full-Range Picture Vocabulary Test (Ammons & Ammons)

Memory-for-Designs Test (Graham & Kendall)

Quick Test (Ammons & Ammons)

Scott, Foresman & Co., 1900 East Lake Ave., Glenview, Illinois. 60025 Bryngleson & Glaspey Articulation Test Cards

Study Questions

1. Give an educational definition of learning disabilities.
2. In what way or ways does this definition distinguish a learning disability from other learning problems?
3. Describe a few educational and behavioral symptoms of the learning-disabled child.
   a. Educational:
   b. Behavioral:
4. Describe the various ways in which a child can exhibit hyperactivity.
5. Briefly describe how the child's hyperactivity may interfere with learning.
6. For referral and diagnosis of a learning-disabled child, list the responsibilities of the psychologist, the pediatrician, the neurologist, the regular classroom teacher, the special classroom teacher, and the parent.
7. Determine the differences between the visually impaired child and the child with normal vision who manifests visual perception problems.
8. Discuss pros and cons of drug treatment for a hyperactive child.
9. Discuss the ways a regular classroom teacher can effectively work with the learning disabilities teacher.

Bibliography

Adelman, Howard S. 1970. "Graduate Training in the 'Specialty' of Learning Disabilities: Some Thoughts." *Journal of Learning Disabilities* 3, no. 2 (February).

Alley, Gordon, and Deshler, Donald. 1979. *Teaching the Learning Disabled Adolescent: Strategies and Methods.* Denver: Love Publishing Co.

Barsch, Jeffrey. 1980. "Community Challenge: New Opportunities for the LD Student." *Academic Therapy* 15, no. 4 (March).

Bennon, Allan, and Denhoff, Eric. 1977. "Validity of Proposed Federal Formula." CANHC-GRAM (February). Los Angeles: California Association Neurologically Handicapped Children.

Clements, Sam D. 1966. *Minimal Brain Dysfunction in Children.* NINDB Monograph no. 3, Public Health Service Bulletin no. 1415. Washington, D.C.: U.S. Dept. of Health, Education, and Welfare.

Cruickshank, William. 1966. *The Teacher of Brain-Injured Children.* New York: Syracuse University Press.

————, and Johnson, G. Orville. 1975. *Education of Exceptional Children and Youth.* 3rd edition. Englewood Cliffs, N.J.: Prentice-Hall.

Deshler, Donald; Lowrey, N.; and Alley, Gordon R. 1979. "Programming Alternatives for Learning Disabled Adolescents: A Nationwide Survey," *Academic Therapy* 14, no. 4 (March).

Federal Register 41, no. 230 (November 29, 1976).

Hammill, Donald D. 1976. "Defining 'LD' for Programmatic Purposes." *Academic Therapy* 12, no. 1, Academic Therapy Publications, reprinted by permission.

Heckrel, John R., and Webb, Susan M. 1969. "An Educational Approach to the Treatment of Children with Learning Disabilities." *Journal of Learning Disabilities* 2, no. 4 (April).

Kass, Corrine E., and Myklebust, Helmer R. 1969. "Learning Disabilities: An Educational Definition." *Journal of Learning Disabilities* 2, no. 7 (July).

Kirk, Samuel A., and Bateman, Barbara. 1962. "Diagnosis and Remediation of Learning Disabilities." *Exceptional Children* 29, no. 2 (October).

Landreth, Garry L. 1969. "Complimentary Roles of the Pediatrician and Educator in School Planning for Handicapped Children." *Journal of Learning Disabilities* 2, no. 2 (February).

Learning Disabilities Due to Minimal Brain Dysfunction. 1970. Bethesda, Md.: National Institute of Health.

Marsh II, George E., and Price, Barrie Jo. 1980. *Methods for Teaching the Mildly Handicapped Adolescent.* St. Louis: The C. V. Mosby Company.

McCarthy, James J., and McCarthy, Joan F. 1969. *Learning Disabilities.* Boston: Allyn and Bacon.

Minskoff, Gerald. 1969. "Notes of Federal Activities in Learning Disabilities." *Academic Therapy* 5, no. 1 (Fall).

Morrison, Dr. James. 1971. Kansas Association for Children with Learning Disabilities, pamphlet.

Myers, Patricia, and Hammill, Donald D. 1969. *Methods for Learning Disorders.* New York: John Wiley & Sons.

Rappaport, Sheldon R. 1969. *Public Education for Children with Brain Dysfunction.* Syracuse: Syracuse University Press.

Rice, Donald B. 1970. "Learning Disabilities: An Investigation in Two Parts." *Journal of Learning Disabilities* 3, no. 3 (March).

————. 1970. "Learning Disabilities: An Investigation in Two Parts." *Journal of Learning Disabilities* 3, no. 4 (April).

Slingerland, Beth H. 1969. "Early Identification of Preschool Children Who Might Fail." *Academic Therapy* 4, no. 4 (Summer).

Stewart, Mark A. 1972. "For Parents of Hyperactive Children." *Expectations* 2, no. 4 (September/October).

Whittlesey, Wes. 1969. "Introduction to Children with Learning Disabilities." Position Paper, Director of Pediatric Services, Oklahoma State Department of Health (April).

Wiederholt, J. L. 1975. "A Report on Secondary Programs for the Learning Disabled." Tucson: University of Arizona.

————. 1976. "Recent Research with Hyperactive Children," CANHC-GRAM. Los Angeles: California Association Neurologically Handicapped Children.

9

the emotionally
and behaviorally maladjusted

Definition

Many theories of personality, child behavior, and remediation presently exist within the framework of a definition-seeking study of the emotionally or behaviorally disturbed child. Our experience indicates that it is extremely difficult to find a definition for the disturbed child. A definition must be relevant to the many different cultures, societies, and moral values. Any single definition doesn't seem to be consistent with the needs of all professionals or theories of treatment.

Kessler (1966) indicated the following guidelines as referral criteria for disturbed children:

1. Age discrepancy. There are ages by which most children have outgrown particular habits and behavior.
2. Frequency of occurrence of the symptom must be considered. One should be concerned when the symptomatic behavior is aroused under minimal stress, which means it occurs very often.
3. The number of symptoms is an obvious consideration. The more symptoms, the more the child is disabled. However, one should not rely exclusively on the criterion of multiplicity of symptoms to judge the extent of psychopathology. It is possible for a single symptom to work so efficiently that all the child's anxieties are taken care of at once. All of his problems may be bound up in the one phobic situation so that there is no spillage into other areas.
4. The degree of social disadvantage is an inevitable determinant of parental concern about children's symptoms. It is easy to see a vicious circle at work where the symptom's effects may tend to perpetuate the symptom.

5. The child's inner suffering is often overlooked. It is often assumed that children's opinion of themselves are based solely on the spoken statements of others. So, if the parents are tolerant, and outsiders do not know about the symptom, the parents may feel that children will not be upset about it. But children are quite capable of judging themselves. Though they may not verbalize their inner distress, they often reveal it to someone who knows them well.

6. Intractability of behavior is implied, in part, in the criterion of frequency. The persistence of symptoms, despite the efforts of the child and others to change them, is the hallmark of so-called behavior disorders.

7. General personality appraisal is the most important criterion, and the most difficult. This criterion has to do with the child's general adjustment, rather than with isolated symptoms.

Before describing abnormal or different behavior, one should have some workable concepts of normal behavior. If one were to describe normal behavior, a judgment must be made concerning one's own values, the immediate environment's values, and national or worldly values. Children are unable to live in a static world today. Their environment and cultures are constantly changing, and the children must learn to switch roles. Behavior and values which are acceptable in one school or city may not be tolerated in another school. Values of children's homes or communities may not be acceptable in their schools. Children must learn early in life that they will have to play many different roles of behavior.

Apparently the most serious concerns are behavior deviations that prevent children from maintaining normal patterns of intellectual, social, and emotional growth in the public schools. Schools have achievement records and tests which supposedly determine normal ranges of progress for various academic subjects. Therefore, certain expectations exist for children with particular age ranges. Rubin, Simson, and Betwee (1966) indicated that children can be identified as failing to make appropriate and significant progress in certain well-established and accepted areas of accomplishment, such as at school. They also feel that necessary patterns of adaption for any given age period may be defined. Deviance from these may be a useful guide to the identification of maladaptation.

Many definitions of disturbed behavior appear to center around children's inabilities to maintain themselves adequately in the home, school, and community. Buhler, Smitter, and Richardson (1966) indicated that in psychological terms, a problem is a hindrance that may disrupt the continuity of the processes within an individual or a group. An example would be a child's problem in school which disrupts the classwork, the cooperation of the group, or the child's own ability to function.

Kessler (1966) writes that the criteria for judging a child's need for help should consider three behaviors—progression, fixation, and regression. We agree with Kessler's view that children are growing, changing, and developing, and as a consequence of this interaction with the world their behaviors are constantly changing. The changes in behavior, though, may be indicated by either a static display, which in effect will cause children to regress because they cannot maintain proper relations if they do not move forward; or they actually may manifest serious regressions, which will result in a significant lag in growth; or they will move forward toward maturity and acceptable growth. Hopefully, of course, all children will move forward. Actually some children manifest behaviors that cannot be tolerated in their schools, homes, and communities.

One must always be aware that some children can succeed in one or more areas (e.g., school) but may be completely debilitated in another area (e.g., home or neighborhood). The child's *total* level of functioning must be considered when determining a definition of a disturbed child. Our experiences have indicated that a definition for an emotionally or behaviorally disturbed child must reflect a child's inability to function compatibly in the total environment. A definition which appears to encompass the total environment defines the emotionally disturbed child as one who cannot emotionally, intellectually, and socially function in a manner that is acceptable to peers, teachers, parents, and legal authorities within the school, home, and community environment.

Prevalence of Emotionally Disturbed Children

It would be an impossible task to determine the actual prevalence of children in the United States who are categorized as emotionally disturbed. Kessler suggested that statistics about the number of children with personality disorders have little significance, because each researcher's criteria for defining them would be somewhat different. We believe that no method at the present time enables all behaviorists to tabulate emotionally disturbed children under the same set of criteria. Consequently, estimates of prevalences in the United States range from 1 to possibly 15 percent of all school children.

McCaffrey and Cumming (1969) reported studies suggesting an expectancy that 5 to 10 percent of all children manifest emotional disturbances. They did urge awareness of the fact that emotional disturbances reported in single surveys may subside within relatively short periods of time, while other disturbances may progress to fixed and accumulative patterns of academic and social failures. Jones (1969) also assumed that definite figures of prevalence are not possible, but he does believe that both incidence and prevalence are high. Jones also indicated that the Subcommittee on Juvenile Delinquency of the United States Senate found that 10 percent of school-age children need psychiatric treatment.

Kauffman (1980) provided significant insight into PL 94–142 as it pertains to emotionally disturbed children. The definition of emotional disturbance provided in the law originated from Bower's (1969) definition.

However, social maladjustment is not a part of the definition. This excludes a large number of children who would profit from appropriate interventions. No specific definition of emotional disturbance has been accepted by professionals. Now, under PL 94–142, there is a definition that, although it is not necessarily accepted by all individuals, will be the standard used for litigations.

In addition, prevalence estimates also seem to be changing. The Office of Special Education has provided an estimate of 2 percent, considered conservative by many. Still, the number of disturbed children being served by special education is less than 0.5 percent. Kauffman presented data to indicate that the lower prevalence figure was not due to emotionally disturbed children being in other categorical classifications, because those incidence figures were also lower than predicted. The lower incidence was also not due to overinflated estimates, since estimates by individuals such as Bower, Rubin, and Balow were based on actual surveys. Kauffman stated that because of very limited funding under PL 94–142 and a tremendous increase in administrative details and paperwork, what has happened is probably an abrupt stop of services at the level which was provided before PL 94–142 became effective. That statement is supported by data which shows that the OSE estimated that only 25 percent of the 2 percent of emotionally disturbed children were being served.

In conclusion, Kauffman made the following observation. " 'Special education,' 'appropriate education,' 'unique individual needs'—these and many of our other notions will not help us make successful plans until we consider in greater depth the more fundamental issues: the purposes of education and schools in our society, the limits of educability, the proper role of government in education, and the designation of agents of educational change."

Presently many professional estimates agree with a number of other association reports concerned with mental health problems. It appears quite likely that these reports, although they use different criteria, have indicated a fairly close estimate of prevalence. This prevalence seems to fall consistently within the 5 to 15 percent range—a conservative range, but one that is in apparent agreement with many different behavioral professionals.

Methods of Identification

Dupont (1969) listed Eli M. Bower's report on a California State Department (1955) study concerned with early identification of emotionally disturbed children. Specifically, the study was aimed at discovering the extent to which a teacher-centered procedure might be employed for identifying disturbed children, and the extent to which information ordinarily obtained by the classroom teacher may be used. The teacher was not involved in the study until the psychiatrist, psychologist, or counselor in each participating school was asked to identify some children who were or had been in treatment by the clinical staff for emotionally disturbed behavior. These children were enrolled in classes selected for participation in the study without revealing to the teacher the criterion for selection. The results seemed to indicate that the teacher's judgment of emotional disturbance is very much like that of clinicians. The implications of this study suggest that the classroom teacher is capable of differentiating the emotionally disturbed children from other children in the classroom.

Nelson (1971) reported a study in which a direct observation technique was used to investigate differences between children classified as conduct disturbed or normal on the basis of ratings given by their regular classroom teachers. The results agree with Bower's study that teachers are capable of identifying emotionally disturbed children in their classrooms with a high degree of accuracy. Nelson also points out that a teacher rating alone is not sufficient for identification of disturbed children, because the rating procedure may be based upon the teacher's standards of normal behavior. It is doubtful that all teachers could agree on normal behavior; there is, therefore, a possibility of an error in the rating assigned to a child. The error could cause a child to be assigned a higher rating simply because he or she represented the upper end of the distribution of an unusually calm class.

Maes (1966) reported that emotionally disturbed children in grades four, five, and six can be identified effectively by a teacher rating scale and a group intelligence test and other sources of information, such as arithmetic achievement, reading achievement, a modified sociometric technique (a class play), and a self-concept inventory. Maes indicated that the teacher rating scale and group intelligence test results can be useful in making decisions relative to referrals to psychologists for individual diagnostic study. Other information such as achievement, sociometric status, and self-concept has little predictive value, but may have value for understanding and meeting pupil needs in the educational setting.

Caplan (1964) reported that experts argue for early case findings on the premise that the earlier treatment starts, the more effective and brief secondary prevention will be. Kessler (1966) added that early detection can be dangerous because without treatment, early detection may lead to a self-fulfilling prophecy. She also relates that alerting parents or teachers to possible future difficulties increases their anxieties, which will reduce their effectiveness unless they are given some directions. Therefore, she feels that without any promise of treatment, early diagnosis may only compound the problem and prove to be a curse in disguise. Methods of identification must be consistent with knowledge available from many different areas of human behavior. Alone, a teacher, psychologist, social worker, psychiatrist, child development specialist, or guidance counselor is not equipped to make a conclusive report on a child's emotional problems. Each person concerned with this child's emotional health should be a contributing member of a team that suggests methods of identification and treatment. We have witnessed diagnoses of children by one professional that were blatantly in error. These errors became visible only after there had been an evaluation review from several professional personnel. Evidence in theory and practice does not support the fact that one person alone has the professional skill to determine the life course of a child. Therefore, an assist from another person who may know something about the child's school, home, or community skills is of great importance in determining whether a child is to be tested or treated for emotional disturbances.

Characteristics of the Emotionally Disturbed

Characteristics of emotional disturbances are so plentiful that one becomes diffusely concerned by trying to tabulate all of them. Apparently, though, each behavioral scientist has a specific method of coding these children into distinct areas of behavior or disturbances. We offer an overview of some practices of characterizing disturbed children. The reader should not conclude that it is an easy process to separate the disturbed from the nondisturbed when both have the same or similar characteristics.

The authors offer brief descriptions of the following classifications in four different categories:

I. Psychoses
  A. Schizophrenia, withdrawn
  B. Manic-depressive illness, depressed
  C. Paranoia
II. Neuroses
  A. Anxiety
  B. Hysterical-psychosomatic
  C. Obsessive-compulsive
  D. Depressive
III. Personality disorders
  A. Antisocial
  B. Passive-aggressive, passive type
IV. Transient situational disturbances
  A. Adjustment reaction of childhood
  B. Adjustment reaction of adolescence

Psychoses

Schizophrenia, withdrawn is marked by disturbances of thinking, mood, and behavior. Alterations in concept formation and the individual's misinterpretation of reality are common. Sometimes delusions and hallucinations occur. Mood changes are ambivalent, constricted, and inappropriate. Loss of empathy with others is commonly found. Schizophrenia is generally described as a thought disorder as distinguished from an affective or a mood disorder.

In the category of withdrawn schizophrenia there are varying degrees of personality disorganization. Schizophrenic individuals fail to test and evaluate correctly external reality. They attend to too many aspects of a situation and are unable to filter out irrelevancies. This results in disturbances in thought processes. Tasks demanding sustained attention and effort are futile. The disorder is also marked by disturbances in reality relationships, concept formations, and intellectual performance. Disorganization and disturbances in associations and thinking also occur. There do not appear to be any clear links between ideas or associations.

Feelings or emotions appear inappropriate to the situation. The individual experiences ambivalent reactions as though pulled in different directions. Disharmony between mood and thought is common. Emotional blunting marked by apathy, and indifference also occurs.

Autistic thinking is found in withdrawn schizophrenia. The individual's thinking and perceiving are regulated by personal wishes rather than by objective reality. In teaching this person, concentration should be placed on relationships with others and with objective reality. Depersonalization or misidentification of self with others is characteristic of schizophrenia. Self-concept should be stressed along with expression of thoughts, feelings, and perceptions.

Scattering, moving from word to word without filling in the gaps for the listener, and forming neologisms, or coining new words are typical of the thought disturbance patterns found in schizophrenia. Stress should be placed in the areas of continuity in thought and feeling, order and sequencing in words and events, and building response sets to aid in relating to external reality.

Ullmann and Krasner (1969) cited a study done by Cameron and Margaret (1951) which describes factors resulting in disorganization in a schizophrenic individual.

1. Interruption of activity (frustration)
2. Environment change (alteration in previously supporting environment)
3. Preoccupation (single theme dominates, all else excluded)
4. Emotional excitement (anger or fear increases errors and muscular tension; destroys fine coordination)
5. Ineffective role taking (unable to see perspective of other person)
6. Situational complexity (new or conflicting demands)

Reactions to situations that are difficult and stressful produce deficits in effective role taking, thought organization, and emotional functioning. Social withdrawal also occurs. Therefore, these situations should be avoided.

Manic-Depressive, Depressed states are characterized by sad affect, psychomotor retardation which may progress to an acute stupor, isolation, withdrawal, and apathy. The person experiences a loss of enthusiasm and feelings of hopelessness and helplessness. Hypochondriacal complaints may be expressed. Guilt over wrongdoings is often expressed. Agitation, restlessness, perplexity, and demands for attention are other characteristics.

This disorder is classified as a primary mood disorder. It differs from a psychotic-depressive reaction, which is more easily attributable to stress. Illusions, hallucinations, and delusions, if present, are usually of guilt-laden, hypochondriacal, or paranoid ideas and attributable to the dominant mood disorder.

In working with such people, activity should be increased so as to lower the level of apathy. A variety of activities should be offered to keep them too busy to think about personal problems. Tasks should be brief as they may have difficulty in concentration over a longer span of time. They should be encouraged to relate with others, and placed in activities involving groups. These children should be given tasks at which they can succeed in order to build self-concepts and ease feelings of hopelessness and helplessness. They should be positively reinforced for behaviors incompatible with those to be modified, while behaviors which reinforce the depression should be avoided.

Paranoia is the gradual development of an intricate, complex, and elaborate delusional system based on and often proceeding from misinterpretation of an actual event. Such people consider themselves endowed with unique and superior abilities. The paranoia is considerably restricted in range and does not interfere with the rest of their thinking and personality.

The range of paranoid reactions is described by terms such as sensitive, cautious, rigid adherence to rules, social isolation, overcriticism of others, self-righteousness, and sometimes delusions of persecution (people out to destroy me), grandiosity (individual is important), and reference (the individual gives personal meaning to events that do not personally apply; belief that others are paying special attention). Other characteristics of paranoia are suspicion, distrust of others, tenseness, insecurity, fearfulness, and a high level of anxiety.

Individuals suffering from paranoia have difficulty confiding in others because they expect to be betrayed. They feel and act hostile. They exhibit behavior which is reaction-sensitive. They react with defensive hostility to certain kinds of situations, personalities, and implied threats. They are over ready to react with counteraggression to experiences that assault their integrities.

Paranoids depend heavily on the defense mechanisms of projection and denial as well as repression. In projecting, they attribute their own unacceptable traits to another person. Because they believe that people cannot be trusted, they withdraw socially and emotionally. They tend to deny responsibility for failures and ascribe them to others. They also deny their own unmanageable hostility which is projected onto others.

Techniques to use in dealing with such people would be to reduce the anxiety level by teaching newer, more appropriate methods of response. They should be confronted with their behavior and its consequences. From this point, alternative and more socially appropriate acts can be developed. They should be provided with new experiences which are contrary to and incompatible with their prior belief system.

These people experience feelings of internal discomfort or anxiety. Through projective thinking, internal discomfort is mistaken for external pressure. This reflects the confusion and difficulty that this individual encounters in locating problems responsible for that discomfort.

Some psychotherapeutic techniques used are persuasion: attempting to convince the paranoid that suspicions, hostility, and grandiosity are unwarranted or unnecessary; confrontation: suggestion or interpretation concerning the behavior exhibited. A rapport should be developed prior to confrontation so that the hostility and suspicion will be diminished and a nonthreatening relationship can be developed.

The person dealing with a paranoid should be honest and avoid keeping secrets. Secrecy will be recognized as an attempt to manipulate, which interferes with trust of the teacher or therapist.

In dealing with the paranoid, one must be dependable and consistent. Failure will give the paranoid an excuse to label the individual as untrustworthy. The teacher or therapist should appear nonthreatening, should accept the paranoid's views without practicing deception, should not argue about the delusions, but simply disagree with them. Direct confrontation concerning the paranoid's behavior may serve to relieve tension.

Neuroses

Anxiety neurosis seems to occur when a person subjectively experiences uneasiness, apprehension, anticipation of danger, doom, and feelings of going to pieces or disintegration. The source of these feelings is unknown to the person. There are experiences of anxious overconcern which may extend to panic and which is frequently associated with somatic symptoms. Anxiety neurosis is distinguished from normal apprehension or fear which occurs in a realistically dangerous situation. The anxiety is not restricted to definite situations or objects.

In a relationship with others, such people express a compulsive need for dependency and symbiosis, aggression and domination, and detachment and isolation. They feel driven rather than moved, that they are not active forces in their own lives, and that they are utterly helpless.

Systematic desensitization is often used in dealing with anxiety neurotics. They need to learn new ways to effectively reduce the anxiety level. Assertion training, which teaches them to take the initiative of standing up for their own rights is used to instill confidence and reduce anxiety.

In working with these children in a classroom, pressure should be kept at a minimum. Competition which would create anxiety should be avoided. They would do well to learn to function in groups as well as to work independently. Control of anxiety, as well as free choice of actions in situations, should be taught.

Hysterical-Psychosomatic neurosis is an involuntary psychogenic loss or disorder of functioning. The symptoms begin and end suddenly in emotionally charged situations and are symbolic of underlying conflicts. In psychoanalytic terms, the symptom formation in hysteria represents the unconscious solution, or attempted solution, of an emotional conflict. The symptoms are a protectiom against the perception of the anxiety and depression associated with the conflict. Often, the individuals express *la belle indifference* with respect to their symptoms. They do not seem to be alarmed by the loss and welcome the opportunity to talk about their symptoms.

In an hysterical-psychosomatic reaction, or a conversion reaction, the anxiety is not experienced consciously but is converted into bodily symptoms. There do not appear to be any physiological or anatomical reasons to explain the dysfunctions.

Precipitating factors which may evoke hysterical reactions are conflicts produced by changes in the individual's life situation. Therefore, the maintenance of a stable environment is essential. Possible resolutions to conflicts which produce somatic symptoms are conscious assimilation resulting in a decisive action on the part of the individual, sublimation into a social activity, work, or some other means of compensation.

Discussions of symptoms or physical disabilities should be avoided, as they tend to positively reinforce the illness. Possible techniques to use in modifying the behavior are aversive stimuli, with the objective of extinguishing the negative behavior; positive reinforcement for desired behavior; rewarding a positive behavior which is incompatible with the behavior to be extinguished; performing the undesired behavior until a ceiling is reached so that the behavior will then decline in frequency; deprivation of a desired activity or reward if negative behavior is produced; and systematic desensitization—all are methods which can be used to shape the person's behavior.

Obsessive-Compulsive neurosis occurs when a person experiences persistent, unwanted thoughts or actions which cannot be controlled. Anxiety and distress are often present. Concern about being unable to control or unable to complete the act is often present.

The anxiety found in this disorder is associated with the persistence of unwanted ideas and of repetitive impulses to perform acts which may be considered morbid by the patients. They may consider these ideas and behavior as unreasonable, but feel compelled to carry out the rituals.

Compulsives display excessive concern with adherence to standards of conscience and conformity. They may be overinhibited, overconscientious, and have great capacity for work; or may be characterized as rigid and lacking in relaxing, enjoyable pursuits. In modifying this behavior, attempts must be directed at inconveniencing the person for undesired behavior to the point where reinforcements for attempts to change it can occur.

Depressive neurosis is an excessive reaction of depression because of an internal conflict, or due to an identifiable event such as a loss of a love object or a cherished possession. Acute feelings of despondency and dysphoria of varying intensity and duration also occur. Foreboding about the future, apathy, and fatigue are other symptoms.

Depression is a disorder primarily characterized by symptoms such as a diminished level of activity, lowered self-assurance, apprehension, constricted interests, and loss of initiative. The reaction is frequently precipitated by a current situation involving a loss to the individual and associated with feelings of guilt for past failures or deeds. The symptoms of neurotic depression overlap those found in psychotic depression.

Operant and respondent conditioning is used in treating a depressed neurotic. Behavior which is antithetical to a depressed role should be reinforced. New response sets must also be taught. Supportive techniques to ease guilt feelings should be employed. Distractions such as books, movies, and television will help. Sleep is another very useful aid.

Personality Disorder

Antisocial personality is characterized by developmental defects or pathological trends in the personality structure, with minimal subjective anxiety and little or no sense of distress. It is seen as a lifelong pattern of action or behavior, rather than a disorder caused by mental or emotional symptoms.

Chronically antisocial individuals are always in trouble, profiting neither from experience nor punishment, and maintaining no real loyalties to any person, group, or code. They are frequently callous and hedonistic, showing marked emotional immaturity, with lack of a sense of responsibility, lack of judgment, and an ability to rationalize their behavior so that it appears warranted, reasonable, and justified.

Impulsivity, shortsightedness, and self-defeating acts mark the person's behavior. Social conditioning is slow; the individual must learn new response sets.

Such people have a pattern of being inconsistently rewarded for diffuse acts. For example, if making amends by being charming is reinforced, they learn well, and become very agile at using charm to manipulate. However, the behavior which makes it necessary for them to manipulate is unaltered.

In working with such people, new response sets must be taught. Appropriate ways of social interaction need to be learned. Attention and care should be directed at *which* behaviors are reinforced; be aware of the manipulation attempts which are common among the personality disorders.

Passive-Aggressive. Passive type is characterized by behavioral patterns of pouting, obstructionism, procrastination, intentional inefficiency, and stubbornness. These behaviors are a reflection of hostility that cannot be expressed openly. Often the behavior is an expression of resentment at failing to find gratification in a relationship with an individual or institution upon which there is overdependence.

Two other subtypes are found under the passive-aggressive personality. The passive-dependent is characterized by helplessness, indecisiveness, and a tendency to cling to others as a dependent child to a supporting parent. Irritable, resentful behavior marked by temper tantrums characterize the second subtype, aggressive.

In working with the passive type, attempts should be directed at discovering more appropriate modes of expressing hostile feelings. Control and expression of feelings should also be developed. New roles by which the person can discover other forms of gratification in relationships should be explored.

Transient Situational Disturbances

Adjustment recreation of childhood is a habit or conduct disturbance which is generally a reaction to an event and is temporary. It is marked by irrational, self-defeating behavior which is atypical of the way the person usually acts or is expected to act. There is no underlying personality disturbance present. An adaptive capacity to return to normal functioning is present. Recession of symptoms occurs when the stress is diminished.

Special attention at a personal level should be given to help work through these problems. Encouragement in relating to others should be stressed. Success should be provided in all areas of work.

Adjustment reaction of adolescence is marked by irritability and depression associated with school failure and manifested by temper outbursts, brooding, and discouragement. This disorder is transitory. Emancipatory strivings, vacillation of impulses, and behavior which resembles personality or psychoneurotic disorders is generally found.

Attempts should be made to help this person work through these problems independently. Solutions should be left up to the individual, who should be encouraged to attempt more appropriate responses to situations and events. Independent action should be stressed.

Chapman (1965) reported that psychoneurosis designates a group of emotional disorders in children which may be divided into different categories of behavior.

1. Phobias: abnormal fears of specific things or situations. Phobias constitute the most common psychoneurotic disturbance of childhood.
2. Anxiety reactions: much tension, varying from mild restlessness to sheer panic; they may be acute or chronic.

3. Obsessive and compulsive reactions: in obsessive reactions the child is afflicted with persistent, distressing ideas which will not go away; in the compulsive states the person feels strong urges to perform repeated physical acts to relieve tension.

4. Conversion and dissociative reactions: various disorders of sensation, movement and special sensory perception. The term conversion reaction is, in general, synonymous with the older term hysteria. The dissociative disorders are clinically related and are characterized by disturbances of awareness or memory, as in psychogenic amnesias.

5. Tics: discrete, repetitive, muscular movements caused by emotional tension. Because mild tics are common in children and have particular characteristics, we shall treat them as a separate category. Tics in adults are often included under the conversion reactions.

Many symptoms may be characteristic of "normal" behavior and these symptoms, even though present, do not cause any functional problems. The same symptoms exhibited in a disturbed child's repertoire may cause considerable distracted behavior. Such things as nail-biting to the "normal" type of symptom may be the overlay of a very serious problem. Each nail-biting session is then a very anxiety-provoking situation. Some disturbed children will not manifest characteristics such as bed-wetting, nail-biting, or thumb-sucking as distinct symptoms of anxious behavior. They will, instead, invest themselves into a personality structure that causes difficulties in their total interpersonal relationships. Chapman has divided what he refers to as interpersonal and personality functioning behavior into three general areas:

1. Personality-pattern disturbances, in which the emotional troubles of the child produce problems in the personality structure. This category includes the depressed child, the passive child, the aggressive child, the compulsive child, and the emotionally insecure child.

2. Acting-out behavior disorders, in which the child acts out hostile feelings in antisocial ways. Examples are running away, stealing, lying, school truancy, fire-setting, use of alcohol and illicit drugs.

3. Disorders of sexual behavior, in which emotional turmoil produces disturbances of sexual behavior, as in homosexuality and transvestism.

Disorders of the learning and training processes of children may cause maladjustment in the necessary skills for communication, social, and academic proficiency. Children are somewhat characterized by their experiential framework. Therefore, if the child's world has been infested with socially inappropriate behaviors he or she will probably gravitate to these behaviors and appear to be a helpless, paralyzed, dependent, noncommunicative child. Chapman (1965) made a three-section division of disorders in training, learning, and speech as possible characteristics of emotionally disturbed children:

1. Adjustment disorders of habit training, in which a socially necessary type of training is not developed, as in enuresis and encopresis. This group also includes thumb-sucking, hair-pulling, and sleep disturbance.
2. Adjustment disorders of learning, including difficulties in mastering the skills of scholastic learning, all of which involve the use of symbols. Examples are reading problems and general learning inhibitions.
3. Adjustment disorders of speech including delayed speech, stuttering, and disorders of speech articulation.

Chapman also divided psychosomatic illnesses into categories characteristic of some emotionally disturbed children. We contend that there really isn't much need to sort out the psychosomatic illnesses into distinct areas. The concern should not be for the specific malingering illness, but should instead be for the fact that the child is ill. The specific kind of illness manifested—asthma, ulcers, hyperventilation, acne, headaches, abdominal pains, chest pains, back aches, etc.—is not as important characteristically as is the fact that the child consistently manifests these illnesses and symptoms when no apparent organistic cause can be determined. The physician will quite likely impress medical treatment upon the child in the same manner as applied to other children. It is interesting to note, though, that disturbed children will manifest varying kinds and degrees of severity of their psychosomatic illnesses. Placebo or medication application will have relatively little effect upon the aches and pains for any significant period of time. Therefore, one should note the frequency and tenure of the illnesses and the child's response to those illnesses.

Autistic Children

The child with infantile autism appears to have no affective awareness of other human beings. This behavior suggests that perception and awareness of mother is absent. There appears to be a total lack of contact with the outside world. An example is a statement by a mother of an autistic child, "She never made any personal contact or appeal for help at any time."

Some authorities believe that infantile autism may be a childhood psychosis in which children lack any capacity to trust or communicate with others. In addition, they may be either mute or have complex disturbances of speech. They could easily be diagnosed as mentally defective if it were not for the ability to handle inanimate objects. Some psychiatrists believe autism is the basic defense attitude of the infant. It seems as though these children cannot tolerate stimulation from the outer world as well as they master their inner isolated feelings. Their thought processes, their highly selective and restricted sensory awareness, seem to overtax their concept of self.

Bernard Rimland (1964) has a thorough formulation of the symptoms of autistic children. He feels very strongly that they neither look, nor are mentally retarded. However, he says that they may appear retarded socially, because of the inability to form relationships. The first inclination by the parents that a child is autistic may be the lack of the usual anticipatory movements prior to being held. Also, there is often a stiffness or a failure to make the usual body adjustments by the child in adapting to being carried or held. There are other disturbing symptoms which appear between the fourth and eighteenth month, such as prolonged rocking, head banging, apathy and disinterest, unusual fear of strangers, obsessive interest in certain toys or mechanical appliances, highly repetitive and ritualistic play, insistence on being left alone, not changing the physical environment, very unusual language behavior, self-imposed isolation or "autistic aloneness," odd eating habits, and suspected deafness. Of these, Rimland believes that self-imposed isolation and insistance on the preservation of sameness are the most widely accepted diagnostic signs.

The speech of the autistic child, if there is speech at all, is very distinctive and indicative of pathology. Autistic children do not learn to speak in single words like "mama" and "dada" and "car." Instead, they may remain mute until their emotional states have reached points at which they are ready to resume speech. They will then begin speech by repeating a whole phrase or sentence (echolalia), the organization of which is commensurate with the general intellectual level at which they are functioning.

The failure to hear, or more explicitly, the failure to respond to auditory stimuli, is part of the child's withdrawal. In a large proportion of autistic children, the apparent deafness is probably because of auditory avoidance, not impaired hearing. They also tend to show visual avoidance by just closing their eyes. Autistic children frequently fail to respond to tactile stimuli. When they are in a severely withdrawn state, a touch intended to attract attention evokes no response. These children have not lost the sense of touch. At times it is quite obvious that they can feel things normally, and they make great use of their tactile senses in manipulating familiar objects. Many children derive pleasure from the feel of surfaces and textures.

It is suggested that these children, having little interest in the world and its people, turn toward their own bodies and their own primitive sensory satisfactions. Ultimately, of course, the deviant behavior in childhood autism must be the result of some kind of abnormal event within the brain such as anatomic, metabolic, or electrophysiologic pathology. Or perhaps it is an attempt by a normal child to adapt defensively against an excessively stressful environment.

Table 9.1 Major Distinctions Between Infantile Autism and Childhood Schizophrenia

	Infantile Autism	Childhood Schizophrenia
Onset and course	Present from the beginning of life.	Disordered behavior follows an initial period of normal development.
Health and appearance	Almost invariably in excellent health, beautiful and well formed, and usually of dark compexion.	These children are almost always described as being the "best child the mother ever had." Generally in poor health from birth. Respiratory, circulatory, metabolic, and digestive difficulties are very common. These children are usually thin, pale, have translucent skin, blonde hair and blue eyes.
EEG	Usually a normal EEG	80% of these children show abnormal EEGs.
Physical responsiveness	Autistic children typically do not adapt their bodies when being carried or held. They are stiff and unresponsive.	These children are noted for their strong tendency to "mold" to those who hold or carry them like dough.
Autistic aloneness	These children are noted for failing to adjust to adults emotionally as well as posturally. They are described as being aloof.	These children are rarely called unresponsive or unappealing. They immediately capture the empathy of the adult who is often seduced into a false evaluation of treatment possibility.
Preservation of "sameness of environment"	This is a cardinal symptom.	Not at all common in schizophrenic children.
Hallucinations	Absence of hallucinations.	Many visual and auditory hallucinations.
Motor performance	Excellent motor ability in both gross body movements, and finger dexterity.	Poor coordination, locomotion, and balance.
Language	Absence of the words "yes" and "I." The word "I" is not used by the autistic child, until about age 7, and then only sparingly.	No difference in the use of the word "I" betweeen these children and the control group.
Idiot savant performance	Unusual memory, musical, and mechanical performances.	Not found in this group.
Personal orientation	Autistic children are described as unoriented, detached, appearing disinterested in events occurring around them. Aloof and oblivious to the environment, then in conflict with it.	These children appear to be disoriented, confused and anxious. More accessible than the autistic child.
Conditionability	Difficult to condition and hard to extinguish.	Easily conditioned.
Twins	Unusual number of monozygotic twins reported.	Not found in childhood schizophrenia.
Family background	Extremely high education and intellectual background and low divorce rate among parents of these children.	71% of the homes of this group are "inadequate."
Familial mental disorders	Strikingly low incidence of mental illness.	Strong familial dependency. Much higher rate of psychosis in the ancestors of schizophrenic children.

Source: *INFANTILE AUTISM: The Syndrome and Its Implications for a Neural Theory of Behavior.* © Bernard Rimland.

There is still considerable confusion and disagreement among authorities about infantile autism and childhood schizophrenia. Some authorities see no difference between autism and schizophrenia. *The Diagnostic and Statistical Manual of Mental Disorders* (1980) does not even include diagnostic criteria for childhood schizophrenia. Infantile autism is listed though, as a pervasive developmental disorder. Rimland (1964) indicated a rather convincing differentiation which is represented in Table 9.1. This table should not be considered as empirically conclusive evidence of the distinctions between childhood schizophrenia and autism, but it is a good assessment guide to aid professionals and parents in discerning the major and obviously different behavioral characteristics of autistic and schizophrenic children.

Dunlap, Koegel, and Egel (1979) provided information from Rimland (1978) which indicates that autistic children typically display a majority of the following symptoms:

1. Lack of appropriate speech
2. Lack of appropriate social behavior
3. Apparent, but unconfirmed sensory deficit
4. Lack of appropriate play
5. Inappropriate and out-of-context emotional behavior
6. High rates of stereotyped, repetitive behaviors
7. Isolated areas of high-level functioning in the context of otherwise low-level intellectual functioning

Autistic children usually have normal appearances. The difficulty in diagnosing autistic children has caused many labels to be applied to them, such as brain damaged, emotionally disturbed, mentally retarded, or aphasic. For this reason Dunlap et al. (1979) focused on describing individual behaviors through an empirical and functional approach which provides information for the treatment intervention. Upon completion of assessment, the focus turns to whether or not the child can be taught.

Education and Treatment of Autistic Children
The basic principle in training and educating autistic children is that the teacher should first try to establish a relationship with the child. This may be accomplished by using whatever activity the child will undertake as a means to bridge the gap between them. One should then try cajoling the child into gradually expanding the aimless and often mechanistic activity into activity that approaches a purpose and eventually an educational skill.

Conventional methods of treatment and orthodox methods of teaching have been tried and proven somewhat unsuccessful. Play therapy and psychoanalysis, conditioning techniques, and intensive teaching have often ended in discouragement and disillusionment. The child fails to improve after endless hours of treatment. Therapists or teachers, unable to accept this failure, tend to regard the child as unteachable and untreatable. They turn their attention to less needy children and ignore the withdrawn autistic child. Treatment for autistic children must begin as early as possible. It is important to treat physical factors also. The child-mother relationship should be improved as much as possible, and efforts to comfort emotional problems within the family must be undertaken. Also, the parents must be aware that taking the child from the home for treatment may cause further feelings of rejection and forms of withdrawal.

When an autistic child has been hospitalized, mother substitutes have been a successful treatment method. The mother substitute is slowly eliminated by the introduction and reappearance of the natural mother. A close contact must be maintained with the substitute and natural mother and child until the child is ready to leave the hospital.

Dunlap et al. (1979) related that the autistic child can be taught through behavior modification, which is especially suited to educational settings: (1) it offers an applied research methodology that focuses on educational needs, (2) its effectiveness can be determined by objective data, (3) it involves parents rather than blaming them, (4) it is based on the basic principles of learning, which can be taught easily to nonprofessionals, and (5) it can succeed in teaching autistic children a wide variety of adaptive behaviors. A number of comprehensive treatment programs using behavior modification have improved the behavior of autistic children. Instruction is usually best on a one-to-one basis, but a gradual increase in group size has been effective for some autistic children.

How should teachers prepare themselves? Dunlap gives two primary ways:

1. Educators should become acquainted with behaviors of autistic children. Some behaviors, and methods for dealing with them, are listed below.
   a. Tantrums and aggression toward self, others, and objects have been eliminated with specialized techniques such as time out, extinction and the use of aversives, and reinforcement for no aggressive behavior.
   b. Elimination of self-stimulation through contingent electric shock, a quick slap on the hand, restraint, positive practice overcorrection, and sensory extinction has been evident. These characteristics must be eliminated for behaviors to improve.
   c. Autistic children exhibit a general unresponsiveness to social stimuli and social rewards. To improve their motivation, attempts have been made to develop new reinforcers, such as sensory stimulation, including music or tickling. The authors completed a study showing that if the educational procedure is designed to increase correct responding, the child's motivation on tasks is increased.

d. Autistic children may have a tendency to respond to only a restricted portion of complex stimuli in the environment. This is commonly referred to as stimulus overselectivity. The development of special prompts has helped teachers to guide autistic children to the completion of correct responses.

e. To increase the generalizing and maintaining of gains made in the therapeutic environment, it appears necessary to identify the stimulus the children selectively respond to and ensure that it is present in extratherapy environments. When this was not done, it was soon found that the children quit responding. A thinning out of reinforcement in the clinic along with occasional rewards in the extraclinical setting corrected this.

2. Teachers should be specially trained in certain teaching techniques.

Both teachers and parents take the role of therapeutic agent in the use of behavior modification. If they are trained in the use of these techniques, they are successful. The importance of such training for both teaching and maintaining appropriate behaviors has led to the development of a number of general training manuals. These provide techniques for presenting instructions, prompts, and consequences. We are gathering data which suggest that the teacher's identification of optimal rates of stimulus presentation can greatly improve children's performances. A continuity of programming between home and school may ensure certain gains in the classroom. Specific teaching procedures, shown empirically to be effective, are becoming increasingly available. The ability to use them can contribute significantly to successful experiences in teaching autistic children.

The teacher should set goals low enough to allow for the slow progress of the autistic child. Autistic children tend to stick to certain levels of educational tasks. The teacher should not lose interest even though children tend to maintain a plateau. One should discover new ways to lead them to appropriate responding and not give up easily.

After the initial teacher-child introduction is made, the child should be gradually introduced into small groups, and put on a rudimentary program or a schedule. After a group process is established, there may be less fear of the outer world and the child may have less reason to ward off reality.

The schooling for an autistic child is best as a part of the normal school system. These children's basic problems are not being able to relate to others. If they are totally segregated into a program consisting only of other autistic children, the milieu purpose would be defeated. A grouping of emotionally disturbed and mentally retarded children in somewhat equal numbers has had some indication for a successful class situation.

Schopler and Olley (1980) indicated that the diagnosis of autism does not provide the information necessary for individualized planning and curriculum. They suggest the use of a developmental assessment procedure, based on the psychoeducational profile by Schopler and Reichler (1979). Schopler and Olley believe that after assessment, the autistic child's IEP often will accommodate existing self-contained classes for mentally retarded or severely handicapped children.

Historically autistic children have gone into trainable-level classes or residential programs. We realize that few autistic children can be integrated into the mainstream of any total school program. Regular class teachers are not equipped to tolerate or work with them. Special educators know little about methods and techniques for teaching them. The teacher's day is usually spent in management programs. Even though autism generally affects few children (4 in 10,000), adequate programs are not provided. Special educators must cast aside the older concepts of care facilities for these children and invest energy and resources into programs that offer maximum development in language, social, and adaptive life.

We visited many special education programs in England during the late 1970s and early 1980s, and one very impressive program was the Community for Autistic People. Sybil Elgar is the Director of the school, which is near Brent Knoll, Somerset, England. This is a residential school that provides a total living concept—work, school, and farm animals that produce considerable staples for the dining room. It is a very structured program, but the students are integrated into many local community activities. We have never seen a program in the United States that remotely compares with the level of functioning achieved by these autistic people in England. The English schools testify to the value of competent residential programs. We in the United States need to take a very evaluative look at the misused concept of mainstreaming, and the avoidance of residential programs.

Parents and teachers must remain aware, though, that autistic children are not suddenly going to become model children. It takes time, patience, energy, and more time.

School Behavior

Many characteristics of emotionally disturbed children should be evident to the classroom teacher. These characteristics may clearly present obstacles to the child's progress or they may remain somewhat subtle. The teacher is exposed to a child for the second largest number of hours in each day, and the child probably is in a position at school to exhibit problems even more obviously than in many home situations. Bower (1969) indicated five different areas from which a teacher could observe visible signs of trouble:

1. An inability to learn which cannot be explained by intellectual, sensory, or health factors.
2. An inability to build or maintain satisfactory interpersonal relationships with peers and teachers.

3. Inappropriate behavior or feelings under normal conditions.
4. A general, pervasive mood of unhappiness or depression.
5. A tendency to develop physical symptoms, pains, or fears associated with personal or school programs.

A study conducted in California by Bower (1969) noted that the emotionally disturbed differ from other children in the following ways: scored significantly lower on group IQ tests, scored significantly lower on reading and arithmetic achievement tests, other children tended to select them for hostile, inadequate, or negative, rather than positive roles in class activities.

Quay, Morse, and Cutler (1966) subjected the Peterson Problem Behavior Rating Scale to a factor analysis on a variety of populations. These studies indicated that three independent dimensions account for about two-thirds of the variance of the interrelationships among problem behaviors. These three dimensions, of course, include activity that may be characteristic of the emotionally disturbed. The first dimension listed aggressive, hostile, and contentious behaviors (also called conduct disorders), unsocialized aggressions, or psychopathologies. The second dimension included anxious, withdrawn, introvertive behavior, which have also been labeled personality problems or neuroticism. The third dimension included preoccupation, lack of interest, sluggishness, laziness, daydreaming, and passivity. The third dimension generally seems to have accounted for much less of a variance than the first two dimensions.

Children's strange behaviors are many times the expression of and hopefully the detection of their problems. They express themselves in many different styles of behavior and will undoubtedly defend the actions as acceptable. Unknown to them and many times to those who are near, they are expressing a need for help through unacceptable behavior. Morse (1969) pointed out the importance of being able to detect the symptoms of the emotionally disturbed. His reasoning is that most disturbed children are still in regular classrooms, and probably will continue there until more and better provisions are made for them. Therefore, he sees the need for the teacher to be able to recognize symptoms which indicate that there is a problem and a call for help.

If teachers and professionals can hear the cry for help from a disturbed child, they should then consider many questions relevant to the child's behavior and background. It should be noted, though, that a child does not necessarily show all the characteristics listed below. These different behaviors may be present in large numbers in some children, and in small quantities in others. We have had experiences with a number of disturbed children, who showed excessive unacceptable behavior through expression of the different characteristics that are listed below. This list is not conclusive, but it does contain a number of important considerations for those concerned with identifying emotionally disturbed children.

1. Does the child express excessive anger?
2. Does the child appear hostile?
3. Does the child have significant academic deficiencies?
4. Does the child appear to maintain acceptable physical hygiene?
5. Does the child appear to receive adequate sleep?
6. Is the child sleepy and bored with school?
7. Does the child appear negative?
8. Is the child exceptionally hyperactive?
9. Is the child significantly withdrawn from peers?
10. Does the IQ score appear to be compatible with the functioning level?
11. Does the child participate in extracurricular activities?
12. Is the child destructive to property?
13. Does the child have temper tantrums in school or at home?
14. Is the child truant or tardy consistently?
15. Does the child appear to be depressed or exhibit suicidal tendencies?
16. Is the child suspicious of the teacher and peers?
17. Does the child appear to have hallucinations or delusions?
18. Does the child complain of physical illnesses?
19. Do moods vascillate from pleasant to unpleasant?
20. Is there indication of sexual preoccupation?
21. Is there indication of stealing, fire-setting, or enuretic behavior?
22. Does the child exhibit sudden emotional outbursts?
23. Is the child's self-image depreciatory?
24. Is the child accident prone?
25. Does the child exhibit regressive forms of behavior?
26. Is the child a perfectionist and succeeds academically?
27. Does the child appear to be a daydreamer?
28. Has the child attended special classes?
29. Has the child had a migrant education program (moved frequently)?
30. Has the child repeated grades in school?
31. Does the child reject all authority figures—school, home, police?
32. Does the child defy structure and school rules?
33. What is the sociological culture of the home?
34. Does the child live in a broken home situation?
35. Does the child appear to be parentally neglected?

These are only a few of the characteristics that may be manifested by a child with emotional problems. They should not be considered in sequence, nor should a child have to possess a certain number of them in order to be disturbed. A determination of functioning level must be related to the seriousness of the actions, the frequency of the behavior, and whether the behavior lasts over a period of time that appears to be excessive.

Narcotics

Many youngsters who are manifesting emotional problems will turn to illegal drugs, stimulants, and narcotics to reduce their problems. Drugs without proper medical supervision will only magnify the disturbed person's internal problems. The authors offer the following information from table 9.2 as a guide to understanding some of the more common symptoms associated with improper drug usage.

Services Available

There appears to be a lack of proper or adequate facilities for emotionally disturbed children. States provide self-contained classrooms, resource rooms, general special education classes, hospital classes (both inpatient and outpatient), and itinerant teachers, but generally the provisions for emotionally disturbed children are quite deficient throughout the United States. Schultz, Hirshoren, Manton, and Henderson (1971) pointed out that education programs for emotionally and socially maladjusted children have existed within a few public school systems, primarily in large cities, for over fifty years. It has only been recently, though, that programs have developed in small school districts with help from the Office of Education Federal Funds. Schultz et al. also indicated an approximate twenty-year growth of classes from a 1948 total of ninety public school programs serving 15,300 children, to a 1966 total of 875 school programs serving approximately 32,000 emotionally disturbed children. It is interesting to note the improvement over that twenty-year period of the number of children being served by ninety schools compared to the number of children served by 875 schools. Evidently, there was a tremendous change in the teacher-pupil ratio.

Presently it would be difficult to arrive at the exact number of services available to emotionally disturbed children, because of the many deceptive means of placing them in school situations. Some children are hidden in regular classes; some are in mentally retarded classes; some are in learning disability classes; and many are school dropouts. A conservative estimate of public and private school and institutional placement would be approximately two hundred thousand children. This estimate, though, represents the number who are probably receiving adequate treatment. It does not include those who are misplaced in other service or categorical areas.

Table 9.2 Common Symptoms of Drug Abuse

Name of Narcotic	Possible Behavior Symptoms	Material Evidence	Physical-Emotional Consequences
Glue Sniffing	Violence, appearance of drunkenness, dreamy or blank expression	Tubes of glue, glue smears, large paper bags or handkerchiefs	Lung/brain/liver damage. Death through suffocation or choking, anemia
Heroin (H., Horse, Scat, Junk, Snow, Stuff, Harry, Joy Powder) *Morphine* (White stuff, Miss Emma, M., Dreamer) *Codeine* (Schoolboy)	Stupor/drowsiness, needle marks on body, watery eyes, loss of appetite, blood stain on shirt sleeve, running nose	Needle or hypodermic syringe, cotton, tourniquet string, rope, belt, burnt bottle, caps or spoons, glassine envelopes	Death from overdose. Mental deterioration, destruction of brain and liver, hepatitis, embolisms
Cough Medicine containing Codeine and Opium	Appearance of drunkenness, lack of coordination, confusion, excessive itching	Empty bottles of cough medicine	Causes addiction
Marijuana (Pot, Grass, Locoweed, Mary Jane, Hashish, Tea, Gage, Reefers)	Sleepiness, wandering mind, enlarged eye pupils, lack of coordination, craving for sweets, increased appetite	Strong odor of burnt leaves, small seeds in pocket lining, cigarette paper, discolored fingers	Inducement to take *stronger* narcotics
LSD (Acid, Sugar, Big D, Cubes, Trips) *DMT* (Businessman's High) *STP*	Severe hallucinations, feelings of detachment, incoherent speech, cold hands and feet, vomiting, laughing and crying	Cube sugar with discoloration in center. Strong body odor. Small tube of liquid	Suicidal tendencies, unpredictable behavior, chronic exposure causes brain damage. LSD causes chromosomal breakdown
Amphetamines (Bennies, Dexies, Co-Pilots, Wake-Ups, Lid Poppers, Hearts, Pep Pills) *Methamphetamines* (Speed, Dynamite)	Aggressive behavior, giggling, silliness, rapid speech, confused thinking, no appetite, extreme fatigue, dry mouth, shakiness	Jars of pills of varying colors, chain smoking	Death from overdose, Hallucinations, Methamphetamines sometimes causes temporary psychosis
Barbiturates (Barbs, Blue Devils, Candy, Yellow Jackets, Phennies, Peanuts, Blue Heavens, Goof balls, Downs)	Drowsiness, stupor, dullness, slurred speech, appearance of drunkenness, vomiting	Pills of varying colors	Death from overdose or causes addiction, convulsions and death as a result of withdrawal.

Ref: I. Taxel, Woodmere, N.Y. 1970

The availability of services is considerably deficient compared to the needs for placement of emotionally disturbed children. A report by the National Institute of Mental Health (1970) indicated that surveys conducted through school systems imply that 2 to 3 percent of the children are in need of psychiatric care. An additional 7 percent are in need of emotional help. A total estimate of all children in need of special programs for emotional problems is conservatively placed at 1,200,000. Therefore, it is quite obvious that the services for emotionally disturbed children are drastically insufficient.

We do not advocate any particular service need, because different children may be served under various kinds of programs. There is a need for all kinds of services, rather than for one specific kind of facility or program. Schultz et al. (1971) discovered twelve specific kinds of services: special class programs, resource room programs, crisis intervention, itinerant teacher program, academic tutoring, home-bound instruction, guidance counselor, school social worker, psychotherapy by school psychologist, psychiatric consultation, public school transportation to nonschool agency, and payment by public school for private school. Hopefully each school system would be able to provide at least one of these services, but realistic observation indicates that these services are not now available to the majority of disturbed children in public schools. Until states fulfill the mandatory special education laws, schools will probably fail to provide the necessary services. Schultz et al. found a general profile in the United States to indicate that the majority of programs for emotionally disturbed children were on a permissive basis. They discovered that special classes were the most often-mentioned service (47 states). Resource room programs (40 states), and home-bound instruction (38 states) were the next most common programs. They also noted that more than half of the states permitted the twelve services previously stated, and that some states prohibited services (specifically, payment to private schools) that other states mandated.

Number of Students Per Class

Many states have laws or state education department requirements on the maximum and minimum number of students permitted in each class or unit of instruction. Generally in the United States it appears that approximately ten students seem to be the maximum load for an individual class. Three as the minimum number necessary for a class appears to be a fairly consistent figure in many states, although, a range from a minimum of three to a maximum of fifteen is found in various school systems. The maximum or minimum number of students also may depend somewhat upon the age and severity of the children's problems. Without question, a teacher should be able to work more effectively with five older students who have already acquired some academic skills than with five very young disturbed children who have not achieved any academic success.

Schultz et al. (1971) also discovered that there were considerable differences among the states in the number of students assigned to a particular staff member. They received information from fifty states which indicated an extremely heavy load in some states for resource teachers—60 students; for crisis interveners—75 students; for social workers—250 students; and for psychologists—700 students. In other states they found extremely small case loads for teaching professionals.

There isn't any magical number of students per class that will ameliorate the problems of working with disturbed children. Logic does dictate, though, that a professional can achieve only limited success if overloaded. Therefore, a reasonable student-teacher or student-professional ratio must be maintained. What is reasonable will have to be determined by the professional and teacher-possessed skills, and by the age and severity of the students' problems.

Eligibility for Special Class Services

Provisions for special class placement are generally the function of the state department of education. States have different criteria which are usually consistent with the particular categorical definitions as described by each state. Eligibility to receive special school services is determined by meeting the guidelines established by the state's department of special education. These procedures for admission are not compatible. Some states may require a psychiatric examination for admission to a special class merely on the advice or recommendation of the school's administration.

Eligibility for admission should dictate that the program is special, and that it does not become a convenient means for the teachers or administrators to sidetrack their problem children. Guidelines for admission should be strict enough to keep children *out* of a class as well as permit them into one. A standard procedure for referral, evaluation, and placement should exist in each state. The procedure need not be common among the states, but it should be procedurally sound if the class or program is to maintain its identity and serve a specific function for emotionally disturbed children.

Many times teachers refer children they think need psychological services, but it may be the teacher's particular problems that become evident, the problem may be the result of that teacher's inability to function. Therefore, the next step should be an evaluative process that determines the child's emotional level of functioning. After adequate evaluation the child may be placed in a special class or returned to the regular program. The recommendation should *not* be made on the basis of the initial referral, whether it came from a teacher, a parent, an administrator, or even a psychologist, unless the report has been reviewed thoroughly with other school or professional personnel.

Educational Planning

The child has received a good evaluation, and he has been referred to the special class program. Now, what are the chances of succeeding and returning to the mainstream of school and life? If children are to succeed, they must have the advantage of sound educational, social, and intellectual planning. They cannot be discarded into a special class to vegetate and deteriorate. They must receive the benefits of experienced personnel, who have reasonable plans for remediation of social, emotional, and academic problems. They should be placed in a situation that best meets their needs, whether it is a contained room, a resource room, or whatever. After a child has been placed, a plan should be developed which is concerned with this particular child's growth. Wood (1968) expressed the need for a therapeutic educational plan that should be considered generally for all children placed in special programs, but should vary in its details with each situation. His suggested plan is as follows:

1. What is the child's educational problem? If the assumption is made that all children should be kept as closely integrated into the regular educational stream as possible, this becomes a question of which of the child's special needs can be met by adjustments within the regular classroom and which require special programming outside the regular class. Perhaps a special placement should be coordinated with part-time placement in a regular class.

2. Are any special conditions of placement necessary for exconcurrent psychotherapy, or medication? Who will be responsible for seeing that these conditions will be met?

3. What educational and management procedures are the regular or special class teacher to use with the child?

4. What period of time is to elapse before the success of the placement is to be evaluated? Who is responsible for making this evaluation and communicating it to the members of the team?

Wood's plan is a general guideline that could be followed with the placement of each child in an emotionally disturbed class, but the plan cannot be effective if individual consideration is not given to each child.

The attending behavior and academic performance of emotionally disturbed children are serious concerns for the classroom teacher. Attempting to increase both areas has been a problem. Attending behaviors have been improved by the use of cubicles; however, academic performance has not been affected. In a study by Haubrich and Shores (1976), cubicles and contingent reinforcement for attending behavior and academic performance were compared. Behavior modification techniques such as baselines, recording of the data by an independent observer, specification of target behaviors, continual measurement, and return to baseline conditions were used. The study involved five upper-elementary school-aged children in a residential center. The authors concluded that the use of contingent reinforcement improved attending behaviors to a greater extent than the use of cubicles, and only the reinforcement contingency improved academic performance. Teachers of the emotionally disturbed are, therefore, encouraged to develop meaningful reinforcement contingencies for both attending behavior and academic performance.

Bullock and Whelan (1971) completed a study relative to teacher competencies which indicated that teachers for emotionally disturbed classes must have adequate training and affectually sound models.* They reported that a competency committee, given the task of defining the specific competencies needed by teachers of emotionally disturbed and socially maladjusted children, made the following recommendations regarding the personal qualities of teachers:

They should be people of good judgement, possess a sense of humor, have the ability to place people and events in proper perspective, have adaptability and flexibility of mind, be conscious of their own limitations and idiosyncrasies, and have a normal range of human contacts outside the daily task of working with problem children.

After a careful analysis of the opinions of the competency committee and those expressed by teachers themselves, several suggestions for teacher training programs were postulated. Rabinow's program relies heavily on psychiatry, psychology, sociology, and communications and education. Schwartz proposed the training of a clinical teacher—one proficient in the diagnosis and remediation of learning and behavioral disorders. Hewett has a hierarchial framework—(a) objectivity, (b) flexibility, (c) structure, (d) resourcefulness, (e) social reinforcement, (f) curriculum expertise, and (g) intellectual model—which he believes to be vital for the teacher of emotionally disturbed children. Mackie, Kvaraceur, and William's program contained the above characteristics also.

Bullock and Whelan drew a comparison between two different groups of teachers of the emotionally disturbed—how each group viewed the competencies which a special study staff chose as important. The participants in the Bullock and Whelan investigation (a) did not view the competencies as being as important as did the original group; (b) viewed themselves as being more proficient in the competencies than did the original group; (c) tended to rank the items similarly to the original group on importance and on proficiency; (d) saw themselves as being less proficient in the items that they rated as being less important; and (e) tended to view themselves as being proficient in the items which they viewed as important.

It is apparent that continued and more intensive research must be undertaken to determine the most important competencies needed by teachers of emotionally disturbed and socially maladjusted children. Without this

*Lyndal M. Bullock and Richard J. Whelan, "Competencies Needed by Teachers of the Emotionally Disturbed and Socially Maladjusted: A Comparison," *Exceptional Children* 37, no. 7 (March 1971). © The Council for Exceptional Children.

research teacher preparation institutions lack scientific data to substantiate their existing programs and to serve as guidelines for program development and expansion.

It is suggested that preparation programs for teachers of emotionally disturbed and socially maladjusted children need to place renewed emphasis on individualized and sequential programming techniques in order to ensure school success for these children. Such an approach calls for teachers with a comprehensive overview of both regular and special curriculum materials for all grade levels. Since a large proportion of these children are below grade level academically, it seems imperative that teachers also have a thorough knowledge of remediation procedures, particularly in the areas of reading and arithmetic. Teachers also need thorough knowledge and understanding of behavioral principles as they apply to the management of these children. Since a multidisciplinary approach is also necessary; teachers need to become aware of other professional personnel and work with them as a team.

During the process of training persons to become teachers of emotionally disturbed children, it has been most difficult to assess these teachers' performances. The national picture shows program training in terms of numbers of courses in common, and of hours spent in practicum and classes. Haring and Fargo (1969) believe further training is necessary. They indicated that a teacher's skills cannot be measured by the courses listed on the college transcript or by the total number of course-hours completed, but rather by the effectiveness of teaching children.

To accomplish this goal, the techniques required are continuous structured evaluation of teacher performance, and clear statements of behavioral objectives. The behavioral objectives recommended by Haring and Fargo have been summarized as follows: (1) to establish procedures of observing, recording, and analyzing behaviors systematically; (2) to assess child performance in four areas—academic, verbal, social, and physical; (3) to assess the child's academic placement and the skill areas which need emphasis while also recognizing preference of activities which are most motivational; (4) to develop systematic procedures for initiation and maintenance of work in specific skills; (5) to demonstrate that the above-mentioned skills can be used with individuals and groups of children.

These criteria for evaluating the teacher were made by the cooperating classroom teacher and by the teacher's self-evaluation. This self-evaluation was enhanced by videotapes so that the teacher could get the full effect of the job done, and reflect and review methods that were used. Using videotape in evaluation is highly recommended.

Evaluation, which in the past has tended to be general and nonmeasurable, can be specific and more effectively done. Through means of observation and evaluation of the end result—children and their performance—a true and accurate evaluation of the effectiveness of a teacher may be obtained.

Parental Considerations

Many years' experience in the field of special education has impressed upon us the realization that parents of exceptional children are generally sophisticated about the specific problems of their children. The majority of parents seem to have genuine concern about these problems. Parents are usually quick to learn all they can about emotional disturbances. They are aware of different behaviors, and they probably are not content to live with them. Consequently, when they do seek help, they are willing to involve themselves with a therapeutic program.

McKinnon (1970) reported a study in which parent and pupil perceptions of special class placement were assessed. His study involved two urban communities where special classes for emotionally disturbed children had been in operation for several years. The program was an accepted part of the school system. This study involved eighty-eight children and their parents. The students had been in special class elementary schools for an average of seventeen months and had an average age of fourteen. At the time of the study they had terminated attendance in classes for an average period of three years. Even though the perceptions were in retrospect, parents were able to recall experiences, and they generally expressed positive views about the special classes. The parents indicated, too, that the teachers were positive also and had a stabilizing effect upon them and their children. They also reported relief when their child was taken from the failing regular class situation and was placed in the special class.

McKinnon's study also indicated that pupils recalled a pleasant and positive experience. Some of the questions that he asked the students drew answers that expressed an understanding of, or an awareness of their problem behaviors. An example is the response most frequently received when they were asked to give reasons for entering the special class. These responses were reflections upon themselves for having tempers and the ways they acted. The second most frequent response was a recognition that they were unable to do the work in the regular classes.

Parents' realistic perceptions of problem behaviors may be the turning point which dictates other constructive behaviors within the child. It should be interesting to note whether the child's behavior has actually changed or whether the parents' perception of the same behavior has changed. Many times parents see what they want to see. Though children seem demonic, parents may still perceive them as angels. Another parent may have a child who functions within a normal curve and yet perceive the behaviors as considerably deviate. Proper or improper behavior may lie in the eyes of the beholder.

Children's Considerations

Apparently the largest majority of children who have experienced a special class settting have realized the advantages of which they may avail themselves. McKinnon (1970) reported that children had generally positive feelings toward academic and craft work in the special classroom. They enjoyed both nonacademic and academic areas where assistance and success were possible. He also reported that a high percentage of the pupils did not like other students in the classes, because they exhibited explosive, unpredictable or "nutty" behavior. We agree with McKinnon that this perception could be their projection of their own "nutty" behavior.

Students sometimes seem to have intellectual understanding of their problems, but they are often unable to benefit from an emotional or affective investment. They are able to tell the teacher of their problems, and sometimes identify those elements of their behaviors that create obstacles for them, but they are unable to present a feeling-level of understanding. A student who is able to integrate intellectual and affective involvement in problem behavior should then be able to master the problems with relatively little assistance. Generally, though the student will manifest intellectual conversations that say, "Yes, I know I do not behave. I know that I cause my parents and teachers problems, but I don't know why." Therefore, they continue their poor behavior, possibly because they know of no other way to say, "Please, help me. I need help."

These children need the structure, supervision, and assistance that are available only in special programs. They will not receive the affective understanding they so desperately need from a traditional education program. Consequently, it should not be difficult to understand why these children, even in retrospect, perceive their experiences in special classes as enjoyable and sound growth periods of their lives. The time spent in special programs has enabled many of these students to be involved in the first successful academic and social experiences that they have ever had.

Residential Treatment

The National Institute of Mental Health (1969–1970) reported that in 1969 there were 261 facilities classified as residential treatment centers. The majority of them were small, privately owned institutions, mostly located in the Northeast Central, Pacific, and Middle Atlantic areas. Approximately two-thirds included special education as a part of their programs. Also, approximately one-third placed no diagnostic restrictions on their admission requirements. Those that had restrictions tended to mention most frequently that mental retardates were not eligible for admission. The National Institute also indicated that nearly twenty-one thousand patients were under care in residential treatment centers during 1969. That number is small compared to the total needs of children throughout the United States. Current estimates indicate that 10 percent of the population needs mental health care. It is

Exceptional children need the services of a variety of institutions, both private and public. (Courtesy of Dr. Nelda Ferguson, Timberidge School, Oklahoma City, Oklahoma.)

quite obvious that residential settings are not sufficient to handle emotionally disturbing problems for the general population. Quite likely the majority of patients seeking care from residential centers were either financially able or qualified for public assistance.

Treatment in residential centers may primarily involve those who are too disturbed to be under treatment in a less intensive environment. Children who manifest behaviors that are destructive to themselves or to others would not normally be handled in a community or school project. Therefore, a number of them will be placed in residential settings. We are not suggesting that there should be a general flow of child admissions to residential settings. Children should be in their home environments if at all possible. Children do not get functionally well if they are confined to a sick environment. They must be exposed to and integrated into a "normal" milieu, which provides them with realistic life conditions.

Institutional settings often separate the children from their families which in some situations is quite therapeutic. This separation also denies the facility the opportunity to work with the parents across geographic barriers. Consequently, the residential center must concentrate on the child, and reconstruct and remediate the problems to such a degree that the child can return home and tolerate parents' child-rearing deficiencies. Parents are requested by some facilities to seek treatment for themselves in their own communities. Home visits by the child or institutional visits by the parents would then allow observations to determine the growth of both parents and children.

Adventure School Playground. (Courtesy of Dr. Robert Phillips, Oklahoma City, Oklahoma.)

We have worked with some children who seem to offer evidence that the greater the geographic separation, the quicker the child responds to treatment. If the child and parents arrange a visit, either at home or at the residential setting, there seems to be a level of anxiety which causes the child to regress. It has also been observed that if children are allowed to have telephone contact with their parents for longer than two to three minutes, disagreements and arguments usually follow.

A practical suggestion for parent and child contact may be that the child should not be forced to call or write to the parents. The parental contact should be made only if the child wishes to do so, and the parents should not have the opportunity to phone or visit unless it is recommended by the staff as therapeutic. If the parents contact the child and have not modified their own problems, they will very likely resort to the attitudes which possibly caused the child's residential placement initially.

Heiting (1971) pointed out that the practice of maintaining close family relationships while the child is in a residential treatment program is advantageous for the following reasons:

1. It helps offset the child's fear of being abandoned, and feelings of being sent away for being a bad person.
2. It helps keep alive the anxiety parents have developed from feelings of guilt and failure in having placed their child away from home—anxiety that can be used in the treatment process to stimulate them to find new and more effective ways of interacting with their children.

3. It keeps the conflict between parents and child active and provides the staff with specific types of behavior on which to focus in helping the child and parent effect change.
4. It forces detached, neglectful parents to acknowledge their responsibilities to the child, or opens the way for steps to provide a substitute family for the child.

A residential setting may be the answer for some children, but not for others. Parents and professionals should examine closely the child's particular needs. Parents should also be aware before they waste their time seeking information about residential treatment, that it is generally very expensive.

Care Responsibilities

Bower (1969) expressed a concern that the care of the emotionally disturbed child is a community-centered problem, not just a school problem. He indicates that the school should cooperate with other civic agencies and campaign actively for complementary programs, such as foster homes, detention homes, day-care centers, and residential settings. Kessler (1966) suggested that social concepts and patterns of comprehensive care offer a good potential, but she sees a danger in that children may be slighted in favor of adults.

The National Institute of Mental Health points out that the community mental health center should provide comprehensive services that are particular to the communities' needs, and services should be provided by the specific community's resources. NIMH defines the following five essential services that a community center should provide:

1. *Inpatient care* offers treatment to patients who need 24-hour hospitalization.
2. *Outpatient care* offers patients individual, group, or family therapy, while permitting them to live at home and go about their daily activities.
3. *Partial hospitalization* offers either day care for patients able to return home evenings, or night care for patients able to work but in need of further care and who are usually without suitable home arrangements. It may include both day and night care and/or weekend care.
4. *Emergency care* offers emergency psychiatric services at any hour around-the-clock, in one of the three units mentioned above.
5. *Consultation* and *education* is made available by the center staff to community agencies and professional personnel.

NIMH also suggests the following services in addition to the basic five:

1. *Diagnostic services* provide diagnostic evaluation and may include recommendations for appropriate care.
2. *Rehabilitative services* include both social and vocational rehabilitation. For example: vocational testing, guidance, counseling or job placement.

3. *Precare* and *aftercare* provide screening of patients prior to hospital admission, home visiting before and after hospitalization, and may make available follow-up services for patients at outpatient clinics, in partial hospitalization programs, in foster homes, nursing homes, or halfway houses.

4. *Training* programs may be provided for all types of mental health personnel who serve the center's patients.

5. *Research* and *evaluation* may be undertaken by the center to evaluate the effectiveness of its program and to analyze the needs of the area it serves.

Care responsibilities should involve many different agencies within a community setting. The public schools will have a major portion of the responsibility simply because they are exposed to almost all of the children in a community. Their effectiveness can increase with their willingness to share their problems and constructively involve other community resources.

Methods and Materials for Emotionally Disturbed Children

There are no method or material panaceas available to teachers. If there is a panacea in teaching it has to come from the values and expertise of the teacher. Unquestionably, the teacher has a tremendous effect upon the child's cognitive and affective world. The traditional application of educational procedures will not enable disturbed children to reach potential growth. The teacher must discover those materials which apply to the problem area of the child, and then those materials must be structured and regulated to an aspirational level that is compatible with the level of growth of the child. Materials are not necessarily the answer to the child's problem; it is instead, the teacher's ability to integrate methods and materials through personal and flexible affective tones.

Aspects of the different behavioral theories are somewhat applicable to the teaching and academic setting of the emotionally disturbed. Professional education and behavioralists should not restrict themselves to one rigid scheme of treatment. One should screen all systems, and use the parts of the different systems that may be applicable to a particular child. A brief overview of some of the different systems or theories of behavior shows resemblances to Freud's original concepts of personality development. The theories which are in use today, even though they include some Freudian concepts, emphasize that their basic principles have application in the emotionally disturbed child's classroom.

Analytic Theory

The analytic theories suggest that the permissiveness and acceptance expressed in a client-centered environment could be advantageously applied in a teacher-child relationship. Naturally, the teacher should not expect a continuous positive therapeutic transference. There will be times of regression in the child which may exemplify severe negative transference of feeling. The general principles of psychotherapy do, though, have distinct applicable qualities of the classroom setting. The child, hopefully, would be able to reduce the conflicts between self and environment through acceptance, respect for the teacher, and the setting-of-limits. Changes in adaptive behavior may occur when children effect changes in the environment or changes within themselves. They may change as a result of the psychophysical (relation between mental action and physical phenomena) reduction of the psychic and somatic conflicts which previously had caused a hypochondriacal symptomatic state of asthenia. Also, adaption to a functional level may happen as a result of the student's choice of a new environment which contributes to a functioning level, rather than restricting it. Sometimes the environment causes children to appear abnormal, when in reality they could function properly in different environments. Therefore, changing their environments may enable them to be acceptable.

Behavioral Theories

Pavlov and Skinner to some extent started the present behavior modification trend that appears to be rapidly spreading throughout the United States. Even though their primary work was years ago and was involved in laboratory settings, they created the basic techniques that have enabled behavior management methods to reach the classroom in the public schools. Behavior modification is discussed in another chapter in this book, but some examples of successful modification methods are described here.

Axelrod (1971) reported a study by Gallagher, Sulzbacher, and Shores with a group contingency procedure to reduce disruptive classroom behaviors of five boys ranging in age from approximately seven to eleven. The study hypothesized that more deviant behaviors existed when a member of the class was not seated. The goal was to eliminate out-of-seat behavior, which in turn should reduce the other deviant behaviors. The students were offered a twenty-four-minute coke break at the end of the day if they did not leave their seats without permission. A chart in the room indicated two-minute segments from twenty-four to zero, and each child's name was marked by a different color of chalk. When a child got up without permission, the teacher would mark off two minutes from the entire class's coke time. The color coding, of course, designated the student involved. The results indicated a reduction in out-of-seat behavior from 69.5 to 1.0 times per day, and a significant decline in disruptive behaviors.

Glavin, Quay, and Werry (1971) conducted a two-year study with children who exhibited severe difficulties in the public school. These children were placed in an experimental special class situation. The first year (1967), the program emphasized the elimination of grossly deviant behaviors and the acquisition of attending behaviors that were preliminary to academic success. The second year (1968), the emphasis was placed on rewards for academic performance. Attractive reinforcers were given for appropriate performance on academic tasks. Various intangibles may have had influence on the results, but a comparison between the 1967 and 1968 data seems to favor the 1968 program as the primary contributing factor for improved academic and behavior performances.

Behavior modification programs are not the total answer to the remediation of problem behaviors, but they provide functional methods that can be systematically applied. Management techniques should never be without the affective levels of warm, human interaction; behavior techniques must be void of rigid, cold, and mechanical application.

Ecological Theory

The ecological theory links the individual and the environment into a single concept. The individual is not separate from the environment; therefore, the problems of the individual become the property of the community. The problems are not dealt with as a single attribute of the child. Consequently, if there are disturbances within the community the individual will be affected by the ecology.

A psychologist who visits a home, classroom, community living space, or the total school and community environment can distinguish behaviors contributive to the child's deviations. The child is also contributing to the system's deficient pattern, but possibly should not be identified as the primary etiology of the disturbed environment. The ecological system presents a pattern of reciprocity which says, "You hurt me, and I'll hurt you."

Lewis (1970) wrote that ecological planning offers fresh insight into ways of helping children with behavior problems. He indicated that ecology tells us that children need more than a good educational program. Ecological planning suggests an enlarged scope that includes the total environment: the people with whom children live and interact regularly. The general program goals in the ecological system would be to remediate behavioral and academic problems. Remediation enables the child to interact appropriately with the environment, which would then cause the environment to interact appropriately with the child.

Sociological Theory

Society appears to be a collection of structures which dictate the needs of individuals. Personal needs seem to have no limitations, but people are commanded to stay within certain norms of behavior that are determined by the majority of society. Consequently, the more limited a particular society's structure becomes, the more obvious the individual's deviation will be. An example of limited structure could be found within the confines of a church setting where a person is to act with certain dignities. If this person were to use profanity, the deviation would be very obvious. If one were a sailor on ship and used profanity the deviation would not be so obvious. Therefore, obviously the controls of society can cause a child to be categorized as a disturbed child. Movies which exhibit pornography may be within the mores in some communities while in others a person may be labeled a sex deviate for attending such movies.

Allergy and Nutrition Theory

This section contains information which lends considerable controversy to the areas of learning disability and emotional disturbance, but we believe in the importance of including the many different approaches to the behavioral sciences. Certainly, there is no mutual agreement on a best theory or practice. Many behavioral scientists have changed directions after years of static practice simply because they were exposed to research which evidenced a valid reason for change.

The following is a summary reprint of research offered by Dr. Philpott's study of food and chemical symptom induction testing.*

Maladaptive allergic or allergic-like reactions can affect any tissue of the body. The majority of the time when the central nervous system is a maladaptive shock organ, the common symptoms of allergy (runny nose, watery eyes, itching skin or hives, respiratory or gastrointestinal symptoms) are not present. In small children there is a more frequent association of common allergic symptoms with central nervous system reactions than in adolescents or adults. If they remain exposed to the substance to which they are maladaptive reacting, their common allergic and allergiclike symptoms will disappear and the central nervous system symptoms will take their place. Thus the milk- or corn-allergic infant may in later childhood be frequently eating dairy or corn products under the assumption of having "outgrown" reactions to these substances, only to have the development of hyperactivity, lethargy, insomnia, dyslexia, short attention span, poor concentration or over- or under-hearing. If the exposure continues, behavior problems can and often do result out of the poor learning of social behaviors. If the stress of the exposure continues further, frank psychosis can result.

Learning problems are frequently due to maladaptive allergic or allergiclike reactions occurring in the central nervous system. The most common cause for these maladaptive reactions is the most commonly used food for the particular person under consideration. Cereal grains (especially wheat, rye and corn), dairy products, sugars (corn syrup, cane and beet), eggs, chocolate, potato and tomato are common offenders. Petrochemical

*Reprinted by permission of William H. Philpott, M.D., Oklahoma City, Okla., 1975.

hydrocarbons and food additives and preservatives are frequently involved. It can be anything other than pure air, pure water or pure salt that the person contacts frequently. Learning problems characteristically occur at the stage of addiction at either the stimulatory contact stage or the delayed timing of three hours or more after contact, which is the withdrawal stage.

Learning problems as defined in such terms as dyslexia or minimal brain dysfunction are viewed as at the extreme left of the continuum with psychosis at the extreme right. Both have a basic organic cause, as truly organic as the well-defined neurological dysfunctions of the nervous system. The qualities of partial function and fluctuation function give them the "soft organic" quality. The qualities of primary, secondary or associated emotion and disordered behavior in these central nervous system allergic reactions have served to overshadow the underlying organicity as far as the education of psychiatrists is concerned. Efficiency demands that we deal realistically with both functional and organic factors but also demands that organicity be given the priority. Once the organicity is handled there still remains the big therapeutic job of corrective education for dyslexia, desensitization of phobias, inhibition of obsessions and compulsions, excitation of motivation, conflict resolution, teaching of social skills, and general personality maturity.

Quotable Quotes

A number of other allergists have documented the many mental symptoms and behavioral problems caused by food additives and food allergies. If mental illness caused by allergies was recognized more, and emotional factors not always sought to explain mental disturbances, a great deal of time and money could be saved, and patients' mental conditions eliminated. There are millions of patients enduring needless suffering. One can only guess at the number of major and minor tragedies that are enacted daily because of misinterpreted symptoms and inappropriate therapy (Rapaport 1970).

Western civilization was created and/or distributed a wide assortment of agents that could conceivably cause damage to the human brain, including food additives, cereal grains, drugs, insecticides, cleaning fluids, tobacco, alcohol, vaccines and microorganisms of various types including viruses. We now know enough about many of these to know that they should not be overlooked in search for the etiology of any disease that affects the brain (Torrey 1974).

Consideration of symptom complexes is important in arriving at an accurate diagnosis of an allergic diathesis. The average specialist becomes so involved in his specialty that he tends to neglect other areas of medical knowledge. Psychiatrists, for instance, are among the greatest offenders in overlooking organic disease, attempting to explain all phenomena on a psychological basis (Campbell 1974).

. . . one must be taught to suspect, for if one does not suspect, he does not test and if he does not test, he does not know (Rinkel 1951).

Certain it is that the psychiatrist and the allergist should work together for the solution of their more difficult problems (Alvarez 1951).

Additionally, we have extracted information from a research paper. "The Physiology of Violence," presented at the Huxley Institute for Biosocial Research, Bowling Green State University, by Dr. Philpott (1976).*

Howard G. Rapaport, M.D. (1976) stated, "It is factually established that one of five school children has a major allergic disease." He views allergy considerations as belonging in the differential diagnosis of causes of learning disabilities.

Starting in 1970 I began to take a serious look at the claims made by some allergists that an assortment of emotional reactions are sometimes observed to occur during deliberate exposure to single foods and chemicals. Under the guidance of the allergists Marshall Mandell, Theron G. Randolph, and Sol D. Klotz, I learned how to test patients so as to induce symptoms during exposure to single items. For food testing patients avoid commonly used foods by a four- to six-day fast using water only or eating only foods seldom used.

The symptoms evoked during testing range in scope from mild to severe and involve numerous physical as well as mental symptoms including psychosis and seizure. The following case histories involving aggression were observed by Dr. Philpott during induction testing of his patients.

A 20-year-old paranoid schizophrenic became quite symptom free by the fourth day of a fast on water only. When test smoking a cigarette he became disoriented, delusional and defied anyone to come near him. It took four men to subdue him and place him in a seclusion room. He was well until two years before when he went off to college at which time he also introduced cigarette smoking.

An 18-year-old paranoid schizophrenic had to be restrained since he would strike out to kill anyone who came near him because he believed they wanted to kill him; so he was attempting to kill them first in self-defense. By the fourth day of his fast he was not delusional and could be trusted about the hospital. At this time he phoned his father stating, "I love you. Please come and see me." When given a test meal of wheat he became hostile, agitated, and phoned his father and yelled into the phone, "I hate you. You made me sick. I don't ever want to see you again." When tested for a reaction to tobacco by smoking a cigarette he became paranoid, hostile, and struck the examiner because he hallucinated horns on the examiner's head and thought the examiner was the devil. It was necessary to restrain him physically. Later he had no memory of the incident.

A 52-year-old woman with a neurotic depression was tested for wheat and developed a stiff neck, tightness in the chest and throat, but worst of all she felt like hitting or punching someone. She was so frightened she might act on these compulsive urges that she went to a room by herself until the reaction subsided.

*Reprinted by permission of William H. Philpott, M.D., Oklahoma City, Oklahoma, 1976.

In a 36-year-old psychoneurotic woman pineapple evoked: irritability, blocking of thought, dizziness, headache. Oranges: violently angry, fought with her son, and loudly told another patient to shut up, following which she became sleepy and her mind functioned so poorly she could hardly carry on a conversation. Rice: she loudly scolded her son for speaking while she was speaking. When the examiner observed that this behavior was a reaction to the test meal of rice she denied it and said she was just teaching her son to be respectful. A few minutes later she began uncontrollable giggling followed by crying. At this time she admitted she was reacting to rice.

A 4-year-old boy with a diagnosis of hyperkinesis had these reactions. String beans: very hyperactive, wanted to fight, coughing. Carbanzo beans: first overly happy followed by hunger and grouchiness. Navy beans: very hyperactive, teasing, and eyes watering. Cod fish: coughing, cried and said he thought there would be a storm, afraid of having nightmares and seeing scary monsters, and afraid his cat would turn into a lion. Carrots: fighting and grouchy. Celery: stomachache, crying and grouchy. Strawberries: angry, hyperactive and coughing. Unrefined cane sugar: irritable, stuffy nose and coughing.

A 12-year-old hyperkinetic boy. Banana: listless, depressed, crying. Then he became aggressive and picked up a stick and tried to hit another patient. Oranges: first singing then tired, impatient, wild and wanted to strike someone. Tomato: irritable, defensive, upset stomach. Rice: hot, silly, teasing and followed by rebelliousness and hyperactivity. Apple: at first he felt stimulated and then started a fight.

A 12-year-old autistic girl grabbed and broke her mother's glasses during a food reaction. In response to another food she picked up a rock used as a door stop and attempted to hit someone.

A 40-year-old schizophrenic woman's response to a sublingual test for petrochemical hydrocarbons using glycerinated exhaust fumes was trying to find a way to kill herself and had to be restrained to prevent suicide. Repeatedly she had attempted suicide by opening the door of the car in an attempt to jump out while the car was going down the road. She would be normal when starting on a ride but within a few minutes she would try to jump from the running car and had to be restrained by her husband. He found a faulty exhaust system on the car which leaked exhaust fumes into the car.

One patient in response to a test for oranges lost his voice and was so irritable he slapped his son. One 60-year-old grandmother argued and fought with her grandchildren in response to a food test.

I could go on and on with case histories that reveal the evidence that objectively observed induction testing of foods and chemicals reveals the cause and effect relation between maladaptive reactions to foods and chemicals in aggressive behavior as well as numerous other physical and central nervous system reactions.

Children may need chemotherapy, play therapy, good nutrition, counseling, or various combinations of these treatments. (Adventure School Playground is courtesy of Dr. Robert Phillips, Oklahoma City, Oklahoma.)

Drugs for Treatment of Emotionally Disturbed Children

Few topics of discussion generate more heat and less light than the proper role of drugs in the treatment of emotionally disturbed children. At one extreme are those who argue that meaningful treatment is possible only by using the insights provided by psychotherapy, and that drugs, if they function as more than placebos, do so only as chemical straightjackets for troublesome children.

At the other extreme there are those who consider drugs to be the agents of choice because they attack the disturbed function at the physiologic level; the place they believe the ultimate pathology lies. This controversy engages the passions of psychologists, social workers, parents, and teachers. But for the empiricists, however, the relevant question is, "What are the facts?"

Historically, the search for drugs to influence behavior or learning, or to induce a feeling of inner calm and contentment, extends far beyond modern pharmacology. Many natural substances such as opium, alcohol, and mescaline have been used to calm, soothe, and increase acceptance of a poor situation or simply cause partial oblivion or sensory dullness. These "cures" are often worse than the illness. Adverse effects of these drugs include habituation, addiction, and loss of personal control.

These natural drugs in "raw" form do not meet the necessary requirements of an effective tranquilizer. The effective tranquilizer should produce rapid therapeutic responses in a majority of cases, without inducting tolerance or addiction. It should have low incidences of toxic effects and side effects. Hopefully, it would not dull the senses or decrease perception or interfere with mental alertness, to any extent (Cruickshank 1966).

The first major group of synthetic drugs to be used in this way were the barbiturates. They offered considerable advantage over the natural drugs, but had one major shortcoming: they dulled the senses and blunted mental response because they are sedatives rather than tranquilizers (Wilson 1964).

Early in the 1940s some favorable responses to the administration of amphetamines were observed. These drugs were known for their stimulating effect on the central nervous system. These are better known commercially as benzedrine and dexedrine.

There was little additional work completed until the 1950s, when chlorpromazine was introduced by French investigators. Since that time, the literature dealing with drugs that affect behavior has grown at an incredible rate. Numerous compounds have been developed and some have emerged without careful study. Unfortunately, to this day there are few well-designed and controlled scientific studies to assess the psychological state of the patient and the relationship to agents under study (Conners 1971).

The decision to initiate drug therapy for children with behavior problems is still a very controversial issue, now complicated by the climate of the times. The psychostimulant drugs do have a place in treatment, but the high rate of placebo effect, the reaction of the public against drug therapy in general, a lack of knowledge concerning long-term effects of these agents, and the possibility of drug abuse are all factors to be considered in the initiation of any drug therapy (Solomans 1971).

Tranquilizers

Tranquilizers are drugs which are used to control anxiety, psychomotor agitation and related symptoms. There are two clinical groups: (1) the major tranquilizers and (2) the minor tranquilzers. The major tranquilizers can be divided ino the phenothiazines and Rauwolfia derivatives. The minor tranquilizers can be divided into diolcarbamates, and diphenylmethanes, and a miscellaneous group.

Additional groups are becoming necessary as new compounds appear. Although this classification is incomplete and tentative, it offers a useful guide. After this general introduction, a presentation of the therapeutic properties of the major and minor groups is possible (Benson and Schiele 1962):

1. A diminution of emotional tension and a reduction of mental activity and agitation
2. An absence of depression of any aspect of cognition
3. A suppression of psychomotor activity and excitement
4. An alleviation or abolition of delusions and hallucinations
5. The reduction or dispersal of mental confusion in psychosis

Pharmacologically, there are distinctions among the tranquilizers. Although many similarities do exist in the action of representative drugs from each group, there are also considerable differences.

The major tranquilizers exert greater autonomic effects (on the nervous system) and, in addition, are prone to induce tremors. The most significant action is their ability to depress the hypothalamus (controls basic drives) without depressing the cortex (senses). The minor tranquilizers differ among themselves in that autonomic blocking activity is more characteristic of the diphenylmethanes while the muscle relaxant action is a prominent effect of the diolcarbamate drugs.

Chlorpromazine (thorazine) was the first major tranquilizing drug introduced which was used to modify behavior. The most remarkable action of chlorpromazine (thorazine) is its ability to reduce the frequency of aggressive agitated outbursts in seriously ill psychotics with relatively less ataxia, skeletal muscle incoordination, and drowsiness associated with bromides and barbiturates. The primary site of action is the central nervous system (Benson and Schiele).

The other major tranquilizers are characterized by one or more of the following:

1. Produces a type of emotional calmness with relatively little sedation.
2. Is capable of producing the reversible extrapyramidal syndrome (outer limbs) characterized by tremors, rigidity, and drooling.
3. The incidence of annoying side reactions is relatively high with the use of this and other major tranquilizers, and serious dangers do exist to some extent.
4. They produce little, if any, dependency or habituation.

Trifluoperazine (stelazine) is at least twice as active as chlorpromazine, but otherwise is similar in its spectrum of action. It produces no drowsiness, but on the contrary has been said to have an awakening effect.

Fluphenazine (prolixin) is, in terms of potency, the most active compound available at the present time. It is considered to be more than twenty times as potent as chlorpromazine (Benson and Schiele). We authors have worked with students who were administered prolixin which has a cramping effect if additional dosages of cogentin are not administered; therefore, it was used to control behavior by withholding cogentin.

One caution should be added at this point. The dosage should be made according to the individual patient—with small dosages in the beginning, to be increased only after evaluation by the physician. With major tranquilizers there is the danger of toxicity and harmful side effects. These two facets should be evaluated before they are prescribed for any patient.

The minor tranquilizers are very widely used and are the preferred drugs in common nervous illness. In many cases, their calming action is sufficient to provide relief during the acute phase of a disorder. In spite of the widespread use and great popularity of the minor tranquilizers, much less is known about them than is known of the major tranquilizers.

Neprobamate (Equanil) has a mild sedative action with muscle relaxing and some anticonvulsive activity. It is the most widely used of all tranquilizers. Although it is a safe compound compared with the major drugs, habituation, ataxis, and skin reactions occur occasionally.

Chlordiazepoxide (Librium) is a potent central muscle relaxant which has sedative and tranquilizing action. It is closely related to the meprobamate in activity, but is much more potent (Benson and Schiele).

The Antidepressive Drugs

The antidepressive drugs are useful in the treatment of psychiatric depressions. Depression varies as much as pain, and like pain is one of man's most common ailments.

The use of amphetamines to alleviate behavioral disorders in children was originally advocated in 1937. In 1958, methylphenidate was first used on children with behavioral disorders, and eventually became even more popular than the amphetamines. When the era of tranquilizers and other psychoactive drugs erupted in the 1950s, the need for effective drug therapy produced many studies, which lacked control and scientific validation (Solomans 1971).

Today, the main problem is the lack of an operational definition of minimal brain dysfunction, learning problems, or deviant or hyperactive behavior. This automatically produces confusion in the choice of medication and the evaluation of its efficiency.

The site and mechanism of the psychostimulant drugs have not been definitely established. They do, however, have a paradoxical effect on many children, especially those with hyperkinetic behavior. Logically, the hyperkinetic behavior should increase with amphetamine. Connors and Rothchild

(1968) stated that the drug action in the hyperkinetic child is not a pharmacologically true paradoxical effect. The stimulating effect of the amphetamines causes an increase in general alertness and excitation along with an increase in the ability to focus attention. Responses to interfering stimuli are then decreased, and the child is more receptive to positive reinforcement from parents and teachers (Solomans).

With emotionally disturbed, underachieving boys, methylphenidate (Ritalan) significantly increased correct responding, decreased reaction time, and hyperactivity; and in the classroom significantly increased attention and cooperation behavior. This was a well-controlled study using laboratory as well as clinical procedures (Solomans 1971).

Side Effects and Addiction

Admittedly, no psychotrophic drug is a panacea. None of these agents attack the etiologic factors which are sometimes unknown, uncertain, or unresponsive, and few bring permanent symptomatic relief.

While most are safe in competent hands, many drugs cause undesired reactions, and the fear of these side effects is frequently a deterrent to the use of both tranquilizers and antidepressants. On this point, psychiatrists with extensive experience have commented, "Irreversible side effects are vitually unknown" (Remmen 1962). "Weighted against the stress of mental disturbance, the inconvenience of most side effects is inconsiderable (Uhr 1960).

In general, there is one major drawback in the group of major tranquilizers: extrapyramidal reactions or Parkinson syndrome. The symptoms include deficiency of will power (abulia), poverty of movement (akinesia), stiffness of muscles (rigidity), masklike expressions, and in nearly every case, tremor, which may be like a fine tremor of the fingers or a violent, coarse trembling (Burke and Hornykiewicz 1969). Although these reactions are not serious, they may be frightening for the patient. They may be controlled by dosage reduction or the use of antiparkinsonian drugs such as benztropine (Cogentin).

Most authorities in this field consider the extrapyramidal syndromes as part of the normal drug action. Their occurrence is an indication that the drug is affecting the deeper brain centers, where much of their antipsychotic activity presumably takes place. Other side effects may be photosensitivity, drowsiness, or fatigue. These also would be a sign that brain functions are being altered by the medication.

The minor tranquilizers, when given in therapeutic doses up to the maximum dosage, have rarely shown the extrapyramidal reactions. Also, serious toxic effects are almost unknown and photosensitivity does not occur. There have been no cases of jaundice or severe dermatitis reported (Benson and Schiele 1962). In children, however, overdosage leads to a very marked central nervous system dysfunction, depression, and prolonged hypotension (Burke and Hornykiewicz).

Another concern is *addiction.* Addiction is a complex and little understood problem in humans. The definition of drug addiction, according to the World Health Organization, emphasizes damage to the individual and society. The person who is habituated will readily self-administer the drug if it is available, but has little tendency to increase dosage and exhibits no physical abstinence syndrome on withdrawal of the drug. Another term applied to this category of drug dependence is psychic dependence. This term suggests that the process is mental as opposed to physical and therefore not measureable (Shuster 1968).

A degree of habituation to the phenothiazines may occur. Patients who, after administration of large doses, cannot get up without suffering anorthostatic collapse are able to do so during the course of continuing treatment. The sudden termination of prolonged treatment with large doses of phenothiazines usually leads to exacerbation of the basic disease. Many authors believe this to be a sign of withdrawal. Domino (1962) stated that there was no reason to assume that phenothiazines induce true addiction (Burke and Hornykiewicz 1969). There are many differing accounts in the literature in regard to the compulsive use of and physical dependence on minor tranquilizers.

In the final analysis the value of tranquilizers and antidepressants depends on the correct and appropriate use of the drugs prescribed, and the practitioners' knowledge. The various groups of drugs themselves counteract specific types of symptoms rather than a specific illness. From the point of view of treatment, it is frequently the quantity, not the quality of specific action that renders the drug of therapeutic value (Uhr 1960).

Antidepressants and Stimulants

Dr. Burack, physician and author of *The New Handbook of Prescription Drugs,* says that Ritalan was first developed in an effort to find a substance with the "mood elevating" effects of amphetamines, minus its drawbacks, but the drug has been a disappointment. It begins to appear that Ritalan may not achieve full separation of amphetamine's desirable and undesirable effects, and amphetamine abusers are beginning to ask for it. The U.S. Food and Drug Administration has urged physicians to exercise extreme caution in prescribing the drug, because of the danger of addiction (*Washington Post* 1970). In the dosage used for children the question of toxicity, noted in the stimulant abuser, is not a critical issue. Unwanted physical and mental effects rarely appear in children when there is cessation or adjustment of dosage. Physicians who care for children treated with stimulants have noted that they do not experience the pleasurable subjective effects that would encourage misuse. They observe that most often they are willing to stop the therapy, which they view as "medicine." These drugs are usually not given to children after age eleven or twelve, when actual risks of experimentation or misuse might become significant (*Education Digest* February 1972).

Summary Listings of Drugs

The use of medication with emotionally disturbed children is a very controversial issue, even though studies have shown that there is a place for medication as part of their treatment. These studies have shown that when the medication is effective, children can organize activities in the direction they wish. Hopefully, other secondary consequences will also appear. These can be better peer relationships, improved self-image, and pleasures from achieving success.

Dosage may require shifting to minimize unwanted side effects, such as loss of appetite and insomnia or the Parkinson syndrome. It cannot be emphasized too strongly that the use of drugs is only one aspect of the total treatment of the emotionally disturbed. Drug administration can improve the symptoms from which the patient suffers, but drugs are not a solution to the environmental problems or mental maladjustment which cause the problem. The child who benefits from the use of psychotherapeutic medications should not be stigmatized. That situation is no different from that of the child who benefits from glasses. And finally, drug treatment should and need not be indefinite, and is usually stopped after age eleven or twelve.

The most important aspect of the drug treatment is correct diagnosis and careful administration of the medication. When drugs are used correctly, they will help most children achieve their desired goals. Some of the improvement is a result of the placebo affect. Oftentimes, just the expectation of a beneficial effect is sufficient to cause a striking improvement, though many times reports of behavior reflect a change in the attitude of the observer.

Some drugs recently discovered are especially effective with children who are quite anxious, depressed, or hyperactive. The physician is the key member of the team whenever medication is involved. He or she should make all such decisions. Other team members—the school nurse, psychologist, teacher, counselor, and parents must work together for more effective results.

Some general conclusions can be drawn about the use of psychotherapeutic drugs. First, improvement in emotional stability and general behavior may occur, but there will be no change in intellectual ability. There are no pills to make children smarter, but pills may alter behavior characteristics. Secondly, behavior changes that do occur are generally more in the terms of degree than of kind. And thirdly, any drugs capable of marked psychotherapeutic action should, of course, be employed with caution, under the supervision and control of a physician who has known the child awhile and can prescribe wisely. (Crawford 1966).

A teacher should be aware of the medication used by the children in her classroom, along with the normal daily dosage and possible reactions to such medication. If a child is being administered a drug with which the teacher is unfamiliar, it would be wise to contact the child's physician to become aware of any possible side effects. To help the teacher become more familiar with drugs, the following list containing only a few of the more commonly used forms of medication has been provided. (Van Osdol, Van Osdol, Shane 1975).

Atarax (Roerig) 50–100 mg daily. Used in management of anxiety and tension and psychomotor agitation in conditions of emotional stress.

　　Side effects: Rare adverse reactions, occasional drowsiness, dry mouth, tremor.

Aventyl (Lilly) Children 10–75 mg daily, Adults 20–100 mg daily. Used in treatment of mental depression, anxiety, tension states. Symptomatic reactions of childhood enuresis, passive-aggressive personality, obsessive compulsive reactions, psychophysiological gastrointestinal reactions.

　　Side effects: Dryness of mouth, drowsiness, tremor, dizziness, blurred vision, restlessness, etc.

Benadryl Hydrochloride (Parke, Davis) Children 20–80 mg daily. Adults up to 250 mg daily. Antihistaminic action. Used to quiet hyperactive emotionally disturbed child.

　　Side effects: Drowsiness, dizziness, dryness of mouth, nausea, nervousness, etc.

Benzedrine (Smith, Kline and French) 5–10 mg daily. To control appetite; stimulatory effect helps restore optimism and dispel fatigue; to control narcolepsy and childhood behavior problems.

　　Side effects: Restlessness, insomnia, over-stimulation, tremor, headache, sweating.

Deaner (Riker) 100–300 mg daily. For learning problems, reading difficulties, shortened attention span. Behavior problems, hyperkinetic behavior, perseveration, distractibility, impaired motor coordination, etc.

　　Side effects: Mild headache, insomnia, transient rash, constipation, tenseness in the neck.

Dexedrine (Smith, Kline and French) Spansule, 30–35 mg, Elizer 2 ½–5 mg (3 to 4 times daily). Control of appetite, childhood neurotic behavior disorders, narcolepsy, mood evaluation.

　　Side effects: Undue restlessness, insomnia, gastrointestinal disturbances, palpitation, headache.

Dilantin (Parke-Davis) .2–6 gms daily. Used in treatment of grand mal and other convulsive states. Controls seizure without hypnotic effects of many anticonvulsant drugs.

　　Side effects: Gastric distresss, nausea, weight loss, sleeplessness, gingival hypertrophy, excessive motor activity.

Equanil (See Meprobamate)

Librium (Roche) 15–40 mg daily. Used for relief of anxiety, tension and apprehension.

> Side effects: Ataxia, drowsiness, confusion, etc.

Mellaril (Sandoz) Children 20–75 mg daily. Adults up to 100 mg daily. Reduces excitement, hypermotility, agitation, apprehension, anxiety, behavioral disorders.

> Side effects: Drowsiness, nocturnal confusion, dry mouth, headaches, nasal stuffiness.

Meprobamate (Rexall) Children 300–600 mg daily, Adults 1200–1600 mg daily. Also *Equanil* (Wyeth) and *Miltown* (Wallace). Used in management of anxiety or tension by tranquilizing action. May help spastic conditions secondary to neurological disorders. Relaxes skeletal muscles.

> Side effects: Drowsiness, rash, occasional visual disturbances.

Prolixin (Squibb) Children 1–2 mg daily. Adults up to 10 mg daily. Reduces anxiety and tension, severe mental disorders, behavioral problems in children. Behavior modifier with sustained and prolonged action. Should be used with caution in patients with history of convulsive disorder.

> Side effects: Jaundice, blood disorders, soreness of mouth and gums. Dystonia (impairment of muscle tone), dyskinesia (pain on movement), oculogyric (movement of eyes).

Ritalin Hydrochloride (Ciba) 20–30 mg daily. Mild stimulant and antidepressant, brightens mood and improves performance. Indicated in chronic fatigue, drug-induced lethargy, psychoneurosis, withdrawn behavior, functional behavior problems in children (hyperactivity, stuttering, etc.).

Stelazine (Smith, Kline and French) Children 1–15 mg daily. Adults 4–20 mg daily. May be used with Thorazine. Relieves symptoms of anxiety whether expressed as tension or apathy.

> Side effects: Drowsiness, dizziness, skin reaction, dry mouth, insomnia.

Thorazine (Smith, Kline and French) 40–75 mg daily. May be used with Stelazine. For agitation, tension, apprehension or anxiety. Behavior disorders.

> Side effects: Drowsiness, dry mouth, nasal congestion.

Tofranil (Geigy) 30–150 mg daily. Used as an antidepressant, may help in "target symptoms" as lack of interest, feelings of inferiority, psychomotor retardation, and inhibition.

> Side effects: Tremor, dizziness, weight gain, dry mouth. Some of these symptoms may show at first and then disappear with continued use.

Valium (Roche)5–15 mg daily. Used for anxiety reactions stemming from stressful circumstances whenever somatic complaints are concomitants of emotional factors.

    Side effects: Fatigue, drowsiness, ataxia, mild nausea, dizziness, headache, diplopia, tremor, etc.

Overview

The total program for emotionally disturbed children is one that may glean aspects of treatment from many different theories of personality and methods of teaching. There are no static techniques or methods that will solve the problems for all teachers. There are some definite affective considerations of which the special class teacher should be aware. The emotionally charged behaviors of children can many times call forth distorted perceptions from teachers. The teachers should not expect an emotionally disturbed child to show abnormal behavior throughout the daily routine. The children may have functionally sound periods of time. The teacher should not be quick to judge children as well and rush them back to regular classes. A good look at the child's total environmental level of functioning is required. Some children may become academic whiz kids and pass all subjects with little effort, but they may still be very sick. Their resources are thrust into the avenue which presents less obstacles. If the academic area is easy, all energy goes into studies and there is nothing left for the rest of the environment. That level of functioning, even though comfortable for the teacher, is not a manifestation of good mental health. The teacher should remain somewhat suspect of the children. It is not reasonable to believe that a teacher can befriend a child, buy her a coke, and believe that suddenly all problems will disappear. As a teacher, you will have to prove again and again that you are trying to help the children because they will test your tolerance repeatedly until they really feel that you are trustworthy. A teacher should want to like the children, but don't assume that a display of love and affection will relieve the child's problems. The child may be one who cannot afford to be loved, and will reject all your efforts to get close, because this child has many times experienced the same reaction: when she loves someone, she gets hurt. Therefore, love to this particular child may represent pain. The teacher should expect to receive aggressive behaviors from the children. These aggressions may be displaced, or they may be deliberately aimed at the teacher authority figure. Either way they are, again, the means for the child to test the teacher's responses.

    Generally, one of the best approaches to any teaching situation is to use just plain good common sense. There are no magical cures, and people were raising children long before Freud and the other behavioral scientists. Many parents and teachers developed some good products. Maybe Billy the Kid's mother missed, but so have a lot of other parents and teachers in this contemporary world.

Study Questions

1. Define the emotionally disturbed child and cite the complete reference data which you have used.
2. How do you personally assume that public schools provide for emotionally disturbed children?
3. Describe the type of training which should be required of a teacher who is planning to teach emotionally disturbed children.
4. Compare the paradoxical similarities and distinct differences between learning disabled and emotionally disturbed children.
5. Discuss the pros and cons of drug therapy for the emotionally disturbed child.
6. Determine the relationship of environment and/or heredity to emotional disturbances. Cite your references.
7. List your preferences of types of services available for the emotionally disturbed child; discuss and defend.
8. In what ways can parents effectively work with their emotionally disturbed child?
9. List three or four symptoms of emotional disturbance. Discuss and cite references.
10. What is the role of the psychologist, psychiatrist, regular class teacher, special class teacher, and the parents in providing services for the emotionally disturbed child?

Bibliography

Axelrod, Saul. 1971. "Token Reinforcement Programs in Special Classes." *Exceptional Children* 137, no. 5.

Alvarez, Walter C. 1951. *The Neuroses, Diagnosis and Management of Functional Disorders and Minor Psychoses.* Philadelphia: W. B. Saunders.

Benson, Wilbur, and Schiele, Burtrum. 1962. *Tranquilizing and Antidepressant Drugs.* Springfield, Ill.: Charles C Thomas.

Bower, Eli M. 1969. *Early Identification of Emotionally Handicapped Children in School.* Springfield, Ill.: Charles C Thomas.

Burke, F., and Hornykiewcz, O. 1969. *The Pharmacology of Psychotherapeutic Drugs.* Heidelberg: Springer-Verlag.

Buhler, C.; Smitter, F.; and Richardson, S. 1965. "How Can Disturbed Children Be Identified?" *Conflict in the Classroom,* ed. N. J. Long; W. C. Morse; and R. G. Newman. Belmont, Calif.: Wadsworth Publishing Co.

Bullock, Lyndal M., and Whelan, Richard J. 1971. "Competencies Needed by Teachers of the Emotionally Disturbed and Socially Maladjusted: A Comparison." *Exceptional Children* 37, no. 7 (March).

Campbell, M. Brent. 1974. "Neurological and Psychiatric Aspects of Allergy." *Otology Clinic North America* 7:3.

Caplan, Gerald. 1964. "Patterns of Parental Response to the Crisis of Premature Birth: A Preliminary Approach to Modifying Mental Health Outcome." *Principles of Preventive Psychiatry.* New York: Basic Books.

Chapman, A. H. 1965. *Management of Emotional Problems of Children and Adolescents*. Philadelphia: J. B. Lippincott Co.

Conners, Keith C. 1971. "Recent Drug Studies with Hyperkinetic Children." *Journal of Learning Disability* 4: 471.

Crawford, John E. 1966. *Children with Subtle Perceptual Motor Difficulties*. Pittsburgh, Pa.: Stanwix House.

Cruickshank, William M., ed. 1966. *The Teacher of Brain Injured Children*. Syracuse: Syracuse University Press.

Dunlap, Glen; Koegel, Robert L.; and Egel, Andrew L. 1979. "Autistic Children in School." *Exceptional Children* 45, no. 7.

Dupont, Henry, ed. 1969. *Educating Emotionally Disturbed Children*. New York: Holt, Rinehart & Winston.

Eisenberg, Leon. 1969. *Educating Emotionally Disturbed Children*. New York: Holt, Rinehart & Winston.

Glavin, John P.; Quay, Herbert C.; Annesley, Fredrick R.; and Werry, John S. 1971a. "An Experimental Resource Room for Behavior Problem Children." *Exceptional Children* 38, no. 2.

Glavin, John P.; Quay, Herbert C.; and Werry, John S. 1971b. "Behavioral and Academic Gains of Conduct Problem Children in Different Classroom Settings." *Exceptional Children* 37, no 6.

Haring, Norris G., and Fargo, Geoge A. 1969. "Evaluating Programs for Preparing Teachers of Emotionally Disturbed Children." *Exceptional Children* 36, no. 3.

Haubrich, Paul A., and Shores, Richard. 1976. "Attending Behavior and Academic Performance of Emotionally Disturbed Children." *Exceptional Children* 42, no. 6.

Heiting, Kenneth H. 1971. "Involving Parents in Residential Treatment of Children." *Children* 18, no. 5.

Jones, Edward V. 1969. "A Public Health Approach to Emotional Handicap in the Schools." *The Journal of School Health* 39, no. 9.

Kauffman, James M. 1980. "Where Special Education for Disturbed Children Is Going: A Personal View' *Exceptional Children* 46, no. 7 (April).

Kessler, Jane W. 1966. *Psychopathology of Childhood*. Englewood Cliffs, N.J.: Prentice-Hall.

Lewis, Wilbert W. 1970. "Ecological Planning for Disturbed Children. *Childhood Education* 46, no. 6.

Maes, Wayne. 1966. "The Identification of Emotionally Disturbed Children." *Exceptional Children* 32, no. 9.

McCaffery, Isabel, and Cumming, John. 1969. "Some Dimensions of Emotional Disturbance." *Educating Emotionally Disturbed Children,* ed. Henry Dupont. New York: Holt, Rinehart & Winston.

McKinnon, Archie J. 1970. "Parent and Pupil Perceptions of Special Classes for Emotionally Disturbed Children." *Exceptional Children* 37, no. 4.

Moyer, K. E. 1975. "The Physiology of Violence; Allergy and Aggression." *Psychology Today,* July.

Morse, William C. 1969. "Disturbed Youngsters in the Classroom." *Today's Education* 58, no. 4.

National Institute of Mental Health. 1969–70. *Mental Health Statistics,* series A., no. 6. National Clearing House for Mental Health Information. Residential Treatment Centers for Emotionally Disturbed Children.

Nelson, Michael C. 1971. "Techniques for Screening Conduct Disturbed Children." *Exceptional Children* 37, no. 7.

Philpott, William H. 1974. "Maladaptive Reactions to Frequently Used Foods and Commonly Met Chemicals as Precipitating Factors in Many Chronic Physical and Chronic Emotional Illnesses." *New Dynamics of Preventive Medicine*. New York: Intercontinental.

———. 1976. "Methods of Relief of Acute and Chronic Symptoms of Deficiency-Allergy-Addiction Maladaptive Reactions to Foods and Chemicals." *Clinical Ecology*, ed. Lawrence D. Dickey. Springfield, Ill: Charles C Thomas.

———. 1975. "Organic Continuum Between Children with Hyperkinesis and Learning Disabilities and Adults with Psychosis as Demonstrated by Food and Chemical Symptom Induction Testing." Oklahoma City.

———. 1976. "The Physiology of Violence: The Role of Central Nervous System Maladaptive Responses to Foods and Chemicals in Evoking Antisocial and Violent Behaviors." Bolling Green, Ohio: The Huxley Institute for Biosocial Research of Ohio, Bolling Green State University.

Philpott, William H.; Neilsen, Ruth; and Pearson, Virginia. 1976. "Four-Day Rotation of Foods According to Families." *Clinical Ecology*, ed. Lawrence D. Dickey. Springfield. Ill.: Charles C Thomas.

Quay, Herbert C.; Morse, William C.; and Cutler, Richard L. 1966. "Personality Patterns of Pupils in Special Classes for the Emotionally Disturbed." *Exceptional Children* 32, no. 5.

Randolph, Theron G. 1965. "Descriptive Features of Food Addiction: Addictive Eating and Drinking." *Quarterly Journal Study Alcohol* 17:189.

Rapaport Howard G., and Flint, Shirley H. 1976. "Is There a Relationship Between Allergy and Learning Disabilities?" *Journal School Health* 46, no. 3 (March).

Rapaport, Howard G., and Linde, Shirley Motter. 1970. *The Complete Allergy Guide*. New York: Simon and Schuster.

Remmen, Edmund et al. 1962. *Psychochemotherapy*. Los Angsles: Western Medical Publications.

Rimland, Bernard. 1964. *Infantile Autism*. New York: Appleton-Century-Crofts.

Rimland, Bernard. 1979. *Infantile Autism: The Syndrome and Its Implications for a Neural Theory of Behavior*. Century Psychology Series. New York: Irvington Publishers.

Rubin, Eli Z.; Simson, Clyde B.; and Betwee, Marcus C. 1966. *Emotionally Handicapped Children and the Elementary School*. Detroit: Wayne State University Press.

Schopler, Eric, and Olley, J. Gregory. 1980. "Public School Programming for Autistic Children." *Exceptional Children* 46, no. 6.

Schultz, Edward W.; Hirshoren, Alfred; Manton, Anne B.; and Henderson, Robert A. 1971. "Special Education for the Emotionally Disturbed." *Exceptional Children* 38, no. 4.

Shuster, Charles R. 1968. *Behavioral Pharmacology*. Englewood Cliffs, N.J.: Prentice-Hall.

Solomons, Gerald. 1971. "Guidelines on the Use and Medical Effects of Psychostimulant Drugs in Therapy. *Journal of Learning Disability* 4: 471.

Telford, Charles W. 1977. *The Exceptional Individual*. 3rd ed. Englewood Cliffs, N.J.: Prentice-Hall.

Torrey, E. Fuller; Torrey, Barbara B.; and Burton-Bradley, Burton G. 1974. "The Epidemiology of Schizophrenia in Papua New Guinea." *American Journal Psychiatry,* 131:5.

Uhr, Leonard. 1960. *Drugs and Behavior*. New York: John Wiley & Sons.

Ullman, Leonard P., and Krasner, L. 1969. *A Psychological Approach to Abnormal Behavior*. Englewood Cliffs, N.J.: Prentice-Hall.

"Use of Stimulant Drugs for Behaviorally Disturbed Children: Report of a 1971 Conference." *Education Digest*. February, 1972.

Van Osdol, B.; Van Osdol, William R.; and Shane, Don. 1975. *Learning Disabilities K-12 Manual.* Moscow, Idaho: Idaho University Press.

Washington Post, June 29, 1970.

Wilson, John R. 1964. *The Mind.* New York: Time, Inc.

Wood, Frank H. 1968. "The Educator's Role in Team Planning of Therapeutic Educational Placements for Children with Adjustment and Learning Problems." *Exceptional Children* 34, no. 5.

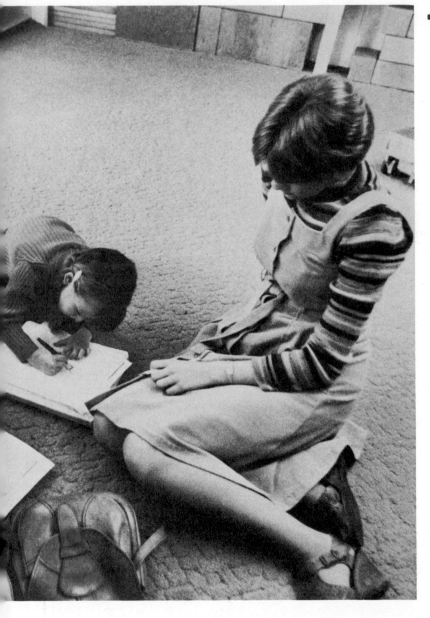

10

practicum—an integral part
of special education

Introduction

College students who are entering the field of special education should have some awareness of the type of training they are about to enter. Although from the college catalog a student can see that practicum experiences are part of a program, specific information related to this particular area is most pertinent.

We have included a chapter on practicum for several reasons. First, this experience is an essential feature of a comprehensive training program in the field of special education. A training program which does not require practicum experiences will not "arm" students with sufficient information to be able to perform adequately on the job.

Secondly, experience of practicum is also important because this is another way in which special services can be provided for exceptional children. Special projects can be prepared by the college student for implementation in a practicum setting. These projects may provide services which would not otherwise be available.

Thirdly, practicum courses for special education teachers indicate the experiential direction of many college training programs. No longer does the college training program provide lecture courses which fail to include any application of the skills which are supposedly learned. Many training programs are establishing procedures to evaluate future teachers through performance in working with exceptional children. The important point is that college students may be able to progress successfully through the training programs as far as theory courses are concerned; however, they may not be able to work effectively with children in a classroom or other settings. By providing many experiences in practicum situations, the staff of the special education training program can observe and evaluate a college student's ability to work with children in a real-life setting. The implementation of practicum experiences is referred to as a performance-based training program.

Most universities and colleges which offer training in the field of special education are now involving students in a variety of practicum settings. The inclusion of practicum in addition to student teaching has become essential in order to prepare well-trained professional personnel. This has been the most practical method universities and colleges have had for bridging the gap from the university classroom to the "real" world. Practicum provides an additional aspect above and beyond the more traditional approach of providing only student teaching experiences.

Although the literature on the subject of practicum for the training of special education personnel is rather limited, several reports regarding these efforts have been published. The primary purpose of this chapter is to synthesize some of these reports and discuss the wide range of purposes and implications regarding meaningful student practicum experiences.

Purposes of Practicum

In several universities and colleges, theory, practicum, and student teaching for the special education major are not easy to establish, nor are colleges able to provide continuous experiences throughout the student's college training program. Detailed descriptions of practicum are discussed by Shane (1970), Anderson and Little (1968), and Shane and Manley (1971). Although programs such as these are essential for the adequate training of special education personnel, a more sequential and comprehensive practicum program is required.

One of the first reasons practicum is essential is to provide a meaningful method of permitting the student to become a part of the selection process. In the past, special education personnel have attempted to recruit students from the high schools into the fields of special education. Once recruited, these students were not seen in the training program until their junior year. Practicum provided as early as the freshman or sophomore year is an absolute necessity if the potential special educator is to have an appropriate information base before declaring a course of study. For example, as a freshman, a student may be assigned a practicum with a type of exceptional children. That experience should enable students to realize if they are interested and comfortable enough in that situation to pursue a major in special education.

In addition to providing an effective means of recruitment, the practicum should and can be offered as an elective to students throughout the campus. By providing actual contact with exceptional children, with special education teachers, with other personnel, and with a seminar for discussions of the practicum, a more appropriate awareness of exceptional children is also given to those who plan to enter other professional fields. They can also become more effective members of the interdisciplinary approach to solving the problems of exceptional children. These students can enhance the total approach to the education and training of the exceptional child by contributing knowledge from their own fields. This can help to make future special education professionals more aware of potential contributions from other professional personnel.

The purposes described above are certainly sufficient if one is attempting to justify the reasons why practicum should be offered. However, just as important also, is the way in which the university practicum experience in special education can implement more of a noncategorical approach to the training of future teachers, counselors, supervisors, administrators, diagnosticians, and other supportive personnel.

When teachers enter the field of special education, they seldom have a "neat" categorical group of children. Teachers who have taught exceptional children or worked with them in capacities other than teaching, know that many exceptional children have more problems than just the primary problem for which they were placed in the special education setting. Many graduates are employed in positions other than that for which they were specifically prepared on the college level. A variety of practicum experiences, individual studies, and student teaching can provide some introductory experiences with a cross-section of exceptional children. This variety can be further enhanced by requiring a seminar once a week in order to give students the opportunity to discuss their experiences with their college supervisors.

Another purpose of practicum throughout the college students' careers is to provide experiences which call for actual involvement with children. Becoming involved with exceptional children through tutoring, counseling, or just individual contact will better prepare the college student for student teaching as well as a professional career. If students in special education enter student teaching with a background of three or four practicum experiences, they are more familiar with materials and methods which have been effective with different children, and have an increased knowledge of skills that can be applied more easily and more confidently.

A minimum of four hours' credit in practicum for undergraduate and graduate students should be required. This requirement definitely helps to join theory and practice and provides a more practical approach in the total training program. For example, a freshman student who declares special education as a major, should be encouraged to enroll in a practicum at least by the third or fourth semester. As students progress through course work in special education, they should take practicums that are directly related to a special education course in which they are currently enrolled. If students are taking the introductory course in mental retardation, a practicum with mentally retarded children is appropriate. Then, if they later take a course in the area of learning disabilities, that practicum should be with children who have learning disabilities. Therefore, they have the opportunity to see the children who are being discussed in the course, the special education teachers in operation, and the instructional materials that are being used. This approach adds to the noncategorical emphasis described earlier and also offers a compatible integration of theory and practice.

Graduate students should have a wide variety of practicum throughout their programs. They should be required to complete four credit hours of practicum—one credit hour of practicum should require three hours per week or sixty-four hours per semester of field work—and may receive additional experiences by requesting a practicum assignment through an individual study. As programs in special education progress, graduate students should have greater flexibility in choosing a practicum assignment. Plans should be developed to assign graduate students to rural school systems in nearby areas to provide a program that exposes them to children from rural areas in addition to the metropolitan area.

Services Provided Through Practicum

It is well known that there continues to be a shortage of qualified personnel in special education. Part of the emphasis in practicum is, therefore, to provide the potential manpower among student groups to the population of exceptional children. Although not completely trained, or certified, the undergraduate students in any program are certainly capable of providing services on an equal basis with voluntary aides who are used widely in some areas. Many graduate students have had teaching experience prior to entering a training program and are well qualified to provide services to exceptional children.

A training program in special education at the university level should tend to help the university become more service-oriented to the local communities by providing services to public schools, private clinics, psychiatric wards, guidance clinics, and other special programs. Recognizing that they must have a period of observation prior to working with an individual or a small group of children in a special setting, the majority of students do become "involved" in providing services during their assignments. This aspect of the program should tend to provide many services of supplementary nature to exceptional children.

Graduate students in rural school systems could help to provide screening services for students who are having learning or adjustment difficulties. Also, these students can help personnel of the rural school systems discuss, consider, and plan cooperative agreements that will provide better programs for exceptional children.

Upon completion of their theory, practicum, and student teaching programs, students should be well trained. They will have had ample time to apply their skills, and receive supervision from a university staff during their assignments.

Implications of Practicum

In modern teacher training, students also have a very strong desire to become involved—not only in working with children, but also in the program of training. The type of practicum offered, plus the continuity of the practicum experiences, should certainly keep students involved with staff members in small group discussions about a wide variety of programs in order for the program to move one step closer to meeting the needs of college students.

Through practicum, students have opportunities to apply the skills they have learned and to "test" a variety of approaches they have studied. Therefore, a training program becomes more of a "testing" experience for the student in self-evaluation.

Implementation of Practicum

Practicum may be implemented in a variety of ways. Several university training programs have courses which are titled "Practicum." In other situations one may have to be more specific in a course title such as "Introductory Experiences in Special Education." One may also use practicum as individual study or as an internship. In a few cases, one hour of a three-hour required course could be used as an assignment in practicum. The main point is that practicum can, through some existing means, be implemented as an integral part of the total training program.

The inclusion of practicum as an integral part of special education training programs is essential in the training of future teachers and other professional personnel. It is, in all probability, the most effective means available to provide a practical orientation in teacher training.

An advantage in practicum is the flexibility which it offers by assigning students to settings which provide services to different types of exceptional children. Students, therefore, can have meaningful experiences in gaining first-hand knowledge regarding the wide variances in personality and learning characteristics of exceptional children. As knowledge of practicum increases, and as more community services are initiated, training programs will continue to improve.

Bibliography

Anderson, R. M., and Little, H. A. 1968. "A Practicum Oriented Teacher Education Program." *Education and Training of the Mentally Retarded* 3, no. 2.

Shane, Don G. 1970. "Introductory Experiences With Handicapped Children." *Education and Training of the Mentally Retarded* 5, no. 2.

Shane, Don G., and Manley, Max W. 1971. "Undergraduate Practicum Experiences in Special Education." *The Teacher Education Division Newsletter* 8, no. 1 (Fall). The Council for Exceptional Children.

11

teachers, administrators, and parents

Accountability

A discussion of the varied school personnel essential to providing educational services for exceptional children should include emphasis on accountability. Accountability certainly applies to the special education teacher and the teacher education program. Although accountability is still an evolving concept, and probably should remain so, the emphasis seems to be increasing and the abilities and characteristics of special education teachers seem to be related directly to this concept. For study and comparative purposes, the new teacher may also benefit from a discussion of the abilities and characteristics of practicing teachers. A few suggestions regarding accountability of special education programs may serve as guidelines for the teacher's efforts to develop effective instructional programs for exceptional children.

The role and responsibilities of the special education teacher are changing. Special education teachers may be the primary people in the school who influence the personal, social, and vocational development of exceptional children, but they certainly cannot provide the required services in isolation. They are no longer viewed as self-contained classroom teachers. They must be prepared to assume responsibilities of diagnostic teachers, resource teachers, crisis teachers, or other related capacities. In addition to the various roles to which a special education teacher may be assigned, the comprehensive planning and programming necessary for exceptional children require the services of other school personnel and the support of the children's parents.

The term *accountability* is not new to people in education. Administrators, school boards, and the entire educational community have not been able to escape the concept of accountability. Accountability is a management concept. It involves agreeing upon objectives, deciding upon the input to achieve the objectives, and measuring the output to determine the degree to which the objectives have been met. The application of accountability to all aspects of the educational system is increasing. This will certainly require thorough study if the concept of accountability is to be meaningful, not only to educators, but also to the children who are directly involved.

Accountability can be viewed as an administrative concept, or a branch of technology through which one can make education more effective. Education can use this technique constructively with careful planning; however, a haphazard approach could apply too much pressure on everyone concerned. Accountability may be viewed as a process which can provide feedback regarding the extent to which a particular procedure or program has been effective.

Other ideas have arisen from the concept of accountability. Merit pay, performance contract, turnkey approach (a type of performance contract), educational auditors, voucher systems, and Project Yardstick emerged for the purpose of increasing accountability (Hyer 1971).

The call for accountability came from the President of the United States, Congress, agencies of the federal government, school boards, teacher training institutions, the taxpayers, and the classroom. Theodore A. Dolmatch, president of the Pitman Publishing Corporation said, "Asking for accountability is a legitimate response of government, which wants to know how efficiently its money is being spent" (Stocker and Wilson 1971).

The emphasis on accountability has implications for teacher training institutions with special education programs and also for the teacher of exceptional children. The purpose of this chapter is to concentrate on the implications of accountability for colleges and universities and special education teachers in the public schools.

Implications for the Teacher of Exceptional Children

The special education teacher is accountable for specific areas of education. The following are included: academic preparation and continuing professional growth, concern and knowledge about exceptional children, effective communication with other school personnel and parents, involvement in community activities, and provision of an environment which maximizes opportunities for each individual to learn. Special education teachers are accountable to themselves, their students, the teaching profession, and the public (Stocker and Wilson 1971).

In order to accomplish a desired level of accountability, a special education teacher should have certain characteristics. The ability to mobilize and sustain a high level of energy is one specific characteristic. A high energy level is considered important because to provide an individualized program for six to ten children is a difficult task. When these children are exhibiting a variety of learning and behavioral problems, the assigned task is even more difficult. The management of a classroom can be extremely exhausting to any teacher, but even more so to a teacher with little energy (Reger, Schroeder, and Uschold 1968).

A special education teacher must be alert and responsive. These characteristics are important because teachers must continuously be aware of each event in the classroom and be able to respond quickly and appropriately. A teacher who does not attend to disruptive behavior in the initial stage will expend more effort to correct the behavior as it increases. It is more economical for everyone concerned to stop disturbances as soon as possible. The ability to observe systematically the children in the classroom is essential in controlling discipline as well as instructional planning. Without skilled observation, the teacher will have serious difficulties in planning the environment needed by the majority of exceptional children.

Personal stability and self-control are also essential. These characteristics are mentioned because of the naive misconception that a teacher of exceptional children appears to enjoy wallowing in problems of emotion, brain damage, or physical defects.

Special education teachers should develop an orientation toward being a teacher that emphasizes such concepts as educational therapy. They should develop a sound educational philosophy and be interested in individualized instruction. Behavioral change is the main concern of a special education teacher and this factor can be a teacher's answer to accountability. Teachers are agents who assist in behavioral change—and behavioral change results in learning (Reger, Schroeder, and Uschold).

A teacher of exceptional children should be aware of negative traits. The following characteristics are considered to be unfavorable: being sentimental toward the exceptional child; believing in permissiveness in that exceptional children are allowed complete freedom in self-expression; seeking frequent counsel of other professionals for help in planning the daily instructional program; becoming easily upset over insignificant events, and having little understanding of the relationship which should exist between children and the curriculum. Less accountable teachers think of working with exceptional children as a glamorous opportunity to sacrifice themselves to society.

Besides having positive general characteristics and being aware of negative traits, a teacher should demonstrate the following positive characteristics on the job. A teacher must develop a meaningful understanding of children. Learning to form a working relationship with children, and describing them verbally is essential for the purpose of providing an appropriate instructional program. A demonstration of a grasp of the relationship between children's needs and the curriculum is an important ability of an accountable teacher of exceptional children. An inexperienced teacher may choose one reading series or method, but the experienced teacher has a grasp of individualized instruction and chooses many materials and approaches. The teacher will observe each student's needs and search for materials or techniques to meet these needs. The accountable teacher is knowledgeable of materials such as those described in *Instructional Materials and Resource Materials Available to Teachers of Exceptional Children and Youth* (1969), which has over 460 pages of resource materials.

Also, a special education teacher should have the ability to communicate with parents about their children in descriptive, informative language. Discussions should be in a language which parents can understand. For example, if a child is having a reading problem, a teacher should not tell the parents why the child cannot read, but rather what is being done to help the child's reading. The ability to communicate in direct understandable language with parents and meaningfully discuss children is a complicated but necessary asset for accountability (Reger, Schroeder, and Uschold 1968).

A teacher who is not accountable will not effectively manage children and will often resort to the use of labels or technical terms in an effort to explain their behavior. Too much emphasis will be placed on the use of hardware or other novel devices with no understanding about their pertinence to the needs of children. The teacher who has not become accountable will, in addition, hesitate to upgrade teaching skills through in-service training or supervisory activities (Reger, Schroeder, and Uschold 1968).

If a special education teacher does not have these positive characteristics, acquiring them should be a goal. Teachers have usually acquired these positive characteristics and there are seldom any major problems. Where training institutions have not prepared teachers by developing these positive characteristics, there is a problem, especially in the area of accountability (Reger, Schroeder, and Uschold).

Behavioral Objectives

A special education teacher, like a regular classroom teacher, is searching for means of becoming adequately accountable to peers, the public, the students, and to self. The public is requesting more concrete evidence of the teaching-learning process (*Scholarship Program* 1971). In order to meet the challenge, teachers, as well as administrators, curriculum planners, members of boards of education, and researchers are beginning to use behavioral objectives.

"Behavioral objectives are statements which describe what students will be able to do after completing a prescribed unit of instruction" (Kibler, Barker, and Miles 1970). For example, a behavioral objective for an exceptional child for a unit in arithmetic might be as follows: The emotionally disturbed child will be able to work correctly at least five out of eight long division problems with four digits in five minutes. Behavioral objectives serve two functions. They allow teachers to design and evaluate their instruction, and they communicate the goals of the instruction to students and to those who are responsible for evaluating their teaching.

In the preparation of behavioral objectives, a special education teacher needs to consider four factors: (a) selection, (b) classification, (c) analysis, and (d) specification (Kibler, Barker, and Miles). A teacher determines what a student is able to do before selecting objectives, which are based upon what the student should be able to do after accomplishing the assigned unit and completing educational requirements.

After the objectives are selected, a teacher must classify them. The classification may focus on a desired behavior such as the acquisition of knowledge, comprehension of knowledge, or analyzing and evaluating information (Kibler, Barker, and Miles).

After objectives have been selected and classified, the teacher must determine what each student will be expected to do. This step needs to be accomplished in order to match objectives to individual students and to demonstrate the achievement of objectives. In an analysis of selected objectives, a teacher chooses important stimuli to which a student responds positively, notes the responses made, and measures them to determine how well the objectives have been met. (Kibler, Barker, and Miles).

The type, the conditions, and the criterion of behavioral objectives will be specified by a teacher and a description of observable behavior must be stated. For instance, a teacher will decide if a student is to demonstrate a mastery of writing, solving, identifying, or describing. One must specify under what conditions a student will demonstrate the objectives and what criteria will be implemented. This will involve questions such as: How many problems must be correctly solved? How many principles will be applied? In what length of time will a task be correctly completed? (Kibler, Barker, and Miles).

A special education teacher can discover individual needs through behavioral objectives. Such objectives encourage a well-structured class, not a program which is rigid and stale. Also of value, a pretest and posttest can be compared to illustrate to what extent learning has taken place. The greatest value in using behavioral objectives is that teachers can evaluate each student individually in comparison to their own objectives. This eliminates evaluating each student on the basis of competitive student performances or subjective information.

There are several controversial issues regarding behavioral objectives with which teachers should be acquainted. In using objectives, it is difficult to specify objectives for a unit which the teacher has not previously taught or for a group of children who have never been seen. Even though difficult to plan and implement, behavioral objectives can still serve as a means for developing appropriate instructional programs. A special education teacher plans the objectives to meet individual needs, rather than attempting to limit teaching to specific academic course content. If one finds that the objectives are inappropriate, one must evaluate the entire plan and make decisions which will enhance the child's progress. This entails a study of the behavioral objectives to determine if the steps for a student's learning are improperly sequenced, too advanced, or too easy. Continuous evaluation is essential if behavioral objectives are to be helpful in establishing a system of appropriate accountability.

Critics of behavioral objectives say that a teacher may decide that all students should be required to achieve the same objectives. Special education programs should orient their students toward individuality and thus avoid requiring the same achievement of all students.

Critics also hesitate to implement behavioral objectives because a teacher has a choice of deciding whether all students should be required to achieve the same level of mastery for each objective. The well-trained special education teacher is aware of Frank Hewett's developmental sequence of goals including attention, response, order, exploratory, social, mastery, and achievement levels. Teachers of emotionally disturbed children, as well as teachers of mentally retarded, and learning-disabled children, should incorporate this methodology into their educational program. Through this approach, a teacher should be aware of the individualized performances of each student (Hewett and Taylor 1980). If teachers of exceptional children are accountable, they will implement and rely on behavioral objectives.

The incorporation of accountability in all phases of educational programs should result in improved instruction and services for exceptional children. As suggested by Vergason (1973), accountability would not only improve education but would provide a means whereby parents could legally demand appropriate educational services for their child. Parents could also be required to accept adequate educational services for their child.

If accountability requires improved planning and data to support pupil progress, then school administrators will be required to provide appropriate means for the teacher to accomplish the specified objectives. In short, Vergason's discussion has many implications for teacher training institutions, administrators, practicing teachers, parents, and publishing companies with respect to the increasing development and application of accountability.

Guidelines in the Evaluation of Teacher Training Programs and Instructional Programs for Special Education Teachers

Evaluation is an involved, complex, and ongoing process. Various facts about a system or program are accumulated which must be integrated and interpreted. Evaluation, as used in this chapter, is a procedure used in determining the effectiveness of teacher training programs and the instructional programs for special education teachers. It is a system or a process of examining information relevant to a particular program for the purpose of making meaningful decisions about that program. If used appropriately, evaluation should be a major factor in the achievement of planned changes rather than change based solely upon opinion (Guba 1968).

An evaluation team must focus on several aspects of a training or instructional program. The team will have to examine factors which may be described as the context of the program, factors which may be considered as input, processes used in the operation of the program, and the product or output of the program (Guba). Each of these factors is related to all the others. The evaluation of one factor must lead to the evaluation of all factors if recommendations for changes are to be meaningful.

Planned changes in training or instructional programs, which exist to benefit exceptional children, must be based upon such a comprehensive approach. Obviously, an evaluation of only the input into a program would be insufficient. The results of input must be measured by the extent to which a program meets its objectives. In essence, evaluation should attempt to ascertain the importance of factors such as the staff, the training of the staff, costs, the scope and depth of the curriculum, supportive systems through supervisory or consultant personnel, practical activities, such as field trips or practicum experiences, and the degree to which program objectives (output) are met. A partial evaluation may result in premature and unwarranted changes.

Implementing an evaluation system for teacher training programs and the instructional program of special education teachers implies that changes are needed. With change in mind, the evaluation team must first identify areas where change is needed and focus attention on them. Once a need or problem has been identified, a response is called for. For instance, what can be done about a curriculum program? Has anyone else done anything about effective curriculum programming? Does anyone have any ideas? Is there any research on curriculum programs? After it is determined that a change is needed, one needs to decide what change should be attempted (Guba 1968). This is the first step the evaluation team must take, but the team must also continuously use self-evaluation. For example, the team must be careful to avoid change for its own sake. To what extent is a change *warranted* at this time? That is the primary question the team must ask itself. Abraham Kaplan (1964) once said, "Give a small boy a hammer and he will find that everything he encounters needs pounding."

The administrative team must also study all aspects of its recommendations before submitting them to a board or group for implementation. For example, if a certain change is recommended, are the monies required for it currently available? Are the necessary professional persons who may be recommended for employment available? The final analysis of any recommendations for change must be evaluated to determine if the program personnel being evaluated can implement the recommendations. Recommending changes that are currently beyond the ability of the personnel involved will accomplish nothing other than frustration and discouragement. Gradual improvements which are presently feasible are much better approaches than demands for sweeping changes which, for the most part, would be impossible to incorporate.

Evaluation ultimately brings the subject of behavioral objectives into focus. Only worthy evaluation will trace everything back to improved student performances. The proper methodology of evaluation is the methodology of research. Evaluations should be designed as experiments are designed, in that data is collected and interpreted as for research. However, research and evaluation differ in their objectives. For instance, research is concerned with universal true knowledge, and controls must be carefully observed. Evaluation will do none of this (Guba).

A few evaluation methods have already been mentioned. A closer examination of these methods is needed for a more thorough understanding. "Context evaluation is concerned with providing information about the context or setting within which the educational activity is taking place" (Guba). In this case, the context of the special education department and the classroom for exceptional children is the context. The evaluation team, obviously, must have a starting point. To illustrate: At what level of achievement is Jimmy presently functioning? After determining this factor, the evaluation team should establish limits, choose subareas or topics to explore, and gather the desired information.

Secondly, "Input evaluation has to do with decision alternatives, their delineation, and their relative worth" (Guba). Input evaluation is making a decision about the problem. In doing this, the administrative team will have developed certain specifications based on context evaluation. The team is to assess each specification and decide which one will have the highest payoff potential. There will be several specifications which the evaluation team must explore if the evaluation is to be comprehensive.

Process evaluation is a type of guidance system in that it signals whenever the program is off course and provides a mechanism of protection. It is also the stage where further refinement and extension of the problem is handled.

"Product evaluation is concerned with final outcomes. The decision here is whether or not the item being evaluated should be retained, eliminated, or altered in some way" (Guba). In the final analysis, an evaluation should be made for the purposes described above. The general criteria are as follows:

1. Internal validity
2. External validity
3. Reliability
4. Objectivity
5. Relevance
6. Significance
7. Scope
8. Credibility
9. Timeliness
10. Pervasiveness (Guba)

In the near future, administrative evaluation will be part of every ongoing program in the field of special education. If professional educators approach this area with specific concerns regarding the learning and adjustment of handicapped children, then perhaps the evaluation systems will be effective. If there is anxiety regarding teaching positions or other professional positions, then the product of the ongoing evaluation will not bring about the chanqes required for the development of appropriate instructional programs for exceptional children.

Personnel in Programs for Exceptional Children

Educators in the field of special education have advocated that many persons are needed in order to deliver appropriate and comprehensive services to exceptional or handicapped children. The special education teacher cannot continue to function in isolation and accomplish all the tasks required to habilitate or rehabilitate handicapped children. In recent years there has been a trend to recognize that professional personnel must be trained to work with handicapped children in settings other than the classroom. This has come about because the needs of handicapped children have been identified through research and practical experiences. More handicapped children have also been identified. Where children are recognized as having learning or adjustment problems, additional supplementary services are indicated.

Regular Class Teachers and Exceptional Children

Many exceptional children are in the regular classroom. These children are often unrecognized by the regular class teacher, administrators, and counselors. Teachers may teach information the "normal" students already know. Consequently, the exceptional child, whatever the exception may be, falls below the mean to the lower end of the normal curve, and fills a statistical quota for the teacher's "F" grades. The exceptional child's academic or social failures enable the teacher to place a sampling of grades from "A" to "F." They also justify the teacher's concept that some students are aware socially and some students are "misfits." Therefore, the exceptional child balances the normal curve, and the teacher has a proper class distribution of academic and social skills. The grade distribution may indicate deceptively that the teacher and the methods of teaching are compatible with the general school population. Obviously, that observation is only justified at the exceptional child's expense. The child is recognized not as one who has problems, but one who is unwilling to learn and participate.

The first avenue which will offer the exceptional child mobility has to come through a teacher's awareness of the child's ability levels. Ability, not disability, must be stressed. Awareness by the teacher of the "real" child, not the expected child, must be emphasized. The child's problem *is* the teacher's problem. Excuses for the child's or teacher's inabilities will only

Regular classes may help integrate exceptional students into least restrictive environments.

prolong the problems. Therefore, regular class teachers should be knowledgeable of the many different kinds of exceptional children and the specific academic and social ramifications of these exceptionalities. No panacea exists, but the teacher who approaches exceptional children in the regular classroom with intense empathy, resourcefulness, and problem orientation will proceed toward a constructive outlet of reasonable expectations.

Many states require that all school personnel complete a college credited introductory course on exceptional children. This course will not serve as closure for a long existing problem, but the course will enable school professionals to open doors which have been closed to exceptional children. The parents who have expressed their legislative and certification demands for the introductory course obviously are aware that *all* teachers, at least, should be intellectually aware of the different exceptionalities.

Regular class teachers and other school personnel are not expected to become proficient in methods and techniques, but they should be able to realize aspirations and expectations that are compatible with the levels of growth of the exceptional children. The simple realization that the exceptional child can grow and develop can bring about the application of realistic objectives and personal consideration of a child's abilities. One note of caution. Don't confuse empathy with sympathy. Exceptional children do not wish for sorrow to be expressed to them. These children are aware of their exceptionalities and ask only that the teacher bestow upon them the same limits and structures that are reasonable for them relative to their peer relationships. The regular class teacher will discover that exceptional children ask for no favors. They want to be as similar to the other children as possible.

Sometimes the regular class teacher who has not had contact and training with exceptional children will mistakenly offer assistance when the child needed firm structure. Exceptional children need assistance; but there are times when they should have the opportunity to discover their own abilities. There is no possible reason for humiliation or subserviency by the teacher and other children. We realize that teachers generally do not acknowledge pity toward an exceptional child, but the teacher may feed back unintentionally a subjective message of discomfort to which the child responds defensively. This response may express anger, self-pity, hate, or aggression. Simply, the child will maintain an equilibrium which affords a resemblance of comfort. If someone depreciates the exceptional child socially or intellectually, a natural response will be to "get even." Therefore, regular class teachers need to be aware of each child's manifested problems, real or imaginary.

As Public Law 94–142 is fully implemented during the 1980s, regular teachers will be responsible for a part of the educational program for many different exceptional children. Special educators will be complementary to their programs, and cooperative efforts should restore respectability to the lives of exceptional children. If all educators aid each other, rather than strive for isolated teaching autonomy; the total school program will profit. However, if teachers maintain a selfish certificate independence, the entire school system will suffer. Surely, educators, psychologists, counselors, and administrators are not so naive that we should expect each regular class teacher to have the necessary skills to be a certified special class teacher. We do expect, though, that each regular teacher will assume those parts of an exceptional child's education that are compatible with the traditional aspects of the regular classroom setting.

The regular teacher will not have extended preservice training in special education, but the present emphasis upon in-service training should enable teachers to become acquainted with various procedural and technical methods, which will supplement their teaching skills for and services to exceptional children. Teachers should have professional interests which create an intense need to learn more ways to help their children. We are teachers; consequently, we should have some innate motivation that is not preceded by administrative demands. Administrators don't motivate teachers or students; motivation comes from within oneself, not from someone else.

Therefore, teachers, you have no cop-out. If you are a teacher, regular class or special class, then your label as a teacher and the fact that you successfully completed a teacher training program demand that you strive for proficient teaching of *all* children. The job demands long hours and resourceful, creative alertness. You constantly must be aware of the realistic and pseudo concepts of school programs. You must be able to separate your personal self from the intense school demands placed upon you, and refrain from defensive tactics that will only aggravate fellow teachers, administrators, and parents.

Resources are plentiful for the regular teacher who is serving exceptional children. Most of the special education personnel we have mentioned are available to assist regular teachers. These persons can provide assistance for instructional planning, for parental counseling, and for discipline matters. For the teacher in a rural area, the primary resources are the principal, the special education teacher(s) in the school system, the remedial reading teacher, and the persons from the regional education resource centers.

It is not feasible to suggest the precise supportive services a regular teacher may need. Supportive services depend upon the learning characteristics of the individual and the specific learning objectives of the teacher.

Most regular teachers will need assistance in learning how to modify their instructional programs. This modification includes formulating appropriate instructional objectives for the exceptional child, and learning how to select or to construct educational materials that support the instructional objectives. The accommodation of the exceptional child in a regular class will take time, energy, and the support of knowledgeable professionals.

In addition to modifying the instructional program, regular class teachers may need assistance in changing their attitudes toward exceptional children. Changing attitudes about the learning characteristics of an exceptional child may be the most important task for the regular teacher. To make these changes, the teacher needs the services of professional supportive persons.

The objectives of this book are reflected in the title. Whatever your chosen area of teaching, you should be introduced to exceptional children. We cannot offer information which will enable you to be a proficient special educator, but you have been exposed to many different aspects of exceptional children. Your awareness of and introduction to these children should give you the opportunity to be a better teacher, because you now recognize symptoms, characteristics, strengths, and limitations manifested by exceptional children. Awareness of these children should ease your anxieties and instill the need to go to the library and regional centers to gather resources which offer the information necessary to assess your past or present theories, practices, and concepts of education. Then, as a regular teacher, adopt a cooperative perspective of education for *all* children; because you are a teacher of *all* children.

Special Education Counselor

The position of special education counselor in the public schools is a recent concept. This additional position will greatly enhance services for handicapped children since the increase in counselors in public schools has failed to keep pace with the demand for counseling services. Most counseling training programs have not emphasized the inclusion of pertinent information in working with disabled students. Counseling of exceptional children has usually been provided by the special education class teacher (Fine 1969), and that is still true into the 1980s.

The training of regular school counselors seldom prepares them to provide services for exceptional children. With a lack of information and training, such as a practicum experience with exceptional children, the school counselor hesitates to work with this group of the school population (Patterson 1969). A review of the professional literature indicated that there were only sixteen instances of school counselors providing some type of counseling for exceptional children (Cormany 1970).

Students who are placed in a special education class need professional counseling services for a variety of reasons. They have experienced frustration and failure prior to placement in special education to the extent that their self-concepts are seriously damaged. Parents may have feelings of guilt or place too much or too little emphasis on the child's problems and, therefore, inadvertently create more frustration for the child (Fine). These problems may have existed for one or more years and the child will need long-term counseling services to help adjust and improve functioning. As exceptional children grow older they may be confronted with experiences which add to their frustrations and their adjustments. As a result, they need counseling services to help them confront "new" situations.

A recognition of the counseling needs of exceptional children may place regular school counselors in a difficult position. They may agree that children who have learning, adjustment, or physical problems are in need of continuous counseling services, but typically this group of children constitutes approximately 5 to 10 percent of the total student population. Therefore, counselors are faced with the problem of deciding whether to expend most of their time and energies with a small group for whom they have usually been inadequately trained to provide service, or whether they should attempt to serve all of the school population. For these and other reasons, the need for a special education counselor is slowly being recognized.

The state of Texas created a position of special education counselor. This position is described as follows: "To provide educational and vocational guidance to students with limited personal guidance. Philosophically the intent of this position is described as liaison between pupil, parent, and teacher and between home, school and community" (Hansen 1971). In addition, the person who becomes a special education counselor is trained to provide counseling services for parents in order to help them make an adjustment in their feelings and their treatment of their disabled child. Training develops counseling techniques which help exceptional children in their personal and vocational adjustment (Hansen).

Special education counselors should also be trained in the area of group counseling. Group counseling of exceptional youngsters has been an effective procedure and saves time. Group counseling can also bring to the fore indications of children who may need more intensive individual counseling.

To effect changes in a child's adjustment to the environment and the classroom, peer groups may be used to supplement the services of the counselor. Children may react more positively to counseling services if supplemented by peer interaction. The use of peers as helpers in group counseling sessions was successful for a group of children who had adjustment problems. The initial training of the peer helpers took only three hours. The investigation was conducted over a period of nine weeks, during which the peer helpers received additional training once a week. The findings indicated that the peer helpers were successful in supplementing the services of the counselor (Kern and Kirby 1971). Additional research should provide more insight regarding the effectiveness of group counseling and the use of peer groups in counseling.

If the training of peer groups is not feasible within a school program, consider the training of volunteer groups to assist in the provision of counseling services. A program was initiated in Auburn, Maine, to incorporate community volunteers into a school guidance program to assist exceptional children. This program was developed because many children needed services which the school system could not provide through existing professional staff. Pamphlets describing the program and emphasizing the need for volunteers were distributed throughout the community. During the first year of the program, thirty-two adults, of whom twenty-nine remained for a second year, provided additional services for children. The program emphasized the development of a relationship between an adult and a child and did not merely attempt to train the volunteers as tutors or teacher aids. From this program came a description of general characteristics which adults should possess to be most effective in counseling sessions: (1) a sincere desire to be a part of the program and to be of service to a child, (2) a sense of humor, (3) understanding and acceptance of children, (4) enthusiasm, (5) flexibility, and (6) a well-balanced personality (Muro 1970).

Recognition of the need of special education counselors continues. The factors mentioned above should become a part of the training program for those pursuing this position. School systems will have to make decisions regarding the number of exceptional students who can be effectively served by a special education counselor. This may entail considering a special education counselor as an itinerant resource person serving more than one school building. A special education counselor should also be trained to assist the special education and regular classroom teacher in classroom counseling services.

Diagnostic Teachers

Diagnostic teachers are essential if resource centers, learning laboratories, and precision teaching are to be effective with exceptional children. A person trained as a diagnostic teacher must be able to integrate diagnostic information to the extent that an appropriate instructional program may be developed for a particular child. A diagnostic teacher must be able to systematically evaluate the effects of an instructional program and be willing to change the program to accommodate the learning characteristics of the child. Training must also include the careful planning, sequencing, and development of teacher-made materials. In addition, a diagnostic teacher will serve as a liaison person to the classroom teacher and must be able to communicate with others in the school program regarding effective procedures and materials. Because of the short time a diagnostic teacher may spend with children, a person in this position should also be afforded the time and opportunity to conduct follow-up services with former students. Follow-up services are essential for the reevaluation of progress and effective implementation of the prescribed instructional program which the diagnostic teacher has prepared.

The lack of trained special education teachers is a primary reason for developing the position of a diagnostic teacher. If children with learning and adjustment problems are to be served adequately, it will require more than one model, such as the self-contained classroom with a qualified special educator. The growing demand for classroom space is, of course, another reason why the services of a diagnostic teacher may be an effective procedure. To provide effective and economical services, two or more school systems may want to explore the possibility of a cooperative school agreement similar to that developed by three communities in Virginia. These communities wanted to improve and extend existing services for exceptional children. After studying their problem, feasible plans, financing, and available professional staff, these communities applied for and were awarded a grant to implement the models of the diagnostic-prescriptive teacher and the crisis-resource teacher (Tenorio amd Raimist 1971).

Diagnostic-Prescriptive Teacher

A diagnostic-prescriptive teacher must be a trained observer of behavior. When a classroom teacher requests the services of a diagnostic-prescriptive teacher, the first phase of the referral process involves observation of a child's behavior in the classroom setting. This provides a realistic basis for initially collecting data regarding the child. A diagnostic-prescriptive teacher will also obtain personal information about the child during initial observation. This may include factors such as age, sex, grade, recent achievement test scores, and primary learning difficulties.

A diagnostic-prescriptive teacher first decides on assisting the classroom teacher to modify approaches or materials. If this is not feasible or does not help, then the child is temporarily assigned to the diagnostic classroom.

In the diagnostic classroom, the diagnostic-prescriptive teacher will, through experimentation, decide what approaches and materials are appropriate for a child, formulate a prescription, and confer with the classroom teacher about the implementation of the prescription. Periodic follow-up contacts are made with the classroom teacher to effect any changes needed to meet the child's needs (Tenorio and Raimist).

Crisis-Resource Teacher

A crisis-resource teacher provides services similar to those provided by a diagnostic-prescriptive teacher. A primary difference is that the crisis-resource teacher must be immediately available. The needs of a teacher or a child would be of a critical nature and the crisis-resource teacher would have to be constantly "on call." Given the immediacy of the situation, a crisis-resource teacher needs to be a very skilled person in order to make appropriate decisions. The decision may involve counseling, changing environmental consequences of the classroom, or helping the teacher to select and use an appropriate technique (Tenorio and Raimist 1971).

It seems, from the description of the crisis-resource teacher given by Tenorio and Raimist, that every elementary and secondary school should be assigned a person who would fulfill this function. Otherwise, situations which require immediate action could not be appropriately met. A school system could establish target schools to which the assignment of a crisis-resource teacher would seem most feasible. This could be accomplished by surveying all schools within the district to obtain pertinent and current information about the problems of teachers and children. A crisis-resource teacher could also be assigned full-time to one school building for a specified period of time, (i.e., nine weeks) and serve approximately four schools during the school year. Granted, this would not be as effective as having one crisis-resource teacher for every school building. Flexibility would be absolutely necessary for any school system planning the effective use of a crisis-resource teacher.

Consulting Teachers

The use of a consulting teacher is not as recent as other trends in special education. A consulting teacher is also referred to as a helping teacher or supervising teacher. This position often requires additional certification requirements beyond those of a classroom teacher. However, some states have no criteria established for the qualifications of a consulting teacher. In states without certification requirements, a local school system generally promotes a classroom teacher based upon performance and years of experience.

Efforts to determine the number of teachers with whom a consulting teacher can work effectively have not been too successful. One would not usually find specific information relative to this situation in the job description of a consulting teacher. Questions proposed in attempts to solve this problem involve such factors as follow: How often should a consulting teacher visit a classroom teacher? How many schools should a consulting teacher serve? Is a consulting teacher a resource person to whom children can be referred for evaluation or reevaluation? Should consulting teachers expend the majority of their time visiting classroom teachers, or in developing in-service training programs? To what extent should a consulting teacher be assigned administrative duties? Answers to these questions may determine how effective consulting teachers can be in helping to improve the instructional program, which is the primary task they must confront.

A program organized in Vermont is an example of one in which consulting teachers served as resource persons for classroom teachers. The University of Vermont, the Vermont State Department of Education, and five school districts near the university trained a number of elementary teachers as specialists in behavior modification and its application to exceptional children. They were trained over a two-year period in the many facets of behavior modification, including training to help classroom teachers apply principles of behavior modification in the classroom. The program also included the assignment of the consulting teachers to the university for the purpose of training future and present teachers in behavior modification (McKenzie et al. 1970). Specific training of consulting teachers is a different approach in an attempt to aid the classroom teacher in implementing appropriate techniques.

Paraprofessionals

Since the need for qualified staff in special education has not kept pace with the identification of children who need special services, school systems have begun to train and use paraprofessionals to help classroom teachers deliver services to handicapped children. Paraprofessionals may be parents, volunteer adults, high school youths, or college students. A school system may provide long-term training for paraprofessionals or on-the-job training, depending upon the extent to which these persons are to become involved with exceptional children. A few school systems have provided for an additional paraprofessional in special education and regular education classrooms through the position of teacher aid.

A paraprofessional may be required to provide a variety of services. A handicapped child may need special tutoring in one area which the classroom teacher cannot consistently provide. Here the paraprofessional can be quite helpful—relieving the teacher of a special responsibility. A paraprofessional may also develop and present projects which focus on the development of manipulative skills, physical education programs, art projects, or language skills. With very little supervision from the classroom teacher, the paraprofessional can conduct such activities and be quite successful in contributing to the instructional program.

Karnes, Teska, and Hodgins (1970) conducted a three-year experiment to compare the performance of professional teachers to that of adult and teenage paraprofessionals in teaching preschool-age children from economically and educationally deprived families. The adult paraprofessionals were black mothers with no previous teaching experience. The teenage paraprofessionals were girls in a high school work-study program. The emphasis in the content of the lessons was on language development as exemplified in the Illinois Test of Psycholinguistic Abilities. All were trained, and their effectiveness, as compared to that of the teachers, was based upon the children's performances on standardized tests. The results indicated no significant differences in the progress of the three groups of children. However, the teenage paraprofessionals were considered to be less satisfied with their experiences.

Mothers have been trained as paraprofessionals with their own preschool-age children. The training was conducted by a demonstrator who went to the home and demonstrated play activities with the child. The play activities centered around verbal interaction. The ultimate objective was to increase intellectual functioning. Since the beginning of the program in 1965, follow-up studies have been conducted. These studies have indicated increases in cognitive functioning through gains in IQ points and achievement test scores, which were up to grade level during the first year of school (Levenstein 1971).

Another interesting project using parents to help young children increase their learning skills was developed by the Far West Regional Laboratory in 1970. The concept of a toy library was established through this project. Parents were trained in the selection and use of toys with their children and could then go to the toy library and borrow educational toys. From this program, parents began to see their children and the educational process differently. Other materials could be provided in the library and loaned to parents to use at home. These libraries could be established in the public schools, giving parents relatively easy access to the materials and training in their use (McDonald 1971).

Programs involving parents as paraprofessionals, similar to those described above, could have a tremendous impact on special education programs. Children from families with limited incomes and limited resources could be helped to overcome some of their learning deficits prior to entering school and thus be better prepared. Parental attitudes toward their children could also be modified so that children would develop better attitudes toward the learning process.

Paraprofessionals have also been used extensively in institutional settings for the mentally retarded. Institutional or residential facilities for the mentally retarded, and for all exceptional children are usually understaffed. Projects which require one-to-one activities or even small group activities have been difficult if not impossible to organize.

Paraprofessionals in the residential facility must be trained at the facility to be cognizant of the tasks they will confront. A project involving training language specialists for institutionalized mentally retarded children who were functioning at a low level was successful in training and using paraprofessionals and also in increasing the skills of the children (Guess, Smith, and Ensminger 1971).

Considering all of the trends regarding programs and personnel discussed in this chapter, the special educator can no longer complain about a lack of programs or a lack of personnel. The programs or personnel may not presently exist in a particular area. However, there are ways to provide some services which are within the grasp of a community with respect to both finances and manpower. This chapter has by no means attempted to present all of the unique ideas for increasing and improving services for exceptional children, but perhaps the reader has gained insight into the problems and ways to resolve them and provide meaningful programs.

Administration of Programs for Exceptional Children

The administration of programs for exceptional children is the responsibility of all local, state, and federal governmental agencies which are related to the development and implementation of such programs. A close examination of the administration of such programs would probably reveal that the school principal is the primary school person involved in promoting adequate programs.

The School Principal

The school principal is considered to be the person who determines the attitude and sets the tempo for the total educational program in a school. The principal is the educator who encourages flexibility, innovations, and the use of appropriate techniques to improve all services, particularly those offered exceptional children.

In order to implement effectively procedures and more flexible approaches, the educational leader should have some basic information regarding exceptional children. The principal needs such information in order to work effectively with the teachers and the parents. A survey of school principals would probably show that only a very few have completed any course work pertaining to the exceptional child. In fact, such a survey was conducted by Bullock (1970). Of ninety-two principals only 12 percent had taken more than one course in special education, and 65 percent had elected no courses in special education.

The principal may be the key person; however, the total program requires a coordinated effort by the entire administration—the teachers, the parents, and appropriate community agencies (Melcher 1972). The emphasis must be on developing a program which is child-centered and not merely based on administrative decisions. The special education teacher operating in isolation may still exist, but this type of program is not comprehensive and lacks the variety to meet the needs of exceptional children. In other words, operating programs for exceptional children without support and cooperative efforts of school personnel, parents, and community agencies severely limits the possible effects of the program. All teachers and children can benefit from cooperative efforts and sharing of procedures and skills.

Cost Factors and Other Related Aspects

Of course, the provision of special services for exceptional children always adds to the cost of a school system. Many school boards and school administrators hesitate to develop or expand services for exceptional children because of the "excess" cost. These actions may be based on the realistic fact that there is a lack of monies to support programs. Frohreich (1973) compiled data regarding variables such as administration, teachers, supplies, counseling, transportation, which increase the costs of providing services for all types of exceptional children. The information was based on surveys conducted in school systems which provided exemplary programs, and may well serve as a guide to beginning or expanding programs. All school administrators, directors of special education, and special education teachers should study this report in detail.

In addition to cost factors and variables pertinent to establishing good programs, the acceptance of exceptional children in the schools should be emphasized. Programs for exceptional children are required in order to prevent the possible total or partial loss of an individual's potential, and also to prevent the costly factors which are created when programs are not provided. The exceptional child, regardless of abilities or difficulties, is a worthwhile human being. If specialized teaching, counseling, and equipment are required, programs of quality offering these services and materials should be provided. Developing human resources or at least preventing their loss should be a mandate for all educational programs.

An important factor in providing exemplary programs for exceptional children is the selection of the best teacher available for a particular group. Again, the role of the principal is paramount in making this decision. A well-trained special education teacher can provide a more meaningful and realistic instructional program, and also serve in the capacity of a resource person to the other teachers in the building. If instructional programs and other supportive areas are to be improved, the special education teacher must have the training essential for making worthwhile contributions.

The administration of special education programs and the role of the administrator may not appear to be very meaningful to the college student preparing to enter the field of special education. These aspects are, however, of utmost importance when the practicing teacher seeks support from the administration and doesn't receive it, or asks for additional monies for supplies and equipment and is refused. It can be most discouraging to new teachers to discover that the children with whom they are working are devalued and merely tolerated within the school programs.

Directors of Special Education

The position of director of special education is certainly not a new one. Special education has had directors of programs on the state level for many years. As special class programs in the public schools have grown, the position of director has been added to the school staff.

School systems will continue to have a need for qualified and well-trained directors of special education as legislation provides for the establishment of additional classroom teachers and resource persons for exceptional children. Developing sound procedures for referring and evaluating children with exceptional abilities or disabilities, hiring competent staff to provide services, and involving the staff in seeking appropriate federal and state funding for special projects will require a specialist who can function as a director of special education.

The director of special education is responsible to teachers of exceptional children for promoting and developing ongoing in-service education programs and special workshops. Teachers should be assisted in the appropriate referral and use of community agencies, and in the development of curricular materials. The director may be of considerable value in interpreting the program for exceptional children to all school personnel, parents, and the general public. The director is responsible for building a sequential, comprehensive program, and for the development of a good professional library. In addition, the director of special education has the responsibility of keeping the school administration informed of the needs for personnel, classrooms, transportation, diagnostic and evaluation procedures, and methods for the evaluation of the total program.

With such a variety of responsibilities, the director of special education must be well trained and have a good experiential background with exceptional children. An example from one state regarding the specifications applicable to the director of special education is presented below.

Legislation in the state of Ohio provides for the position of director of special education. This provision includes the requirements for certification and describes the primary functions of the director of special education as leadership and supervision. Specific duties listed are as follows: (1) planning and program development, (2) administration and program coordination, (3) staff selection and development, (4) budgeting and fiscal control, and (5) program evaluation and reporting (Kern and Mayer 1971).

A majority of special education programs have developed certification requirements for a director of special education. A survey of all fifty states concluded that an educational program for directors of special education should include courses in administration, education foundations, psychology, guidance, and research. The training should also include a practicum or internship in special education administration, certification in a teaching field, and a master's degree with emphasis in the field of special education (Kern and Mayer).

Parents of Exceptional Children

Aspects regarding parents have been discussed in the chapters on the specific types of exceptional children and will not be repeated. However, the parents of exceptional children are a very important link in the provision of educational services, and further delineation regarding parents is worthy of consideration. Parents are influential in the diagnosis and evaluation of their children, and their support of programs is essential. Supplementary services which parents may provide in the home or through a community agency are extremely beneficial to their children's education and training.

The problems of parents of exceptional children are multidimensional and individualistic. There is no static answer. There is no magic formula in dealing with their problems. The problems of the parents or the child must be approached when the problems arise, and we must discontinue the position of waiting and seeing before intervening. Several types of counseling services on a continuous basis must be provided for families. As more professionals become oriented to the problems of parents of exceptional children, perhaps our services will become more available and more meaningful to them and to their children.

School administrators, counselors, therapists, and teachers must be cognizant of the wide variety of problems which families may have with their exceptional children. These problems vary from difficulties within the family unit to difficulties which derive from external attitudes or pressures. Knowledge regarding family problems has to be directed to the specific family; however, a discussion of possible difficulties may serve to set up guidelines in providing counseling services.

Parents of exceptional children will exhibit a variety of reactions depending upon many emotional variables that exist in themselves and in the family unit. There are exceptions to any generalizations; therefore, persons working with parents of exceptional children must be knowledgeable in the area of human dynamics and be aware of the parents with whom they are dealing. The parents' reactions may vary from frustration to fear, anxiety, hopelessness, exhilaration, despair, shame, guilt, and a variety of other responses. One should recognize that parents may react defensively to the fact that they have an exceptional child, because of other people's reactions toward them. These parents did not request an exceptional child. They have had to deal with many different parental experiences which other parents will never realize. Some parents may close themselves to their environment, and depend entirely upon their own inner resources to meet the daily needs of their child and to cope with their daily frustrations and fears. Parents may close their environments because they have tried and failed to obtain any services from different community agencies. Consequently, they have given up their search for particular services and have tried to serve as their own resource. This experience may lead to a very frustrating situation for the parents and the family.

Fortunately, though, some parents of exceptional children receive appropriate services as well as appropriate information regarding their child, the extent to which their child might be disabled, and the ways in which they can promote positive development in their child. Community agencies provide parents with resources for their family needs and enable them to be realistic and emotionally healthy toward their child and their home situation. This positive attitude of the parents may be ideal, and ideality is becoming more possible as a result of federal legislation and community action programs.

Professionals sometimes seem to forget to listen. We should let parents tell their stories in their own words about how they perceive the abilities and the needs of their child. Too often teachers, counselors, principals, medical doctors, psychologists, and other professionals indicate that they know the answers and know more about the child than the parents know. They do not listen to cues which express how the parents perceive the growth and development of their child, or which community services they already have explored for their child. They hesitate to give much credence to the abilities and insight of parents. Listening is one of the key factors, and regardless of how knowledgeable we think we are, parents do have something to contribute. Parent contributions may serve as guidelines for us regarding extended services from which the exceptional child might benefit.

Communicating With Parents

It is incorrect to assume that the implementation of Public Law 94–142 and other federal and state legislation has created ideal situations for all parents of handicapped children. While there have been many cooperative placement and IEP team meetings, and services have increased for many handicapped children and youth, there are still situations which are not favorable for parents or their children.

In a case study reported in the August, 1980, issue of *The Exceptional Parent,* some of the possible conflicts between school and parents regarding assessment and placement of a child were presented. In the school principal's initial contacts, the parents were advised to obtain an independent evaluation of their child if they so desired. The parents followed this suggestion, and the outcome was that they disagreed with the findings of both evaluations.

In the school meeting, the father reported that there were too many people in the room, only two of whom he recognized. The school staff read their reports, and the father perceived that they were really communicating with each other; they had little regard for the parents other than asking if they had questions after reading each report. The father indicated that the staff had used professional language which he did not understand; therefore, he could not ask questions. The father refused to sign a form regarding the staff's recommendations not only because of a lack of understanding, but also because the staff's recommendations and the private assessment's recommendations were different.

The staff's concern regarding their child had caused the father to remember all of his difficulties in school, such as fighting other children and arguing with teachers. The mother had recalled her difficulty expressing herself verbally in the classroom. The parents also perceived their daughter's difficulties as a direct reflection on their child-rearing practices.

School officials must recognize that there are problems in communicating with many parents of handicapped children, and that training is required to improve these skills. Increased efforts must also be made to improve communications among the variety of school personnel.

As professionals, we should realize that increased concerns and programs for school-age handicapped children do not automatically continue for those beyond school age. For exceptional young adults, there are gaps in programs or no programs at all. Michaelis (1980) reported the many frustrations experienced in twenty-four years of fighting to obtain services for her son, who is mentally retarded. Now that her son is over twenty-one years of age, he is no longer eligible for the services provided under Public Law 94–142. Dr. Michaelis, a university professor in special education, is being told now that her son needs a group home and adult services, and that if these programs are acceptable to her, she will have to fight for them.

Michaelis reported that Jim entered a work study program which provided an IEP stating that he would be given a half-day school experience and job training experiences such as learning to ride a bus. Instead of following the IEP, the teachers were teaching the Dolch words and telling time which Jim had known since age ten.

Michaelis was unable to get Jim in the one group home in the county because it was full and had a waiting list of over 200. Nor was it possible to get him in the local sheltered workshop because it was full. The workshop staff also indicated that he was too high intellectually to qualify for their services. Jim's mother finally obtained a vocational evaluation. However, the staffing was held at a time during which she could not attend. After nine months of waiting, no results of the staffing were ever communicated to Dr. Michaelis.

After many frustrations and disappointments, the end result was that Jim was sent to another state to live with his maternal grandparents. They could get him in the local sheltered workshop because they had been in the community for years. So in this case, after contacting school officials, workshops, vocational evaluators, employers, and the local association for retarded citizens, a retarded young adult had to be separated from his immediate family in order to receive appropriate services.

Special education teachers spend a good share of their time communicating with parents and have not often been prepared adequately for this role. Expectations of parent conferences do not always coincide with the realities. This is particularly true when teachers are meeting with parents of culturally diverse exceptional children.

Parents of culturally diverse gifted and handicapped children have not generally been thought capable of working cooperatively with school personnel. They do not meet the "average" model as parents because of the size of their families, their language differences, and their economic situation. Many professionals recognize culturally diverse populations to include only those from minority groups, such as blacks, American Indians, or Mexican Americans. A large population group is often neglected: the Caucasian families who are culturally diverse. It should be acknowledged that few, if any, children from culturally diverse families are considered for placement in programs for gifted children. Many of these children are placed in programs for the mentally retarded or emotionally disturbed.

The parents of culturally diverse exceptional children have many needs which have been neglected by school personnel. Marion (1980) stated that these needs include the following:

1. Need for information.
2. Need to belong.
3. Need for positive self-esteem.

These needs can be met by special education teachers and other school personnel by using language which parents understand, recognizing that they have not received information about Public Law 94–142 and other legislation, and that they do not know the methods of assessing and placing children or the programs available for them. Teachers also need to include these parents as active participants in parent groups, rather than seating them as isolated spectators or totally excluding them. Parents should be helped to apply their energies and skills in productive ways which will assist them in meeting their frustrations, angers, and isolation.

One of the intentions of Public Law 94–142 is to make parents equal partners in the education process. This includes parents of culturally diverse exceptional children. Meeting their needs will take time but will improve programs for these children and parental attitudes toward school programs.

The same information gap experienced by parents of culturally diverse exceptional children is often experienced by parents of preschool handicapped children. A model which meets this need is the Transdisciplinary Service Delivery Model (Woodruff 1980) used in Project Optimus in Massachusetts.

The model described by Woodruff focuses on four different aspects of program implementation. The first step is including the parents as a part of the interdisciplinary team in assessing the child. The assessment is done with all members of the interdisciplinary team sitting in a circle and one member serving as a facilitator. The facilitator provides activities for the child which will lead to an assessment of language skills; cognitive functioning; fine and gross motor skills; and social, emotional, and self-help skills. This is referred to as the "arena" method by Woodruff and provides an effective means of including the parents. It also saves time; parents are not asked the same questions by every team member as would be done through individual assessment meetings.

The next three phases involve diagnosis and goal setting, planning and program implementation for the child and family, and evaluation of the program and the child. Throughout these phases, parents are always included. One member of the team is designated as the primary person responsible for the established goals and for working with the parents in the home. Designating one team member as the primary intervener reduces confusion on the part of the child and parents and increases communication.

The planning and program implementation is monitored consistently. Then the evaluation examines the progress being made by the child, the family, and the team member who is the primary intervener. The evaluation phase is continuous. A total reevaluation of the program and child is made every three months.

This comprehensive approach in all four phases of program development is unique in that communication is more effective and program evaluation is of primary concern. Efforts to revise goals and improve all services offered to preschool handicappd children would increase parent communication and the effectiveness of programs.

Imber, Imber, and Rothstein (1979) developed a model program which could be effective in teacher-parent communication and improve the progress of children in the classroom. The program has three phases, which apply behavior modification techniques. Phase one is collecting baseline data. This informs the teacher about the current functioning level of the child in completing seatwork assignments (other tasks or skills are appropriate to examine and improve). The second phase is a teacher-child conference during which the teacher praises the child for current appropriate behavior and informs the child that a praise note will be received when seatwork reaches an 80 percent accuracy level. Phase three requires a teacher-parent phone contact and writing to parents to explain the praise note. Parents are requested to praise their children immediately when they present the praise note; to place the note in a highly visible place in the home; to praise the children in front of other family members; and to encourage them the following morning to repeat the successful performance. In their application of the model program, Imber and his colleagues observed that all the children involved made progress and maintained their progress through intermittent reinforcement for the remainder of the school year. Teachers must be willing to take the time to collect baseline data, write the praise notes, consistently provide systematic praise for appropriate behavior, and take time to develop parent communication. If the techniques are successful as observed in student progress, then the time and effort are worthwhile.

The Learning Disabilities Clinic at Coney Island Hospital (Pope 1980) exemplifies the factors previously discussed regarding parents and professionals. The staff of this clinic provides test interpretation, problem-solving group sessions, training of parents to be tutors, and assistance to parents in developing good home management skills. They locate community resources, teach child development, and provide training in developing coping skills for social pressures and conflicts in the school. The main emphasis at the clinic is to provide services for parents and their children who have learning disabilities. The parents are viewed and accepted as collaborators in a joint effort. The staff does not use technical language and approaches their work in a nondogmatic, nonauthoritarian fashion. Other agencies could profit from the approaches of this clinic's staff, by using parents as collaborators and training them to perform tasks at home which correspond with their children's developmental stage.

The Family

We should be concerned about the needs of each member of families of exceptional children. At times the parental reaction is considered to be of primary importance and we overlook the importance of how other members of the family have reacted, grown, and developed after having lived with an exceptional child. We may, for example, find that the family is very compatible. This unity may serve as a resource for all of the family, including the exceptional child.

The family that develops a positive attitude toward the exceptional child may experience a closer relationship and warmth than many other families in the general population. Other siblings may learn the real meaning of sharing and cooperating. The family may learn new avenues of communication, which reflect good experiences. Of course, the realization of the exceptional child as a family member and the growth and development of meaningful family relationships will be continuous. Functional acceptance and living with the exceptional child in the family may be a very slow process for some members of the family. In some instances the child may be rejected by some members.

Regardless of the appearance of the family situation, counseling services for individuals in the family, and perhaps the whole family, would be beneficial. This counseling should, of necessity, be provided by a skilled counselor, rather than by teachers who have neither the time nor expertise. The recognition of the need for counseling may suggest that the teacher serve as a liaison for making the initial contact for the services.

A family may overestimate the abilities or prognosis of their exceptional child, because they have observed their child functioning and relating to a known, comfortable environment. The family may outwardly demonstrate that they have learned to cope quite successfully with their exceptional child, but their coping may be an overprotecting device instead of a positive way of enhancing growth and development.

The parents may tend to keep the child in the home environment. Consequently, the child has very limited public exposure. If the child is permitted in public with parents or other family members but is protected from others, the child is unable to develop and explore new environments. This type of situation may be seen in the school environment when the child is overly dependent upon the teacher, and the parents are intervening consistently on the behalf of the child. This situation is difficult, but the teacher or other school personnel should provide an environment in which the child can explore and develop meaningful relationships with peers and begin to establish independence.

No one knows all the decisions that should be made to enhance development to the fullest extent. We do know, though, that some exceptional children come to school after having experienced too much pseudo-warmth and unity in the family, which has the overall effect of overprotection. We may see overprotection exhibited by the family. The child is not permitted independent action because the parents or other family members provide for all the child's needs.

The exceptional child does not need overprotection. Families need to reach a happy medium in providing an environment in which the child can grow and develop without looking for a magic formula. At times parents become so frustrated in living with an exceptional child, that their child is physically and psychologically abused. Exerting undue pressure on the child, demanding tasks that are beyond the present developmental stage, becoming frustrated because of the extra financial burden or the emotional burden may cause the parents to punish the child severely. They may verbally abuse their child, or consistently react negatively creating an environment in which the child's potential will be seriously hampered. Part of the abuse may be caused by the parents' responses to the way society has reacted to exceptional children. Expressing pity or hopelessness to the parents because of the situation which controls their lives provides no support. Society's general refusal to provide services, or to recognize that the exceptional child is a human being with rights and learning potential, certainly contributes to the parents' hostilities toward their environment.

Parents and Professionals

Professional persons are concerned with the future of the exceptional child. Will the child receive the structure necessary for future life development? Even though parents may have that concern for their child, they primarily direct their efforts toward daily living behaviors and daily development of skills. Living with an exceptional individual day by day is very demanding, and that experience creates different concerns for parents from those often demonstrated by professionals. Consequently, counseling services for parents and families should be aware that the family may need as much assistance and direction in their daily living with their child as they do in their planning for future potential.

Counseling services must be kept in the proper perspective. We must listen when we are working with the parents and families of exceptional children in order to discover the primary concern at a particular point in time. What kind of help are they seeking? Unless we listen to the family, we will not know their primary concerns. The present problem of the parents may be perceived to be so severe that they will not be able to listen to any other type of discussion.

Another counseling suggestion is to consider whether or not the parents will be able to follow through with the guidelines offered to them. Sometimes parents do not have the inner resources required to pursue a suggestion regarding their child's education or training program. They may be exhausted because of the futile attempts they have made in the past. Previous attempts may have limited results, not because of the child's characteristics, but because the parents have not had adequate training to carry out the counselor's or teacher's suggestions. Sometimes, we are also inclined to think that one suggestion or one counseling session is sufficient because the problem and solution appear obvious to us. Assuming that one counseling session is sufficient for the parents of an exceptional child is ridiculous. Also, we cannot assume, simply because we can tell parents the resources to which they should go and the services they should obtain, that they will in fact use these resources and services.

Emphasizing the need to listen to parents may appear to be common sense. However, true listening and comprehension require skill and even training. According to information discussed by Kroth (1975) there are four types of listeners. They are (1) the passive listener, (2) the active listener, (3) the passive nonlistener, and (4) the active nonlistener. Passive listeners provide ample opportunity for parents to discuss a situation or feelings. Active listeners actually enter into discussions by asking for clarifications or more elaborate explanations. Passive nonlisteners hear the message but miss feelings of anger, frustration, failure, or fatigue; their basic information is correct but they miss the true meaning of the message. Active nonlisteners don't hear any of the messages; they are actively involved in presenting their own messages. In a parent-teacher conference both parties may present their personal concerns, but neither party really listens to the other if both are active nonlisteners.

In addition to the types of listeners, Kroth also discussed deterrents to listening. All teachers should note these deterrents and remember them when conferencing with parents. The deterrents include fatigue, strong feelings regarding a child's behaviors, class performance, and attitudes. Certain words may also be a deterrent to listening. Terms such as *mental retardation,* or *emotional disturbance* can provoke such strong feelings that parents stop listening. Teacher domination of the parent-teacher conference may be a deterrent to listening, in that the parent is required to be a passive listener and may soon become an active nonlistener. Environmental conditions which are distracting or extremely uncomfortable will lessen the ability to listen and negatively influence the conference. For example, having the parents sit in very small chairs may be so uncomfortable that the parents focus on the discomfort rather than the conference. Writing during the conference may or may not influence the flow of the meeting. Teachers must observe the influence of writing with different parents and adjust to the demands of the situation.

All the suggestions provided by Kroth are relevant to the previous discussions regarding communicating with parents of exceptional children. There is no doubt that attention to these factors will improve parent-teacher conferences.

In some situations parents of exceptional children may not be willing to change. They may not be willing to pursue any type of resource or service recommended. They may feel satisfied with the way their child is functioning. They may deem it inappropriate for them to make any changes in their own life-style. They may insist that it is up to the school, the clinic, or community resources to provide the services and make the changes necessary for their child. They have done all they can or will do and they are not going to do any more. Of course, this emotional discharge is some of the limited hostility we may experience from a few parents. When parents do not cooperate, then the primary responsibility of the community resource is to offer developmental assistance to the child. The parents may or may not be cooperative, but either way the community resource should be prepared to perform the bulk of the services.

Many other contacts with parents will be made by school personnel in parent-teacher conferences. School personnel should inform parents of positive growth and accomplishments, and not just contact parents when the children are having problems. School personnel must be able to recognize when they are not adequately trained to provide counseling for severe problems in the family unit. Again, appropriate referral should be made for situations which are beyond the training and abilities of school personnel.

Residential Centers

Many parents of exceptional children may be confronted with the possibility of placing their children in residential centers for the emotionally disturbed, the deaf, the blind, or the mentally retarded. The placement may be necessary because of a lack of appropriate programs in the community, or because of the severity of the child's difficulties. This type of placement should never be a routine suggestion, but should be the last resource to which one refers parents. The community or a nearby community should be thoroughly explored for possible services before recommending placement in residential facilities.

Avoiding residential placement is not a direct criticism of residential centers, because many have excellent programs. The factors of primary importance are to keep the children with their families and within their communities if at all possible. If the severity of the children's problems, or the insufficiency of family and community resources are such as to warrant residential placement, then the best and nearest program should be sought. For accurate and detailed information, the parents should be encouraged to visit, or at least communicate with the facility prior to making formal application. Suggesting this type of placement for exceptional children may also result in the need for professional counseling services for the parents.

Parents as Teachers

The previous discussion of paraprofessionals includes information pertaining to parents as teachers. School personnel should always consider requesting parents to work as paraprofessionals or as teacher aides. In addition, school personnel may ask parents to provide supplementary or extended educational services for their children in their own homes. Requesting parents to be a part of the educational process must include an evaluation of the possible effectiveness of this procedure. For example, the parents may place undue pressure on their children to perform, and so cause more difficulties. Instead of assisting their children academically, parents may be requested to take them to places in the community which would strengthen their awareness and knowledge of their environment. It is also appropriate to ask parents to provide their children with the time and a suitable place in their homes to pursue school-related activities with some degree of privacy and quiet. Perhaps just helping the parents accept their children's exceptionalities and recognizing the children as unique persons may alleviate some of the parents' frustrations regarding these children.

In short, school personnel have tremendous responsibilities in the development of the relationship between home and school. Every effort should be made to help the family with their exceptional children to the extent that the parents and other family members can contribute in a positive manner to the children's total growth and development.

Considering all of the programs and persons that have been discussed in this chapter, the special educator can no longer complain about a lack of programs or a lack of personnel. The programs or personnel may not presently exist in a particular area, but, as discussed, there are ways to implement ideas for the provision of services which are within the grasp of a community with respect to finances and manpower. This chapter has by no means attempted to present all the ideas which can be developed to increase and improve services for exceptional children, but perhaps the reader has gained insight into the ways in which meaningful programs can be provided.

Study Questions

1. In what ways can a regular class teacher contribute to a program for exceptional children?
2. Describe the type of parent-teacher conference which would exist if both parties were active non-listeners.
3. What is the role of the crisis teacher?
4. Write a brief summary of at least four references which pertain to improving communication with parents.

5. What is the role of the diagnostic teacher?
6. What is the role of the special education counselor?
7. List the ways in which a teacher might help a school principal to become more knowledgeable about special education programs.
8. How may paraprofessionals be trained and used effectively in programs for exceptional children?
9. Because of mandatory legislation, how has the parents' role relative to child services changed?
10. How are behavioral objectives related to teaching exceptional children?
11. In addition to the areas discussed in the chapter, list the types of services which are needed by exceptional young adults.
12. What are the cooperative needs among special class teachers, regular class teachers, administrators, and parents for services?

Bibliography

Bullock, Lyndal M. 1970. "An Inquiry into the Special Education Training of Elementary School Administrators." *Exceptional Children* 36, no. 10 (Summer).

Cormany, R. B. 1970. "Returning Special Education Students to Regular Classes." *Personnel and Guidance Journal* 48, no. 8 (April).

Fine, M. J. 1969. "Counseling with the Educable Mentally Retarded." *The Training School Bulletin* 66, no. 3 (November).

Frohreich, Lloyd E. 1973. "Costing Programs for Exceptional Children: Dimensions and Indices." *Exceptional Children* 39, no. 7 (April).

Guba, Egon G. 1968. *Evaluation and Change in Education.* Bloomington, Ind.: National Institute for the Study of Educational Change.

Guess, D.; Smith, J. O.; and Ensminger, E. E. 1971. "The Role of Non-professional Persons in Teaching Language Skills to Mentally Retarded Children." *Exceptional Children* 37, no. 6 (February).

Hansen, C. E. 1971. "The Special Education Counselor: A New Role." *Exceptional Children* 38, no. 1 (September).

Hewett, Frank, and Taylor, Frank D. 1980. *The Emotionally Disturbed Child in the Classroom.* 2d ed. Boston: Allyn and Bacon.

Hyer, Anna L. 1971. "From Gold Stars to Green Stamps." *Audiovisual Instruction* 16, no. 5 (May).

Imber, Steve C.; Imber, Ruth B.; and Rothstein, Cary. 1979. "Modifying Independent Work Habits: An Effective Teacher-Parent Communication Program." *Exceptional Children* 46, no. 3 (November).

Instructional Materials and Resource Materials Available to Teachers of Exceptional Children and Youth. 1969 and 1972. The University of Texas at Austin.

Kaplan, Abraham. 1964. *The Conduct of Inquiry: Methodology for Behavioral Science.* San Francisco: Chandler Publishing Co.

Karnes, M. B.; Teska, J.; and Hodgins, A. S. 1970. "The Successful Implementation of a Highly Specific Preschool Instructional Program by Paraprofessional Teachers." *Journal of Special Education* 4, no. 1 (Winter-Spring).

Kern, R., and Kirby, J. H. 1971. "Utilizing Peer Helper Influence in Group Counseling." *Elementary School Guidance and Counseling* 6, no. 2 (December).

Kern, W. H., and Mayer, J. B. 1971. "Certification of Directors of Special Education Programs: The Results of a National Survey." *Contemporary Education* 42, no. 3 (January).

Kibler, Robert J.; Barker, Larry R.; and Miles, David T. 1970. *Behavioral Objectives and Instruction*. Boston: Allyn and Bacon.

Kroth, Roger L. 1975. *Communicating with Parents of Exceptional Children: Improving Parent-Teacher Relationships*. Denver: Love Publishing Co.

Levenstein, P. 1971. "Learning Through (and From) Mothers." *Childhood Education* 48, no. 3 (December).

McDonald, P. 1971. "Cross Currents: Parents, A New Resource." *Teaching Exceptional Children* 3, no. 3 (Winter).

McKenzie, Hugh S.; Egnar, Ann N.; Knight, Martha F.; Perelman, Phyllis F.; Schneider, Betsy M.; and Garvin, Jean S. 1970. "Training Consulting Teachers to Assist Elementary Teachers in the Management and Education of Handicapped Children." *Exceptional Children* 37, no. 2 (October).

Marion, Robert L. 1980. "Communicating with Parents of Culturally Diverse Children." *Exceptional Children* 46, no. 8 (May).

Melcher, John W. 1972. "Some Questions from a School Administrator." *Exceptional Children* 38, no. 7 (March).

Michaelis, Carol T. 1980. "Things Are Worse Now: A Parent's Perspective." *The Exceptional Parent* 10, no. 4 (August).

Muro, J. J. 1970. "Community Volunteers: A New Thrust for Guidance." *The Personnel and Guidance Journal* 49, no. 2 (October).

Patterson, C. H. 1969. *Rehabilitation Counseling: Collected Papers*. Champaign, Ill.: Stipes Publishing Co.

Pope, Lillie. 1980. "Clinician and Parent: Partners for Change." *Academic Therapy* 15, no. 4 (March).

Reger, Roger; Schroeder, Wendy; and Uschold, Kathie. 1968. *Special Education: Children with Learning Problems*. New York: Oxford University Press.

Scholarship Program. 1971. U.S. Department of Health, Education, and Welfare.

Stocker, Joseph, and Wilson, Donald F. 1971. "Accountability and the Classroom Teacher." *Today's Education* 60, no. 3 (March).

Tenorio, S. C., and Raimist, L. I. 1971. "A Noncategorical Consortium Program." *Exceptional Children* 38, no. 4 (December).

————. "The IEP Conference: A Problem for Parents," *The Exceptional Parent* 10, no. 4 (August).

Vergason, Glenn A. 1973. "Accountability in Special Education." *Exceptional Children* 39, no. 5 (February).

Woodruff, Geneva. 1980. "Transdisciplinary Approach for Preschool Children and Parents." *The Exceptional Parent* 10, no. 3 (June).

trends and services
in the field of special education

The objective of this chapter is to acquaint the reader with services and trends in the field of special education. Approved methods which have been effective in teaching exceptional children include the resource center, precision teaching, behavior modification, and physical education. Emphasis is also being placed on the reintegration of exceptional children into regular classes, preschools for handicapped children, and the teacher's position in diagnostic-remedial activity.

Many model programs and methods are currently in operation and have proven effective in improving programs for exceptional children. There is also evidence that the ability to gain community understanding and participation in special education programs can greatly benefit our exceptional children. A goal, therefore, should be to implement these techniques and incorporate these needed paraprofessionals into the field of special education.

Integration of Exceptional Children in Regular Classes (Mainstreaming)

Many definitions of mainstreaming are available in the literature. We have chosen the following definition, which was approved in April, 1976, by the Delegate Assembly of the Council for Exceptional Children.

Mainstreaming is a belief which involves an educational placement procedure and process for exceptional children, based on the conviction that each such child should be educated in the least restrictive environment in which his educational and related needs can be satisfactorily provided. This concept recognizes that exceptional children have a wide range of special educational needs, varying greatly in intensity and duration; that there is a recognized continuum of educational settings which may, at a given time, be appropriate for an individual child's needs; that to the maximum extent appropriate exceptional children should be educated with non-exceptional children; and that special classes, separate schooling, or other removal of an exceptional child from education with non-exceptional children should occur only when the intensity of the child's special education and related needs is such that they cannot be satisfied in an environment including non-exceptional children, even with the provision of supplementary aids and services.

405

Placement of a child in a special education class should never, except in an extreme case such as the trainable mentally retarded, be considered a permanent decision. The majority of school systems have programs which are designed to prevent permanent placement by including a requirement for retesting children within a period of one year. In the past, school personnel usually did not have the time or the manpower to conduct reevaluations of each child. In many situations, after a child was placed in a special education class, the door closed and no consideration was given for returning the child to regular classes even on a part-time basis. With the implementation of Public Law 94–142, the doors of the special education class will remain open and children will be reassessed periodically. Problems in reevaluation are evident. Cormany (1970) indicated that even though psychological evaluations of many students recommended for special education class placement suggested a one-year follow-up for reconfirmation, a period of five years or more had elapsed without further evaluation. These conditions contribute to the many questions which have arisen concerning the use of psychological testing and the labeling of children. In our opinion, however, undue delay in reevaluation is not always the fault of the psychometrist or psychologist. The classroom teacher has a definite responsibility to schedule children for reevaluation and to evaluate them informally in the classroom.

The concept of labels and categories has caused many educators and parents to respond quickly to the panacea called mainstreaming. Anyone who has taught or worked with exceptional children realizes that labels don't originate necessarily from special education classes, psychologists, or teachers, simply because someone has a file which spells out handicapped. Many children get their negative labels by sitting in regular classrooms without benefit of special resources. They exhibit intellectual, physical, or emotional behavior which is different. They become obvious to other children; then these other children and sometimes even teachers and administrators call the exceptional child weird, dumb, retardo, stupid, shy, dyslexic, aphasic, crippled, blind, deaf, illiterate, etc. These labels come from the "mainstream" of school, not from special classes. Be very careful before you give blanket approval to the concept of mainstreaming. Realize the child's success perspective in a special class and the possible unreasonable demands of the regular class. Mainstreaming will not work unless it truly offers the child the least restrictive environment for learning.

Children in special education classes need counseling and guidance when plans are made for their return to the mainstream of education. This process, in the majority of cases, should slowly and gradually program the child back into regular classes. Therefore, instead of immediately placing the child in the regular mainstream of education, success should be experienced in one class and then gradually in other appropriate classes. An administrative decision to move a child from special education classes directly into regular classes without counseling the child, or providing successful experiences will result in failure and frustration.

Perhaps an example will emphasize this concern. A child who is referred for special education placement often has been exposed to many failures prior to being assigned to a special class. The frequent exposure to frustrating failure experiences damages the self-concept to the extent that the child may learn that it is safer to cease functioning rather than risk failure. In essence, this means the special education teacher, after the child is placed, must focus on learning problems and on helping the child to regain self-confidence. After a period of readjustment and relearning, the child may be ready for at least a partial return to the regular class program. Unless the child is helped to view this experience as nonthreatening and one in which the child can function without renewed threat to self-concept, the child may fail purposely in order to return to the security of the special class. Therefore, the exceptional child's ability to function in a regular classroom program is only one of the factors to consider when the child is reintegrated into regular class programs.

Cormany (1970) reported on a successful approach to the problem of reintegration. This program provided counseling services and role play for one group of students and reassigned a control group to regular class programs with no preparation. The experimental group consisted of fifteen students, none of whom failed in the regular class programs after preparation through counseling services. Over one-half of the control group of fifteen students failed in their reintegration experiences and had to be returned to special class programs.

Yates (1973) reported an in-service laboratory/experiential approach for preparing regular classroom teachers for the reintegration of exceptional children into regular education. Actual experiences in working with exceptional children improved the acceptance of regular classroom teachers in comparison to a control group of teachers who received no practical experiences. The post-test attitudes of the experimental group of teachers regarding exceptional children indicated that students with less obvious handicaps could be successfully mainstreamed.

The reintegration of exceptional children into the regular education program is not going to be an easy process and should never be considered as merely an administrative matter. If educators expect exceptional children to be successful and functional in the mainstream of educational programs then efforts such as those by Cormany, Yates, and others will have to be extended. Educators must consider what happens to children who are returned to regular classes, rather than how palatable special class placement may be for teachers.

Certainly mainstreaming may be considered a worthwhile concept to promote. For too many years there has been a certain mystique surrounding the exceptional individual which has resulted in avoidance or fearful reactions. The exceptional individual has been isolated from the rest of the world and has been misunderstood and discriminated against. The exceptional child in the mainstream of education should be recognized as a human being who has many of the same feelings, attitudes, and abilities of the so-called normal child. Perhaps this recognition alone will enhance the life chances of the exceptional child and encourage more normalization.

Individualization in the regular classroom is an absolute must if the concept of mainstreaming is to be effective for an exceptional child. Individualization may be easier to accomplish on the elementary level than on the secondary level. However, very little individualization can be implemented when an elementary teacher has forty children each day. Individualization of instructional programs is a very difficult process. Without appropriate resources the classroom teacher cannot accomplish this task adequately.

In the elementary school a child may progress both academically and socially to an extent that further modifications in the instructional program are not necessary. Elements of progress may be attributed to the elementary school level curriculum, special learning centers, interest centers, and the open-classroom program. Consistent reevaluation of the child is required to determine whether progress is continuing and if mainstreaming remains a good decision. If the child is reevaluated and there are serious deficits in learning, then schools are not providing appropriate programs through the process of mainstreaming.

Individualization for a secondary school teacher who has from 150 to 200 children each day can be overwhelming. At the secondary level, where academics are stressed to a greater extent, individualization is a very difficult process. Fewer resource persons who are familiar with the educational needs of exceptional individuals are available for the secondary school teacher. This tends to make mainstreaming more difficult.

If an exceptional child in secondary school is mainstreamed and quits school because of low grades or extreme frustration, then mainstreaming obviously is not effective for that child. Closely supervised follow-up evaluations must be provided at the secondary level to examine the effects of mainstreaming. If results of a follow-up indicate that a large majority of exceptional children dropped out of secondary school, then under Public Law 94–142 they would become an unserved population group. If this group became unserved, school personnel would begin to reemphasize the formation of special secondary programs much like we experienced in the late 1950s and early 1960s.

Mainstreaming the secondary-level educable mentally retarded may be inappropriate for many reasons. For example, work-study programs for this group have indicated very positive results since the late 1950s. Many of those at the junior or senior level are included already in such elective classes as industrial arts, physical education, home economics, music, etc., and their work experiences add tremendously to their integration into society.

Eliminating current work-study programs for the educable mentally retarded youngster and providing mainstreaming as their only program option is very questionable. Clark (1975) presented the following reasons for this objection:

1. We have no empirical evidence on adolescent retardates to indicate that movement from a partially developed approach (but demonstrably more effective than previous programs) to a new, untried approach is appropriate.

2. The curriculum focus of mainstreaming at the secondary level is not congruous with what has been identified as the needs of the adolescent retarded.

3. The basic assumptions posed for secondary special education programming do not indicate that regular secondary programs or tracks are appropriate.

4. Career education concept programs are not yet adequately established in junior or senior high schools.

5. Support personnel for vocational education teachers, the group most obviously needed for an appropriate mainstreaming approach, are not available.

6. The inflexibility of junior and senior high school policies and goals is not predictive of success for this population.

We agree with the reasons presented by Clark. We also believe that these same reasons may apply to many children who have serious learning disabilities or emotional problems.

The importance of mainstreaming is difficult to assess, because there are so many different opinions about it. Blatt (1976) suggested that in the process of debating mainstreaming we are forgetting the important factors in teaching and learning. Blatt indicated that the important factor in appropriate education is the interaction between child and teacher—not mainstreaming, the curriculum, or even the type of class provided.

Blatt expressed a real concern about the development of educational programs. We really have no education without meaningful interactions between the child and teacher. Consequently, we need to enhance teacher-child interactions in conjunction with mainstreaming to improve our efforts at integrating exceptional children in regular classes.

Special resource teachers should continue to provide services when a child is mainstreamed at the elementary or secondary level. Mainstreaming should not remove all or the majority of the child's support and direction from a special class teacher. They should continue to help the child learn and to monitor behavior. They should not serve only as tutors for the child in regular class subjects. If educators condone the special resource teacher as a tutor in regular class subjects, then special education training will have to change to meet this need. The special lab teacher must be afforded the opportunity to provide special instruction.

An important aspect regarding mainstreaming is the training and present class size of the regular class teacher. A teacher who is overloaded already will not have the time to provide for the needs of an exceptional child. A regular class teacher who has sincerely referred a child for placement in a special program may have that child returned to the regular class because of mainstreaming. A concern to evaluate is whether that particular teacher is prepared to provide an instructional program for the child, and if not, whether that teacher will be forced to modify both approach and attitude and accept the child back into the classroom. This is not realistic planning for the teacher and for the child.

The development of class programs for children with learning disabilities has resulted in the realization that all exceptional children do not need a self-contained class program to help them with their learning or adjustment problems. Part-time placement in learning laboratories and short-term placement in self-contained classrooms have helped many such children to reenter successfully the mainstream of education. Such educational planning has gained acceptance for other types of exceptional children. As temporary special class placement for many types of children with learning problems gains wider acceptance, the role of many special education teachers will change. The special education teacher who has fewer children and has had specialized training to work with specific learning problems should be accepted as a resource person for the entire school. The instructional program certainly should not be considered a program for "those dummy children" or "those sick children," but a program designed specifically for helping children to work to their capacities, to overcome some learning deficits, or to learn to circumvent some learning problems. With these services, they may reach levels of functioning that are commensurate with their abilities.

We suggest that exceptional children who are mainstreamed should have an advocate who will follow them throughout the remainder of their school careers. Martin (1972) stated that a large majority of handicapped children would be unemployed or underemployed during the years of 1972 through 1976. Therefore, if mainstreaming eliminates vocational training during the school years for the exceptional youngster, the unemployment and underemployment rate for the 1980s will continue to increase.

For one educator, mainstreaming seems to have proven itself already. Ensher (1976) stated:

Mainstreaming works! It works when a child, failing to achieve as expected, spends a portion of [the] day in a special class setting and is thereby maintained in a regular grade. It works when another child moves from a segregated environment to a regular school. Mainstreaming works when a special class child participates in the nonacademic activities of the regular school. It has achieved its ultimate end when all education is special and no child beyond its pale. In practice, mainstreaming provides alternatives and reconciles varied levels of ability. Indeed, the exemplariness of education is bound intimately to the accommodation of variance, not as something "special," but as routine and in the course of ordinary responsibilities.

Perhaps enough evidence is presently accumulated to indicate that mainstreaming does work and that all education is "special." We prefer to see the evidence and to examine the research that has been and will be conducted on the long-range effects of mainstreaming on children.

In the *Special Education Newsletter* (1976), Yale psychologist Edward Zigler is quoted as urging a special appropriations committee to consider funding research to discover the effects of mainstreaming. Zigler noted that large amounts are being spent in the name of mainstreaming, and we have no idea as to the effects of this practice. In fact, future research may tell us that mainstreaming was no more than a passing fad. Some of Zigler's concerns should be concerns of educators who lend strong support to a practice without any data to indicate that it is better than what is being provided.

One of the primary factors to consider in mainstreaming is that the decision should be an educational decision, not an administrative one. The purpose of mainstreaming should not be to save money, to find an easy way to provide services, or to serve as the only way to provide appropriate educational services for exceptional children. If an exceptional child is considered for mainstreaming, the special education teacher, school counselor, principal, school psychologist, parents, and the regular class teacher(s) should be a part of the process. Prior to mainstreaming or integrating an exceptional child, an assessment should be made regarding how that child will be able to perform academically and socially in the regular classroom. If children are mainstreamed without exploring their functioning level for the regular class, it would be an injustice to them, to the regular class teacher, and to the children in the regular classroom.

Albert Shanker (1980), president of the American Federation of Teachers, provided some serious criticisms of PL 94–142. He concludes that research conducted to date does not indicate that mainstreaming is an appropriate alternative. During 1980, the Office of Special Education, U.S. Department of Education, conducted several studies on mainstreaming; however, the results of those studies are not yet available.

Teacher training, particularly through in-service programs, has been inadequate generally in assisting teachers to adjust their programs to the needs of handicapped children. Teachers are also neglected in the due process guidelines provided in PL 94–142; due process for them is not a part of the law. According to Shanker, PL 94–142 has not been fully funded, but school districts are still required to provide the services. The end result is that schools are violating the law. When these violations are recognized, the court cases will deplete funds further. The overall effect will be a drastic cut in regular programs so that services for the handicapped will be provided. All interested parties are encouraged by Shanker to send the inadequacies of PL 94–142 to Congress in order to obtain full funding and also bring about changes in the law as necessary.

Rather than mainstreaming all handicapped children, Shanker recommends the guidelines for mainstreaming prepared by the American Federation of Teachers:

1. All children cannot benefit from a mainstream setting.
2. Mainstreaming should be decided on an individual basis, based on the special student's readiness and the capabilities of the regular class teacher to meet individual needs.
3. Advance notice should be given to regular teachers before placement of special children in their classrooms.
4. Staff development programs prior to placement in the regular class and continuous support and training are necessary.
5. Placement decisions should have input from regular teachers.
6. The special student and regular students should have a transitional period for preparation and adjustment to the placement.
7. Regular classes which have handicapped students should be smaller if individualization is going to be possible.
8. Certified special education teachers must be retained to teach children in special classes and provide assistance to regular teachers.
9. Special and regular teachers must have support professionals, such as counselors and psychologists, available.
10. Release time should be given for consultation with support personnel.
11. Classroom materials, equipment, and facilities must be modified to the needs of handicapped students.
12. Scheduling should be accomplished to meet the needs of handicapped children rather than serve the needs of the school program.
13. Continuous evaluation of student placement and progress is necessary.
14. Special funds should follow the handicapped child even in mainstream situations.

We agree in part with the basic principles of mainstreaming, because many children have been placed in special classes without appropriate justification, and many are in need of special modifications which have not been provided in their school curriculum. Incidence studies indicate that 60 to 75 percent of all exceptional children are receiving some special services through special education programming; therefore, it is very interesting to observe the tremendous emphasis toward mainstreaming when the other 25 to 40 percent are already in regular classrooms and have never been in isolated special classes. The national figures of the total number of exceptional children versus those receiving special services indicates a question whether educators have overemphasized mainstreaming as the best way to serve all exceptional children.

Is mainstreaming a fad or a serious step in the planning of educational programs? Does the emphasis upon mainstreaming imply that any good teacher can teach any child? Can the regular class teacher with minimum training in two or three courses or in-service sessions accommodate the exceptional child? Does mainstreaming mean that all educators must become special educators in order for the educational system to work for exceptional children? These questions have not been answered and perhaps will not be answered in any short period of time because of the many variables involved in mainstreaming.

The advent of mainstreaming requires that educators examine the factors relevant to the education of *all* children. Unless administrators, counselors, parents, psychologists, and regular and special class teachers are willing to work and plan together for meaningful and appropriate changes in educational environments, mainstreaming will not be effective, and continued implementation will further deteriorate educational programs.

Diagnostic-Prescriptive Methods

The development and implementation of diagnostic-prescriptive methods is a relatively new endeavor in special education. These methods are not static or rigid in their development or implementation. One may find differences in the application of one approach being used in the same school system or perhaps even in the same school building. Such experimentation and modification should continue if the needs of exceptional children are to be met appropriately.

Flexibility should be paramount in the development and use of diagnostic-prescriptive methods. Without flexibility, programs can become stale, enthusiasm lost, and needs of children neglected. Certainly diagnostic-prescriptive methods are not "the answer," but such approaches can definitely enrich instructional programs for exceptional children as well as teacher training programs.

Perhaps through learning about diagnostic-prescriptive methods, educators are also discovering more about the many factors involved in developing individualized instructional programs. Even more important are the discoveries about the many facets of the learning process.

Resource Centers

One of the approaches in diagnostic-prescriptive methods is the use of a resource center. A resource center may be located (1) within a single school building to serve the children from that school, children from a particular section of a metropolitan area, or all of the children within a small school system or, (2) within a single building to serve teachers from one school system, one state, or a regional area. The purpose of the center will, of course, determine its size and the group of children or teachers whom it may serve.

One important type of resource center is the regional resource center intended to serve teachers who are having difficulty teaching their handicapped children. These centers were authorized by Title VI of the Elementary and Secondary Education Act of 1965 as amended. The program offered through the center may help the teacher to select instructional materials and appropriate methods in order to attempt to meet the current needs of the child as described by the diagnosis and prescription (Moss 1971).

The personnel of a resource center designed to help teachers become more effective with handicapped children may conduct a variety of services. Handicapped children may be referred to the center for a more thorough educational diagnosis and may even remain at the center so that a well-planned teaching approach that will match the diagnosis-prescription may be designed for them. Teachers may also go to the center to see the instructional program in operation with a particular child. In addition, the teacher's instructional program can be evaluated by the staff of the center in order to determine if changes are warranted. If children need more intensive services, the center staff can prepare an experimental teaching program, teach the homebased teacher how to implement the program and, after a short period of time, return the children to their own schools. If any aspect of the program is not effective, the child or the planned instructional program can be reevaluated (Moss).

Of course, as proposed by Moss, such a center would require the services of many trained professionals. Such a center would use the team approach in planning and developing instructional programs for handicapped children. In addition, specialists would be required to conduct comprehensive diagnostic evaluations. Liaison personnel would also be needed to make contact with the public schools and to communicate with them regarding the total services being offered. Evaluators of the center program would also be needed so that the effectiveness of the center program could be disseminated to professionals in the field.

Similar approaches have been developed in many states through the organization of regional educational service centers. These centers are not as directly involved in preparing instructional programs for handicapped children as the centers proposed by Moss. However, they do serve teachers of many exceptional children in a variety of ways. The centers provide expert consultant services by conducting in-service training sessions or by taking an in-service training program to the school. Many of these centers also have an instructional materials center from which teachers may borrow materials for a period of approximately two weeks. For school systems which cannot provide diagnostic services, the center provides personnel for the purpose of conducting evaluations and writing prescriptions for teachers to use. In addition, many of the centers loan films, filmstrips, videotapes, and records.

School systems help to support the centers by paying for services. The formula requires payments based upon the enrollment of the school system. These centers have been very effective in bringing programs and services to teachers where such programs may otherwise be very limited, if not impossible.

Diagnostic Procedures in the Classroom

The classroom teacher of exceptional children must become actively involved in the diagnostic-prescriptive program. It should be clearly understood that, at the present time, every teacher cannot expect to receive consistent services from a resource center such as those described above. Therefore, to enhance the learning of exceptional children, the teacher is obligated to learn as much as possible about classroom techniques for diagnosis and designing effective instructional programs. These procedures are by no means easy to learn or implement and special education teachers will find that their energies and talents are even more in demand to develop more appropriate individualized programs.

Smith (1969) developed an approach intended to help special education teachers understand their role in diagnosing and teaching the exceptional child. He developed five levels of diagnostic-remedial activity teachers can follow for identifying the nature of educational disorders in children. The first step involves assessing the child at a very early age to determine if there are any difficulties (physical problems, etc.) which are interfering with the learning process. After the child has been evaluated through step one, then evaluations should be made to determine the existing learning problems. If any weaknesses in learning are indicated by achievement tests, the teacher needs to probe further to determine if the weaknesses are evident in the child's classroom performances and if so, to what extent. Questions of particular importance in this step involve such areas as how the child approaches a particular learning task and what skills are being used to accomplish the task. The next important step is to analyze what may be the reasons for the learning problems. Do they involve difficulties in perceiving or in assimilating material? Is the instructional program properly sequenced? Conclusions reached from this analysis will be tentative, but will provide an objective means for the teacher to use in planning an appropriate program for the child. The last step involves the testing of the tentative conclusions reached through step four. Of course, the plan proposed by Smith is not intended to be a means of finalizing any instructional program provided for a child. The five steps require a consistent approach to evaluation and ongoing reevaluation of the instructional program. Through such a plan, the teacher can be the initial diagnostician and possibly the remediator of many problems children have.

Precision Teaching

A third trend in special education in the field of diagnostic-prescriptive work is precision teaching. Ogden R. Lindsley, Professor of Education at the University of Kansas, shaped and developed the idea in response to the needs of exceptional children as reported by their teachers.

In 1965, at the University of Kansas, he began the practice of collecting daily frequency records of students' performances to see if this information would be of help in monitoring instruction, evaluating curriculum, or teaching in special and regular classes. Based upon experiences in using precision teaching, Lindsley's group discovered that the frequencies of behaviors had to be recorded daily within the classroom setting. The recording of behaviors is done on a standard chart which has a six-cycle design for recording of an adequate range of behaviors which may occur once a day or as frequently as 1,000 times a minute. The use of a standard chart makes the recording more objective on the part of the teachers, facilitates the sharing of data with other teachers and administrators, and gives an ever-ready, ongoing report system to the parents (Lindsley 1971).

From the standard chart, through individualized planning, every child is given an individual curriculum. This system provides a more meaningful program for each child, which is intended to help accomplish instructional objectives and improve functioning. In addition, the child is involved in the process of selecting instructional materials, and behaviors are objectively recorded for the purpose of efficiently planning programs according to current needs. (Lindsley).

Inner behaviors as well as outer behaviors are recorded by the system of precision teaching. Attempts are made to record such behaviors as success thoughts, anxiety feelings, joy, love, and compassion. Although still in developmental stages, the use of precision teaching to record inner behaviors could have many profound implications for programs for exceptional children as well as for other programs (Lindsley).

The standard charts used in precision teaching may also be used with gifted children who are not challenged by the instructional program. The gifted child may be making all A's, but the program may not be adequately designed to motivate the child to put forth real effort in learning. The charts may be used to help determine special abilities in a single academic area and, therefore, to help plan a curriculum which is more appropriate to the child's abilities and present needs. Further development of precision teaching could be instrumental in helping educators to plan appropriate instructional programs, which for all practical purposes, could make better use of nongraded programs (Lindsley).

Precision teaching can be learned easily by the classroom teacher and can serve as a supplement to the program already being offered. Precision teaching can also help teachers determine changes more objectively by observing the child's improvement in appropriate behaviors and the elimination of inappropriate behaviors. Thus, special educators have another means to efficiently supplement and enhance teaching approaches and instructional materials (Lindsley).

Behavior Modification

Behavior modification has become an established approach in classrooms for exceptional children. Although it is established as an effective process for changing behaviors of both exceptional and normal children, many teachers attempt to use behavior modification procedures without really understanding what they are doing and without using the objective techniques which are so much a part of this method. One cannot study merely the surface aspects of behavior modification and then use the procedures effectively. The use of behavior modification requires considerable study on the part of the teacher, or any other person, in order to insure that appropriate changes are effected. If one does not grasp all of the factors of behavior modification, one may, in fact, be rewarding inappropriate behaviors without realizing it.

According to Ullmann and Krasner (1965), "Behavior modification is the application of the results of learning theory and experimental psychology to the problem of altering maladaptive behavior." In essence, this definition refers to the planned and systematic control of human behavior for the purpose of helping people become more functional, improve academic achievements, improve social relationships, and control behavior. According to the behavior modifier, all behavior is learned; therefore, through consistent and systematic procedures, old behavior may be unlearned and more appropriate behavior learned.

The use of behavior modification requires that the practitioner be objective. The focus is on observable behaviors, not on behaviors which may be "internal." One must objectively record a child's behavior, preferably with other observers also recording behavior, in order to test for reliability. Then, from the baseline record of the child's behavior, decide upon the use of behavior modification. In other words the behavior to be modified must be chosen by objective methods, not by a random sampling technique. The appropriate selection of reinforcement techniques also requires some time and effort on the part of the teacher. An excellent description of selecting reinforcement techniques is presented by Birnbrauer, Burchard, and Burchard (1970). This description can be easily followed by a classroom teacher.

The use of token reinforcement has become quite common in the modification of children's behaviors. This system has gained acceptance because it saves the teacher time in the appropriate dispensing of rewards. It is also

Ramps for swimming pools provide access to the child in a wheelchair.

effective in providing for immediate rewards and will also help young children learn to delay gratification. Several studies of the use of token reinforcement in behavior modification have been reported by Axelrod (1971).

An excellent review of studies which have involved behavior modification procedures has been prepared by Axelrod. These studies pertain to children who are severely mentally retarded, educable mentally retarded, emotionally disturbed, and learning disabled. The behaviors studied include academic and social behaviors, disruptive behaviors, and following instructions. For those who want a fairly comprehensive review of the current use and effectiveness of behavior modification, this is an excellent resource.

Behavior modification should not be viewed as a panacea for the learning problems of exceptional children. If used appropriately, this technique can definitely supplement the special education teacher's instructional program. The use of positive reinforcement for appropriate or desired behavior often has been interpreted as nothing more than using common sense. Certainly behavior modification is the use of common sense. However, if a teacher does not learn objectively how to observe, describe, record, measure, and shape behavior consistently and systematically, efforts in using this approach will, in all probability, be totally ineffective.

Many concerns about ethics of behavior modification have been expressed in the literature and also to us in person. Ethical considerations are important and must be taken into account when one is using this approach. The appropriate use of behavior modification is a very powerful technique for controlling human behavior. In the field of special education, behavior modification procedures can be effective in implementing appropriate objectives for children. Rather than viewing this technique as a method of indiscriminately controlling behavior, special educators must regard it as a

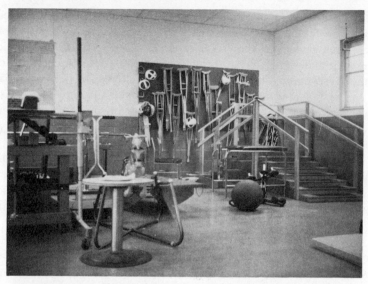

A large variety of materials are required for children with physical handicaps. (Courtesy of June Maddox, Children's Convalescent Center, Bethany, Oklahoma Public Schools.)

technique which will aid them in helping children to develop or improve behaviors which are essential in the process of learning and becoming more functional in everyday living.

This text cannot devote excessive space to the area of behavior modification. Any person using this text in a teacher training course may certainly expand upon the material presented here. A few years ago there were very few references in the professional literature to behavior modification. Today, one may find references in the professional journals dealing with exceptional children. There is also a journal devoted exclusively to the field of behavior modification *(Journal of Applied Behavior Analysis)*. These references as well as several books on the market will provide sufficient information for any interested student. Certainly this technique will continue to grow in emphasis and application.

Physical Education and Motor Development

There is a trend in special education to include physical education and motor development in the curriculum for all types of handicapped children. Perhaps these two areas should be presented as separate programs. However, we have decided to cover them together as related fields of development in the classroom program for handicapped children.

The increased emphasis on physical education for the handicapped has existed for some time. The federal government has encouraged this emphasis by sponsoring workshops and programs which have demonstrated particular techniques and designed physical fitness programs for the exceptional child. In addition, several pamphlets have been published on various essential aspects in the planning of a program. Although an increased emphasis in physical education has been in existence, the majority of teacher training programs have not provided enough preparation in this area for the physical education teacher or the special education teacher.

Musgrove (1971) said the problem can be solved by an interdisciplinary approach involving the special education teacher and the physical education teacher. The teamwork approach would be employed in a public school setting by providing instruction in the special class and then applying the skills learned through activities in the gymnasium.

Physical education activities are a must for the majority of exceptional children, many of whom have been overprotected at home for various reasons or have not had the opportunity to play and develop an interest in physical education. Children who have spent their formative years in the inner city or the ghetto areas are particularly less likely to have had meaningful experiences in play activities, or in activities which may be considered developmental physical education. These are the primary reasons why children who are mildly retarded, learning disabled, emotionally disturbed, or even physically disabled need physical education activities from the elementary through the secondary school years. Many of these children will obtain employment during young adulthood and will need particular physical skills in order to perform effectively. Teachers must, therefore, provide appropriate experience in physical education for handicapped children through the development of teamwork (Musgrove).

Many attitudes can be enhanced by involving exceptional children in physical education activities. Perhaps for the first time, in some of their lives, these children may be taught concepts such as taking their turn, working cooperatively with others, learning the basic application of various rules and why rules are important in play activities. In addition, these activities may enable some handicapped children to become actively involved in an experience which has concrete meaning. A teacher should be able to analyze many different physical education activities and provide ways in which the "academic" program can come alive for the children. For example, many games readily lend themselves to the development and use of number skills and the use of sequencing with respect to the various activities in a classroom. Sequencing may be included as the teacher helps children to emphasize the first step, the second step, the third step, and so on in the playing of a particular type of game. In some instances, appropriate physical education activities can supplement activities the teacher may plan for the development of rhythm and enhancement of body awareness. Many of these activities will help to promote appropriate attitudes for classroom behaviors and may even be extended to help the child develop appropriate behaviors for adult functioning (Musgrove).

During the past few years, physical education activities for exceptional children have become an essential feature of the total program. Special education teachers often need help in planning and implementing these activities. However, the physical education instructor should not be expected to provide the program alone. Special education teachers should know their children well enough to make decisions regarding activities which may be too demanding either physically or mentally. For example, a game with rules which are too numerous or too complicated may be entirely above the mental abilities of the average mildly mentally retarded child. For the child with learning disabilities, the activity may require motor skills which are too detailed or too refined for the present stage of development. The games or activities should not be so simple that children are not motivated to participate or unchallenged with the tasks, but certainly there should be activities in which the children can be successful. The academic program may have consistently presented nothing but frustration and failure for the exceptional child, and physical education should not add to the learning problems or self-concept problems that the exceptional child may already have.

Motor skills are somewhat different from physical education activities. Both are instrumental in the development of skills of coordination, but they do differ. Physical education activities may focus on gross motor coordination, while motor skill training may involve fine motor coordination which includes a variety of areas.

Training in motor skills should never be viewed as absolutely mandatory for every child. The teacher should also be aware that training in motor skills will not necessarily improve the child's functioning in any other area of development. Appropriate training to help children develop motor skills, or improve some area of functioning such as visual perception, take considerable time on the part of the teacher in the planning process, as well as in the conducting of the program. On several occasions we have seen teachers attempting to use a motor skill training program with a group of thirty to forty children in one setting. There were so many children involved that the teacher could not possibly determine the extent to which the *individual child* was appropriately performing the task or learning from the experience. For a school administrator or a director of special education to order special education teachers to have motor development exercises as a daily part of the curriculum is also unnecessary. This may cause teachers to put together rapidly a motor development exercise lacking in the objectives or structure that would enable children to benefit from the experience.

Educators should be familiar with the extensive work of Kephart, Getman, Cratty, and others like them, who have prepared testing materials and motor development exercises for children. These professionals have also contributed much to our understanding of the importance of movement and the development of body and motor awareness. A good example of the importance of motor development training is commented upon by Cratty, who indicated that motor development exercises which do not require thought may help the child to increase physical strength, but will not help to develop an awareness of the body and how the body relates to space (Cratty 1967).

A good program in motor development will include visual-motor development, the development of body awareness, the systematic exploration of various concrete objects, movement of the body through a variety of situations, and orientation skills. As classroom teachers develop programs designed to help exceptional children develop motor skills, they must plan for specific objectives and include activities that accomplish these objectives, just as they do in the academic programs. Motor development training must be taken seriously if it is to have significance for the children.

The Talented Among Minority Children

Rather than automatically and erroneously assuming that children of disadvantaged or minority groups have limited learning potentials, there is a trend toward discovering and implementing techniques which would identify minority group children who are talented. Much of this effort is focused on obtaining more positive information regarding cultural aspects of minority groups and making adaptations or modifications of teaching and curricular approaches.

Compensatory education programs have been in existence for some time, and the results have been quite promising. Educators and researchers have discovered positive information regarding the learning styles of culturally diverse children. In many cases, techniques and approaches have been developed which enhance their learning. According to White (1971), these techniques include the following: providing concrete applications of material learned, using listening centers, using many audiovisual materials, and making colorful presentations. The primary consideration which White mentions is that this is the beginning of the teaching approach; it should progress gradually to more abstract learning such as problem solving. Although many programs within the total Head Start, Follow Through, and other compensatory education programs have been successful, relatively few educational modifications have actually been implemented which capitalize on the learning strengths and potential talents of culturally diverse children.

A review of studies which focus on searching for the talented among minority groups indicates that the majority of programs for these children are remedial. However, this review also presents pertinent information from many researchers which indicates that the primary deficiencies in schools which serve minority groups are in teaching and curricular modifications (Renzulli 1973).

Early intervention programs are a must for preschool handicapped and culturally diverse children.

Renzulli discusses several assessment procedures developed for the purpose of exploring talents other than academic talent. These instruments are appropriate for use with minority or disadvantaged children and include such instruments as the *Torrance Tests of Creative Thinking* (Torrance 1966) and the *Sub-Cultural Indices of Academic Potential* (Grant and Renzulli 1971). Through the use of such instruments, as well as others mentioned by Renzulli, educators may become more aware of the talents of culturally diverse children and, as a result, begin to plan and implement more effective teaching and curricular modifications.

In conclusion, it seems very appropriate to give further consideration to this area, which should become a primary focus for many educators, by discussing preschool programs for handicapped children. Early education programs are essential for the majority of culturally diverse children. Through the continued development of preschool programs which include parent involvement and training, and a search for talent among these children, the status of culturally diverse children may be improved considerably.

Preschool Programs for the Handicapped

The Handicapped Children's Early Education Assistance Act (1968) provided for the development of model preschool and early education programs for handicapped children. In 1969, twenty-four organizations received a total of about $1 million in U.S. Office of Education grants to establish model preschool and early education projects for handicapped children. At that time, Edwin W. Martin Jr., Acting Associate Commissioner, Bureau of Education for the Handicapped noted:

For the first time, these children will have an opportunity to begin the process of becoming responsible citizens in a society that is assuming responsibility at an increasing rate for all its children—including the handicapped. More than half of the children can have their handicapping conditions lessened—or in many cases, prevented—if they receive appropriate educational and related services at an early age. The challenge is here and the education community must respond. ("Breakthrough. . ." 1970)

As a result of financial assistance through federal legislation, many school systems and university programs have begun to emphasize early childhood education for the handicapped. In view of the importance of early experience in the development of a child, particularly a handicapped child, it seems that early education for handicapped children can and will provide programs that will change the lives of a great many children. Education of the preschool handicapped child must focus on structure and have specific objectives which will lead toward cognitive development. One of the primary difficulties of many handicapped children is that they have not learned how to learn. Thus, the preschool program must provide structured environments and activities if the objective of increased functioning is to be met. In the majority of situations a structured approach will emphasize language development and preparation for later learning. Many examples could be cited; however, the study of Karnes, Hodgins, and Teska (1968) will serve. They report that handicapped children who were taught language development through a structured approach had greater gains in language functioning and cognitive development than those who were involved in more traditional preschool programs.

Realizing that a structural approach, a language development approach, a cognitive development approach or combination of all of these approaches is essential to preschool programs for handicapped children, perhaps our emphasis should turn toward a pressing need beyond preschool programs. How will elementary school programs need to be structured in order to maintain gains in the development of handicapped children? Improving the functioning of the preschool handicapped child is, of course, a very significant achievement. However, the development of programs beyond the preschool level, which will maintain improvements and enhance further development, is a goal which educators must point toward immediately.

Guidelines for the identification of preschool handicapped children are presently not well established. Out of forty-four states responding to a survey conducted by Lessen and Rose (1980), there were seven with specific definitions, nineteen with no present guidelines other than PL 94–142, fourteen using existing categorical definitions, and four using miscellaneous criteria. There were variations as well in the ages of children for whom services were available. The age ranges were from birth to six years, three to five years, below twenty-one years, and age ranges left to the discretion of the local school district. As indicated in this survey, more efforts must be made to establish acceptable definitions and program guidelines and objectives for the preschool handicapped.

Children from birth to three years of age were not included in PL 94–142, which is an interesting omission since the law is titled "Education for All Handicapped Children Act." Hayden (1979) presented evidence concerning the need for early intervention programs by quoting McDaniels, who stated that programs for the preschool handicapped should begin at one year of age and that age three was too late for intervention. Using 1977 U.S. population estimates, which indicated that there were 9,626,000 children from the ages of zero to three, there would be 1,636,420 handicapped children (using a 17 percent incidence estimate) in that population. Of that number, approximately 25 percent were receiving services. Certainly one should hope that there will be a decrease in handicapping conditions from zero to three years of age during the 1980s, and that a larger percentage will be receiving services. However, there is a tendency for handicapping conditions to be increasing among this population group partially because of family disintegration, child abuse, accidents, lack of immunization, and lack of public awareness. For example, Hayden reported that there were 1.8 million mothers in 1977 who admitted leaving their preschool age children at home alone while they were at work. Use your imagination to consider the effects of this practice on intellectual, social, and emotional development. Hayden commented on our lack of concern and programs by stating:

A basic problem is that children's needs do not fit our budget. Do we really want to know just how good or how bad a job we are doing or do we want to continue to offer excuses and raise questions that detract attention from our piecemeal, too-little-too-late, penny-wise-and-pound-foolish, exclude-rather-than-include approach to solving these problems? (Hayden 1979)

The need for preschool programs for the handicapped from birth to age three is very evident; many problems could be solved during this time, and others could be prevented. Intervention has shown that preschool handicapped children do profit from early education programs. There are many efforts being made to improve the situation through such programs as the Handicapped Children's Early Education Programs network funded by the Office of Special Education. This funding is considered to be seed money in that initial grants are awarded with the contingency that the recipients will set goals for obtaining other funding after three to five years. In 1969–70, there were 23 programs funded and there were 214 grants in 1978–79. Of the original 23 programs funded, 18 (86 percent) were still in operation seven years after the first funding and were obtaining their funds from private sources, universities, local education agencies, and medical centers. This information suggests under specific sets of conditions, seed money can be effective in establishing on-going programs (Swan 1980). In addition, four states have mandated provisions for the birth onward population, model programs are being developed, and there has been a world-wide growth in concern for infants. Contributions from many different disciplines are increasing our knowledge of early infancy. Efforts thus far, however, are only a beginning (Hayden).

As indicated earlier, preschool programs for the handicapped are not fully mandated by PL 94–142, because of the section which states that if an existing state law or practice prohibits providing school services to handicapped or nonhandicapped children from age three to five, then services do not have to be provided. PL 94–142 does provide an incentive grant for preschool handicapped children and authorizes $300 per child per year for school services. However, in 1979 the appropriation amounted to only $75 per child (Cohen, Semmes, Guralnick 1979).

Preschool handicapped children are receiving services through the Handicapped Children's Early Assistance Act (PL 90–538), mentioned previously, the Education Amendments of 1974 (PL 93–380), and the Head Start, Economic Opportunity, and Community Partnership Act of 1974 (PL 93–644). These acts require that school services be provided, but no time lines are required as they were for the older age ranges. In Head Start programs, 10 percent of the funds received must be allocated for preschool handicapped children (Cohen, Semmes, Guralnick).

The four acts mentioned above have resulted in growth in programs and services. As of 1978, thirteen states had mandated educational services for preschool handicapped children (ages three to five) but all of them are not receiving services (Cohen, Semmes, Guralnick). Many children in the age range of birth to five are still unserved because families don't qualify for Head Start programs, states haven't been required to provide time lines for providing services, and states have not mandated the services.

State Implementation Grants from the Office of Special Education are another source of funds for implementing comprehensive planning for services for preschool handicapped children. In 1978–79, twenty-three states received funds through this grant program. The grants are for a two-year cycle and are in addition to the Preschool Incentive Grants provided through PL 94–142 (Carter et al. 1980).

The State Implementation Grants do not provide direct services to children but assist states in the development of state-wide programs for the preschool handicapped. The areas of concern for developing comprehensive programs for these children include the following:

1. System development—delivery systems
2. Needs assessment—census, curriculum, personnel needs
3. Planning—goals and objectives
4. Program management—policies, procedures, and evaluation
5. Coordination of resources—interagency agreements
6. Personnel training—inservice activities
7. Parent involvement—parent contributions and training

Illinois has combined its State Implementation Grant and the Preschool Incentive Grant for the development of a delivery system and the provision of services to the preschool handicapped. Preschool programs for the handicapped down to age three are mandated in Illinois. The mandate and combination of the two grants have provided services to over 20,000 preschool handicapped children, the screening of vision and hearing for children from three to five, a study of the transition practices from the preschool programs to kindergarten and lower elementary school programs, parental involvement, and the total service delivery system. Illinois is no doubt a leader in this area (Carter et al.).

Questions which should be considered in the total field of education in relation to this problem include: To what extent must the educational program during the early elementary school years be changed to further enhance the development of handicapped children? How can teachers in the field or in training receive information about the program a preschool handicapped child has had and the effects of this program? If a highly structured approach were provided similar to that of Bereiter and Englemann, will the structure need to be continued during the early elementary years and, if so, to what extent? If a preschool program has helped a handicapped child increase skills in language development, how can the need for further development be communicated? How can the first-grade teacher be assisted in the selection of appropriate approaches and materials to enhance this development? Based upon past experiences in attempting to reintegrate handicapped children into regular education, what problems, if any, will we meet when those who have "graduated" from preschool programs attempt to reenter the regular education program? It seems that in-service training of school administrators and regular teachers is essential if concern for the preschool handicapped child is going to be felt throughout the school community. The prevention of "wash out" effects of the efforts of preschool programs for handicapped children seems to also be a matter for considerable concern.

In summary, our concern is that preschool programs for handicapped children should have significant effects on the development of appropriate changes in the existing instructional programs of elementary schools. If the early childhood education programs are to be successful over a period of years, the personnel of these programs must become influential in bringing about changes within programs to which the handicapped child will be assigned during the elementary school years.

Special education has progressed through many changes in recent years. New changes will develop as more information is obtained about effective program modifications for exceptional children. The job of developing and improving special education programs should never become stagnant or static. There are many challenges with which all special educators will be confronted, and the new special educator must become a vital part of this process. Changes in philosophical approaches and educational programs are necessary, not for the sake of change, but to improve services for individuals.

Predictions regarding the future of special education have been made by many professionals. Perhaps one of the best discussions of this topic focuses on predictions about the year 2000 and special education. In this discussion Leo Connor indicated the following:

For special education all of this should add up to a greater struggle for mastery of its own world—but with more effective weapons, greater satisfaction, more tangible gains, better instruction, more effective evaluations, tighter teamwork, saner diagnoses, perceptive teachers, insightful supervisors, decisive administrators, revolutionizing researchers, and exhilarating professors. Literally, I mean that the seeding and tilling will be more difficult but the harvesting should be more bountiful and satisfactory. (Connor 1968)

Study Questions
1. How do current services and trends in special education affect the role of regular classroom teachers?
2. Contact a local school district and briefly report on the evaluation procedures used for determining the effects of mainstreaming on children, teachers, and parents.
3. How can a resource center assist a regular class teacher in the instruction of an exceptional child?
4. What are the five levels of diagnostic remedial activity as proposed by Smith?
5. Through library research, prepare brief paragraphs on at least five techniques used in behavior modification.
6. In using behavior modification, what would be the teacher's primary areas of focus?

7. Describe your personal concept of mainstreaming.
8. Contact your state education agency and report on your findings regarding your state's program for preschool handicapped children. Include guidelines for assessment, program development, and age ranges served.
9. As a regular or special class teacher, briefly describe how you believe mainstreaming will affect you in the classroom.
10. Why should we emphasize preschool programs for the handicapped?
11. Describe an adaptive physical education program which would be appropriate for one or more types of handicapped children.
12. Why should compensatory education programs exist for talented minority children?

Bibliography

Axelrod, S. 1971. "Token Reinforcement in Special Classes." *Exceptional Children* 37, no. 5 (January).

Bereiter, Carl, and Englemann, Siegfried. 1966. *Teaching Disadvantaged Children in the Preschool.* Englewood Cliffs, N.J.: Prentice-Hall.

Birnbrauer, J. S.; Burchard, John D.; and Burchard, Sara N. 1970. "Wanted: Behavior Analysts." In *Behavior Modification: The Human Effort,* ed. Robert H. Bradfield. San Rafael, Calif.: Dimensions Publishing Co.

Blatt, Burton. 1976. "Mainstreaming: Does It Matter?" *The Exceptional Parent* 6, no. 1 (February).

"Breakthrough in Early Education of Handicapped Children." 1970. *American Education* 6, no. 1 (January-February).

Carter, Julie Anne; Imhoff, Charlene; Lacoste, Ronald; McNulty, Brian; and Peterson, Pamela. 1980. "The Implementation of Statewide Early Education Plans: A Two-Year Report." *Education and Training of the Mentally Retarded* 15, no. 1 (February).

Clark, Gary M. 1975. "Mainstreaming for the Secondary Educable Mentally Retarded: Is It Defensible?" *Focus on Exceptional Children* 7, no. 2.

Cohen, Shirley; Semmes, Marilyn; and Guralnick, Michael J. 1979. "Public Law 94-142 and the Education of Preschool Handicapped Children." *Exceptional Children* 45, no. 4 (January).

Connor, Leo E. 1968. "Reflections on the Year 2000." *Exceptional Children* 34, no. 10 (Summer).

Cormany, R. B. 1970. "Returning Special Education Students to Regular Classes." *Personnel and Guidance Journal* 48, no. 8 (April).

Cratty, B. J. 1967. *Movement Behavior and Motor Learning.* Philadelphia: Lea and Febiger.

Ensher, Gail L. 1976. "Mainstreaming: Yes." *The Exceptional Parent* 6, no. 1 (February).

Grant T. E., and Renzulli, J. S. 1971. *Sub-Cultural Indices of Academic Potential.* Storrs, Conn.: University of Connecticut.

Hayden, Alice. 1979. "Handicapped Children, Birth to Age 3." *Exceptional Children* 45, no. 7 (April).

Karnes M.; Hodgins, A.; and Teska, J. 1968. "An Evaluation of Two Preschool Programs for Disadvantaged Children: A Traditional and a Highly Structured Experimental Preschool." *Exceptional Children* 34, no. 9 (May).

Lessen, Elliott I., and Rose, Terry L. 1980. "State Definitions of Preschool Handicapped Populations." *Exceptional Children* 46, no. 6 (March).

Lindsley, Ogden R. 1971. "Precision Teaching in Perspective: An Interview with Ogden R. Lindsley." *Teaching Exceptional Children* 3, no. 3 (Spring).

Martin, Edwin W. 1972. "Individualism and Behaviorism as Future Trends in Educating Handicapped Children." *Exceptional Children* 38, no. 7 (March).

Moss, J. W. 1971. "Resource Centers for Teachers of Handicapped Children." *Journal of Special Education* 5, no. 1 (Winter-Spring).

Musgrove, D. G. 1971. "Physical Education and Recreation for the Handicapped—An Interdisciplinary Approach." *Contemporary Education* 42, no. 3 (January).

"Official Actions of the Delegate Assembly at the 54th Annual International Convention." 1976. *Exceptional Children* 43 no. 1 (September).

Renzulli, Joseph S. 1973. "Talent Potential in Minority Group Students." *Exceptional Children* 39, no. 6 (March).

Shanker, Albert. 1980. "Public Law 94–142: Prospects and Problems." *The Exceptional Parent* 10, no. 4 (August).

Smith, Robert M. 1969. "Collecting Diagnostic Data in the Classroom." *Teaching Exceptional Children* 1, no. 4 (Summer).

Special Education Newsletter 15, no. 1 (September) 1976. National Catholic Educational Association.

Swan, William W. 1980. "The Handicapped Children's Early Education Program." *Exceptional Children* 47, no. 1 (September).

Torrance, E. P. 1966. *Torrance Tests of Creative Thinking: Norms-Technical Manual.* Princeton, N.J.: Personnel Press.

Ullman, Leonard P., and Krasner, Leonard, eds. 1965. *Case Studies in Behavior Modification.* New York: Holt, Rinehart & Winston.

White, William F. 1971. *Tactics for Teaching the Disadvantaged.* New York: McGraw-Hill.

Yates, James R. 1973. "Model for Preparing Regular Classroom Teachers for 'Mainstreaming.' " *Exceptional Children* 39, no. 6 (March).

appendix a testing

Minimum Testing Guidelines

Testing and the dependence upon certain tests for placing exceptional children appear to become more controversial each year. Test use and misuse has and will remain. We, affirm, though, that there should be a baseline before one can adequately provide services. Many variables must be considered relative to the intent of each child's testing. There should be consideration for and mutual understanding of the child's needs among teachers, parents, and psychologists when testing information is shared.

Considerable attention has been directed toward the pro's and con's of IQ testing. Mandated school provisions for all exceptional children will involve even more dissent about testing procedures. The reader must understand that IQ testing is not a solitary means of evaluation. IQ tests must be used with other tests. A child should not be placed in a special program on the basis of one IQ test. Therefore, we offer the following testing guidelines as a minimum protocol for special class placement or referral for additional testing. If the examiner detects information that may indicate hearing, sight, physical, emotional, or speech problems; learning disabilities or mental retardation, the child should be referred, through the administrative procedures of the school, for either additional testing or for a staffing as prescribed by law to determine appropriate class placement.

The following abbreviations are commonly used by psychologists and other examiners in test write-ups. Personnel who work with students from ages three to twenty-one should become familiar with these terms.

IQ	Intelligence Quotient
PQ	Perceptual Quotient
DQ	Development Quotient
DAP	Draw-A-Person Test
PPVT	Peabody Picture Vocabulary Test
VAKT	Visual-Auditory-Kinesthetic-Tactile
Vis. Dis.	Visual Discrimination
Aud. Dis.	Auditory Discrimination
ITPA	Illinois Test of Psycholinguistic Abilities
WISC-R	Wechsler Intelligence Scale for Children—Revised
WAIS	Wechsler Adult Intelligence Scale
WPPSI	Wechsler Preschool & Primary Scale of Intelligence

Binet	Stanford-Binet Form L-M IQ Test
Zero or Ceiling Age	Binet—Level at which all items were not passed
Basal Age	Binet—level at which all items passed
LA	Learning Aptitude
MA	Mental Age
CA	Chronological Age
GE	Grade Equivalent
MMPI	Minnesota Multiphasic Personality Inventory
16-PF	Sixteen Factor Personality Test
H-T-P	House-Tree-Person Test
T.A.T.	Thematic Apperception Test
C.A.T.	Children's Apperception Test
WRAT	Wide Range Achievement Test
CTMM	California Test for Mental Maturity
CAT	California Achievement Test
SIT	Slosson Intelligence Test
PMA	Primary Mental Ability Test
db	Decibel—hearing measurement
Hz	Hertz—hearing measurement
fq	Frequency range—hearing measurement
P.T.A.	Pure Tone Average—hearing measurement
S.R.T.	Speech Reception Threshold—hearing measurement
20/20	Visual Acuity Measurement
SMR	Severely Mentally Retarded
PMR	Profoundly Mentally Retarded
MR	Mentally Retarded
TMR	Trainable Mentally Retarded
EMR	Educable Mentally Retarded
EMH	Educable Mentally Handicapped
TMH	Trainable Mentally Handicapped
L.D.	Learning Disabilities
E.D.	Emotionally Disturbed
P.S.	Partially Sighted
H.H.	Hard of Hearing
P.H.	Physically Handicapped
C.P.	Cerebral Palsy
M.H.	Multiple Handicapped
M.B.D.	Minimal Brain Dysfunction

Basic Preschool Testing Protocol

IQ Tests

WISC-R/WPPSI	or	Binet
SIT	and/or	CTMM
PPVT		Draw-a-Person

Perceptual Tests

ITPA	and/or	Frostig (Vis. Discrim.)
Wepman (Aud. Discrim.)	and/or	Purdue Perceptual Motor Survey

Achievements

Peabody Individual Achievement Test	and/or	Wide Range Achievement Test

Social Adaptive and Developmental Behavior Tests

Denver Developmental	or	Burks' Behavior Rating Scales (Preschool)
Preschool Attainment Record	and/or	Vineland Social Maturity Scale
Burks' Academic Readiness		

Basic Elementary Testing Protocol

IQ

Binet	or	WISC-R
SIT	and/or	CTMM
Draw-a-Person	and/or	PPVT

Perceptual Tests

Purdue Perceptual Motor	or	ITPA

and/or

Bender-Gestalt	Burks' Behavior Rating Scale for Organic Dysfunction	Frostig	Wepman Auditory Discrimination	Memory for Design

Achievement Tests

Peabody Individual Achievement Test	and/or	WRAT

Social Adaptive Behavior Tests

Burks' Behavior Rating Scales	and	House-Tree-Person

Basic Elementary and Adolescent Testing Protocol

IQ Tests

Binet	or	WISC-R or WAIS
Draw-a-Person	and/or	PPVT
		SIT

Purdue Perceptual-Motor   or   Hiskey-Nebraska
Survey

and/or

Bender-Gestalt Memory for Design Burks'   Wepman   Others
Behavior   Auditory
Rating   Discrimination
Scale for
Organic
Dysfunction

Achievement Tests
WRAT

Social Adaptive Behavior Tests
Burks' Behavior Rating   and   House-Tree-Person
Scale
"16" Factor Personality   and/or   Guilford/Zimmerman
Temperament
Survey

The choice of which battery to administer depends on three major factors.

1. Basic areas for evaluation for planning remediation
2. Child's level of energy
3. Amount of time for testing

Intelligence Tests
I. *WISC-R—Wechsler Intelligence Scale for Children—Revised*
WAIS—Wechsler Adult Intelligence Scale—16 C.A. and over
Scores: Verbal IQ; Performance IQ; Full Scale IQ
Subtests: six (6) verbal; five (5) performance
A. *Verbal Subtests:* Wechsler
1. *Information*—designed to find limits of child's general information
a. This is considered to be information acquired in "non-teaching" situations, although much of it could be learned in school.
b. Reflects cultural level of home life. Reflects conversational level of home life.
(1) This information would be imparted through conversation and natural interaction of children with parents or others in their environment.
c. One's general information is considered to be closely related to one's total IQ.

2. *Comprehension*
   a. Tests common sense.
   b. Success depends on a certain amount of practical information and general ability to apply and evaluate past experiences.
   c. Valuable in detecting emotional instability.
      (1) Bizarre responses to social situations, etc.
   d. Reflects something about the social and cultural background.
3. *Arithmetic Test*—deals with a child's ability to solve math problems.
   a. No pencil and paper are permitted, although the child uses fingers or whatever for counting.
      (1) Use procedure should be noted, because it will show need for concrete materials in this area.
      (2) Indicates child's ability to handle abstractions and to what degree.
      (3) Indicates ability to organize.
   b. Math aptitude is indicative of mental alertness; children who do poorly on this test often have problems with other subjects. This test is valuable in the evaluation of educational abilities, particularly when considered with information score.
   c. Information—math scores frequently are accurate estimates of child's scholastic achievement.
   d. Problems on this test may also be due to anxiety level.
4. *Digit Span*
   a. One of the least effective tests.
   b. A good rote memory may be practical in many instances, but it is not necessarily an integral part of global intelligence.
5. *Similarities*—a kind of general intelligence test in which responses indicate logical thinking processes.
   a. One of the best indicators of general intelligence when considered with vocabulary.
   b. Shows ability to categorize and analyze quickly; although untimed, the test does not dwell unnecessarily on these items.
6. *Vocabulary*—a good measure of intelligence.
   a. Evaluates learning ability, verbal resources, and general range of ideas through the number of words known.
   b. A brain-damaged person will often retain words that reflect a past level of performance, but not actual functioning ability.
   c. The vocabulary test can also estimate the extent of a child's mental deterioration.

B. *Performance Subtests*
   1. *Picture Completion*—identifies missing part of picture.
      a. Particularly good for determining intelligence at lower levels.
      b. Measures basic perceptual and conceptual ability as these relate to visual recognition and identification of familiar objects and forms.
         (1) In a broader sense it also indicates the ability to distinguish essential from nonessential detail.
      c. This test has been found to have the highest general intelligence loading of any of the performance tests.
   2. *Picture Arrangement Test*
      a. A series of pictures which, when put in correct sequence, tell a story.
      b. Measures "social intelligence," ability to comprehend and reconstruct sequence in fairly common social situations.
      c. Persons doing well on this test are usually of average or above average intelligence even though they do poorly on other tests.
   3. *Block Design*—ability to perceive and analyze forms and patterns—an excellent test of general intelligence.
      a. Lends itself to qualitative analysis.
         (1) Examiner observes *how* the child approaches the task and may as a result tell if, and how, the child has a problem.
      b. Brain-damaged persons have particular difficulty with this test, and with repeated efforts cannot complete the designs.
   4. *Object Assembly*—little correlation with general intelligence.
      a. Its contribution to the total score is mainly qualitative.
         (1) by observing the person the examiner can have some idea concerning the thinking and working habits.
      b. Three (3) factors also relate:
         (1) spatial orientation
         (2) visualization
         (3) figural selection
   5. *Coding*—matching and reproducing symbols.
      a. Most consistent loadings in nonverbal organization and memory.
      b. The speed and accuracy of performance are of primary importance on this test.
      c. Children with reading problems may be handicapped as they respond slowly.
      d. Unstable persons may also do poorly.
II. *PPVI (Peabody Picture Vocabulary Test*—Untimed (average time, however, is 15–20 minutes)
   A. Provides rapid and objective scoring for conversion into MA, IQ, and percentiles.
   B. Measures receptive (hearing) vocabulary and "verbal IQ."
   C. Correlates best with WISC scores for children in high 70s and low 80s.

D. May be used with a child's level of understanding of abstract terms with visual clues—many children may score low on vocabulary portions of WISC or Binet but their "understanding" vocabulary may be demonstrated as higher by using PPVT.

III. *Goodenough-Harris Drawing Test (DAP)*
  A. A good test of conditioned or learning responses.
  B. Procedure: Child draws a person on 8½ × 11 plain paper
  C. Scoring: Details of drawing determine age (MA); from the MA the IQ may be determined
  D. Children with L.D.—particularly reading problems—have problems with the DAP Test
     1. We don't know if this is because of problems of self-concept, revisualization, or the inability to organize a complex structure.

Perceptual Tests

I. *Illinois Test of Psycholinguistic Abilities (ITPA)*—for children under ten (10) years of age.
  A. To detect specific language abilities and disabilities.
  B. The design originated from Hull's formulations coupled with Osgood's psycholinguistic model.
  C. Psycholinguistic ability is measured in three (3) dimensions:
     1. Levels of organization.
     2. Psycholinguistic processes.
     3. Channels of communication.
  D. Levels of organization—functional complexity of the organism.
     1. Varying levels required for various activities.
     2. Two (2) levels are important for language acquisition.
        a. Representational level—activities that require the meaning or significance of linguistic symbols.
           (1) Tests:
               (a) auditory reception (auditory decoding)
               (b) visual reception (visual decoding)
               (c) associational (auditory-vocal association and visual motor association)
               (d) expression—(verbal expression = vocal encoding) (manual expression = motor encoding)
        b. Automatic-sequential level—activities that require the retention of linguistic symbol sequences and the execution of the automatic habits chain.
        b. Automatic-sequential level tests used:
           (1) Automatic
               (a) grammatic closure (auditory-vocal automatic)
               (b) visual closure

(2) Sequential
    (a) auditory memory (auditory-vocal sequencing = digit span)
    (b) visual memory (visual-motor sequencing)
E. *Psycholinguistic Processes* specifies the acquisition and use of all the habits necessary for normal language usage. There are three (3) main sets of habits:
  1. *Reception*—understanding through visual or auditory linguistic symbols or stimuli.
  2. *Association*—manipulating linguistic symbols internally; tests are word association tests, analogies tests, and similarities and differences tests.
  3. *Expression*—expressing oneself in words or gestures.
F. *Channels of Communications*—the sensory-motor path by which linguistic symbols are transmitted, received, and responded to.
  1. The ITPA is divided into two (2) parts:* Reception and Response.
    a. Pure receptive ability requires only a mode of reception = hearing or sight; how the subject responds has no relevancy in receptive tests.
    b. Pure expressive ability requires only a mode of response—speech, gesture.
    c. Associative ability, or any combination of abilities, requires the *interaction* of all the channels of communication.

II. *Purdue Perceptual-Motor Survey*
A. *Not a test*—A survey which allows the examiner to observe a broad spectrum of behavior within a structured situation.
B. *Purpose*—to detect (not diagnose) perceptual-motor development as observed on a series of behavioral performances. Designed for children in grades 2–4, but may be used with MR's; norms were established on children between ages six to ten years.
C. Easy to administer; little or no equipment.
D. *Description:* twenty-two items; divided into eleven subtests measuring motor development. Primary concern: laterality, directionality, and skills of perceptual-motor matching.
E. *Use*
  1. Discovers weak areas that may not be tapped through tests of linguistic ability.
  2. Used primarily to indicate areas for tutorial needs, including remediation using physical education programs and academic tutoring.

*There are nine (9) subtests of psycholinguistic ability. Primarily, these tests are used to determine deficiencies and to direct planning or remediation. By indicating *abilities and disabilities* a psycholinguistic profile should lead to program planning utilizing the child's assets in overcoming areas of deficiency.

III. *Marianne Frostig Developmental Test of Visual Perception*
   A. Areas measured—Five specific areas:
      1. Eye-motor coordination
      2. Figure-ground discrimination
      3. Form constancy
      4. Position in space
      5. Spatial relations
   B. Use: intended primarily for preschoolers, but the test may be used very effectively in helping detect specific areas of visual perception weaknesses in first and second graders.
   C. Frostig has a sequential remediation program based on this diagnostic instrument.
IV. *Wepman Auditory Discrimination Test*
   A. Used for identification at early elementary level of children who are slow to develop auditory discrimination.
   B. Makes a differential diagnosis of reading and speech difficulties in older children.
V. *Hiskey-Nebraska*—for children *over* age ten (10)
   A. A test of learning aptitude designed to evaluate the learning ability of deaf children. The revised test was expanded to cover age norms for the hearing as well.
   B. It was standardized with children ranging in age from two years six months to seventeen years five months. The Hiskey has tests for psycholinguistic abilities. Since norms are established on children above ten years—which is the maximum age range of the ITPA—this test supplements the battery on evaluating linguistic weaknesses of older children. The subtests below are given to children ranging in age from three (3) years to ten (10) years.
      1. *Bead Pattern*—visual memory and visual memory for designs.
      2. *Memory for Color*—visual memory and memory for visual pattern.
      3. *Picture Identification*—perception and visual discrimination.
      4. *Picture Association*—conceptual ability to see similarities between different visual stimuli.
      5. *Paper Folding*—a visual motor ability which also involves sequencing.
   C. When used in conjunction with such tests as the WISC and the Binet, these subtests are practical for discovering L.D. These are administered to children of all ages:
      1. **Visual attention span*—sequence picture objects (similar to visual memory on ITPA).
      2. *Block Patterns*—perceptual organization; depth perceptional spatial relationships.
      3. **Completion of Drawings*—visual closure; detail analysis.
      4. *Memory for Digits*—memory for sequencing visual digits.

*These subtests are used more often.

5. *Puzzle Blocks*—perceptual organization and spatial relationship.
6. **Picture Analogies*—similar to visual association on ITPA. Measures ability to see relationships between different visual stimuli.
7. **Spatial Reasoning*—similar to spatial relationship on Frostig.

D. For children over age ten (10) the Hiskey-Nebraska subtests—especially the picture analogies, spatial reasoning, visual attention spans, and completion of drawings—may confirm the seriousness of visual motor dysfunction suggested by a low WISC coding or other low performance scores. Since the WISC or Binet is nearly always used and since both have digit span tests and tests using blocks, the choice of the visual attention span, the completion of drawings, the picture analogies, and the spatial reasoning subtests, can avoid duplication and add efficiency and thoroughness in testing.

VI. *Memory for Designs Test*—(Presents geometric design and child reproduces it from memory.)

A. Scoring is negative = "0" is satisfactory; "1–3," the higher the score the poorer the performance.
1. Total score (raw) will give approximate rating of "normal," "borderline," or "critical," (possible borderline damage).

VII. *Bender-Gestalt Test*

A. Maturational test of visual-motor gestalt functions

B. Purposes
1. Diagnostic information relating to:
   a. retardation
   b. regression
   c. loss of function
   d. organic brain defects in children and adults

C. Procedure: Untimed
1. Test card designs remain before the individual for reference in copying; memory is not a factor.

D. Scoring
1. Distortions of shape
2. Rotations
3. Integration
4. Perseveration
5. Norms are provided in Koppitz scoring to 11 years old.

Achievement Tests

I. *Wide Range Achievement Test (WRAT)*

A. Measures
1. Reading—word recognition and pronunciation *(only)*
2. Spelling—reproducing words or letters by audio cues
3. Arithmetic—computation

*These subtests are used more often.

B. Test was designed as a supplement to IQ tests and behavioral tests.
C. Has no age limit.
D. Determines instructional levels for school children.
E. Two levels
   1. Level I—to age eleven years
   2. Level II—eleven years and older
F. Scores: Three (3) kinds
   1. Grade level
   2. Percentiles
   3. Standard scores
G. Time: Approximately thirty (30) minutes
H. Clinical analysis of L.D., and MA-CA compatibility

Note: See also Bush, Wilma Jo, and Waugh, Kenneth W. 1976. *Diagnosing Learning Disabilities,* 2nd Ed., Columbus, Ohio: Charles E. Merrill Publishing Company.

appendix b agencies, associations, and organizations relative to exceptional children

For information concerning specific exceptionalities, parents, teachers, and interested personnel should write to the following:

Alexander Graham Bell Association for the Deaf, Inc.
1537 35th St., NW, Washington, DC 20007

American Academy for Cerebral Palsy
University Hospital School, Iowa City, IA 52240

American Academy of Private Practice in Speech Pathology and Audiology
P.O. Box 53217, State Capital Station, Oklahoma City, OK 73105

American Association for Health, Physical Education and Recreation
1201 16th St., NW, Washington, DC 20036

American Association for the Education of the Severely/Profoundly Handicapped
P.O. Box 15287, Seattle, WA 98115

American Association of Psychiatric Clinics for Children
250 W. 57th St., Room 1032, Fish Building, New York, NY 10019

American Association of Workers for the Blind, Inc.
1151 K St., NW, Suite 637, Washington, DC 20005

American Association on Mental Deficiency
5201 Connecticut Ave., NW, Washington, DC 20015

American Corrective Therapy Association, Inc.
811 St. Margaret's Road, Chillicothe, OH 45601

American Foundation for the Blind
15 W. 16th St., New York, NY 10011

American Heart Association, Inc.
44 E. 23rd St., New York, NY 10010

American Occupational Therapy Association, Inc.
600 Executive Blvd., Rockville, MD 20852

American Orthopsychiatric Association, Inc.
1790 Broadway, New York, NY 10019

American Physical Therapy Association
1156 15th St., N.W., Washington, DC 20005

American Printing House for the Blind
1839 Frankfort Ave., Louisville, KY 40206

American Psychological Association
1200 17th St., NW, Washington, DC 20036

American Rehabilitation Counseling Association of the American Personnel
and Guidance Association
1607 New Hampshire Ave., NW, Washington, DC 20009

American Schizophrenia Foundation
Box 160, Ann Arbor, MI 48107

The American Speech and Hearing Association
9030 Old Georgetown Rd., Washington, DC 20014

Architectural and Transportation Barriers Compliance Board
Room 1004, Switzer Building, Washington, DC 20201

Association for Children with Learning Disabilities
5225 Grace St., Pittsburgh, PA 15236

Association for Education of the Visually Handicapped
919 Walnut St., 4th Floor, Philadelphia, PA 19107

The Association of Rehabilitation Centers, Inc.
7979 Old Georgetown Rd., Washington, DC 20014

Closer Look
National Information Center for the Handicapped
Box 1492, Washington, DC 20013

The Council for Exceptional Children
1920 Association Dr., Reston, VA 22091

Council of Organizations Serving the Deaf
4201 Connecticut Ave., NW, Suite 210, Washington, DC 20008

Epilepsy Foundation of America
1828 L St., NW, Washington, DC 20036

Goodwill Industries of America, Inc.
9200 Wisconsin Ave., Washington, DC 20014

International League of Societies for the Mentally Handicapped
12, Rue Forestiere, Brussels-5, Belgium

International Society for Rehabilitation of the Disabled
219 E. 44th St., New York, NY 10017

Joseph P. Kennedy, Jr. Foundation
719 13th St., NW, Suite 510, Washington, DC 20005

Muscular Dystrophy Association of America, Inc.
810 Seventh Ave., New York, NY 10019

National Center for Law and the Handicapped
1235 N. Eddy St., South Bend, IN 46617

The National Association for Gifted Children
8080 Springvalley Dr., Cincinnati, OH 45236

The National Association for Mental Health, Inc.
1800 N. Kent St., Arlington, VA 22209

National Association for Music Therapy, Inc.
Box 610, Lawrence, KS 66055

National Association for Retarded Citizens
2709 Ave. E. East, P.O. Box 6109, Arlington, TX 76011

National Association of Hearing and Speech Agencies
919 18th St., NW, Washington, DC 20006

National Association of Sheltered Workshops and Homebound Programs
1522 K St., NW, Washington, DC 20005

National Association of the Deaf
814 Thayer Ave., Silver Spring, MD 20910

National Association of Social Workers
2 Park Ave., New York, NY 10016

National Committee for Multi-Handicapped Children
239 14th St., Niagara Falls, NY 14303

National Council for the Gifted
700 Prospect Ave., West Orange, NJ 07052

National Council on Crime and Delinquency
44 E. 23rd St., New York, NY 10010

The National Easter Seal Society for Crippled Children and Adults
2023 West Ogden Ave., Chicago, IL 60612

National Epilepsy League, Inc.
116 S. Michigan Ave., Chicago, IL 60603

National Federation of the Blind
218 Randolph Hotel Building, 4th and Court Sts.
Des Moines, IA 50309

The National Foundation—March of Dimes
1275 Mamaroneck Ave., White Plains, NY 10605

National Hemophilia Foundation
25 W. 39th St., New York, NY 10028

National Network of Learning Disabled Adults
P.O. Box 3130, Richardson, TX 75080

National Rehabilitation Association
1522 K St., NW, Washington, DC 20005

National Society for Autistic Children
306 31st Street, Huntington, WV 25702

National Therapeutic Recreation Society
1700 Pennsylvania Ave., NW, Washington, DC 20006

The President's Committee on Employment of the Handicapped
U.S. Department of Labor, 1111 20th St., NW, Washington, DC 20210

President's Committee on Mental Retardation
Washington, DC 20201

Southern Regional Education Board, Special Education Division
130 6th St., NW, Atlanta, GA 30313

United Cerebral Palsy Associations, Inc.
66 E. 34th St., New York, NY 10016

U.S. Public Health Service, Health Services and Mental Health Administration, National Institute of Mental Health
5454 Wisconsin Ave., Chevy Chase, MD 20015

U.S. Public Health Service, National Institutes of Health
HEW South Bldg., Rm. 5312, Washington, DC 20201

Social and Rehabilitation Service, Assistance Payments Administration
330 Independence Ave., SW, Washington, DC 20201

Social and Rehabilitation Service, Children's Bureau
330 C St., SW, Washington, DC 20201

Social and Rehabilitation Service, Office of Research, Demonstrations, and Training
HEW North Bldg., Rm. 3315, Washington, DC 20201

Social and Rehabilitation Service, Rehabilitation Services Administration
330 Independence Ave., SW, Rm. 3139 D, Washington, DC 20201

Western Interstate Commission for Higher Education, Special Education and Rehabilitation Program
30th St., University East Campus, Boulder, CO 80382

Photo Credits

Author Index

Horwitz, Elinor, 141
Huberty, Thomas J., 54
Hutt, Max, 65
Hyer, Anna L., 370

i

Imber, Ruth B., 394
Imber, Steve C., 394
Inzer, Lenore C., 99, 101
Issacs, Anne F., 120, 124, 130, 143
Itard, Jean-Morc-Gaspard, 4

j

Jacobs, John C., 120
Jenkins, E., 231
Johnson, G. Orville, 17, 19, 20, 148,
190, 198, 200, 266, 289
Jones, Edward V., 309
Jordan, Thomas E., 80, 94, 95

k

Kaplan, Abraham, 375
Kappman, Marion, 21
Karnes, M., 386, 424
Kass, Corrine E., 250
Kauffman, James M., 309, 310
Kelling, Kent, 102
Kephart, N., 421
Kern, W. H., 382, 389, 390
Kessler, Jane W., 307, 308, 309, 311,
340
Khatena, J., 121
Kibler, Robert J., 372, 373
Kidd, John, 54
Kirby, J. H., 382
Kirk, Samuel A., 109, 148, 163, 164,
252, 258, 261
Kliment, Stephen A., 154
Klotz, S. D., 346
Koch, Richard A., 93, 96
Koegel, Robert L., 323, 324
Kokaska, Charles, 73
Koller, James R., 54
Krasner, Leonard, 313, 417
Krippner, Stanley, 123, 124
Kroth, Roger L., 397, 398

l

La-Coste, Ronald, 426, 427
Lahay, M., 244
Lainer, Harriet, 244
Landreth, Garry L., 292
LaVor, Martin, 29

Lehning, Thomas W., 22
Lessen, Elliott I., 425
Letlow, Helen, 139
Levenstein, P., 386
Levitt, Harry, 242
Lewis, Wilbert W., 343
Libby, B. P., 62
Lilly, Stephen, 14, 20, 23
Lindsey, Jimmy D., 184
Lindsley, Ogden R., 416, 417
Lippke, Barbara A., 178
Little, H. A., 364
Lohr, F. E., 231
Lowenbraun, Sheila, 224
Lowrey, N., 284, 288
Lunde, A., 224
Lytle, William G., 131

m

McCaffrey, Isabel, 309
McCarthy, James, 27, 28, 29, 30, 297
McCarthy, Joan F., 27, 28, 29, 30,
297
McDonald, P., 386
McKenzie, M. S., 385
McKinnon, Archie J., 336, 337
McNulty, Brian, 426, 427
Maes, Wayne, 311
Mandell, M., 346
Manley, Max W., 364
Manton, Anne B., 329
Marion, Robert L., 393
Marsh, George E., 284, 288
Martin, Edwin, 11, 21, 29, 410, 424
Martin, Richard, 237
Maurer, Steven, 179, 182
Mayer, J. B., 389, 390
Meade, M., 96
Melcher, John, 43, 387
Mercer, Jane R., 102
Michaelis, Carol T., 392
Miles, David T., 372, 373
Minskoff, Gerald, 249
Mitchell, Patricia B., 128, 129
Monekeberg, Fernando, 98
Moore, G. Paul, 235
Moores, Donald F., 224
Morrison, James, 250, 267, 290
Morse, William C., 327
Moss, J. W., 208, 414
Moss, M., 208
Mowery, Charlane, 245
Muro, J. J., 382

Murphy, Diane, 184
Musgrove, D. G., 420, 421
Myers, Patricia, 266
Myers, R. E., 143
Myklebust, Helmer R., 250, 254, 258

n

Nash, William R., 132, 133
Nelson, Michael C., 311
Newby, Hayes A., 203, 206, 208, 210, 212

o

Olley, J. Gregory, 325
O'Neill, John J., 205
Orhtmann, William, 24
Osberger, Mary Joe, 242

p

Pasamanick, Benjamin, 93
Patterson, C. H., 381
Pauls, Mariam D., 203
Perkins, Stanley A., 96
Peterson, Pamela, 426, 427
Philpott, W., 344, 346
Plowman, Paul B., 123, 130, 131, 132
Polser, Charles M., 58
Poorman, Christine, 184
Pope, Lillie, 395
Porter, Hahlon E., 74
Price, Barrie Jo, 284, 288
Price, Marianne, 40, 42
Purkey, W. A., 143

q

Quay, Herbert C., 255, 258, 327, 343

r

Raimist, L. I., 383, 384
Randolph, T. G., 346
Rapaport, H. G., 345, 346
Rappaport, Sheldon, 289, 300, 301
Regan, Richard R., 40
Reger, Roger, 21, 370, 371, 372
Rellas, A., 139
Remmen, Edmund, 352
Renzulli, Joseph S., 120, 121, 422, 423
Replogle, Anne, 245
Reynolds, Maynard, 14, 30
Rice, Donald B., 262
Rice, J. P., 143, 262

Richardson, S., 308
Rimland, Bernard, 321, 322, 323
Rinkel, H. J., 345
Robinson, Dale O., 223
Robinson, Halbert B., 57, 66, 93, 99, 162, 163
Robinson, Nancy, 57, 66, 93, 99, 162, 163
Rose, Terry L., 425
Rosenberg, Harry E., 74
Rosner, Stanley, 143
Rothstein, Cary, 394
Rubin, Eli, 308, 310
Ryan, Bruce, 245

s

Sabatino, David A., 102
Sawrey, James M., 68, 119, 120, 138, 189, 191, 198, 200, 203, 229, 230
Scheflin, Rhonda, 29
Schiele, Burtrum, 350, 351, 352
Schopler, Eric, 325, 326
Schroeder, Wendy, 370, 371, 372
Schultz, Edward W., 329, 331, 332
Schwartz, Louis, 25
Semmes, Marilyn, 426
Shane, Don G., 16, 66, 355, 364
Shanker, Albert, 411, 412
Shores, Richard, 333
Shuster, Charles R., 353
Silverman, Franklin H., 236, 237
Silverman, R. Richard, 202, 203, 205
Simmons, F. Blair, 208, 209
Simson, Clyde B., 308
Sisk, Dorothy, 118
Slingerland, Beth H., 261
Smith, J. O., 387
Smith, Linda H., 120, 121
Smith, Robert M., 415
Smitter, F., 308
Solomans, Gerald, 349, 351, 352
Sontag, Ed, 179, 180
Stainback, Susan, 179, 182
Stainback, William, 179, 182
Sterling, Gail R., 223
Stern, M. J., 124
Stewart, Mark A., 269, 278
Stocker, Joseph, 370
Strickland. Stephen R., 110
Swack, Myron, 151
Swan, William W., 426

Subject Index

c

cane training, 196
care, inpatient, outpatient, emergency, hospital, 340
care responsibilities, emotionally disturbed, 340
categorical versus general aid, 29
cerebral palsy, 161
cerebral palsy speech, 241
characteristics of teachers of learning disabilities, 299
characteristics of the emotionally disturbed, 312
characteristics of the gifted, 123
characteristics of the hearing impaired, 204
characteristics of the learning disabled, 263, 264, 265, 266, 267, 268, 269
characteristics of the mentally retarded, 60, 65
characteristics of the speech impaired, 230
child find, 18
children's considerations, emotionally disturbed, 337
chronically ill children, 147
classroom characteristics, disadvantaged, 103
cleft palate speech, 241
college programs for learning disabled students, 289
color deficiency vision, 194
communicating with parents, 391
communication devices, 170
community centers, 17
community services for mentally retarded, 77
community services for visually impaired, 200
comprehensive plan for programming, 24
conductive hearing loss, 210
congenitally deaf, 203
Congentin, 352
consulting teachers, 384
continuum of services for handicapped children, 15, 16
correlation between prematurity and IQ, 94
cost factor—special education, 388
counseling services, 397
creative or productive thinking, 121
Crib-o-gram, 208
crisis-resource teacher, 384
crossed eyes (strabismus), 194
culturally diverse, 422
curriculum development in special education, 25

d

deaf-blind children, 160
deafness, 202
Deaner, 355
decibel (db) loss, 203
defective speech, 229, 230, 231
defects in rhythm—stuttering, 235
Defining "LD" for Programmatic Purposes, 251
definition of emotionally disturbed, 307
definition and estimates of prevalence, gifted, 117
definition and incidence, multiply and severely handicapped children, 180
definition of learning disabilities, 249
definition of speech impaired, 229
definitions, physically disabled and chronically ill, 148
degree and certification programs for teachers of learning disabilities, 294
delayed language, 239
delayed speech, 238
denasal speech, 234
depressive neurosis, 317
developmental picture of premature infants, 94
Dexedrine, 355
diabetes, 165
diagnostic-prescriptive methods, 413
diagnostic-prescriptive teacher, 383
diagnostic procedures in the classroom, 415
diagnostic teachers, 382
diet, 279
Dilantin, 355
directors of special education, 389
disability versus handicap, 149
disadvantaged children, introduction, 91
disadvantaged gifted, 109
disadvantaged gifted, identification of, 108

456   Subject Index

hearing impaired, skills, 222
hearing impaired, special training for
    teachers, 224
hearing losses among babies, 208, 209
hearing problems and concerns, 212
hearing surgery, 219, 220, 221
HEW proposed rules for learning
    disabilities, 258
Hiskey-Nebraska Test, 439
homebound instruction, 167
homebound or school-to-home
    instruction, 18
hospital or special settings, 17
hospital teaching, 167
Hurlin method, 191
hyperactive children, 263, 266, 269
hyperactive symptoms, 270
hyperactive treatment, 270
hyperopia (farsighted), 194
hysterical-psychomatic neurosis, 316

i

Implementation of Public Law
    94–142, 37
implications for the teacher of
    exceptional children, 370
impulsiveness, 265, 267, 270, 276
individual education plan (IEP), 40,
    41, 243, 244, 392, 393
individual education plan, resources for
    development, 42
individual needs, 373, 404, 416, 421
infantile autism, 322, 323
inherited hearing problems, 213
inner ear loss, 217, 218
integration into regular classes, 405
intelligence of visually impaired, 201
interdisciplinary approach, 149
intermediate special class, 70
introduction, disadvantaged children,
    91
IQ, 117, 118, 120, 122
IQ tests, 431, 432, 433
issues and trends in placement of
    exceptional children, 23
itinerant teaching, 21
ITPA (Illinois Test of Psycholinguistic
    Abilities), 437

j

junior high special class, 70

k

Keyboard Strip Printer KSP-1, 175
kinds of giftedness, 121

l

lab classes, 21
labels, 398
labels and categories, 14
language disorders, 237
Lapboard Strip Printer LSP-1, 175
leadership ability, 122
learning disabilities, secondary
    programs, 283
learning disability testing, 284, 286,
    294
legislation for exceptional children, 27
leisure time, 79
Librium, 351, 356
linguistic diversity, disadvantaged, 104
long-term effects of prematurity, 95

m

mainstreaming, 184, 405, 406, 407
malnutrition and education, 101
malnutrition and poverty, 96
malnutrition and pregnancy, 99
malnutrition, growth of the brain, and
    IQ, 100
manic-depressive, 314
maternal factors related to
    prematurity, 93
medication, 151, 152
Mellaril, 356
Memory for Designs Test, 440
Meniere's syndrome, 214
mentally retarded, characteristics of,
    60, 65
mentally retarded children, definition,
    49
mentally retarded children, estimates
    of prevalence, 55, 56
mental retardation, methods of
    identification, 57
Meprobamate, 356
methods and materials for emotionally
    disturbed, 341
methods of identification, emotionally
    disturbed, 310
methods of identification, gifted, 120
methods of identification, learning
    disabilities, 261